Mekong–Gaṅgā Axis

# Mekong–Gaṅgā Axis

*Editors*

**Pankaj Mittal**
**Ravi Bhushan**
**Daisy**

*Editorial Advisor*

**Kapil Kapoor**

BPS Mahila Vishwavidyalaya

PRINTWORLD
Publishers of Indian Traditions

**Cataloging in Publication Data — DK**
[Courtesy: D.K. Agencies (P) Ltd. <docinfo@dkagencies.com>]

**Mekong-Gaṅgā axis** / editors, Pankaj Mittal, Ravi Bhushan, Daisy ; editorial advisor, Kapil Kapoor.
p. cm.
Includes bibliographical references and index.
ISBN 13: 9788124608197

1. India – Relations – Southeast Asia – Congresses. 2. Southeast Asia – Relations – India – Congresses. 3. Southeast Asia – Civilization – Indic influences – Congresses. I. Mittal, Pankaj. II. Bhushan, Ravi, 1974- III. Daisy. IV. Bhagat Phool Singh Mahila Vishwavidyalaya.

DDC 327.54059 23


*First published in India,* 2015
**ISBN 13: 978-81-246-0819-7**



*Published by:*
**Bhagat Phool Singh Mahila Vishwavidyalaya**
Khanpur Kalan, Dist. Sonepat (Haryana)

*and*

**D.K. Printworld (P) Ltd.**
*Regd. Office: Vedaśrī,* F-395, Sudarshan Park
(Metro Station: Ramesh Nagar)
New Delhi – 110 015
*Phones:* (011) 2545 3975; 2546 6019; *Fax*: (011) 2546 5926
*E-mail:* indology@dkprintworld.com
*Website*: www.dkprintworld.com

Printed by : D.K. Printworld (P) Ltd, New Delhi

# Foreword

I AM glad to know that the Centre for Indic-Asian Studies (CIAS) is publishing its second book titled *Mekong–Gaṅgā Axis*. Indeed it is a privilege for me to share my thoughts with the readers through this foreword.

The CIAS, established as one of the youngest Area Study Centre of the University Grants Commission of India at Bhagat Phool Singh Mahila Vishwavidyalaya in 2011, is making significant contribution to the research on Indo-Asian issues of Culture, Literature, Economy, Society, Politics, History, Science, Art and Heritage. The two international conferences organized by CIAS on "India–Korea Relations: Past and Present" and "South-East-East Asia and India: Historical Interconnections in Art, Architecture and Culture of Laos, Thailand, Cambodia and Vietnam" have truly been academic events of international standard. The participating scholars in these conferences, I am told, discussed various issues pertaining to South Korea, Vietnam, Cambodia, Laos, Thailand, Sri Lanka and their historical–cultural relationships with and among each other and the discussions will go a long way in further developing the cultural, social, political and diplomatic relationship between these two societies. I believe these scholarly deliberations would facilitate formulation of India's foreign policy towords the countries of this region.

This book which is appropriately titled *Mekong–Gaṅgā Axis* carries the scholarly papers presented during the conference. While going through the papers and discourses of eminent and erudite scholars from the world over, I could sense the eclectic nature of the themes discussed during the conference. The horizon of topics discussed ranges from theatre to commerce and has in its ambit areas as varied as History, Science, Literature, Language, Anthropology, Culture, Economics and Geography by renowned scholars from different countries. The discourses, I am sure, are definitely an invaluable contribution to the existing knowledge on South-East Asia.

I take this opportunity to applaud and appreciate the untiring efforts put in by CIAS and in particular its erstwhile Director and internationally acclaimed scholar of Indian knowledge systems, Prof. Kapil Kapoor, in bringing together the scholars from world over and making the conference happen. I also put on record the key role played by Dr Daisy, Dr Ravi Bhushan and Dr Babita in the planning and organization of the conference and putting together the manuscript for publication.

I congratulate the CIAS and thank all the esteemed scholars whose papers have been included in this magnificent book.

*Best Wishes*

**Prof. (Dr) Asha Kadyan**
Vice-Chancellor
Bhagat Phool Singh Mahila Vishwavidyalaya
Khanpur Kalan (Sonipat), Haryana

# Preface

A PREFACE is an exercise in the poetics of recall, of memory, a time to bring to mind all those who made this book possible.

Dreams they say happen only in sleep. But sometime they climb down to earth and bless some beings. I have been fortunate that I have actually *lived* a dream in the *siddha* village of Khanpur Kalan, a dream that lasted more than four years. Goodness was the stuff of that dream – the dream is over but the goodness of Khanpur still lives in my heart and mind, the goodness of beautiful, loving benign human beings. Goodness of those with whom I worked those four years – Dr. Ravi Bhushan, Coordinator of the Centre for Indic-Asian Studies, always a younger brother to me for all my small and big problems, Dr. Daisy of the University's Woman College, like a daughter to Mrs. Kapoor and me with her warm love and care in summer and winter, Joginder-ji with his smiling face and the *laḍḍoo*s he brought in the marriage season from his village for Mrs. Kapoor who is so fond of those village *laḍḍoo*s, the late Sunita who always knew when I needed warm water and what kind of tea will do me good. And our Ms. Meena, always Minu for me and Mrs. Kapoor, our daughter, who was always so concerned about both of us as only a daughter can be, about our food, our health and our general well-being.

And there was ever smiling Rinu, our Ph.D. student, who would feed the best *burfī* to us all and who was attending to the participating scholars all the time taking care of their small problems with an endearing smile. May Bhole Baba bless her!

We can never dream of repaying their goodness.

It was this beautiful family that in a new, nascent rural girls' university enacted, what would appear almost impossible for a rural university off the main road, two international conferences in the pioneering area study Centre of Indic-Asian Studies in 2012 and 2013, conferences that brought together an array of scholars from Bhārat and abroad. The first was about the rich historical India–Korea relations and the Centre has already published the proceedings of that conference. The second conference was an exploration in India's more than a millennia old relationship with the South-East–East Asian region, the land along the two banks of the River Mekong, the river that echoes the name of Gaṅgā and not unexpectedly the culture of the four countries Cambodia, Laos, Thailand and Vietnam – on the banks of Mekong – have native cultures markedly inflected by Indian culture over centuries. This area earlier subsumed under Bṛhat Bhārat (Greater India) has now assumed considerable geo-political importance and much significance for India and therefore this conference was an effort to re-ignite that age-long relationship. The cooperation received from the embassies of these countries was most encouraging, and more encouraging was the enthusiasm with which so many scholars from these four countries responded to the Centre's request and participated in the deliberations. Their presence along with noted Indian scholars made it a truly educative experience for all. The range, the diversity of topics discussed, gives an idea of the multi-dimensional, interactive relationship that characterizes this region, a relationship that still exists.

In the now changed geo-political situation, this volume we expect shall contribute to a better appreciation and closer relationship between Bhārat and Mekong countries in the time to come.

The students loved the experience of listening to so many scholars and they were great hosts to all the scholars, serving them and attending to their comforts and needs.

This volume shall be an enduring testimony to the love and care that mark all aspects of life in that noble village – Khanpur Kalan. I am sure Bhagat Phool Singh-ji, the great social revolutionary who founded the seed institution of this university, the girls' school in 1936, is happy in his eternal abode with this small token exercise in ideas in the village he loved and by and for the girls whom he loved even more.

**Kapil Kapoor**

# Asia as Culture Cluster

*Kapil Kapoor*

WE are thankful to our friends who have come to support us in these reflections on South-East Asia, an area of great importance for India. The scholars from outside India, and from India, responded to our request and agreed to participate in the deliberations and grace this occasion. Indeed this is a privilege for us.

The Centre for Indic-Asian Studies, the only Area Study Centre in the region, deals with ancient things and relationships. Having such a centre in one of the youngest universities has some significance. The entire Asian region is permeated with "pastness". To make visible the "pastness" of the present we are in fact trying to recreate and reveal this pastness. There have been waves of relationship among countries of this region. We want to reawaken ourselves. There is a need for reawakening of ourselves. Unfortunately we in India are unaware about ourselves and we know little about those who are ours. It is the scholars like those present here who have consistently discovered India and Indians. We need to reconnect with the landmass known as Asia. We have become like a kite which has drifted away and is lost. We need to relocate ourselves where we belong. Our goal is de-territorializing Asia and this is a shared concern. Today political boundaries have become an overwhelming reality. This reality of political boundaries should be put under a lense. Political boundaries are shifting boundaries. If we want to affiliate with others we shall think in terms of cultural clusters in which the boundaries are either not there or very tenuous. Asia is a culture cluster. We need to rediscover this. We in Indian universities have not tried to rediscover. Scholars in foreign universities discuss and tell us about ourselves. Learned Prof. Byrskiji from Poland for example taught us *Nāṭyaśāstra* here some months back. The current scholarship of ethnographic thinking has separated people. We now must believe in the scholarship of affinity and promote synthesizing models of thinking. Indian mind must begin using transcendental models of thought and that is what our instinctive goal is in CIAS. Our aim is to make it a living experience for our students. The young scholars must recognize the priority of knowing ourselves. This is the goal and theme. Movements of ideas across globe shall be promoted — the notion of immigration and migration was not there earlier. There were movements of art and culture and peoples and they lived in a world without political boundaries.

We are thankful to our learned friends such as Prof. Shiv Vajpayee, former Professor of History in California University, USA, who was to join us but due to ill health could not come. He has sent his discourse on world systems developing in an earlier time, what we today call "globalization". We are grateful to Prof. S. Kalyanaraman for sharing his monograph on Indian ocean community.

*Keynote Address*

# India's Cultural Relations with South-East Asia

*J.C. Sharma*

INDIA's cultural relations with South-East Asia are one of the most fascinating fields of history. This interaction, which precedes the beginning of the Christian era, has left an indelible impression on almost every aspect of life in a number of countries of the region. It would not be an exaggeration to say that this intercourse has been a vital factor in shaping the history of this area. The most unique feature of this interaction is that it has been entirely peaceful. There is probably no other example in the history of mankind of such cross-fertilization between different cultures and people for over two millennia without any involvement of military force.

I was fortunate to have the opportunities to see the depth of this vibrant relationship during my various postings in South-East Asia. Hindu–Buddhist monuments of South-East Asia bear silent testimony to the two millennia of peaceful and mutually beneficial Indo–South-East Asian interaction. Awareness and knowledge about the monuments is not only important for the study of history, art and culture of this region but it is also helpful in understanding South-East Asia of today.

The civilization and culture of South-East Asia in general and Cambodia in particular have three major elements — the indigenous, Indian and Chinese. The seed of the culture and civilization of most of the countries in South-East Asia is undoubtedly indigenous. It has cross-fertilized with two great civilizations of Asia, India and China. No doubt there has been lots of cross-fertilization among various indigenous cultures of South-East Asia.

During my postings in both Cambodia and Vietnam, I used to often say that Cambodia and Vietnam have had three major foreign influences — the French, Chinese and Indian. There is, however, a fundamental difference or the nature of the intercourse. The unique feature as I mentioned in the beginning of my talk is that the Indian influence has been without any involvement of the military force.

The depth of our relationship was not systematically studied by our own scholars. The credit for making us aware of our long history of interaction definitely goes to the colonial scholars. There is a galaxy of French scholars and explorers who have made extraordinary contribution to the study of culture and civilization of Cambodia. Francis Gamier, E. Aymonier, Lunet D. Lajonquiere, Sylvain Lévi, Groslier, A. Bergaigne, Barth, H. Parmentier, Philips Stern and a host of others spent their lifetime studying the civilization of Cambodia and its relations with other cultures particularly the Indian culture. We owe much of gratitude to George Coedes who was undoubtedly the doyen of scholars in this field. Similar contribution to the study of South-East Asia was made by the great Indian scholar R.C. Majumdar. *École Française d'extrême-Orient* (EFEO) has been the centre of research, which has nurtured scholars since its inception.

To this learned audience, I need not give the very well-known history of the early contacts between India and Cambodia. I don't like to repeat the story of arrival of Kaundinia and his marriage to Princess Liyue Vi (Somā). With this story begins a fascinating saga of nearly two millennia of interaction between our two countries.

The seed of Khmer genius nurtured by Indian ideas produced one of the most glorious civilizations and, the greatest symbol of which is Angkor Vat. The two millennia of this cross-fertilization has left its imprint on almost every aspect of life in Cambodia. It would be difficult to cover every aspect in the short duration of one lecture. I would, therefore, draw your attention to some of the salient areas of our civilizational and cultural links.

**Art of Writing**

It is not my intention to take either the Indologist or Orientalist point of view. The views of early scholars are best summed up in the following quotation born the Sylvan Levi in his famous work *L'Inde Civilisatrice: Apercu Historique:*

> The expansion of Indian civilization to those countries and islands of the Orient where Chinese civilization, with strikingly similar aspirations seemed to arrive ahead of it, is one of the outstanding events in the history of the world, one which has determined the destiny of a good portion of mankind. "Mother of Wisdom", India gave her mythology to her neighbours who went to teach it to the whole world. . . . *Mother of law and philosophy, she gave to three-quarters of Asia a god, a religion, a doctrine and art. She carried her sacred language, her literature, her institutions into Indonesia, to the limits of the known world, and from there they spread back to Madagascar and perhaps to the coast of Africa, where the present flow of Indian immigrants seems to follow the faint traces of the past.*

The Orientalist based their work on the basis of glut of India-oriented material available at the time of their research. In subsequent years the new material and research brought South-East Asian personality in much balder relief. The Orientalist point of view brought a sharp response from South-East Asian scholars in the wake of the new research and independence of the colonies. Since I am not an academic and not a scholar in the true sense of the term, I would not take Indocentric or South-East Asia position. Though I do to a great extent agree with Paul Mus who stated that there existed a broadly similar culture from Coastal South China to India. No matter how great the foreign ideas without the local genius they could never flower as they did in Cambodia.

For a generalist like me it would be difficult to give a detailed in-depth exposure of our cultural and civilization links. I would, therefore, mention some salient areas of our interaction.

In my view the most everlasting contribution of India to South-East Asia is the art of writing. Apart from introducing India, this art of writing also enabled the people of South-East Asia to get equipped with Indian linguistic materials to develop their own vernacular and compose many beautiful original works. There is hardly any doubt that much of the cultural heritage of South-East Asia would have been lost forever if its people had not adopted at an early stage the Indian art of writing. There is no doubt that all the major scripts of South-East Asia which today look very much different from those of India, owe their common origin to the late variety of the Indian Brāhmī scripts.

The oldest reference to books and archives of South-East Asia occurs in the Chinese texts. We read in the history of the Tsin dynasty (CE 265–410) that Funan had archives and books and alphabets resembling those of the Hu, a tribe of Central Asia, who used a script of Indian origin. Similarly, the History of the Liange Dynasty (CE 502-55) tells us that a Chinese mission came to Funan between CE 535 and 545 to collect Buddhist texts and monks for China. The king of Funan sent the monk Paramārtha or Guṇaratna of Ujjayinī with 240 bundles of Buddhist texts to China, of which he translated 70 texts into Chinese.

I will not go into the question of the edge or provenance of the early scripts of Funan and Cambodia. Different scholars have reached different conclusions interestingly enough based on the same source material. The Chinese have referred to a Kouen-Louen (Kun-Lun) writing script as well as Kun-Lun language and Kun-Lun merchants and pilots. They seemed to apply this term to ethnolinguistic entity. It appears that the Kaliṅga script and Kaliṅga people definitely had considerable influence on the scripts in South-East Asia including Funan and Cambodia.

**Religion**

We accept the views of Paul Mus about the existence of a similar civilization from southern China to India. We must also agree with his view that similar form of cult and nature worship existed in this entire region. With local characteristic and variations the Indian religious ideas and beliefs were superimposed on the existing cults and spirit of nature worship. There was an amalgamation of a native deity of the soil residing in a high place with the Indian god of the mountain Giriśa (Śiva). The concept of Maheśvara definitely developed because of Indian influence. Most of the Brāhmanical gods and goddesses were well known and worshipped in some form or the other in Cambodia. Indian and Sri Lankan monks also introduced Buddhism. It flourished both alongside Hindu Island subsequently on its own throughout the Khmer history. Today Buddhism is much more potent in Cambodia and Thailand than probably anywhere else in the world. Though Cambodia was exposed to all major forms of Buddhism, Theravāda Buddhism has greater influence in the society. There is enough epigraphic and other evidences of the presence and powerful role of brāhmaṇa priests in the Cambodian history. There is

also evidence that the Cambodians were fully familiar with all the major religious treaties including Vedas, Vedāṅgas and Vedāntas. The Hindu trinity of Brahmā, Viṣṇu and Maheśa was highly respected in Cambodia.

**Sanskrit and Pāli Studies**

The Khmers had acquired mastery of both Sanskrit and Pāli. Chinese history of Tsin dynasty (CE 265–419) refers to the fact that Funan had books, archives and that alphabet resembling those of the Hu, a tribe of Central Asia using a script of Indian origin. The history of Liang Dynasty (CE 502-56) mentions that a Chinese Mission came to Funan between CE 535 and 545 to collect Buddhist and monks for China. The king of Funan sent the monk Paramārtha with 240 bundles of texts. In China of which he translated 70 texts into Chinese. We also know that the Chinese took 1,350 Buddhist manuscripts after defeating Śambhu of Champa. The oldest Sanskrit inscription Vo-Canh has been found in Champa though many scholars believe it was an inscription of Funan. The impact of classical Sanskrit literature of India was felt from third to fourteenth century in Funan and Kamboj. It is well known that the Khmer scholars were familiar with the Sanskrit grammar and metres. Long texts have been composed in classical Sanskrit. Any numbers of inscriptions justify the familiarity of Cambodians with the well-known Indian authors.

The Sanskrit inscriptions written *by* eminent scholars are always written in different Sanskrit metres and these start with the famous Vo-Canh inscription, dated in about the third or fourth century CE. These inscriptions are usually written in flawless Sanskrit but it is not certain if all these charters were written by the brāhmaṇas or members of the royal family alone and the Hinduized Khmers had no share in their composition. The unornamental style of the Khmer epigraphs would however induce one to believe that the former was the case. It is interesting to observe in this connection that some of the inscriptions were couched in the Gauḍī-style prevalent in Bengal, as for instance, in the Vat Thipedi inscription of King Īśānavarman II, dated in 910. The long compounds, exaggeration (*atyukti*) and alliteration (*anuprāsa*), which are the principal characteristics of this style, are found in several other inscriptions. One specimen of hybrid Sanskrit composition is found in an inscription and, like its class, it lacks in grammar, metre, etc.

The hundreds of Sanskrit inscriptions written in the Kāvya style underlining the tremendous literary effort made by the Sanskrit scholars of Kambuja. By itself, it is a phenomenon, and no country outside India is known to have made comparable effort in this direction. H.B. Sarker examined about 58 Sanskrit inscriptions of Kambuja, for which the necessary details are available, in chronological order, from the earliest times to 1005, to study their prosodical structure and found that the most popular metres, in order of priority, were the following: *śloka* or *anuṣṭubh* (39), the group *upajāti, indravajra* and *upendravajra* (37), *śārdūlavikrīḍita* (24), *vasantatilakā* (18), *śragdhārā* (14), *mālinī* (10), *varṇasastha* (5), *pṛthvī* (3), *mandakrāntā* (3), *vaitālitya* (2), *aupachandaśika, svagata* and *triṣṭubh,* one each. By comparing the frequency of these metres with those used in the *Raghuvaṁśa, Kumārasambhava, Kirātārjunīya, Bhaṭṭikāvya, Māghakāvya* and *Naiṣadhīya,* the dates of which range between the fourth and tenth century, we find that the popularity of metres in the Sanskrit inscriptions of Kambuja had no relation to the general popularity of the metres the contemporary India had.

The royalty including several princesses of the royal house, as well as brāhmaṇas, have left behind hundreds of Sanskrit inscriptions in Funan–Champa–Kambuja. Princess Tilakā, for instance, received the title of Vāgīśvarī Bhagavatī on account of her profound knowledge. Similarly, Queen Indradevī who "surpassed in her knowledge the knowledge of philosophers" composed in faultless Sanskrit a panegyric on her deceased younger sister who was the first queen. Scholars have been described as proficient in the Vedas, Vedāṅgas, Vedāntas, Brāhmaṇas, Sūtras of the Taittirīya school, the six systems of philosophy, as well as the Buddhist philosophy, Nyāya, Dharmaśāstras, including *Manu Saṁhitā*, the epic literature, the Purāṇas, Tāntric literature, Buddhist Jātaka stories, the grammar of Pāṇini, particularly the *Mahābhāṣya* of Patañjali, *Kāśikāvṛtti* as well as *gāndharva-vidyā,* i.e. music, Dhanurveda or archery, Cikitsāśāstra or medicine, etc.

It is interesting to note that the fame of many Indian authors had travelled to far-flung Kambuja. In the eastern Baray inscription of King Yaśovarman I, we come across the name of Vātsyāyana, while in another inscription of the same period, Pravarasena has been described as the author of *Setubandha*. The poet Bhāravi is also

mentioned in verse 31 of the eastern Baray Stele inscription of the same king, while Guṇāḍhya, the Prākṛta author, is mentioned in verse 69. Besides, the same inscription describes Viśālākṣa as the author of a *work* on Nīti, while Sura is referred to as having humiliated a rival name Bhīmaka. Jina also probably been referred to as the writer of one of the *pūrvas* named *Kalyāṇa*. Verse 70 also mentions the name of the poet Mayūra. The references to so many writers in one region undoubtedly indicated the brisk study of Sanskrit literature during the reign of King Yaśovarman. When we remember that the inscriptions in which the names of these authors occur have been written in the north Indian script, one may well believe that the transmission of these works to Kambuja might be due to the north Indian immigrants or travellers, whose number must have been considerable.

The four Vedas and Vedic literature do not however figure in Kambuja inscriptions before the seventh century. It is, however, interesting to observe in this connection that none of the charters of Kambuja, written in the native Khmer language, has ever used the expression *veda*, but only *caturvidyā*s, as if the use of the term *coda* outside Sanskrit texts would constitute a sacrilege. The study of Vedic literature is mentioned, as stated above, from the seventh century onwards and King Sūryavarman I (1102-50), for example, has been described as proficient in the Vedāṅgas. If the royal family was the patron of Sanskrit learning, it was the brāhmaṇas who shed lusture on it and there is hardly any branch of Sanskrit learning that they did not study thoroughly. The Vedas, Vedāntas and Vedāṅgas were studied in detail. The Vedāṅgas, it may recall, included discipline in pronunciation, metre, ritual, grammar, lexicography as well as astronomy, and various references to them occur in the inscriptions of Kambuja. In many cases, the name of the individual scholars who were proficient in Vedic literature has come down to us. A Śaiva brāhmaṇa called Śakrasvāmin figures in an inscription of CE 713 as well as versed in the Vedānta and the Taittirīya. If we are guided by references in the inscriptions, it would appear as if the study of the discipline under the Taittirīya School, which began not later than CE 635 was vigorously pursued even in the beginning of the eighth century.

The branches of literature referred to above and some others proliferated in the Angkorean period (CE 800–1150). Apart from studies of the Vedic literature which continued unabated, at least up to the reign of King Śrīndravarman (1307), the studies of Pāṇinian grammar, philosophy, the Purāṇas, Mīmāṁsās, Nyāya, Dharmaśāstras, etc. were pursued vigorously. King Yaśovarman (CE 887–900) is said to have composed a commentary on the *Mahābhāṣya* of Patañjali. Brāhmaṇa scholars like Vidyāviśeṣa, Vidyāpuṣpa, Bhāgavat Rudra, Bhūpendra-paṇḍita, Amarabhava, Caitanyaśiva and others, too many to be mentioned, figure in Kambuja inscriptions as masters of grammar. Some rules of sanskrit grammar bearing on *prakṛti, pratyaya, ādeśa, guṇa, vṛddhi*, etc. including actual quotations from Pāṇini (1, 4, 58, 59, 80), are found in the inscriptions. Besides grammar, the study of which was most extensively organized in Kambuja, the scholar Vidyāviśeṣa is said to have mastered the Vaiśeṣika system of Kaṇāda, Nyāya system of Gautama (Akṣapāda), Sāṁkhya system of Kapila and texts on Buddhism. The Horāśāstra (astrology) and the Siddhāntaśāstra were also studied by the Kambuja scholars. We cannot determine for want of adequate data, if these claims were justified, but the very fact of their mention signifies that these were studied, if not extensively, at least in the circle of the specialists.

The role of *Manu Saṁhitā* in South-East Asia and its island-world was without any doubt unique. A text of Bṛhaspati significantly states that the injunction which is not supported by *Manu Saṁhitā* is not to be accepted, because, the essence of the Vedas or Śruti has been reflected therein. It is not therefore surprising that the Kambuja inscriptions have not only referred to the law-code in several places, but the actual quotations given are the same.

### Indian Epics, Purāṇas and Buddhist Texts

Among epics and Purāṇic works, the most popular were, of course, *Rāmāyaṇa* and *Mahābhārata*. A record dating from the sixth century CE tells that the brāhmaṇa Somaśarman, a brother-in-law of King Bhavavarman I, had dedicated a copy of *Rāmāyaṇa* and a complete copy of *Mahābhārata* as well as the copy of a Purāṇa for daily recitation before the deity named Tribhuvaneśvara. In the following century, a manuscript of the Sambhava section of the "Ādiparvan" of *Mahābhārata* was deposited at the temple of Bhavainana. The inscriptions also refer to many well-known episodes of the epics, of which some have been portrayed in bas reliefs. Scholars proficient in the recitation of *Rāmāyaṇa* and *Mahābhārata* as well as "numerous Purāṇas . . . without omitting any one" have been referred to in the inscriptions. There might be some exaggeration, but there is hardly any doubt that a substantial number of works of the Epic–Purāṇic genre were studied in Kambuja. Among the scholars who were specially proficient in the study of epics or recitation thereof were Śivasoma, Vāgīśvarapaṇḍita, Kavīndrapaṇḍita, etc. It is believed by some scholars that a concise and an enlarged version of *Mahābhārata* existed in Kambuja, as Ravīndrapaṇḍita is said to have explained *Mahābhārata* in the developed text (*vistāra*). Allusions to many epic stories, as also those from the *Harivaṁśa*, not only occur in the inscriptions, but many well-known episodes from the epics, such as the churning of the sea, the *svayaṁvara* of Draupadī and the Rāmakathā have been immortalized in the temple reliefs of Kambuja.

As the royal house of Kambuja worshipped for many centuries the Devarāja-liṅga; the deities of the Śaiva Tāntric pantheon were specially honoured. The famous Sdok Kak Thom inscription of Udayādityavarman II, which is of unique importance for the history of Kambuja, furnishes certain details regarding the study of some Tāntric texts during the reign of King Jayavarman II (CE 802-50). Jayavarman had invited Hiraṇyadāma "well versed in magical science" to perform a ritual according to Vrah Vinasikha, and taught Vrah Vinasikha, Nayottara, Sammoha and Śiraścheda to Śivakaivalya. The record further tells us that "he recited them from beginning to end in order that they may be written". The inscriptions also tell us that the doctrines of the Śaivite sect of the Pāśupatas and of the Vaiṣṇavite sect of the Pāñcarātras were taught by competent professors. Among other treaties, *Śiva Saṁhitā*, Śaivite *yoga* manuals, *Śivadharma*, *Guhyaṭīkā*, etc. have been mentioned. Buddhist texts were also studied in ancient Kambuja, but these were not in the scale of Sanskritic studies. Of such texts, inscriptions refer to the *Pratītyotpādana*, *Brahmaghoṣa* and *Saddharma-arṣabha*. These, described as Gāthāveda, seem to be the sacred books and songs of the Buddhists. A commentary on *Tattvasaṁgraha* as well as texts called *Madhyavibhāha*, *Paramitantra*, etc. have also been mentioned. The teaching of doctrines of the Yogācāra school was undertaken by some scholars. Yajñavarāha, the great *guru* of King Jayavarman V, has been described in an inscription as proficient in the doctrines of Buddha. The promulgation of some Pāli inscriptions also attests the growing popularity of Hīnayāna Buddhism in royal circles in the last days of Kambuja's greatness.

It is interesting to observe in this connection that the reputation of many authors of India had travelled to Indo–China and inscriptions make particular mention of such authors as Vātsyāyana, Guṇāḍhya, Pravarasena, Bhāravi, Viśālākṣa, Sura, Bhīmaka, Jina and Mayūra. The reference to so many Indian authors during the reign of King Yaśovarman doubtlessly indicates brisk literary activity in the Kambuja towards the end of the ninth century CE. There are also some folk tales of Kambuja which closely resemble those of India in structure and details.

**Art and Architecture**

We are all aware of the give and take that took place in the field of art and architecture between India and South-East Asia, particularly Cambodia. Among the Indian schools, the Amarāvatī, Gupta, Pallava and Pāla phases of art have left their impact in varying degrees on the art and architecture of South-East Asia. The Amarāvatī School which flourished during second and third century, influenced the art and architecture of South-East Asia to a great degree. This was because the Indianized settlements were taking place in this very period. Buddhist missionaries brought with them a number of Buddha images to Funan and the neighbouring Champa. The Gupta school of art which was at its peak from fourth to seventh century has also left deep impression on Khmer and Cham Art. The Indianized pre-Khmer art of Funan flourished between the fifth and seventh century, while the classic Khmer art flourished between the ninth and twelfth century. The Pallava school of art, which prevailed from 600 to 800 and Pāla or Sena school of art, which prevailed from 800 to 1200, have also left their influence on the art of South-East Asia including Cambodia. The Khmer art had developed its own personality and had discarded some of the Pallava motives like the Mokar-torna Lintel, the Caitya-windows and the Hans motifs. Coḷa school of art, which had a very powerful presence in India, has had only marginal impact on the art of South-East Asia, though some scholars believe that some of the Brāhmanical images of Funan were influenced by the south Indian art.

**Dharmaśāstras and the Rule of Law**

I have already mentioned about the study of *Manu Saṁhitā* and other treatises in Cambodia. Several references to *Manu Saṁhitā* occur in

Khmer inscriptions. In the verse 36 of Loley inscription it is stated that the king learnt his duty to the subject by taking guidance from Yogīśvara and that princes prostrating before him made him look as if he was another Manu. Two quotations from *Manu Saṁhitā* occur in the inscriptions of Yaśovarman. The first quotation states, "Of the acquired qualities, the greatest is learning, according to Manu", the second quotation states, "Wealth, kinship, age, pious, depths and in the fifth place, learning — these command respect in the ascending order of importance".

The inscriptions of Vet Prah Einkosai and Vat Baset Pillar also referred to Manu. Several Stelae have described that kings were adept in the Dharmaśāstras.

The inscriptions of Kambuja also throw some light on the proceedings of the law-courts of the country. After a complaint was lodged in the court, the court's "reciter of the Dharamaśāstras" (Indian law books) quoted Sanskrit texts relevant to the case and all legal points of the case were covered by Sanskrit terminology, but the factual presentation of the case was made in vernacular. Native legal proceedings were thus set up in the framework of Indian legal system. It must, however, be emphasized that local customs, practices and beliefs remained important in the Khmer jurisprudence and legal system.

### Varṇāśrama

There was some influence of Indian *varṇa* system on Cambodia. However, the Cambodians were much more flexible. There is evidence of movement from one *varṇa* to the other in several texts. The Buddhist influence on the Khmer society may have also played a role in diluting the *varṇa* system.

### Slavery

Some forms of slavery mentioned in Indian texts have also been mentioned in Cambodia. However, the practice of slavery appears to have been more prevalent in Cambodia than in India.

### Devarāja

The scholars have discussed in detail the divinity of the Khmer kings and the nature of their relation with the Devarāja cult. The very intimate relation between the ruling king and the Devarāja established by him in his mountain temple, amounting to identity and complete unification of the king with the godhead after death is generally acknowledged. Several views have been expressed about the concept of Devarāja. In fact, some scholars believe that it is only the name of a rite. There is little doubt that the concept of Devarāja has been influenced by Indian thoughts and practices. Similar concepts have also existed in central India and in some form in south India.

**Conclusion**

I have tried to give a glimpse of the wide-ranging links between the culture and civilization of Cambodia and India. It must be stated with all the emphasis at my command that the Khmer genius is primarily responsible for the flowering of this great civilization. I am in agreement with Adhir Chakravarty that there existed a fairly good societal structure when Indians came in contact with Khmers. The civilizational links have developed a sense of familiarity and some commonality of culture. Because of these links we share similar values and thoughts. It is hardly surprising that even in the modern times Indian films are very popular in Cambodia.

I would like to conclude with a poem by Ravindranath Tagore:

**To Java**

*When we tied golden threads of kinship*
*round each other's wrist*

*That ancient token, grown pale,*
*has not yet slipped off they right arm,*

*And our wayfaring path of old*
*lies strewn with the remants of my speech.*

*They help me to retrace my way to the inner chamber of thy life,*
*where still the light is burning that we kindled together*
*on the forgotten evening of our union.*

*Remember me, even as I remember thy face,*
*and recognize me as thine own,*

*The old that has been lost, to be regained and made new.*

— Translated from Bengali

*Inaugural Address*

# Let Us Reconnect!

*Lord Diljit Rana*

IT is an honour for me to be here and a privilege to visit this wonderful university. Since I met Dr (Mrs) Pankaj Mittal, Vice-Chancellor of BPS Mahila Vishwavidyalaya in Sanghol, I have been hearing about BPS Mahila Vishwavidyalaya. The spirit with which the original institution at the heart of the university, the Gurukula, was established in 1936 by Bhagat Phool Singhji, with the same spirit I have established educational institutions in Sanghol to help the rural boys and girls. It looks to me that such institutions can work together in this area.

Though India has become independent politically, we have not really become independent. We need economic and cultural independence. The vision of freedom fighters was to get total independence for India and Indians. They wanted independence of thought and restore true democracy and our rich past. Even today, there is a wide gap between urban and rural population.

Elite class in India collaborated with Britishers and focused on cultural colonialism. We shall educate our youth to make them culturally independent and to have pride in our past. We need to awaken our population about our past. Political independence shall be more democratic and take along population below poverty line. The aim of education should not be merely to provide employment, rather education should help in turning our people into good citizens who are responsible and duty bound. We should move away from British legacy of producing clerks and babus.

World economic system works against poor countries. Here is a classic example. The West first went on safari and shot tigers and later established World Wildlife Fund. Who is helping whom? Global warming is on increase just because of over consumption by the West. Colonizers made us poor and then offered grants. Indian society lives in harmony but is disconnected at all levels. There is need to reconnect. Our education shall address these serious concerns.

Thank you and it is a privilege being with you. I strongly believe that there is a need for us to reinvent our past and link with our neighbouring countries who were, at different phases in time, stake holders in our cultural moorings.

With these few words, I officially inaugurate this seminar.

# Contents

# Acknowledgement

It is our pleasure and privilege to present this book *Mekong–Gaṅgā Axis*, a set of lectures delivered in the International Conference on "South-East-East Asia and India: Historical Interconnections in Art, Architecture and Culture of Laos, Thailand, Cambodia and Vietnam" held during 18-20 January 2012 at BPS Women University, Khanpur Kalan. This was the second international conference organized by the Centre for Indic-Asian Studies in which many eminent professors/ scholars from outside India presented their research papers on the said aspects of the respective countries. To name a few, we were privileged to have Prof. Do Thu Ha (Vietnam), Dr Alexander Zorin (Russia), Dr Hawon Ku (South Korea), Dr Tran Phuoc Phuong Thao (Vietnam), Ms Prapassorn Posrithong (Thailand) and Mr Komang Santhi Arsa (Indonesia). We express our gratitude to all our esteemed contributors who acceded to our requests and created time from their extremely busy schedules to come and grace the occasion by their participation in the conference.

We shall always be grateful to Lord Diljit Singh Rana, MBE, Baron of Malone, House of Lords, UK for having accepted our invitation to be the Chief Guest and grace the occasion. We are also deeply grateful to Prof. M.K. Byrski, University of Warsaw, Poland for being an inspiration throughout the conference. We are also indebted to Prof. Balram Singh, Director of Center for Indic Studies at UMass Dartmouth, USA for benefitting the participants by delivering his wonderful lecture on SKYPE. We are extremely thankful to renowned Prof. Shiva G. Bajpai, former Director of Asian Studies, California State University, Northridge for being very kind to send us his contribution through a brief note as he could not be present in the conference due to his health condition.

We are particularly grateful to Late Prof. J.C. Sharma, IFS for being kind to deliver the keynote address in the conference. We are very sorry that he is not around to see the book.

We are thankful to the university administration for facilitating the conference in every possible way. We extend our special thanks to our dear colleagues Dr Babita and Dr Paramba Shri Yogmaya of CIAS for extending help thoughout the conference in every way. We are thankful to our research scholars Ms Rinu Yadav, Ms Farhana and Ms Sonia Kathuria who worked hard day and night to make the conference a success. We are also thankful to Mrs Mina Malik and Mr Joginder for extending complete support during the conference.

We are indebted to our Hon'ble Vice-Chancellor Prof. (Dr) Asha Kadyan without whose constant support, *Mekong–Gaṅgā Axis* would not have come out.

Above all, we are thankful to our dear and revered Prof. Kapil Kapoor, the then Director of Centre for Indic-Asian Studies, working with whom has really been enriching and inspiring for us. He has been a real guide, a mentor, a *guru* in showing us the way throughout during the conference and while editing this (book).

And finally we are very grateful to Sh Susheel Mittal of D.K. Printworld, who has taken a great interest in this book and has enriched the book with excellent publishing values.

**Editors**

# 1

# The Role of Classical Indian Theatre in Spreading the Cultural Influence of India to South-East Asia

*M. Krzysztof Byrski*

MAY I begin in a somewhat roundabout way? It has been since quite some time that I had been preoccupied with an idea of comparing Europe and India. For I insist that it is only fair to consider the whole of Europe as a proper counterpart of India, since none of the single European countries equals India in the size of its territory and in the ethnic variety of its population. Only Europe as a whole can match India on these counts. Even then the population of European Union is only little more than one-third of the population of India. The best description of the relationship of the two entities is in the form of an oxymoron — the twins unlike civilizations. For on many — so to say — structural counts they are like twins, while so far as their character goes, they are very much unlike each other as indeed any twin sisters would be. The main culprit for this difference is the average annual temperature,[1] which made Europeans desperately look for additional sources of energy and for the ways to store it. Thus emerged the technological civilization characterized by unbridled development, which is responsible for unprecedented spread of its tenets and its fascinating products all over the world. On the contrary the same

1 The average annual temperature differs immensely. In India the maximal one is + 26.8° C and minimal is + 18.10° C. The European one in turn is + 17.11° C and – 8.08° C. The important difference is that in most of Europe — for well over half a year — the climate is lethal for an unclad man.

temperature factor, responsible for the fact that practically all year long people living in India do not need additional sources of energy for heating their homes and for dispersing darkness of long wintertime nights, accounts for diametrically different attitude. Consequently in India the concept of *dharma* had been formulated, which lays stress on sustainability that makes people accept natural conditions and adjust rather than try to change these conditions with the help of technology.

Now the question arises whether at any time this particular model of Indian civilization had been comparable to the European model, which is attractive to the wider world? If this question is answered in the affirmative, we can add to the list of similarities of the two civilizations yet one more important item — their universal appeal transgressing the boundaries of their original birthplace. But could the civilization, which shared with art its attitude towards progress and development, consequently refusing to treat them as the only valid criterion, appear attractive to world at large? The answer is most certainly an emphatic yes!

"The impact of ancient India on the rest of Asia was, as it is well known, one of the most powerful exertions of cultural and religious influence in world history", writes Faubion Bowers, while surveying Asian dance and drama.[2] We believe that similar lack of urgency regarding the need for man-made additional and perennial sources of energy, as that one which characterizes India, was mainly accountable for the readiness with which the countries of South-East Asia yielded to the influence of Indian civilization. But this certainly was not the only reason of influence of the Hindu and subsequently also Buddhist doctrines that reached as far as Japan. It also cannot be held responsible for the attraction of decimal system of mathematics, which was readily accepted in Europe. The high sophistication of Indian philosophical and religious thought, the holistic concept of human existence and free from doctrinaire approach, understanding of reality so characteristic of the Vedic thought[3] must have been highly valued and willingly embraced. Even more so it must have been the particular aesthetic sensitivity that made Indian art and architecture

[2] Bowers 1956: 4.

[3] *ekaṃ sat viprā bahudhā vadanti* ।

so immensely attractive. Consequently the whole of South-East Asia became dotted with the temples and *stūpas* bearing distinct marks of Indian influence. "The splendid sculptural and architectural remains of the old kingdoms of Indonesia", writes Vincent Smith, "show the harmonious assimilation of Indian styles and motifs to those native to the region."[4]

Besides its vibrant social life became replenished with performing arts which constitute a living testimony of the fascination of South-East Asians with the Indian art perception. J.C. Sharma in his excellent study of Hindu temples in Vietnam writes:

> India's cultural relations with South-East Asia are one of the most fascinating fields of history. The interaction, which precedes the beginning of the Christian era, has left an indelible impression on almost every aspect of life in a number of countries of the region. It would not be an exaggeration to say that this intercourse has been a vital factor in shaping the history of this area.[5]

One cannot put it more succinctly and pointedly.

The role played in this process by performing arts cannot be underrated. There is no country in South-East Asia that has not welcomed Indian influence in this respect. Faubion Bowers writes:

> Certain broad dramatic principles stemming from this Indian past now are hallmarks of all Asian drama.[6]

Burma borrowed its dance–drama forms "from neighbouring India and Indianized Siam".[7] *Saṅgīta* — a Sanskrit term is used to denote classical theatre of Thailand.[8] The shadow play known as *Wayang Kulit* was "introduced to Indonesia along with other aspects of Hindu culture during great period of Hinduization".[9] Even Japanese theatre seems to be at least partly indebted to Indian influence.[10] Surapone

---

4 Smith 1958: 187.

5 Sharma 1997: XIII.

6 Bowers 1956: 19.

7 Ibid.: 110.

8 Ibid.: 150.

9 Ibid.: 218.

10 Ibid.: 321.

Virulrak holds that "practicum of Thai dance and drama is very similar to those mentioned in the *Nāṭyaśāstra*". Further on, he insists that although the Thai translation of the treatise of Bharatamuni is quite recent, nevertheless dance teachers and students all along have been strongly influenced by this compendium and Śiva Naṭarāja is considered to be supreme authority so far as Thai dance and drama go while "performers wear amulets of Bharatmuni around their necks for blessing and protecting their performances".[11] Naturally the question arises what might have been the reason of this fascination? Which intrinsic features of classical Indian theatre can be accounted for its popularity in South-East Asia? We are aware that in this respect we have to rely heavily on deduction rather than on hard proofs. But it is a very exciting challenge.

The best starting point for our query is Bharatamuni's definition of theatre:

> *yo 'yam svabhāvo lokasya sukhaduḥkhasamanvitaḥ* ।
> *so 'ṅgādyabhinayopeto nāṭyamityabhidhīyate* ॥ — *NŚ* I.116

> The nature of the human world with its happiness and its despair endowed with leads[12] such as body-lead, etc. is called theatre.

Thus this type of theatre has an ambition to be a faithful mirror of the human world (*loka*). It therefore had to address itself to the most vital, universal aspects of human existence and consequently might have had an appeal, which could transcend the precincts of its proper cultural milieu. Especially that according to ancient Indian theoreticians the reality that is created on the stage by actors has a unique character. The question to be answered concerns the proper character of this reality. Let me repeat here what I spoke about during the international seminar on "Word and Image" held at the India International Centre in November 2012:

> It is Abhinavagupta,[13] who in his commentary to the *Nāṭyaśāstra* tries to grapple with the problem of the nature of theatrical reality.

---

11 Virulrak 2012: 75.

12 *Abhinaya* traditionally translated as "acting", literally means "a lead". We shall return to this problem later.

13 Gnoli 1956.

> He asks the question, whose reality is the one with which we deal on the stage of theatre? Is it the reality of the hero or is it the reality of an actor who acts as a hero? Or is it the reality of a spectator? Certainly it is none of the three! Thus, he holds that in theatre we deal with the fourth type of reality — the reality, which is "departicularized" and can be appropriated exclusively by none of the three participants of the event. It should be therefore termed as universal (*sādhāraṇa*) reality, created by an actor and a poet and perceived by a spectator, all three are indispensable to bring to life *nāyaka* on the stage. When watching performance spectators are supposed to identify themselves emotionally with what is going on. Such identification is called *tanmayībhāva*. In such way spectators experience real emotions but generated by *sādhāraṇa* stage reality, therefore such emotions are also *sādhāraṇa* (non-particular). It is for this reason that negative emotions such as fear, disgust, anger and pity are enjoyed as Bhayānaka, Bībhatsa, Raudra and Karuṇa *rasa*s similarly to love, mirth, heroism and wonder enjoyed as Śṛṅgāra, Hāsya, Vīra and Adbhuta *rasa*s.

No doubt such an art must have been extremely attractive to the audiences of South-East Asia for the simple reason that their emotional disposition must have been very much akin to that of the denizens of South Asia, i.e. of India. The more so that

> . . . theatre in Asia is conceived of primarily as a performing art, the text is not accorded priority, and there is little tendency to look first at a play in terms of its meaning. The theatrical art is regarded as a whole. Thus the meaning of a play may be stated through elements of form, or conversely, certain meanings will imply expression through certain forms. . . . In Asian theatre, colour, rhythm, harmony, and balance are legitimate concerns of artist and audience.[14]

This is the common ground, which most probably can be accounted for this phenomenal advance of Indian art of theatre in South-East Asia.

Let us now consider the third element of the definition of theatre quoted above: ". . . *so 'ṅgādyabhinayopeto* . . ." (*NŚ* I.119). ". . . endowed with leads such as body-lead, etc. . . ." The term *aṅga* (body) is the key concept here, intimately connected with the term *abhinaya* —

---

[14] Brandon 1972: 4-6.

commonly translated (with lot of justification) as "acting". Both these terms signify, so to speak, physical dimension of theatre, without which it cannot function. Similarly to our world, that also cannot exist outside its material nature. The two terms in question, i.e. *āṅgika* (bodily) and *abhinaya* are essential for it has to be stressed that *āṅgika* cannot be limited only to gesture. All the three remaining modes of acting (*vācika, sāttvika, āhārya*) can be activated only and exclusively with the help of actor's body. This is why the *Nāṭyaśāstra* declares that there is no such action (*karman*), which cannot be met with in theatre (*NŚ* I.116). Action in everyday life means exertion of the body also that exertion, which is required for speaking (*vācika*) together with all those extra verbal subtle means of expression (*sāttvika*) also serving communication. The same concerns all paraphernalia used by the actor such as costume, make-up and stage props.

Now, let us look again at the term *abhinaya*. It connotes the specific mode of realizing *karman* on the stage of theatre. Sanskrit *abhi*+√*nī* means "to conduct towards", "to bring near" and even "to enter into".[15] Very interesting in this connection is the definition of the term that is to be found in the *Nāṭyaśāstra*.[16] N.P. Unni translates this passage in the following way:

> The root √*ṇīñ* with the preposition *abhi* means "to come face to face" or "ascertainment", since objects are being carried towards this direction, it is called *abhinaya*. Further, since the objects are represented by means of gestures of the body and limb — both main and ancillary — it is again designated as *abhinaya*.

So the term in question denotes a unique way an actor in his role of a hero, i.e. (*nāyaka*) a **leader** (*abhināyati*) **leads** (*sic!*) the audience towards such a state of mind, which in actual life accompanies the particular action represented on the stage. The impression upon the minds of the audience has to be sufficiently strong and lasting so as to make them reach such a level of identification (*tanmayībhāva*) that

---

[15] Monier-Williams: 64.

[16] *abhipūrvas tu ṇīṅ dhātur ābhimukhyārthanirṇaye* ।
*yasmāt padārthān nayati tasmād abhinayaḥ smṛtaḥ* ॥
*vibhāvayati yasmāc ca nānārthān hi prayogataḥ* ।
*śākhāṅgopāṅgasaṁyuktas tasmād abhinayaḥ smṛtaḥ* ॥ — VIII. 6-7

will enable them to fully participate emotionally in what comes to pass on the stage. In actual life it is usually the state of our mind and our emotional requirements that make us to embark upon suitable action. In theatre the order is reverted. Carefully designed by the poet–dramatist actions enlivened by the actor are meant to make us react according to preconceived pattern of five *sandhis*. So an actor — as the leader of performance is supposed to be a sort of an expert-behaviourist, who knows what should be done on the stage and how in order to evoke intended reactions and lead us towards the intended goal. At this moment it has to be added that this is by no means the ultimate goal of theatre, which according to Kālidāsa is "the delightful sacrifice for the eyes of the *kāmapuruṣārtha*".[17]

We have already invoked on these pages the concept of *sādhāraṇīkaraṇa,* the departicularization of the stage reality, which is responsible for the fact that both positive emotions as well as the negative ones are tasted with equal delight by the audience. Is it love (*śṛṅgāra*) or disgust (*bībhatsa*)! In this context one is tempted to ask why theatre has been described as *hitopadeśajanana* (*NŚ* I.113). What sort of good instruction one gets in theatre. Certainly one can emulate the behaviour of the heroes of a play especially when they are of the stature of Rāma, Kṛṣṇa or Arjuna. But this seems to be a less important side effect. The most important lesson comes from the fact that each member of the audience is made to experience the nature of human existence (*svabhāvo lokasya*) with its happiness and despair (*sukhaduḥkhasamanvitaḥ*) feeling the same *ānanda* — satisfaction that a fully realized *yogin* experiences?! How comes?! Well, thanks to the process of "departicularization" (*sādhāraṇīkaraṇa*) he may enjoy equally both positive as well as negative emotions. Since such experience is at all possible within the precincts of mundane existence, albeit in theatre, it means that in real life man can acquire similar distance too and treat even negative emotions afflicting him also with similar equipoise. This is possible thanks to the good offices of an expert actor-leader (*nāyakaḥ*) who with the help of four "leads" (*abhinayāḥ*) leads a spectator, who thus is encouraged to live his life in such a way that he may discover that the true nature of emotions he experiences is their

---

17 *Mālavikāgnimitra* I.4. This is how I interpret the Sanskrit: *kāntam kratum cakṣuṣām.*

*rasatva,* the essence of which is the awareness of the Absolute — the *saḥ* of *Taittirīyopaniṣad,* tantamount to the state of *jīvanmukti.* It is therefore not surprising that such a highly refined art might have earned so enthusiastic an appreciation also outside the country of its birth and especially in South-East Asia.

## References

Bowers, F., 1956, *Theatre in the East,* New York: Thomas Nelson & Sons.

Brandon, J., 1972, *Traditional Asian Plays,* New York: Hill & Wang.

Gnoli, R., 1956, *The Aesthetic Experience According to Abhinavagupta,* Roma.

Monier-Williams, M., 1899, *A Sanskrit-English Dictionary,* Oxford: Clarendon Press.

Sharma, J.C., 1997, *Hindu Temples in Vietnam,* New Delhi: Sankalp Publication.

Smith, V.A., 1958, *The Oxford History of India,* Oxford: Oxford University Press.

Virulrak, S., 2012, "Thai Practice and Discourse on Bharat's Natyashastra", in *Word and Image Seminar,* New Delhi: The Raza Foundation.

# 2

# Concepts for the Revival of Traditional Links between India and South-East–East Asia for Global Leadership

*Bal Ram Singh*

ESSENTIAL cultural values of India and South-East–East Asia are primarily common philosophy and traditions, which emphasize human interactions with nature, self-reflection for harmony with others, and leading a life of freedom and independence. In modern times these values are still valid but the narrative is not controlled by indigenous population. Indian philosophy as reflected in epics *Rāmāyaṇa* and *Mahābhārata*, and absorbed throughout South-East and East Asia need to be re-narrated in modern context socio-economic and political life. The idea of democracy needs to be reformatted for the culture and traditions of the region. Alternative models for economic systems need to be developed with the ingredients of indigenous culture. Spiritual traditions of human as an extension of nature needs to be practised in harmony with the environment. These practices need to be developed for leading the world into a sustainable living.

This article describes common geographical and historical connection of India with South-East and East Asia region, and describes common concepts of Indian philosophy and traditions to suggest ideas for revival of links between India and South-East and East Asia. Example of Balinese Hinduism practices will be used to compare essential values of Indian traditions not necessarily practised in India today yet being preserved in Bali through village and traditionally family practices in business, religious rituals and respect of nature. Some of the practices are in contrast to what is viewed as Hindu practices in India. India needs as much reform as the rest of the world. A regional approach with common tradition may infuse the needed impetus for the ultimate leadership East can provide to the global community.

## Geographical and Population Links between India and South-East and East Asia

In addition to being contiguous landlocked link of India to most of the South-East and East Asia, the region historically also had sea links and technologies to remain connected. This is important for trade and movement across the region, and has been used for hundreds if not thousands of years. India is located at the west horizon of the South-East and East Asia, both literally as well as figuratively. India is the crossroad of East and West, and given its climatic proximity with East, it tends to be part of the East narrative rather than the West. Latest population genetics results make even deeper connection between India and the rest of the world, including South-East and East Asia, as the genetic pool of most of the world originates from India (Braun 2011), after initial migration from Africa (see *fig*. 2.1).

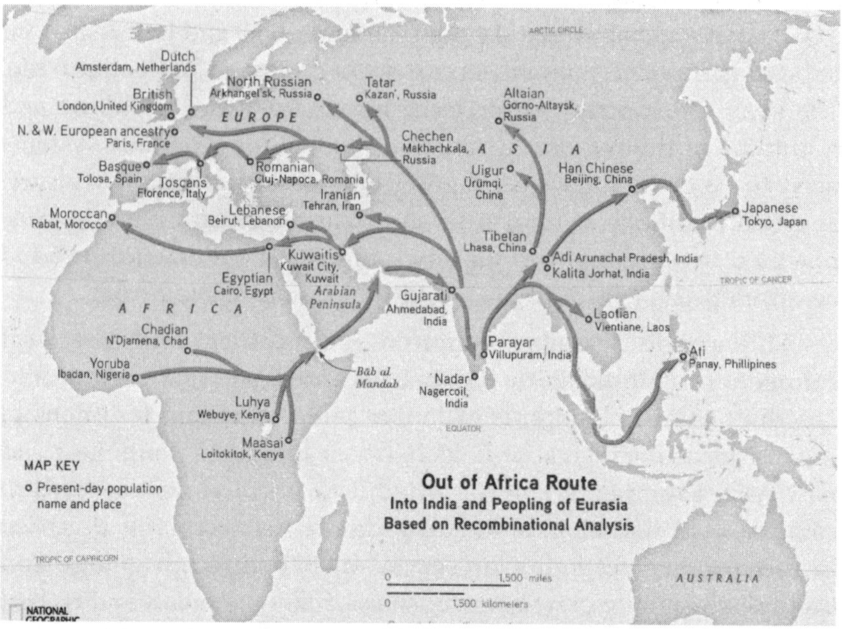


*fig*. 2.1: The map showing original migration of human population from Africa to India, which then becomes of source of population of the rest of the world. The map taken from http://www-03.ibm.com/press/us/en/photo/35881.wss

**Historical Cultural Connections**

India has historically had cultural links with the countries in South-East and East Asia. India's value systems have been adopted throughout the world in ancient times. For example, despite Thailand officially being a Buddhist country, it continues to relish in the essential human values of *Rāmāyaṇa* through its *Khon* and *Lakhon* forms of drama-dance tradition based on *Ramakien*, the Thai version of *Rāmāyaṇa*. The current king of Thailand is known as Rāma IV. In Indonesia, *Rāmāyaṇa* and *Mahābhārata* govern much of the social and cultural milieu, despite Indonesia being the largest Muslim population in the world. At a traffic roundabout on one of the busiest arteries of Jakarta city stands a monumental sculpture facing the central bank on one side and the national monument on the other. It depicts Kṛṣṇa and Arjuna in a chariot drawn by several horses (*fig.* 2.2). The sheer size and magnificence of this famous scene from *Mahābhārata* has no parallel even in India. Cambodia that hosts the largest Hindu temple, Angkor Vat in the world, has had several indigenous Hindu kings, and it had Sanskrit as its national language between sixth and twelfth century. Vietnam had Hindu kingdom of Champa between second and fifteenth century. Other countries, including China, Japan, Laos and Malaysia have been under heavy influence of India for spiritual, cultural, political and economic practices for millennia.

*fig.* 2.2: An sculpture showing the chariot of Arjuna and Kṛṣṇa from the epic *Mahābhārata* at a roundabout in Jakarta, Indonesia

**Essential Concepts**

The essential concepts of life in South-East and East Asia region have several elements which are common with those of people in India.

1. *Harmony with Nature* — Since natural climate is cooperative and helpful to humans, people in this region have very positive attitude towards nature. Nature worshipping, celebration of seasons, harvests and beauty, and general abundance of natural resources (fertile land and ample water) reflect appreciation of the nature.
2. *Ancestor Worship* — This practice is common throughout the region, reflecting a common value of appreciating elders in life and after death. Such a practice creates a culture of strong bond within the family, and care that both elders and youngsters receive.
3. *Karma Theory and Reincarnation* — Traditionally, this entire region accepts karmic consequences and their redemption through reincarnation. Although such concepts are dubbed as religious beliefs they have tremendous social, psychological and economic impacts on the society. Such concepts make people responsible for their own action, minimizing state and government interference and expenses to run a society.
4. *Freedom and Independence* — The whole region has diverse population involving multi-ethnic, multi-linguistic and multi-religious groups. In addition to reflection of a freedom of diversity, living of people in harmony also indicates their relative independence. Although it is not examined extensively, such a practice of living requires an entirely different kind of mindset than what is created from the Western practices in life. For example, independence can be achieved only through self-reliance, and only independence can lead to freedom. This necessarily needs smaller units of living, such as villages. Furthermore, due to relatively isolated village life, people need to be innovative and entrepreneurial to lead a meaningful life. Interestingly, the entire region reflects this way of living where countries still have nearly 70 per cent of their population in rural areas. This protects

environment as well as human population from exploitation by either corporations or governments.

**Traditions and Practices**

As is true with any society that has a reasonable span of existence, essential concepts are turned into traditions and practices for ease and continuity. Following are examples of such traditions in South-East and East Asia which are also common with India.

1. *Small Governments and Local Traditions* — With small village community and traditionally small kings, it has been possible to govern to community through developing traditions of social norms, economic practices and family values. The advantage of traditions over policies and laws is the universal knowledge and practice of traditions, allowing universal enforcement of values which are more fair and effective, and thus more readily acceptable. However, due to the domination of the West through colonization over the past centuries the traditions of the East have come under heavy pressure and face obliteration.
2. *Role Models from Stories of Epics* — Although heroes from stories and legends have been common inspirations throughout the humanity, there is a remarkable emphasis on heroes of epics, particularly *Rāmāyaṇa* and *Mahābhārata,* for people in South-East and East Asia. Origin and stage of these epics being India puts this very large proportion of the world population under heavy influence of Indian culture and traditions. Assuming that these values were not imposed through subjugation, it would reflect the presence of extraordinary human values in the stories and characters so much that they transcend religious barriers in Buddhist Thailand and Muslim Indonesia. In modern times, this tradition has been lacking although there have been examples of personalities like Mahatma Gandhi, Mother Teresa, Nelson Mandela and Martin Luther King Jr. The reason may be the emphasis on democratic majority and minority opinions, which presents an average of a phenomenon no one can exactly associate with. Heroes of epics or legends are like case studies which allow for individual association

and inspiration, making it a better motivation for individual transformation.

### Elements of Links of India with South-East and East Asia

There are several critical elements that link India to the entire region of South-East and East Asia. These include Sanskrit-based languages, climatic commonality leading to common food and clothing, and cultural concepts based on ideals of the two great epics, *Rāmāyaṇa* and *Mahābhārata*. However, these links have rarely been emphasized by the governments in modern times.

There are conflicts between different countries within the region, which are mostly territorial or those related to chauvinistic domination or Western political ideas being employed to show superiority. A system based on their own ethos, culture and traditions is not in place. India holds a key position and must carry a responsibility for developing, modernizing and rejuvenating many of the fundamental human values which had served the humanity for millennia. But it will need an introspection first, and a determined reformation second and finally willingness to join hands with the nations in South-East and East Asia to advance and implement a modernized system based on ancient values and traditions. India does have a very sophisticated articulation of the essential system in its literatures and scriptures, which are unparalleled in the world. However, a proper analysis and understanding of these texts are needed first.

The system of governance in ancient India differed from Western democracy; but there are many instances of righteous kings who considered the interests of their subjects with utmost sincerity. India's Bhārata name comes after king Bharata who ruled over 8,000 years ago an India that encompassed from east of Iran to Indonesia. King Bharata was son of King Duṣyant (a descendant of King Manu through latter's daughter Ilā) and Śakuntalā, the daughter of sage Viśvāmitra. A major story of King Bharata is that he is the first known king who did not choose any of his nine sons as the heir, rather a well-qualified commoner since he found none of his sons as qualified to be a king. Such a legacy is an important one to remember in today's world, both within and without India, as so many rulers even in democratic system tend to promote their offsprings into the political system.

However, that is not to say that all the kings were nobles, and there were obviously problematic kings. There are stories of numerous major wars within the land of Bhārata (two major ones form the basis of epics *Rāmāyaṇa* and *Mahābhārata*), which were not fought for expansion of territories or power, but to right the wrong as the overriding factor. In other words, these wars were fought to assert *dharma*. These stories and values are obviously common with people in South-East and East Asia, and there is no doubt that these will receive sympathetic and favourable responses.

The concept of *dharma* provides a framework for much of the cultural values that have been propounded in the epics of India. There are many definitions of *dharma*. Quite often though it gets translated as religion, which is quite contrary to the original as well as even pragmatic meaning of the word *dharma*. According to sage Kaṇāda, who provided the idea of the atom around 700 BCE, *dharma* is that which governs the birth and death of everything. This is a not just a secular definition of *dharma* but a scientific one. It refers to all those forces involved in governing appearance and disappearance of material and non-material things in this universe. When the meaning of *dharma* properly understood, one has no choice but to turn to the nature to experiment and acquire the true meaning of *dharma*. This is a legacy of India that can so readily be utilized to unite India with rest of the world, although more so and more readily with people of South-East and East Asia.

The understanding and practice of *dharma* are subscriptive as opposed to prescriptive, and apply to every aspect of life and living. So, there is a *dharma* of a son, a daughter, a father, a mother, etc. as much as the *dharma* of a tree, air, water, etc. People are generally free to subscribe to their own *dharma*, as they understand it from the experience of their family, community, natural environment and, of course, education. At the highest level, India does not have a record of injunctions for or against a given type of behaviour or practice. With a long experiment and experience for a society like India that has retained its continuing civilization for at least 10,000 years, many of its collective experiences have become traditions (translation of a Sanskrit word, *paramparā*, which refers to great knowledge). With passage of time, the basic meanings of many of the traditions got misunderstood or the traditions themselves became limited to rituals, which have caused much of social stagnation and at times problems for the society. Nevertheless India's fundamental principles moored in *dharma* remain eternal, the basic foundations of its traditions strong and essence of its practices fairly universal. This will be the crucial element in linking India to South-East and East Asian countries in modern times.

### Indian Culture of Tolerance

In the midst of turmoil we face today in the world, a major Indian tradition of celebrating diversity would do a great deal in promoting peace and prosperity. An article entitled "Want to Prosper? Then Be Tolerant" was written by Paul Johnson, a prominent British historian and author in *Forbes* magazine (Johnson 2004). The article pointed out the economic value of being tolerant. This is a welcome observation that must be promoted and pursued with vigour to open at least an alternative front to deal with the current turmoil in the world. India's tradition, particularly the Hindu tradition of tolerance, has been exalted by Johnson to make his point that whenever a society develops tolerance, there is prosperity in the society. He makes two contrasts to send his message home. One is the communist/Marxist mindset pervasive in the 1950s, 1960s and part of the 1970s in China (under Mao Zedong), and until the 1980s in India (under the Congress party). It is notable that as a result of Congress party in power for the past ten years, with first five years having communists on its piggyback as outside supporters of the government, India is no longer considered an upcoming economic superpower. In accordance with Johnson's theory, and with partial success in communists manipulating the government substantial retrogressive results are apparent the India. Second, Johnson draws upon focus on the escalation of intolerance in the Islamic society and increase in poverty in many Islamic countries such as Iraq, Iran and Saudi Arabia. The traditional culture of rational tolerance and acceptance of diversity in India and South-East and East Asia could provide a common platform for economic plans and principles for the world. The tolerance and appreciation of diversity have been the hallmark of even Western world for the past fifty years or so.

## Global Outreach of India

As the globalization is taking its roots throughout the world, India needs to review and rejuvenate well-established ancient systems of social, economic, cultural, scientific and political values. This would require extensive overhaul of thinking within the intellectual and political class, with complete overhaul of education system and substantial global effort in presenting India's value-based narrative.

Fortunately, the list of India's outside admirers is long and cuts across all sections of life — Albert Einstein, Neils Bohr, Erwin Schrodinger, Max Müller, Mark Twain, Will Durant, Martin Luther King Jr., George Harrison, David Frawley, Robert Blackwill, Bill Clinton, to name a few. What is so unique about India that it has remained at the zenith of philosophy, science, music and culture for thousands of years? The answer lies among other things on the nature's benevolence on India. India's geography, geology and demography provide natural settings for human learning, leading to the philosophy of its diverse culture and traditions. India is the only country blessed with the highest mountain peaks of the Himalayas on one end and the lowest level of earth on the other (the ocean), with numerous geological formations in between. India is the only country on earth which witnesses six clear and distinct seasons during the year. Such crisp variation in seasons and weather could support many diverse species of life in India. Sharing of at least part of this climatic condition with South-East and East Asian people makes it easier to communicate this common human experience.

## The Major Players of the Region

South, South-East and East Asia regions have four key countries (*fig.* 2.3) which have substantial influence in the region as well as in the world. Japan is obviously an economic power of decades now, but has a distinct culture. China has become a giant with its enormous population and economic strength. It is also a military force. Indonesia has the largest Muslim population in the world, and has cultural ties with many countries. India as an upcoming country with its trained workforce and deep ancient philosophical system that provides moorings to all the countries in the region. A combination of Hindu kings, Buddhism, epics of India and many trade relationships, India holds a respectable position in the region. Nalanda University being a centre of learning and scholarship for intellectuals in this entire region during ancient times still holds, as demonstrated by its revival (Rajghatta 2008) through collaborative efforts of several countries in this region (Japan, Singapore, China, etc.). While this establishes India's role as the centre of intellectual and philosophical unity, it does not mean there are no differences among these countries even on intellectual level, nor should there be. Differences are the unending strength that can be tapped to build a diversified portfolio of this region, where India can play the role of unifier. However, this has not been a focus of India which needs to be changed. What form or shape that change will take is not clear. India is currently under the Westernization mode. It will have to be on this course for a while before turning its direction. Two other countries, Japan and China, underwent this course, and have survived as cultures, keeping hope alive for Indian course as well.

Sun Yat-sen, the philosophical architect of China's Westernization had no hesitation in recommending that China should learn from the West:

> Chinese civilization has been around for several thousand years now, while Western civilization has only been around a mere several centuries. Chinese people cannot change a past civilization into a modern one. This is why people say that China is the most conservative and that is the reason for its accumulated poverty . . . we, the modern people of China, are all useless, but if in the future we use Western civilization as a model, we can easily turn weakness into strength, and the old into the new. I think that everyone should go to the West and find something new, then go to the East and find something old, and if we Chinese can bring this about, then there will be nothing hard about the old turning into the new.

Even Japan's economic position today may be attributed to its early decision to Westernize itself. Japanese Meiji reformer, Yukichi Fukuzawa, said:

> Our immediate policy, therefore, should be to lose no time in waiting for the enlightenment of our neighbouring countries in order to join them in developing Asia, but rather to depart from their ranks and

> cast our lot with the civilized countries of the West. We should deal with them exactly as the Westerners do.

This attitude may in part have been responsible for the brutal treatment of Chinese population by Japanese rulers during their occupation of China.

To easternize their relationship India and China made a very promising start in 1954 by agreeing to the Five Principles (Panchsheel) of Peaceful Co-existence as the basis for developing relations between states. These principles provided for peaceful co-existence, mutual respect for each other's territorial integrity and sovereignty, non-aggression, non-interference in each-other's internal affairs, and recognition of equality and mutual benefit. These principles formed the basis of non-alignment movement (NAM) that attracted most of the countries in the world who wanted to keep away from the erstwhile Soviet and American blocks. However, first of all, the Panchsheel principles had nothing that was exclusively Eastern in it, and second the Panchsheel principles were not effectively

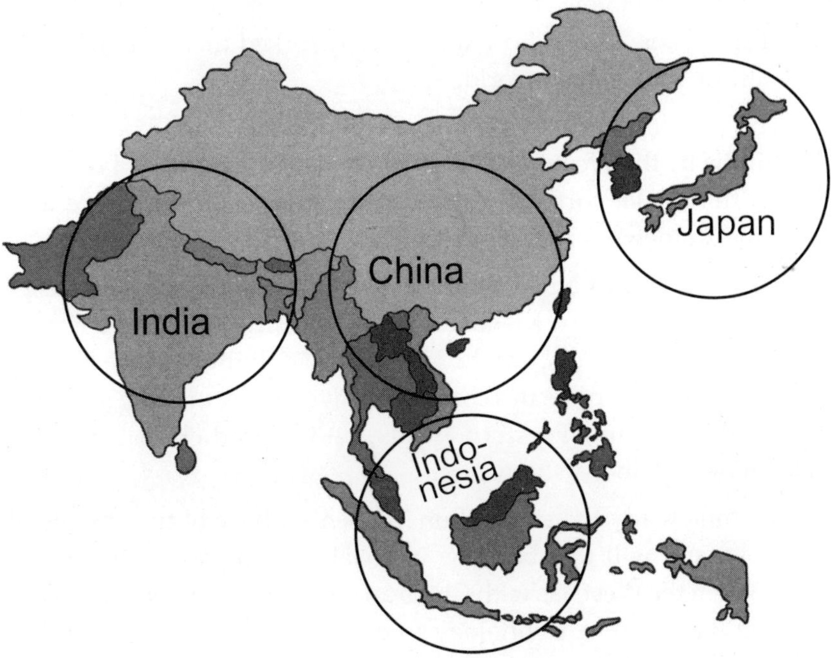


*fig.* 2.3: Key regions of South, South-East and East Asia

implemented, and the 1962 war between India and China shattered any dream of an Eastern leadership to the world affairs. It is possible that these principles are still a framework of the Western world.

China has much better link to India directly through the masses, and that relies on thousands of years of culture rather than communism, another failed Western concept. Relations between China and India are more likely to grow on the foundation of culture and tradition rather than economic "competition" of each other by vying to the standards and definition of the Western world. Economic growth is important, but it must be attained with cooperation rather than cut-throat mentality of competition, because that inevitably leads to distrust and ego clashes. For the Eastern world to succeed globally, India–China relationship is important to not only become a model but also provide a framework for other countries in the region to work with.

Western world has historically made plenty by creating clashes amongst different peoples. Their attempt to create a wedge has worked to their advantage for at least 500 years, and it has all come through the economic channel in the beginning, assuming a military dimension later. That is how colonialists worked their way into India and rest of the Eastern world.

The question is whether China and India, recently clubbed together as Chindia by the Western economic interest groups, would recognize this in time, take corrective measures, and lead their future away from the framework of Western binary vision.

This is going to be a tall challenge, given the history of Eastern world, as outlined by Kishore Mahbubani, the Dean and Practice Professor of Public Policy at the LKY School of Public Policy, National University of Singapore, in a comprehensive review of India's relations on the Eastern and Western fronts, and a prediction for India's independent path for the future.

Is China ready to listen to Sun Yat-sen's advice of turning the old into new, and will that be done in collaboration with India? Part of the problem the West has with China and India may be not that Chindia will use the Western technology to enhance their GDP and military power (they remain assured of their superiority for another half century or so), but to turn their old into new, which may be too hard for the West to compete with.

There is a great deal of debate whether India will represent the Western or the Eastern viewpoint. Some Westerners actually like to think that the Eastern world starts after India. This is primarily because of Sanskrit, the ancient yet still in use, language of India being considered as the origin of the Indo-European languages, and a now virtually defunct Aryan Invasion Theory advanced by colonialists to relate Indian civilization to the European civilization.

In the words of Mahbubani:

> India's role as it emerges as a great power may therefore be quite different from the roles played by Japan and China. Japan tried to demonstrate forcefully that it could be as good a member of the Western club as any Western nations. China, by contrast, has made no effort to prove that it can be as Western as any other Western society.

**Possible Future Moves**

In the final analysis, India in collaboration with China and Japan will have to engage countries in the South-East and East Asia beyond current framework of nation state concept defined by the Western world, yet utilize the opportunities present within the current framework of international concepts and conditions. For example, globalization as a concordant *mantra*, although as old as the human history, has been a frontier phrase for many years now, albeit mostly for the benefit of multinationals. However, due to the advent of Internet communications and information, globalization now seems to have unexpected and totally unintended repercussions on the existence of the nation state concept for world organization. Today, globalization seems to undermine the nation state concept at its core, and threatens the role of political masters much the same way as the colonial masters or slave masters. The long yearning for freedom from masters is finally inching towards its final steps. This reality can be utilized by India and countries in South-East and East Asia, which have promoted the sense of multiple ideas to exist together peacefully.

Western world's treasured concept of democracy and diplomacy can be recast to create a more just and free world without the instrument of constant manipulation to have a zero sum game. For democracy, Mahatma Gandhi had a totally different idea than the state of nation states we see in the world today, i.e. at each other's throat pretending diplomacy. Gandhi said,

> Democracy must in essence, therefore, mean the art and science of mobilizing the entire physical, economic and spiritual resources of all the various sections of the people in the service of the common good of all.

There is a great need to develop the concept of democracy further to let people become independent and free from constant control of corrupt rulers.

Concern about the environment pollution and a sustainable planet is opening the mind for a new way of global thinking. Public in the West is becoming restless with impending global warming and planetary doom. While Western governments keep pointing fingers at India and China for continuous and potential contribution to greenhouse gases, I believe people in the Western countries where social fabric has become very tenuous are looking up to the Eastern wisdom for a sustainable society living in peace with nature. The challenge for India is to develop ideas outside the box, based perhaps on its millennia-old civilizational wisdom. That will be easier to try with countries of the South-East and East Asia than anyone else, given their shared civilizational values.

There is a need to develop *pañcamantra* (five goals) and *pañcatantra* (five approaches) for the humanity irrespective of caste and creed, for the creation of a new world order beyond political and military clichés. My tentative suggestions for *pañcamantra* would be independence, freedom, pursuit of truth, celebration of diversity and harmony with nature. The *Pañcatantra* to be implemented should be universal health, enlightened education, prosperous living, non-violence and righteous governance.

The structural complementarity in current economic practices of China, Japan and Korea can easily be integrated with South-East and other East Asian countries to work together in providing leadership in the globalized world. China as a historically organized society can provide strong leadership in developing ways to implement the *Pañcatantra*, and India with its very long tradition of philosophy could provide leadership in developing elaborate argument for the *pañcamantra* as a replacement of current paradigm of democracy, human rights, diplomacy, nation states and money-based social security.

## References

Braun, D., 2011, "Modern Humans Wandered Out of Africa via Arabia", National Geographic on 3 November 2011.

Johnson, P., 2004, "Want to Prosper? Then Be Tolerant", *Forbes*, 21 June 2004.

Rajghatta, C., 2008, "Nalanda to move from Ruins to Riches", *Times of India*, 11 May 2008.

Singh, B.R., 2003, "NRIs Can Make or Break India's Greatness", *India New England News*, 15 December 2003.

———, 2006, "Role of the Hindu Diaspora in Bringing India's Traditions to the World", *Swadharma*, Harvard's Hinduism Journal (May) **1**: 33-35.

———, 2007 "A Different Path for a Powerful March of India and China in 21st Century", *Business Herald China*, 13 May 2007.

# 3

# Cultural Heritage of Champa Kingdom in Central Vietnam

## Some Evidences of the Interaction of the Trade and the Religion between India and Vietnam in the Past

*Do Thu Ha*

CHAMPA was an Indic civilization that flourished along the coasts of what is now central and southern Vietnam for roughly 1,000 year period between CE 500–1500. The original Chams were probably colonists from the Indonesian islands, who adopted as their principal vocations those of trade, shipping and piracy. Their cities were ports of call on important trade routes linking India, China and the Indonesian islands.

This article discusses about the cultural heritage of Champa Kingdom in central Vietnam as the evidences of the interaction of the trade and the religion between India and Vietnam in the past. With the artefacts of the civilization excavated from this region, dating back from the seventh century to seventeenth century or even earlier, we would like to introduce that very precious legacy of Vietnam.

The artistic legacy of Champa consists primarily of sandstone sculptures — both sculpture in the round and relief sculpture — and brick buildings. Some metal statues and decorative items have also survived. Much of the remaining art expresses religious themes, and though some pieces would have been purely decorative, others would have served important functions in the religious life of the Chams, which synthesized elements of Hinduism (especially Śaivism), Buddhism and indigenous cults.

The history of Champa was one of intermittent conflicts and co-operation with the people of Java, the Khmer of Angkor in Cambodia and the Dai Viet of what is now northern Vietnam. It was to the Dai Viet that Champa finally lost its independence.

The largest collection of Cham art is on exhibit at the Museum of Cham Sculpture in Da Nang. Substantial collections are housed in the Guimet Museum in Paris, Museum of Vietnamese History in Saigon and Museum of History in Hanoi. Smaller collections may be found in the Museum of Fine Arts in Saigon and Museum of Fine Arts in Hanoi.

Now, where does this interest in South-East Asia originate? It is very simple: it lies in a place that I call the "Fujian Stream". Here, Chinese — mostly from Fuji — and Japanese (though not for very long) travelled along this long coastal stream of traffic — perhaps the world's busiest at the time — to move goods through a triangle of traffic, between Japan, China and South-East Asia.

My paper is organized as follows. In Section I, I give some background about my approaching methods. The Section II, I will talk about some facts of the geographical location of Champa in the past that made this country become an important cross-point on sea routes. In Section III, I present a summary of main influences which India left on Champa's culture. In Section IV, I conclude.

## I. Approaching Methods

Historians distrust other historians, as well as practitioners of other disciplines, when they divide up time and label their periodizations. Do the dates really mark "turning points" or are they arbitrarily imposed upon a continuity? Can an era effectively be labelled as one of "violence" or an age one of "imperialism" without degrading a story that can meaningfully be told only in all its "detailed glory"?[1] The answer, of course, is one of convenience. It is impossible to compose a book without a theme or to analyse a situation without an assumption.

Is international order in modern times rightly described, as by students of International Relation (IR), in terms of "anarchy"? Was it preceded — as might be inferred — by a different order, composed, say, of hierarchy? And if there is such a shift, can it be marked off by dates, even if they are striking or symbolic?

---

[1] The phrase is given in Gould 1986: 64.

Historians are stimulated, but also checked, by the cross-centuries application of descriptions. If "anarchy" may be questionable as a description of the recent or contemporary system of interstate relations, would it have been accepted, or even understood, as apt in earlier centuries of the modern era?

The historian will also wonder if the orders, hierarchy and anarchy, are quite so different in practice as they seem to be in definition, quite so sharply distinguishable. For they have to do with common problems that continue over many centuries, even though the nature of the states that makes up the order may change, their capacities advance, their wealth increases, their population grow.

Both orders, modern and ancient, have, for one thing, to deal with the fundamental issue of interstate relationships, the disparity of power and its shifting distribution. The hierarchical system handles that by an explicit recognition of disparity that is also mutual: if the lesser know their place, they may be able to preserve or even enhance it. The characteristic relationship in such a system may be a lord/vassal or patron/client relationship, and/or the rendering and reception of tribute, always with the assumption that there is an element of obligation on the part of the superior as well as the inferior, that submission is counterparted by protection.

The equivalent in the modern system, anarchy, is far less specific, but it is surely there. States are theoretically equal in their sovereignty, but they are grossly unequal in power. The system works only because in practice the powerful moderate the exercise of their power, and the weaker tune their aspirations to equality. A range of supplementary options may help: the making of alliances, the pursuit of a balance of power, the creation of regional organizations. Tensions come with change, often leading to conflict, even wars, big or small.

Both systems are closely related to matters of allegiance or control. In the ancient system the state did not have the power that the modern state has and seeks. It might be content with a diminished allegiance at least outside its core and with indefinite frontiers. It might control its people loosely, exercising symbolic rather than actual control, its officers exemplifying rather than enforcing appropriate behaviour. It might allow "foreigners" more or less to rule themselves, rather than attempting to assimilate them, or even use them as an instrument of control over others. The modern state looks for more: it seeks definite frontiers, within which citizens or subjects owe it services and taxes, and "minorities" have such rights as an entity ruled by or based on a "majority" sees fit to allow them.

Tackling these issues with a regional approach, and including South-East Asia as a region, are welcome strategies, and, it may be shown, profitable ones. In the past neither public nor scholarly debate was ready to identify it as a region, and even in recent works of generalization or popularization it tends to be bypassed. When it was distinguished in the past, it was often labelled to be "Further/ Greater India", the Nanyang, the Nan-yo. Public events — the Second World War in particular — led to the wider adoption of a more neutral geographical labelling, and it was filled out by both political and academic activities. Histories of "South-East Asia" appeared in the 1950s — magisterially led by D.G.E. Hall's — and the Association of South-East Asian Nations (ASEAN) — its leaders conscious of the past as well as the present — was inaugurated in 1967. It was a diverse region, but that was not a reason for not seeing it as a region either for action or for study. Rather the reverse.

Students of the region, as well as statesmen, both sought commonalities, however, and it may be that it still retains, albeit in modified form, practices inherited from a past that temporally is after all not so distant, even if in the interim the region has been the scene of unprecedented change. One feature of the last 150-200 years is its shift from demographic immaturity: perhaps there were only 30 million people in South-East Asia in 1830. Certainly in the more remote past what counted among the state-builders of South-East Asia had been men rather than land, and the attitudes that established arguably help to account for the contemporary strength of patron–client relationships.

Whether the South-East Asian past is peculiar in this may be doubted: in what became Poland, for example, power came from having a following, and security from being a follower. "Princes described their realm not in terms of acreage but in terms of the people who obeyed their orders, or sought their protection", Norman Davies writes of early Poland.[2]

---

2 Davies 2005: 56.

> Political power radiated from a few centres of authority, whose spheres of influence constantly waxed and waned, and very frequently overlapped. These centres can best be likened to magnets, and the people living in between them, to iron filings pulled hither and thither by fluctuating and conflicting magnetic fields.[3]

What may be special about the South-East Asian region — though still helpful in comparative studies — is its cultural diversity. It was penetrated by a range of peoples, but also subjected (by whatever means) to the influence of two great neighbours (that led to past labelling). What the process of that influence was has been disputed among historians. The generally accepted conclusion is that state-builders in the region borrowed from these cultures, in particular from India. At times, if not more generally, China, however, asserted its primal claim: exceptionally, in the Vietnamese case, in the form of political dominance, more usually in the form of a pattern of tributary relationships.

## II. Geographical Location of Champa

The kingdom of Champa (Cham Pa in Vietnamese or Chiêm Thành in Sino-Vietnamese records) was an Indianized kingdom of Malayo-Polynesian origins and controlled what is now southern and central Vietnam from approximately the seventh century through to 1832. It has the oldest known written Malay language from the fourth century CE, predating Sumatran texts by 300 years (Coedès 1939). Champa was preceded in the region by a kingdom called Lin-yi or Lâm Âp (in existence since CE 192), but the historical relationship between Lin-yi and Champa is not clear. Champa reached its apogee in the ninth and tenth centuries CE. Thereafter began a gradual decline under pressure from the Dai Viet which was then northern Vietnam. In 1471, Viet troops sacked the northern Cham capital of Vijaya, and in 1697 the southern principality of Pāṇḍuraṅga became a vassal of the Vietnamese emperor. In 1832, the Vietnamese emperor Minh Mang annexed the remaining Cham territories.

### GEOGRAPHY OF HISTORICAL CHAMPA

Between the seventh and the fifteenth century CE, Champa at times

[3] Davies 2005: 30.

included the modern Vietnamese provinces of Quảng Nam, Quảng Ngãi, Bình Định, Phú Yên, Khánh Hòa, Ninh Thuận and Bình Thuận. Though Cham territory included the mountainous zones west of the coastal plain and (at times) extended into present-day Laos, for the most part the Cham remained a seafaring people dedicated to trade, and maintained few settlements of any size away from the coast.

Historical Champa was a confederation of up to five principalities, each named after a historic region in India:

- **Indrapura**: The city of Indrapura is now called Dong Duong, not many miles from present-day Da Nang and Hue. Da Nang used to be the city of Singhapura and is close to the valley of My Son, site of many ruined temples and towers. The area once controlled by this principality included present-day Quang Binh, Quảng Trị and Thừa Thiên-Huê provinces.
- **Amarāvatī**: Present-day Quảng Nam province.
- **Vijaya (Champa)**: The city of Vijaya is now called Cha Ban but it lies just a few miles north of present-day Qui Nhon in Bình Định province. For a time, Vijaya principality controlled much of present-day Quảng Nam, Quảng Ngãi, Bình Định and Phú Yên provinces.
- **Kauthara**: The city of Kauthara is now called Nha Trang in present-day Khánh Hòa province.
- **Pāṇḍuraṅga (Champa)**: The city of Pāṇḍuraṅga is now called Phan Rang in present-day Ninh Thuận province. Pāṇḍuraṅga was the last of the Cham territories to be annexed by the Vietnamese.

Within the four principalities there were two main groups: the Dua and the Cau. The Dua lived in Amarāvatī and Vijaya while the Cau lived in Kauthara and Pāṇḍuraṅga. The two clans differed in their customs and habits and conflicting interests led to many clashes and even war. But they usually managed to settle disagreements through intermarriages.[4]

---

4 Rutherford 2006: 256.

## HISTORIOGRAPHY OF CHAMPA

### *Sources for the Historiography of Champa*

The historiography of Champa relies upon three types of sources[5] (http://library.kiwix.org:4201/A/Champa.html - cite_note-1):

- Physical remains, including brick structures and ruins as well as stone sculptures;
- Inscriptions in Cham and Sanskrit on stelae and other stone surfaces; and
- Chinese and Vietnamese histories, diplomatic reports and other texts.

### *Overarching Theories in the Historiography of Champa*

Modern scholarship has been guided by two competing theories in the historiography of Champa. Scholars agree that historically Champa was divided into some five regions or principalities (Pāṇḍuraṅga, Kauthara, Amarāvatī, Vijaya and Indrapura) spread out from south to north along the coast of modern Vietnam and united by a common language, culture and heritage. However, scholars have disagreed on whether the five regions belonged to a single political unit, or whether they were politically independent of one another. It is acknowledged that the historical record is not equally rich for each of the five regions in every historical period. For example, in the tenth century, the record is richest for Indrapura; in the twelfth century, it is richest for Vijaya; following the fifteenth century, it is richest for Pāṇḍuraṅga. Some scholars have taken these shifts in the historical record to reflect the movement of the Cham capital from one location to another. According to such scholars, if the tenth-century record is richest for Indrapura, it is so because at that time Indrapura was the capital of Champa. Other scholars have disputed this contention, holding that Champa was never a united country, and arguing that the presence of a particularly rich historical record for a given region in a given period is no basis for claiming that the region functioned as the capital of a united Champa during that period.[6]

---

5 Vickery 2005: 4ff.

6 Maspero, 1928, represented the thesis that Champa was politically unified. Vickery, 2005: 4ff., challenges that thesis.

### *Sources of Foreign Cultural Influence*

Through the centuries, Cham culture and society were influenced by forces emanating from China, India, Cambodia, as well as from other sources. Initially, the culture of Champa was closely tied to Chinese cultural and religious traditions. In the fourth century, wars with the neighbouring kingdom of Funan in Cambodia and the acquisition of Funanese territory led to the infusion of Indian culture into Cham society. Sanskrit was adopted as a scholarly language, and Hinduism, especially Śaivism, became the state religion. From the tenth century onwards Arab maritime trade in the region brought increasing Islamic cultural and religious influences. Champa came to serve as an important link in the Spice Route which stretched from the Persian Gulf to southern China and later in the Arab maritime routes in Indo-China as a supplier of aloe. Despite the frequent wars between Champa and Cambodia the two countries also traded and cultural influences moved in both directions. Royal families of the two countries intermarried frequently. Champa also had close trade and cultural relations with the powerful maritime empire of Srivijaya and later Majapahit of the Malay Archipelago.

## HISTORY OF CHAMPA

### *Prehistory*

The people of Champa were descended from Malayo-Polynesian settlers who appear to have reached the South-East Asian mainland from Borneo about the time of the Sa Huỳnh culture in the first and second centuries BCE. There are pronounced ceramic, industrial and funerary continuities with sites such as the Niah Caves in Sarawak, East Malaysia. Sa Huỳnh sites are rich in iron artefacts, by contrast with the Dong Son culture sites found in northern Vietnam and elsewhere in mainland South-East Asia, where bronze artefacts are dominant. The Cham language is part of the Austronesian family. According to one study, Cham is related most closely to modern Acehnese.[7]

### *The Sa Huỳnh Culture*

The Sa Huỳnh culture is a late prehistoric metal age society on the central coast of Vietnam. In 1909, about 200 jar burials were uncovered

7 "From Ancient Cham to Modern Dialects".

at Sa Huỳnh, a coastal village located south of Da Nang. Since then, many more burials have been found, at some fifty sites. The Sa Huỳnh shows a distinct regional Bronze Age culture, with its own styles of axes, daggers, and ornaments. Carbon dating has placed the Sa Huỳnh culture roughly the same time line with the Dong Son culture, that is about the first millennium BCE. From about CE 200, the central coast of Vietnam was inhabited by the Chams, who had adopted elements of Indian political and religious culture. Recent researches by Vietnamese archaeologists have shown that the Chams are linguistic and cultural descendants of the Sa Huỳnh people. The uncovered artefacts show the Sa Huỳnh people were highly-skilled craftsmen in the production of jewellery and ornaments made with hard stones and glass. Sa Huỳnh styled ornaments were also found in Thailand, Taiwan and Philippines suggesting they were traded with South-East Asian neighbours, over land and maritime routes. Archaeologists also observe that iron seems to have been used by the Sa Huỳnh people when their Dong Son neighbours were still mostly using bronze.

## LÂM ÂP

To the Chinese, the country of Champa was known as Linyi (林邑) and to the Vietnamese, Lâm Âp. It had been founded in CE 192 in the region of modern Hue by a local leader rebelling against the Han — Chinese. Over the next several centuries, Chinese forces made repeated unsuccessful attempts to retake the region.[8]

From its neighbour Funan to the west, Lâm Âp soon received the gift of Indian civilization.[9] Scholars locate the historical beginnings of Champa in the fourth century CE, when the process of Indianization was well underway. It was in this period that the Cham people began to create stone inscriptions in both Sanskrit and in their own language, for which they created a unique script.[10]

The first king acknowledged in the inscriptions is Bhadravarman, who reigned from CE 349 to 361. At My Son, King Bhadravarman established a god named Bhadreśvara, whose name was a combination

---

8 Lê Thành Khôi 1990: 103.

9 Ibid.: 105.

10 Ngô Văn Doanh 2005: 181.

of the king's own name and that of the Hindu God of gods, Śiva.[11] The worship of the original god-king under the name Bhadreśvara and other names continued through the centuries that followed.[12]

The capital of Lâm Âp at the time of Bhadravarman was the citadel of Siṁhapura (Lion City), which was located along two rivers and had a wall 8 miles in circumference. A Chinese writer described the people of Lâm Âp as both warlike and musical, with "deep eyes, a high straight nose, and curly black hair".[13]

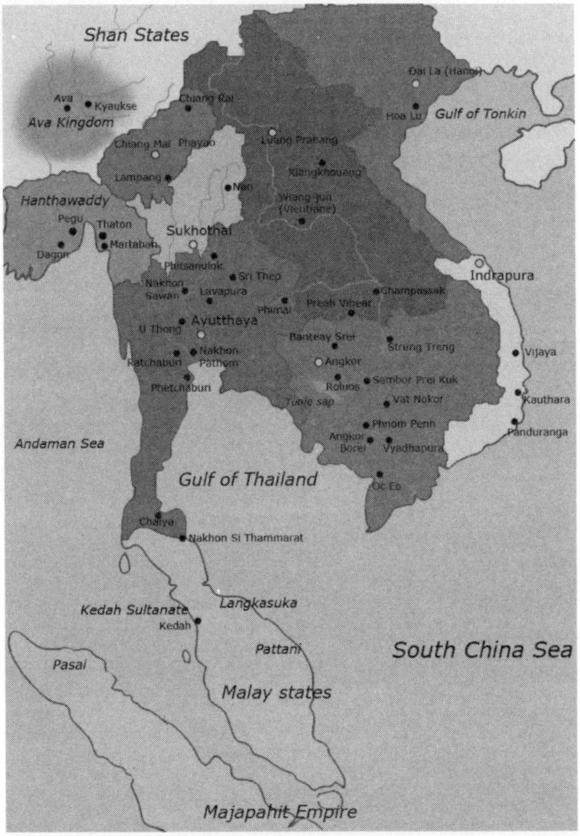


*fig.* 3.1: Asia in CE 800, showing the Champa city-states and their neighbours

---

[11] Ngô Văn Doanh 2012: 31.

[12] Ibid.: 38-39; Ngô Văn Doanh 2005: 55ff.

[13] Ngô Văn Doanh 2005: 56ff.

According to Chinese records, Śambhuvarman (Fan Fan Tche) was crowned as the king of Lâm Âp in CE 529. Inscriptions credit him with rehabilitating the temple to Bhadreśvara after a fire. Śambhuvarman also sent delegations and tribute to China, and unsuccessfully invaded what is now northern Vietnam.[14] In CE 605, a general Liu Fang of the Siu dynasty invaded Lâm Âp, won a battle by luring the enemy war-elephants into an area booby-trapped with camouflaged pits, massacred the defeated troops, and captured the capital.[15] In the 620s, the kings of Lâm Âp sent delegations to the court of the recently established Tang dynasty and asked to become vassals of the Chinese court.[16]

*Source:* Proceedings of the Seminar on Champa, University of Copenhagen, 23 May 1987

*fig.* 3.2: Champa and the southward expansion of Vietnam

---

14 Ngô Văn Doanh 2005: 60ff.

15 Taus-Bolstad 2003: 21.

16 Ngô Văn Doanh 2005: 63.

**Table 2.1: Political Upheavals in Champa from Second Century through 1692**

| *Era/Year* | Kingdom of Lin-Yi* |
|---|---|
| Second-third century CE | Lin-Yi raided Vietnam and southern China in 248 |
| 543 | Champa attacked Vietnam but was defeated by Pham Tu, a general of king Ly Bon |
| 982 | Vietnam force led by Ly Thuong Kiet attacked and pushed Champa's border to south of Hoanh Son (Thanh Hoa) |
| 1069 | King Ly Thanh Tong led Vietnam to invade Champa, sacked Vijaya and took king Rudravarman III (Che Cu) prisoner in exchange for three provinces Dia Ly, Ma Linh and Bo Chanh (present Quang Binh and Quang Tri) |
| 1307 | Vietnamese princess Huyen Tran married king Jaya Sinhavarman III (Che Man) in exchange for two provinces O and Ly |
| 1370 | King Che Bong Nga raided and pilfered Thang Long (Ha Noi). Che Bong Nga was killed in battle in 1382 |
| 1402 | Vietnam invaded Champa. Ho Quy Ly forced king Campadhiraya to concede Indrapura (Quang Nam) and the territory of Amarāvatī (North Champa) to Vietnam |
| 1471 | Vietnamese army led by King Le Thanh Tong captured and destroyed Vijaya. Vietnam annexed the new land as provinces of Thang Hoa, Tu Nghia and Hoai Nhon |
| 1578 | Lord Nguyen Hoang annexed the Cham region of Phu Yen |
| 1653 | Lord Nguyen Phuc Tan captured Cham's region of Kauthara and pushed Vietnam's southern border to Cam Ranh |
| 1692 | Lord Nguyen Phuc Chu annexed the remaining Champa territory as the new prefecture of Tran Thuan Thanh |

* Kingdom of Lin-Yi (Lâm Âp) was recorded in Chinese annals.

Chinese records report the death of the last king of Lâm Âp as falling in CE 756. Thereafter for a time, the Chinese referred to Champa as "Hoan Vuong" or "Huanwang".[17] The earliest Chinese records using a name related to "Champa" are dated CE 877; however, such names had been in use by the Cham themselves since at least CE 629, and by the Khmer since at least CE 657.[18]

---

17 Ngô Văn Doanh 2005: 66.

18 Boisselier 1963: 87.

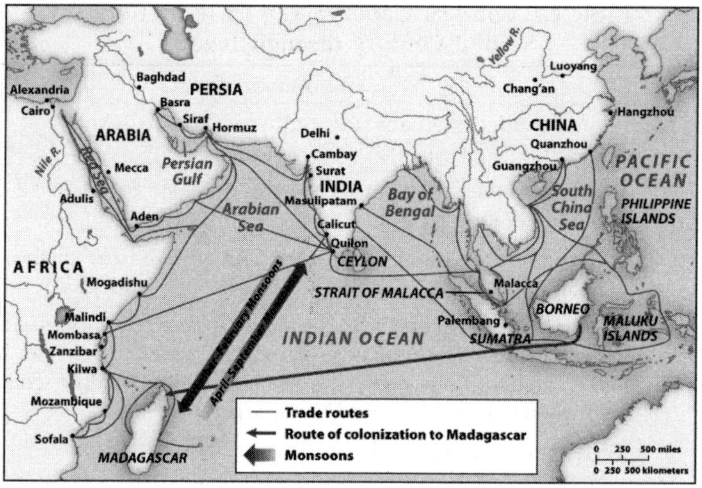


*Source: Ways of the World*, 1st edn., Map 8.2
© 2009 Bedford/St. Martin,
*fig*. 3.3: Spices Routes of Champa

*Champa at Its Peak*

From seventh to tenth century CE, the Cham controlled the trade in spices and silk between China, India, the Indonesian islands, and the Abbassid Empire in Baghdad. They supplemented their income from the trade routes not only by exporting ivory and aloe, but also by engaging in piracy and raiding.[19]

## CHAMPA AND THE SPICES ROUTES

"He who controls the spice, controls the universe." Such were the words uttered by the main character of the movie *Dune* based on the Frank Herbert science fiction epic of the same name. In the story, the spice was the lifeblood of a vast empire. For the leaders of this empire, it was essential that at all times "the spice must flow".

The spice trade of the *Dune* movie was no doubt inspired by the historical trade in aromatics from ancient times to the present. At various periods in history, spices have been as valuable as gold and silver. According to a fifteenth-century saying: "No man should die who can afford cinnamon".

The aromatic substances were even more mysterious as they were connected in many cultures with the idea of a faraway paradise —

[19] Lê Thành Khôi 1990: 109.

Eden. The Muslim writer al-Bukhari wrote that Sumatran aloewood known as 'Ud in Arabic filled the censers of Paradise. Ginger was the other major aromatic of Paradise in Muslim tradition. In the *Travels* of Sir John Mandeville it is said that the aloewood of the Great Khan came from Paradise.

We will show that the famed spices which travelled from Africa to the Arabian traders and from thence to the markets of the classical Mediterranean world had their ultimate origin in South-East Asia. The aromatic trail known as the "Cinnamon Route" began somewhere in the Malay Archipelago, romantically known as the "East Indies", and crossed the Indian Ocean to the south-eastern coast of Africa.

The spices may have landed initially at Madagascar and they eventually were transported to the East African trading ports in and around the city known in Greco-Roman literature as Rhapta. Merchants then moved the commodities northward along the coast. In Roman times, they travelled to Adulis in Ethiopia and then to Muza in Yemen and finally to Berenike in Egypt. From Egypt they made their way to all the markets of Europe and West Asia.[20]

The beginning of the trade is hinted at in Egyptian hieroglyphic inscriptions during the New Kingdom period about 3,600 years ago. The Pharoahs of Egypt opened up special relationships with the kingdom of Punt to the south. Although the Egyptians knew of Punt long before this period, it was during the New Kingdom that we really start hearing of important trade missions to that country that included large cargoes of spices. Particularly noteworthy are the marvellous reliefs depicting the trade mission of Queen Hatshepsut of the 18th dynasty.

The idea of an ancient trade route to the east for spices and also precious metals like gold and silver is not new. The Jewish historian Josephus, writing in the first century CE, offered his explanation of the Biblical story of Solomon and Hiram's joint trade mission to the distant land of Ophir. In his *Antiquities of the Jews,* he said the voyages which began from the Red Sea port of Ezion-geber were destined for the island of Chryse far to the east in the Indian Ocean. Ezion-geber was near the modern city of Eilat in Israel and the trade voyages

---

20 The phrase is given in Gould 1986: 64.

took three years to complete according to the Old Testament account.[21] Where then was the island of Chryse mentioned by Josephus? Greek geographers usually placed it east of the Ganges river mouth. Medieval writings placed it near where the Indian Ocean met the Pacific Ocean. In modern times, Chryse has been equated by scholars with the land known in Indian literature as Suvarṇadvīpa. Both Chryse and Suvarṇadvīpa mean "Gold Island". The latter was also located in Indian writings well to the east of India in the "Southern Ocean" and is identified by most scholars with the Malay Archipelago (the East Indies).

Josephus's theory of voyages to South-East Asia was supported indirectly about a half-century later by Philo of Byblos who translated the History of Phoenicia by Sanchuniathon. This translation was originally considered a fraud by modern scholars, but discoveries from Ras Shamra in the Levant indicate Philo's work was authentic. They are important because they come from a different historical source than the Old Testament account.

Philo records the Phoenician version of Solomon and Hiram's trade mission to Ophir. What is interesting is how Philo's account allows us to interpret some arcane Hebrew passages. He outlines journeys into the Erythraean Sea (Indian Ocean) that took three years to complete. The items brought back from the journey were apes, peacocks and ivory all products of tropical Asia and all included along with other goods in the Biblical account.

Philo's interpretation of Sanchuniathon's history uses words for the products of the voyages which clearly point to tropical Asia unlike the strange terms used 1,000 years earlier in Solomon's time. The romantic idea of distant Ophir may have inspired the explorer Magellan on his circumnavigation voyage around the world in the sixteenth century. The explorer replaced geographical locations in his reference books with the names "Tarsis and Ofir", the equivalent in his time of Biblical "Tarshish and Ophir".[22] He actually set a course on the latitude of one of these locations before reaching the islands of the Visayas from the East.

---

21 Nordhalt 1986: 9.

22 Ricklefs 1992: 665.

In the medieval and early colonial period, commentators on classical Greco-Roman literature first began hinting that the Cinnamon Route might trace eventually from Africa to the east in Asia. Many of the terms used for spices in early works are obscure and can be difficult to identify. The commentators interpreted these terms into the contemporary language at a time when the knowledge of the world had greatly increased. In most cases, we can confidently associate these latter spice names with species that we know today.

Thus, when the ancient writer Pliny mentions *tarum* as a product of East Africa we understand it as aloewood because later commentators translate *tarum* with a word that is no longer obscure: *lignum* aloe "aloewood". By the time of the commentators, the source of the aloewood was already well known. Pliny mentions *tarum* as coming from the land that produced cinnamon and cassia in Africa. But the commentators give it an identity which clearly indicates a tropical Asian origin in their time.

So why were these Asian products turning up in African markets? Pliny is the only writer who attempts an explanation and the related passages have been the source of much scholarly controversy. The details will be discussed later in this paper (it is from one of my books), but the historian James Innes Miller was possibly the first modern scholar to put on his glasses and use Pliny and other evidence to suggest that Austronesian traders had brought spices to African markets via a southern maritime route. Miller connected the spice route with the prehistoric settlement of Madagascar by Austronesian seafarers. Spices from southern China and both mainland and insular South-East Asia were brought by Austronesian merchants whom he associates with the people known to the Chinese by the names Kunlun and Po-sse.

Miller's book was the defining work of his time and it still has a profound influence on historians of trade and seafaring. However, classical historians, philologists even casual graduates of online universities and other scholars have mixed views on Miller's thesis. A number of alternative theories sprung up and Miller was criticized, sometimes rightfully so, with using too many loosely-established ideas to support his argument. One of our main goals will be to use newer evidence along with some apparently missed by Miller to show that, for the most part, his idea of a southern transoceanic route was correct.

In addition to Miller's Cinnamon Route, there also existed a "Clove Route" to China and India. The evidence for these early spice routes comes from every available field including history, archaeology, linguistics, genetics and anthropology. For example, we can show by a process of elimination that a southern route for tropical Asian spices into Africa is historical. The exact details of this route are not known to us from history but the route itself is the only reasonable conclusion given in the historical sources at our disposal. We can then bolster the testimony of history by bringing in supporting evidence from other fields.

One way we do this is to show that certain cultural items that came from South-East Asia, or at least tropical Asia, were diffused first to the south-eastern coast of Africa before moving northward at dates that are supportive of our thesis. One example is the diffusion of the domestic chicken (*Galllus gallus*) to Africa. The oldest archaeological remains of this species may date back to 2,800 BCE from Tanzania.[23] The earliest similar evidence in Egypt is not earlier than the New Kingdom period about 1,000 years later. To support this finding, there is additional evidence provided by the presence of the double outrigger,[24] barkcloth, various types of musical instruments and other cultural items present on the south-eastern African coast. Possibly also the distribution of the coconut crab, the world's largest land-based invertebrate also provides evidence for this early southern contact.

An important factor in ascertaining the old spice routes from South-East Asia is the trail of cloves from Maluku and the southern Philippines north to South China and Indochina and then south again along the coast to the Strait of Malacca. From there the cloves went to Indian spice markets and points further west. This north–south direction of commerce through the Philippines has recently been recognized by UNESCO as part of the ancient maritime spice route. The Philippine–Maluku hub persisted into Muslim times and is chronicled in Arabic historical and geographic writings.

While the Clove Route started in the south, cinnamon trade began in the north. The Cinnamon Route started in the cinnamon and cassia-

---

23 Davies 2005: 56.

24 Ibid.: 30.

producing regions of northern Indo-China and southern China and then likely proceeded from South China spice ports southward during the winter monsoon down the Philippine corridor. The route likely turned south-east at that point to Sumatra and/or Java to pick up different varieties of cinnamon and cassia along with aloewood and benzoin. From south-western Indonesia the voyage then took the Austronesian merchants across the great expanse of the Indian Ocean to Africa.

Linguistically the Clove Route is supported by the distribution of names for ginger in the Malay Archipelago. These appear to have followed the Clove Route from China through the Philippines to the rest of insular South-east Asia.

In the medieval Chinese and Muslim texts we first get specific details about these routes although they probably were unchanged from the ones used centuries or thousands of years earlier. The Chinese records in particular give detailed itineraries including directions and voyage length for each stop along the way to the southern spice markets. Of particular importance are the entrepôts known to the Chinese as Sanfotsi and Toupo. The same marketplaces were likely known to the Muslim geographers likely by the names of Zabag and Waqwaq, respectively.

Like Chryse of the Greeks and Suvarṇadvīpa of the Indians, these entrepôts were a source of wonder and literary romance. In the *One Thousand and One Nights*, Sinbad travels to Zabag on one of his voyages and the islands of Waqwaq are the setting for the adventure of Hassan of Basra. Indian literature also abounds in tales of voyages to the islands of gold by those in search of treasure, either material or spiritual.

From the Arabic literature, we start to learn of first-hand accounts of trade and other voyages by mariners from South-East Asia to Africa. Previously, we had only the vague accounts of Solomon's journey and Pliny's brief descriptions of long sea voyages from or to the cinnamon country. The Muslim works tell us of ships and people from Zabag and Waqwaq coming to African ports for trade and even on occasion to conduct military raids. The records give the impression of well-established trade relationships, but just how long did these long-distance ties exist before the Muslim writings?

We believe that there is a strong case for this trade opening up by at least the New Kingdom period in Egypt. At that time, voyages to the divine land of Punt became more frequent with large fleets bringing back impressive hauls of tribute to the Pharaoh. While the hard evidence is still fragmentary, the quantity and quality of this evidence are still comparable to those of other established theories. We simply come to the most logical conclusions based on the historical records, and how these records should be interpreted based on the evidence.

Rome's discovery of the monsoon trade winds did not have any significant impact as the Roman ships mainly plied the waters between the Ptolemaic port of Berenike and the ports along the coast of eastern Africa and western India. The Romans apparently did not interfere much at these ports and only established minor trading colonies if any in these areas. The wave of Islam into East Africa was probably the strongest factor in closing the southern spice route.

Muslim traders managed to convert the local populations, and in the process, must have greatly complicated pre-existing trade relationships. The Muslim merchants in their dhows moving eastward would have eventually discovered the sources of cinnamon and cassia. Then it was only a matter of time before the caliphate would be able to eliminate the African ports in favour of direct import to Arab entrepôts. This was not an immediate process though.

The Muslim geographers and historians still record trade activity between Africa and South-East Asia in aloewood, tortoise-shell, iron and other products centuries after the Arabs had established themselves on the Tanzanian coast. By the time the Portuguese reached this area though it appears this trade had disappeared. All that was left were traces of the Austronesian contact including the local boats with their outriggers and lateen sails made of coconut fibre.

With the end of the Cinnamon Route and the advent of the European control of the spice trade, the Austronesian component of this commerce almost completely faded away. However, some 3,000 years of spice trade from the New Kingdom to the late Muslim period left a lasting legacy that reshaped the world. The vision of an El Dorado of gold and spices tempted romantics and kings alike. For centuries, the Arabs had controlled the Mediterranean part of the spice trade by keeping secret the monsoon sources of the precious commodities.

Eventually the Roman empire discovered the monsoon routes as opposed to earlier costly voyages that involved closely following the shoreline. However, it took some time before they could discover the real sources of the spices they treasured so much.

When the Alexandrian merchant Cosmas Indicopleustes ventured to find these sources in the sixth century CE, many of these secrets were just coming to light. However, it was a little too late. The meteoric rise of Islam closed off any further European exploration or exploitation of the spice routes. Conversely, a whole new world was opened up for the merchants of the Muslim world. Their newly-found power allowed them to venture deep into Asia as never before. The Islamic texts give the first detailed descriptions of the emporiums of the East. By at least the ninth century, a massive trade ensued between the two regions greatly enriching the Islamic caliphate. Magnificent cities and buildings were constructed throughout the Muslim lands at the same time that Europe sunk into the dark ages. The Arabic writers also tell of great kingdoms and empires of the East including the fabled cities of the Khmers and the island domains of the Mihraj (Mahārāja) of Zabag.

Europe would get another chance centuries later when a charismatic leader arose out of a hitherto unknown nomadic tribe of the steppe. Chingiss Khan, also known as Genghis Khan, rode out of the wastelands of Central Asia with his Mongol armies on epic conquests. Among the empires destroyed in the Great Khan's path was the Islamic Caliphate. The fall of Baghdad again opened the Silk Road and the maritime spice route to the merchants and adventurers of Europe. One of the first to take up the challenge of the East was Marco Polo. The records of his travels along with those of other Europeans who ventured east rekindled the urge to link with the long-lost spice Eden of the East. The Portuguese were the first to take up the gauntlet establishing bases at Goa in India and Malacca on the Malay Peninsula. Others followed including the powerful Dutch East India Company.

The quest for spices and precious metals ushered in what is known as the Age of Exploration. Magellan's personal documents indicated his desire to find the golden islands of Tarshish and Ophir. The explorer Sebastian Cabot was appointed as commander of an expedition "to discover the Moluccas, Tarsis, Ophir, Cipango and Cathay". The fight to control the flow of cloves, nutmeg, black pepper, gold, silver and other commodities led to the circumnavigation of Africa and the world, and the exploration of the Western hemisphere and the Pacific Ocean.

The coming of the Europeans nearly completely excluded the native Austronesian merchants from the trade. The same people who in the Muslim annals were sailing to East Africa to engage in commerce now where often prevented even from participating in merchant activity from city to city or island to island in their own region. Only after South-East Asia freed itself from Western colonialism has this ancient wonderland of entrepôts regained direct control of its own trade again. Today, the nations of the ASEAN have formed a unique organization designed to enhance commerce in the region. Indeed, ASEAN is really the model for the entire Asian region. Even developed Asian nations like Japan and South Korea have looked to ASEAN as the model for regional trade co-operation.

Today, manufactured goods from sneakers to computers are more important exports that spices or precious metals, although these latter

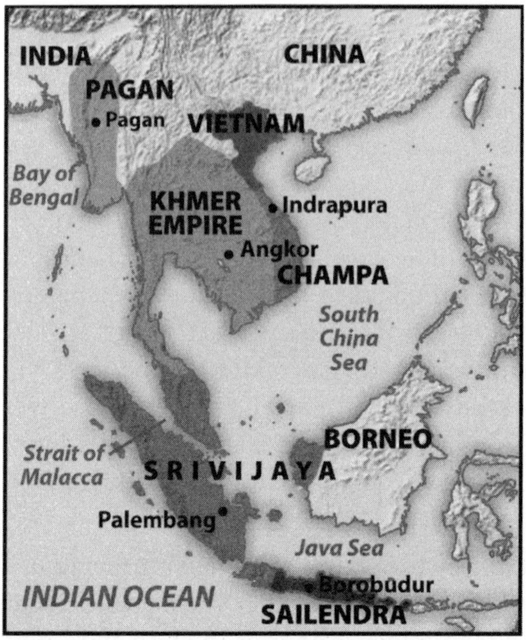


*Source*: *Ways of the World*, 1st edn., Map 8.1,
© 2009 Bedford/St. Martin

*fig*. 3.4: Sea routes led to the creation of various states

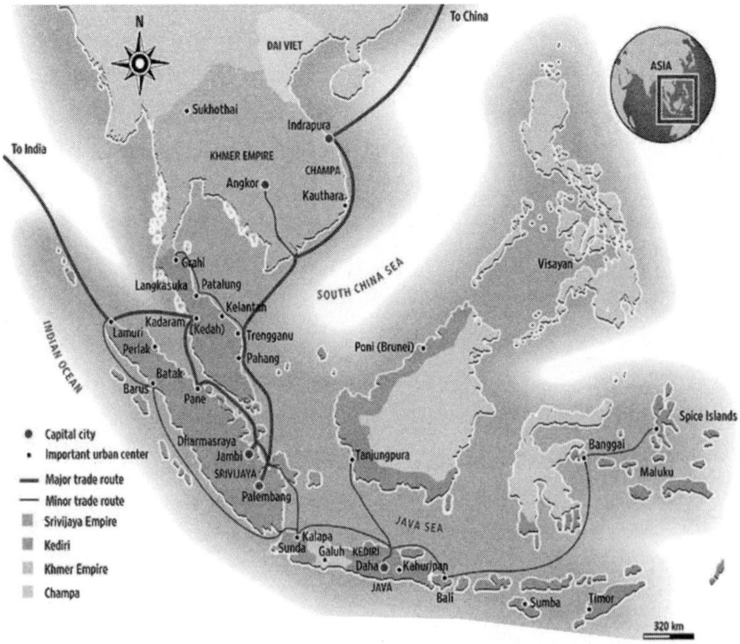


*fig.* 3.5: Trade routes of South-East Asia: Srivijaya, Kediri, Khmer, and Champa around twelfth to early thirteenth century

items continue to hold their own. The region has also come to be a leader in a completely different type of trade — the human trade. South-East Asia is the world's largest exporter of human labour. Seafarers, nurses, doctors, domestics, construction workers, computer programmers and almost every other kind worker including those in illegal trades come from the Philippines, Thailand, Indonesia, Cambodia or other nations in the area and can be found in almost every country of the world.

Many analysts believe the geopolitics of the area will again bring South-East Asia to the centre of the world's stage. Most of the goods shipped around the globe still travel by sea, and South-East Asia is the main hub for trade between Asia and the rest of the world. The volume of trade activity has been growing faster here than any other area of the world and most expect this trend to continue. The region's great natural diversity may again come into play as the ageing populations of the developed world look for new medicines and natural cures from South-East Asia's biological resources.

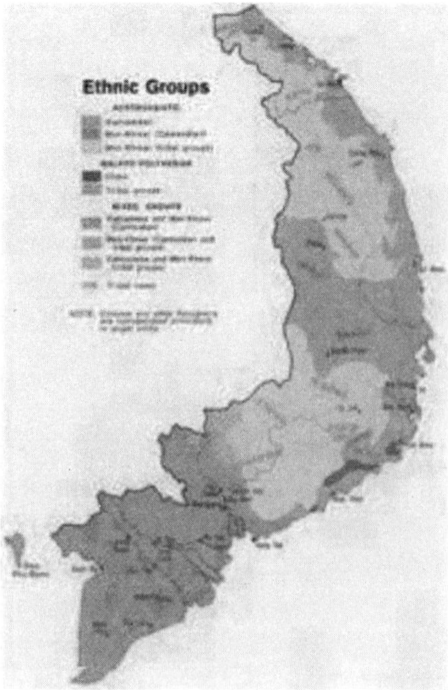


*fig*. 3.6: The linguistic map of Vietnam in the South Vietnam

According to one theory, the great Austronesian migrations of prehistory began with the flooding of the Sundaland continent, which also created the islands of the Malay Archipelago. The region's natural treasures provided the wayfaring Austronesians with items of the trade that became valued in distant lands. Then, as now, a combination of natural forces thrust the people of South-East Asia into a crucial role in the course of world history and Champa was a part of this course.

## III. Main Influences of India on Champa's Culture

### INDIA'S INFLUENCES ON CHAMPA'S LANGUAGES

Of all the ethnic groups that have inhabited the south of Vietnam since ancient times and that have joined the community of Vietnamese peoples since the Ly dynasty (1009–1225), some are from the plains but others had their homes in the coastal regions or high up in the mountains.

With the exception of the Chams and the Khmers who inhabit the Mekong Delta, the other ethnic groups did not have a writing system

**Table 2.2: A Comparative List of Sanskrit Words and Their Derivatives in the Languages Spoken by Ethnic Groups in South Vietnan**

| *Sanskrit Words (Romanized) and their Meanings in English* | *Ethnic Group Words and Their Meanings in English* |
|---|---|
| *bhūmi* = land, country | bhlumi (Ch.) = land, country, village<br>phum (Kh.) = residential land, garden; the smallest administrative unit |
| *śabda* = speech, voice, word, sound | ssop ~ xap (Ch.) = speech<br>xom day (Kh.) = words<br>asap (Ed., Ja.) = speech<br>asap (Ra.) = speech<br>sap (Ko) = speech |
| *śvasana* = spirit, wind, hiss, breathing, respiration | ssuan (Ch.) = spirit<br>raivai (Ka.) = soul<br>suan (Ko.) = spirit |
| *guru* = a wise man, master, worthy | gru ~ kru (Ch.) = master<br>gru (Mn.) = craftsman, handy man<br>mgru (Ra.) = to learn<br>kru (Ra.) = witch doctor<br>pugru (Ko.) = master |
| *devatā* = God | debata (Ch.) = God |
| *jāla* = net, netting | jal (Ch., Ed., Mn., Ra.) = fishing net<br>juo (Ka.) = fishing net<br>jal (Ko.) = fishing net |
| *jaiyak* = victory | chai (Ch.) = to win<br>chaidak (Ch.) = victory<br>jai (Ra.) = to win |
| *karpāsa* = cotton wool | kapah (Ch.) = cotton wool<br>kopaih (Bah.) = cotton wool<br>krapas (Kh.) = cotton wool |
| *marīca* = chilli pepper | amrek ~ mrek (Ch.) = chilli pepper<br>a mareq (Ra.) = chilli pepper<br>proiq (Ka.) = chilli pepper<br>prik (Pa.) = chilli pepper<br>mre (Ko.) = chilli pepper |
| *manuṣya* = man, person | munuih (Ch., Ed.) = man, person<br>monuih (Ja., Ra., Chr.) = man, person<br>manuih (Ka.) = man, person<br>vonus (Ko.) = man, person |
| *nāgarāja* = snake king | karai ~ kirai (Ch.) = dragon<br>grai (Ja.) = dragon<br>rai (Ed.) = dragon |

Cont.

**Table 2.2 (Cont.)**

| *Sanskrit Words (Romanized) and Their Meanings in English* | *Ethnic Group Words and Their Meanings in English* |
|---|---|
| *nagara* = city, country | nugar ~ nukan (Ch.) = region, homeland, country<br>logar (Ra.) = hamlet<br>logar (Ko.) = country |
| *ratha* = vehicle | radeh ~ rideh (Ch.) = vehicle<br>rodeh (Ra.) = vehicle<br>ndeh (Ma.) = vehicle<br>rodeh (Ko.) = vehicle |
| *rūpa* = appearance, body | rup (Ch.) = body<br>rup (Pa., Ed., Ja.) = body<br>rup (Ko.) = body |
| *yakṣa* = demi-god, superhuman being | raksa ~ rak (Ch.) = demon |

of their own until the beginning of the twentieth century. In a language which has a writing system of its own, both its spoken and written forms can provide us with information about the influence of language contact. However, in a language that has no writing system of its own, the only source of this kind of information is its spoken form. This is the case with such Austroasiastic and Austronesian languages as spoken by the ethnic groups now inhabiting the mountains and the highlands to the west of South Vietnam.

Table 2.2 is an incomplete comparative list of Romanized Sanskrit words (taken from the *Sanskrit–Russian–Vietnamese Dictionary*) and their derivatives in the languages spoken by the various ethnic groups in South Vietnam. This list, incomplete as it is, helps us to see more clearly the influence of the Indian language on the languages of the Vietnamese ethnic groups. (All the ethnic groups words that appear on this list have been transcribed into present-day Vietnamese. The abbreviations given in parentheses refer to the various Vietnamese ethnic groups: Ch. = Cham, Br. = Bru, Ed. = Ede, Ja. = Jarai, Ka. = Katu, Kh. = Khmer, Mn. = Mnong, Pa. = Pacoh, Ra. = Raglai, Ma. = Ma, Ko. = Koho. All these ethnic groups use languages belonging to the Austronesian and Austroasian families.)

The list shows that the Sanskrit words that have found their way into the language pack of southern Vietnam belong to both the spheres of spiritual and material activities. The borrowed Sanskrit words, once integrated into the Vietnamese language pack, usually take on new meanings but even these new meanings are not too far removed from the original meanings of the Sanskrit words. Also, the borrowed words usually undergo some phonic changes in accordance with the phonological rules of the borrowing language.

Since the list given above is incomplete, it only gives us a general idea of the problem involved. A more serious and specific research project is needed for a more detailed observation and better understanding of the influence of the ancient Indian language on the Vietnamese language group.

In the lowland and coastal regions, the Indian influence is observed not only in the spoken language but also in geographical names and in the writing systems of the various ethnic groups. All the geographical names common at the times of the ancient Champa kingdom have been either replaced by Sino-Vietnamese names or transliterated into modern Vietnamese. However, with the help of ancient documents and by comparison between the new and the ancient Sanskrit-based names, we can easily detect the relationship between them (Table 2.3).

But the Indian influence is most obvious in the writing systems of the Chams and the Khmers who now inhabit the Mekong River Delta. In the region which was ancient Champa, scientists have discovered hundreds of stelae erected over a period of ten centuries, from the fourth century to fourteenth century (Coedes 1948). These stelae allow

**Table 2.3: A Few Examples of How Old Sanskrit-based Names Have Been Replaced or Transliterated**

| *Sanskrit-based Names* | *Present Names* |
|---|---|
| Śrī Bamui | Dong Hoi |
| Amarāvatī | Tra Kieu (Quang Nam province) |
| Indrapura | Dong Duong (Quang Nam province) |
| Vijaya | Do Ban, Thi Nai (in Binh Dinh province) |
| Kauthara | Nha Trang |
| Pāṇḍuraṅga | Phan Rang |
| Bal Chanar | Ca Na (in Binh Thuan province) |

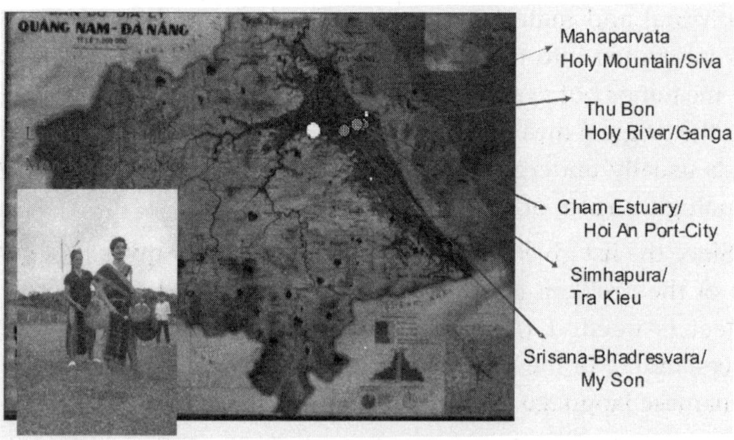


*fig.* 3.7: Quangnam Province's map/former Amarāvatī Champa state

us to examine not only the written form of the ancient Cham language but also how that written form was influenced by the ancient Indian script. Scientists have discovered, too, that during those ten centuries, the Cham script was revised and improved until at last it proliferated into a couple of variants. However, these variants, as well as the other South-East Asian scripts that are typologically similar to the Indian script, can easily be traced back to the Brāhmī script of southern India. One of those variants is the Akhar Thrah script, which is now being used by the Chams in Ninh Thuan and Binh Thuan provinces.

The Khmer script in the Mekong River Delta, like its cousin in Cambodia, originated from the Brāhmī script. At first this Brāhmī script was used to phonetically transcribe the language spoken by the Khmers in the Mekong Delta. Later, it was improved, with some signs modified and new signs added, until at last it became the Khmer script as we see it nowadays.

Beside the Cham and Khmer scripts which originated from the Brāhmī script, the words inscribed on the artefacts found at the excavation site of Chua Vua in Long An province have also been ascertained as belonging to the ancient Indian script. And who knows, in the future, Vietnamese archaeologists, with their enthusiasm, will discover further evidence of similar Indian influence at such new excavation sites as Nam Cat Tien (in Lam Dong province).

## INDIAN INFLUENCES ON CHAMPA'S POLITY

*Maṇḍala* is a Sanskrit word that means "circle". *Maṇḍala* is a model for describing the patterns of diffuse political power distributed among Mueang (principalities) in early South-East Asian history, when local power was more important. The concept of a *maṇḍala* counteracts modern tendencies to look for unified political power, i.e. the power of large kingdoms and nation-states of later history, an inadvertent byproduct of fifteenth-century advances in map-making technologies.[25] In the words of O.W. Wolters, who originated the idea in 1982:

> The map of earlier South-East Asia which evolved from the prehistoric networks of small settlements and reveals itself in historical records was a patchwork of often overlapping *maṇḍalas*.[26]

It is employed to denote traditional South-East Asian political formations, such as federation of kingdoms or vassalized polity under a centre of domination. It was adopted by twentieth-century Western historians from ancient Indian political discourse as a means of

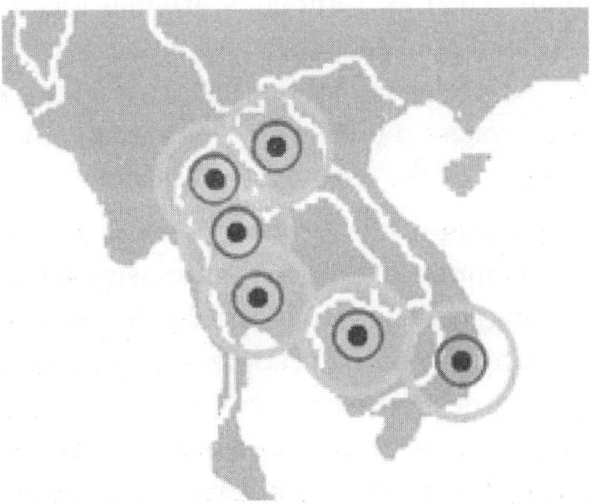

*fig.* 3.8: Intersecting *maṇḍalas c.* 1360: from north to south Lan Xang, Lanna, Sukhothai, Ayutthaya, Angkor and Champa

---

[25] "How Maps Made the World", *Wilson Quarterly*, Summer 2011. Retrieved on 28 July 2011. "Source: *Mapping the Sovereign State: Technology, Authority, and Systemic Change* by Jordan Branch, in *International Organization*, vol. 65, Issue 1, Winter 2011.

[26] Branch 2011: 1-36.

avoiding the term "state" in the conventional sense. Not only did South-East Asian polities not conform to Chinese and European views of a territorially defined state with fixed borders and a bureaucratic apparatus, but they diverged considerably in the opposite direction: the polity was defined by its centre rather than its boundaries, and it could be composed of numerous other tributary polities without undergoing administrative integration.[27]

In some ways similar to the feudal system of Europe, states were linked in overlord–tributary relationships. Compared to feudalism, however, the system gave greater independence to the subordinate states; it emphasized personal rather than official or territorial relationships; and it was often non-exclusive. Any particular area, therefore, could be subject to several powers or none.

The term of *maṇḍala* draws a comparison with the *maṇḍala* of the Hindu and Buddhist world-view; the comparison emphasizes the radiation of power from each power centre, as well as the non-physical basis of the system.

Other metaphors such as Tambiah's original idea of a "galactic polity"[28] describe similar political patterns as the *maṇḍala*. The metaphor of a "solar polity" is preferred by the historian Victor Lieberman,[29] because in the solar system there is one central body, the sun, and the components or planets of the solar system galaxies.[30]

Historically, the main overlord states were Khmer empire of Cambodia, Srivijaya empire of Sumatra, successive kingdoms of Java (Mataram, Kediri, Singghasari and Majapahit), Ayutthaya in Thailand, Vietnam and even China.[31] China occupies a special place in that the other three often in turn paid tribute to China, although in practice the obligations imposed on them were minimal. The most notable tributary states were Cambodia, Lan Xang (succeeded by Vientian

---

27 Dellias 2003.

28 Tambiah 1976: chap. 7.

29 Victor B. Lieberman (Biography), Professor of History, Department of History, appointed 1984, Univ. of Michigan, 4 February 2005. Retrieved on 17 August 2011. "Center for Southeast Asian Studies".

30 Lieberman 2003: 33.

31 Wolters 1982: 27-40, 126-54.

and Luang Prabang) and Lanna. Cambodia, in particular, was described by the Vietnamese emperor Gia Long as "an independent country that is slave of two" (Chandler 1983: 119). The system was eventually ended by the arrival of the Europeans in the mid-nineteenth century. Culturally, they introduced Western geographical practices, which assumed that every area was subject to one sovereign. Practically, the colonization of French Indochina, Dutch East Indies, British Malaya and Burma brought pressure from the colonizers for fixed boundaries to their possessions. The tributary states were then divided between the colonies and Siam, which exercised much more centralized power, but over a smaller area, than hitherto.

The historian Stuart-Fox uses the term *maṇḍala* extensively to describe the history of the Lao kingdom of Lan Xang as a structure of loosely held together "Mueang" that disintegrated after Lan Xang's conquest by Siam starting in the eighteenth century.[32]

The Thai historian Sunait Chutintaranond made an important contribution to the study of *maṇḍala* in South-East Asian history by demonstrating that "three assumptions responsible for the view that Ayudhya was a strong centralized state" did not hold and that "in Ayudhya the hegemony of provincial governors was never successfully eliminated".[33]

Herman Kulke suggests that there were three phases or levels in state formation in South-East Asia: the local, the regional and the imperial. "Very generally speaking, the first step always had to be the successful establishment and consolidation of a solid local power within a limited territory." This he characterizes as "chieftaincy". Next might come the conquest of one or more neighbouring nuclear areas, incorporated not by annihilation nor by administrative unification, but by the establishment of more or less regular tributary patterns. These were the somewhat precarious "early kingdoms". From the early ninth century a small number of what Kulke calls "imperial" kingdoms emerged, beginning with Angkor, which unified two or even several core areas of former early kingdoms.[34]

---

32 Stuart-Fox 1998: 14-15.

33 Wolters 1999: 142-43.

34 Kulke 1986: 5-8.

That word *maṇḍala* was deployed by Stanley Tambiah and in particular by Oliver Wolters, drawing from the Indian political literature and practice that influenced South-East Asia. The former analysed Kauṭilya's *Arthaśāstra*, the only complete work of the Brāhmanic politico–economic literature to be preserved, made notorious for its alleged Machiavellianism by Max Weber.[35] It deals, inter alia, with the maintenance of "state sovereignty" and the conduct of diplomacy, making alliances, making war, according to the *maṇḍala* strategy, in which "circles of kings" formed enemies and allies in actuality or in potentia.

Tambiah also analysed the Buddhist texts. In them *dharma* (righteousness) is an absolute imperative. Its symbol in political life was the wheel (*cakka*) not the sceptre, *daṇḍa*. In his past lives the Buddha admitted that, as a wheel-turning *rājā*, he used violence.

> The *cakkavatti* is depicted as a cosmocrator whose conquest proceeded through the continents at each of the four cardinal points, and whose rule radiated out from a central position either identified or closely associated with the central cosmic mountain of the Indian traditions, Mount Meru.

The *cakkavatti* grants their domains back to the conquered kings when they submit to the basic moral precepts of Buddhism: "in a sense the king *must* let the conquered rulers keep their thrones, since only as a king of kings is he a world monarch". The Emperor Aśoka embraced the model, and he was in turn the model for many South-East Asian Buddhist monarchs.[36]

Before he turns to them Tambiah describes the empire of their exemplar. Aśoka's Mauryan state

> was not so much a bureaucratized centralized imperial monarchy as a kind of galaxy-type structure with lesser political replicas revolving around the central entity and in perpetual motion of fission or incorporation. Indeed, it is clear that this is what the much-cited *cakkavatti* model represented: that a king as a wheel-rolling world ruler by definition required lesser kings under him who in turn encompassed still lesser rulers, that the *rājā* of *rājā*s was more a

35 Tambiah 1976.

36 Ibid.: 40-41, 46-47.

> presiding apical ordinator than a totalitarian authority between whom and the people nothing intervened except his own agencies and agents of control.

The model was "a closer representation of actual facts than has usually been imagined by virtue of misreading the rhetoric".[37]

It was the concept of *maṇḍala*, Tambiah tells us, that led him to invent the label "galactic polities". In a common Indo-Tibetan tradition, *maṇḍala* was composed of a core, *maṇḍa*, and an enclosing element, *-la*, and it was applied to designs, diagrams and cosmological schemes. Representing a cosmic harmony, it was a pattern for the state.

> In the centre was the king's capital and the region of its direct control, which was surrounded by a circle of provinces ruled by princes or governors appointed by the king, and these again were surrounded by more or less independent "tributary" polities.

The capital itself was a *maṇḍala*, with the palace at the centre, surrounded by three circles of earthen ramparts, four gateways at the cardinal points. Each lesser unit replicates the larger, and is more or less autonomous, "held in orbit and within the sphere of influence of the centre". At the margin, however, are "similar competing central principalities and their satellites". The system is "a hierarchy of central points continually subject to the dynamics of pulsation and changing spheres of influence". Territorial jurisdiction was not characterized by fixed boundaries but by fluidity. Behind its cosmology and the "ritually inflated notions we see the dynamics of polities that were modulated by pulsating alliances, shifting territorial control, and frequent rebellions and succession disputes".[38]

The modern literature on these polities has tended not to adopt Tambiah's celestial metaphor. Instead, it might be said, Oliver Wolters presented them in terms of the *maṇḍala* that had set him off in the first place, a word Kauṭilya had indeed used as a geopolitical concept, configuring friendly and enemy states.

---

37 Tambiah 1976: 70.

38 Ibid.: 102, 110, 112-13, 123.

> The map of earlier South-East Asia which evolved from the prehistoric networks of small settlements and reveals itself in historical records was a patchwork of often overlapping *maṇḍala*s, or circles of kings. In each of these *maṇḍala*s, one king, identified with divine and "universal" authority, claimed personal hegemony over the other rulers in his *maṇḍala* who in theory were his obedient allies and vassals.

Wolters borrowed another metaphor from music.

> *Maṇḍala*s would expand and contract in concertina-like fashion. Each one contained several tributary rulers, some of whom would repudiate their vassal status when the opportunity arose and try to build up their own networks of vassals.

Wolters draws attention to two of the political skills required. One was the gathering of "political intelligence", finding out what was happening on the fringe of the *maṇḍala,* so that threats might be anticipated. The other was diplomacy. An overlord had to be able to bring his rivals under his personal influence "and accommodate them within a network of loyalties to himself. . . . Administrative power as distinct from sacral authority depended on the management of personal relationships, exercised through the royal prerogative of investiture", the same skill as attributed to earlier "men of prowess". He had to attract loyal subordinates and preserve their loyalty. "[A]dministrative power as distinct from divine authority had . . . to be shared."[39]

In the Angkor court, as Ian Mabbett writes, there was a "web of obligation and influence. . . . Power was . . . something that arose from relationships and needed to be negotiated".[40] "Bureaucratic apparatuses were mostly Indianized fiction", writes Renée Hagesteijn: "a ruler was dependent on patron–client relations with 'lesser' political leaders".[41] At the centre the supraregional leader had direct relations with the headman. Regional leaders were clients, offered protection, honours, gifts. On the periphery control was "almost lacking".[42]

---

39 Wolters 1982: 16-19; 1999: 27-29.

40 Mabbett 1978: 29.

41 Hegestejin 1985: 139.

42 Ibid.: 102.

What was true of the mainland was true also of the archipelago. In Java, the capital was "the magical centre of the realm", as Soemarsaid Moertono put it,

> but also, from the point of view of state politics, the central region was preponderantly important. . . . The core region was relatively closely knit through the use of a remuneration system of appanages, while the outer regions were more loosely administered.

In the empire of Majapahit, as described in the Nagara-krtagama, there were three regions: Java at the centre, the islands outside it, and countries beyond, like Champa and Cambodia. Later Mataram was composed of the core, *nagaragung*, the outer provinces, *mantjanegara* and *pasisir*, and the lands across the sea, *tanah sabring*. Territorial jurisdiction was "characterized by a fluidity or flexibility of boundary dependent on the diminishing or increasing power of the centre".[43]

It was a form of inter-entity politics that welcomed, utilized and adapted the tradition and practice India had developed. India itself, however, was an exemplar, not an active part of the system. No Indian empire laid a larger claim over the Indianized states of South-East Asia: the subcontinent was perhaps more than a challenge enough. But, given their geographical position, it was not surprising to find that South-East Asian states, largely Indianized though they were, might see their neighbour to the north, the Chinese empire, which had met the challenge of political unification, as the apex of a hierarchy that included them. It was a question of force, but also of accommodation and mutual advantage.

Located in the middle of the International Exchange East–West road, China to India and beyond, and to the Mediterranean, South-East Asia, soon became a focal point of international maritime trade. From the early Christian era, the boats of the residents in the region, the Indian ships and the Arabs along with their culture regularly criss-crossed South-East Asia. On the road of exchange, Champa occupied one of the important and the most favourable positions. The ports of Champa served as the last port before the ships got through the Gulf of Tonkin on the China Sea coast and was the first stop from China to

[43] Moerfono 1968: 111-12.

Malacca, Gulf of Thailand and was closer to the Lower Mekong River Delta in the first seven centuries of Funan kingdom. Most of the sea routes to China and ships from China to Indian ports were passing through Champa. Since an important traffic hub, Champa coast soon became a trading hub. Champa was at the zenith of its glory during 800–1400 CE. During that time, Champa was well known for the trade in spices and silk with such countries as China, Nusantara (Indonesia, Malaysia, Brunei . . . today) and even the Abbasiah kingdom of Baghdad (the country of 1001 nights). Around 800 CE, Champa was known for its very bold and talented traders according to Ismail Hussein, Chairman of National Association of Malaysian Writers (GAPENA). Waters, which today is known as the South China Sea, was formerly known as the Sea of Champa; it served as a regional trade and critical transport route to Champa. The mighty trade and transport of the Champa empire was soon well known not only in Nusantara but also in the whole world. That's why the sea was called Sea of Champa.

The Chams took the right on the sea, and were known to participate and actively engage in international trade flows. They utilized these advantages to develop their kingdom into a regional powerhouse. Commercial marine activities contributed significantly to the survival and development of the kingdom of Champa in the

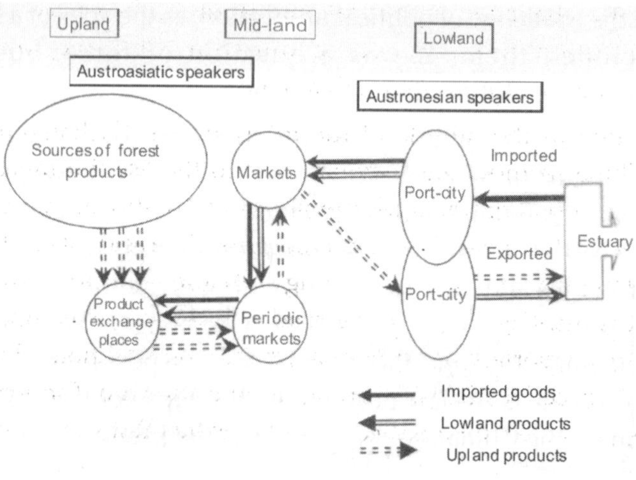


*fig.* 3.9: Network of upland–lowland exchange in central Vietnam

period from the late tenth to fifteenth century. During its development, Vijaya dynasty had been working on building relationships with the nearby island nations. Champa had an increasingly strong integration into the overall development of the history of the whole region. These relationships were really strong. On the one hand, they could strengthen their position throughout the history of the region, on the other hand, they created favourable conditions for expanding trade and made increasingly more powerful entry into the commercial marine sector, making up for the deficiencies of their economy. The Chams were very aware of the trade with foreigners, and facilitated major advantages for them. After Guangdong was destroyed in 758 CE, the traders who were doing business with China were facing difficulty. In fact, from 877 to 951 CE, Champa had no diplomatic relations with China until the end of the chaos. During that time, they promptly got into business with the Arab Muslim traders. As Guangdong was reopened under Later Zhou Dynasty (951-59 CE) and then the Song Dynasty (960–1279), Emperor Shenzong promoted the relationships between the two countries through the Muslim traders in Pāṇḍuraṅga. Muslims became the managers of the downtown in Pāṇḍuraṅga.

The Muslim traders had intimate contacts with the Champa dynasty. Through them there were frequent contacts between Chinese emperor and the king of Champa. There is evidence for Champa sending messengers to China in the year 951. In 958, the official representative of the king of Champa was a Muslim, named Abu Hasan (P's Ho San). He represented Indravarman III (917-60 CE). In return, Chinese emperor sent through him rose water, lamp "Greek fire" and gems. In 961, Abu Hasan returned to China with the new king's letter — Jaya Indravarman I, together with the gifts such as sandalwood, ivory, silk . . . and especially twenty Arab jars. Most of these gifts were the products of Champa, but many other gifts such as "rose water", "Greek light" were Arab goods which were certainly not the commercial products brought by the Arab traders. There were a lot of commercial products obtained from the commercial ports of Champa. About the export goods trade of Champa in this period, we can refer to the types of goods exchanged and traded at Hoi An Port, and other ports, such as Thanh Ha (Hue), Salty Water, Thi Nai (Binh Dinh). . . . During the seventeenth and eighteenth centuries, these ports again came into limelight as the economy of Champa prospered.

About the produce in central Vietnam in the sixteenth century, we find mention in *Ô Châu cận lục* (烏州近- — meaning *Notes about Recent O Chau*):

> . . . ivory, horn, incense, white incense jade, incense bowl, white brocade, blue brocade, buffalo leather, resin, horn, deer skin, deer velvet, the tail feathers of birds, pheasant tail feathers, pepper, honey, yellow wax, rattan. . . .

The products of this type, mostly forest products, should be considered as the specialties of Champa in the last century collected from the mountains and exchanged through the residents of the plains. It shows the strong relationship between the Champa kingdom with the mountainous ethnic groups who were probably living on the upper river side. Keeping strong relationships between Champa kingdom and the mountainous ethnic group ensured relative balance in economic development — marine economy, agriculture and forestry economy. With these products, the Chams were able to maintain commercial and trade relations with other countries in the region. Some scholars explain that the Champa Kingdom's economic model was known as an "exchange system along the river".

In this, "riverside exchange system", a coastal area as a commercial centre, was often located in an estuary. This was also the centre of commercial transactions and international connection points between the rivers of the surrounding area. There were also centres upstream, that were the collection point of goods originating from distant places on the river. These goods were produced in villages in the upstream domain and the upstream market was not in session. Then these goods were gathered in the centre of the Maṇḍala having its own coast. China Sea chronicles from the period of Northern Song Dynasty (960–1127 CE) reveal that in the tenth century formed the sea route connecting the Philippine islands and waters, North coast of the island of Borneo and Champa. According to those chronicles, by 977 CE, Brunei authorities had sent gifts to the Chinese empire and emissaries, and the delegation informed the court of the empire that the May-i (island Midoro) was far from Borneo by thirty days if travelled by a boat. A 1003 record suggests that gifts of Africa to the Philippines and China were sent through Butuan. Song chronicles also describe the history of north-eastern Mindanao as "a small country in the sea of Champa in the east, beyond May-i, having regular contacts with Champa, but rarely with China".

Many centuries later, commercial goods were transported from central Vietnam along the road of north Borneo, as evidenced by shipments abroad from Pandanan in the south-west Philippines. We cannot find any evidence of direct relationship between Africa, Philippines and China, at least until the beginning of the Ming Dynasty. But with the regular and quite unique contacts from Champa, it seems that Champa was acting exclusively in its relations with Africa and the Philippines for a long time (from tenth to thirteenth century). Thus, the trade and tribute of Africa to the Philippines perhaps, up to China took place through Champa. Guangdong ceramics perhaps was traded from China to Champa and then to Butuan. Champa's role as an intermediate hub between China and pottery domain resided in the eastern edge of the South China Sea such as May-i and Butuan Borneo.

In 1007, Butuan claimed with the Emperor of China to receive a similar position as Champa, but denied the request on the grounds that he wasn't under dependence of Butuan like Champa. Only in the thirteenth century, the contact path of Luzon and the new Fujian became popular, before which all trade with China used to happen through Champa. Most likely, the boat ran on a sea route Butuan–Champa, because during this period boats and sailing craft of Champa were of good quality and their sailors were experienced. Champa took advantage of their intermediate position among Africa, the Philippines and China to promote trade activities. The Sea of Champa can be considered a "playground" of the ethnic Malayo Polynesien. Traces of this event still can be found in areas such as the Malaysian State of Kelantan. The renowned trade between Champa and Malaysia at that time was so intense that this land (Kelantan state) was called "the Chepa stop". Chepa here is pronounced as Champa dialect of Kelantan–Pattani. King Tra Hoa Bo De (1342-60) belonged to the twelfth dynasty of the Vijaya clan. He advocated economic development, and kept peaceful relations with Vietnam and Khmer. His Kingdom stretched from northern Hoang Lien Son range to south of Dong Nai of the present Champa. East Sea, west Lao, west Kinh were highly developed and were active in fishing, growing rice (they had rice varieties: short-term, drought-resistant, 2 crops/1 in the famous South-East Asia), Sa Huỳnh pottery, sculpture and industrial production (copper and brass). They developed brilliant and powerful boat fleets, managing a hard waters pa (East Sea) of 3,500,000 km$^2$ with large supply of goods for most part of East Asia, and three fleet on the Indian Ocean, is famous for frankincense, ivory, pepper, brocade, bird nests, pearls. . . . They (Tra Hoa Bo De King and his people) exported thousands of elephants for the soldiers in the battles fighting back the invasion of Khmer and Vietnamese in their territory (Majumdar 1985, III: 4-8, 21-26). Like most other South-East Asian nations, Champa had strong initiative in integrating the regional trade system to compensate the gaps in its economy, transforming external economic potential into different parts of its territory. It was found that Champa had sufficient goods to meet the needs of the Chinese market and West Asia. Champa with its advantages of geographical location, strong boat fleet, as well as commercial items of value, not only had become a hub of goods (entrêpot) for the major markets in the world, but also an important supplier of goods for the regional and international commercial trade. That ability actually became the strength and a foundation for the entire economy of Champa. The secret sources at Butuan from where Champa purchased the products of the Philippines and Africa throughout the centuries weren't known to the Chinese merchants. The Chams were able to hide the exact

*fig*. 3.10: Cham gold

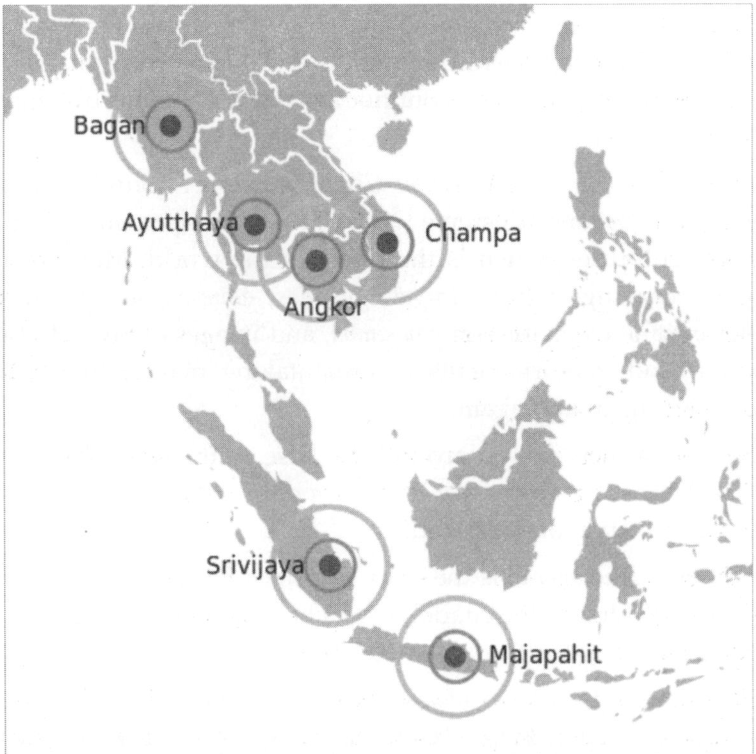


*fig.* 3.11: The main *maṇḍalas* (political formations) of South-East Asian history: Champa, Srivijaya, Khmer, Bagan, Majapahit, Ayutthaya. *Circa* fifth–fifteenth century CE (author: Gunkarta)

location of Butuan. Champa wanted to keep it a secret because it was where gold production was large. Secret excavations in Butuan for gold and gold brass by Champa were also hidden from the Chinese.

With the strong integration of international trade flows into its system, Champa for a long time remained a commercial powerhouse in the region, acting as a regional centre — the central collection and distribution of goods to regions such as South Asia, West Asia and the Middle East.

## INDIA'S INFLUENCES ON CHAMPA'S RELIGIONS

### *Hinduism in Champa*

Champa was profoundly influenced by Hinduism and many of the Cham towers, built as Hindu sanctuaries, contain *liṅgas* that are still worshipped by ethnic Vietnamese and ethnic Chinese alike. After the fall of Champa in the fifteenth century, most Chams who remained in Vietnam became Muslims, but continued to practise various Brahmanic rituals and customs.

*Hindu Gods Found in Cham Museum:* Cham Museum is founded in 1915 by the Ecole Francaise d'Esreme Orient. It has the open-air collection of Cham sculptures which is the finest in the world. Many of the sandstone carvings (altars, *liṅgas*, *garuḍas*, *gaṇeśas*, *sarasvatīs*, sea monster *makara*, elephant-lion *gajasiṁha*, and images of Śiva, Brahmā and Viṣṇu) and altar ornaments are breathtaking; making this a place one can visit again and again.

The four scenes carved around the base of the seventh-century Tra Kieu Altar tell parts of the *Rāmāyaṇa* epic and are influenced by the Amarāvatī style of south India:

*Scene A* (16 characters) tells the story of prince Rāma, who broke the sacred bow (Rudra) at the citadel of Videha thus winning the right to wed King Janaka's daughter, princess Sītā.

*Scene B* (16 characters) shows the ambassadors sent by King Janaka to prince Rāma's father, King Daśaratha, at Ayodhyā. The emissaries inform King Daśaratha of the exploits of his son, present him with gifts and invite to Videha to celebrate his son's wedding.

*Scene C* (18 characters) shows the royal wedding ceremony of Rāma and Sīta and the three princes — brothers of Rāma — marrying princess Sītā's cousins).

In *Scene D*, 11 *apsaras* (heavenly maidens) dance and present flowers to the newlyweds under the guidance of the two *gandharva* musicians who appear in the beginning of Scene A.

*Hindu Gods in Po Klong Gari Cham Towers:* Phan Rang-Thao Cham's famous landmark is Po Klong Gari, also known as Po Klong Girai (*girai* means dragon). The four brick towers, constructed at the end of the thirteenth century during the reign of Cham monarch Jaya Siṁhavarman III, were built as Hindu temples and stand on a brick platform at the top of Cho''k Hala, a crumbling granite hill covered with some of the most ornery cacti — one kind of plants (cactus), this side of the Rio Grande.

Over the entrance to the largest tower (the *kalan* or sanctuary) is a carving of a dancing Śiva with six arms. This bas-relief is known locally as Po Klaun Tri — The Guardian of the Temple Tower — and is famous for its beauty. Inside the vestibule is a statue of the bull Nandī (also known as Kapil Ox), symbol of the agricultural productivity in the countryside. Under the main tower is a *mukha-liṅga*, a *liṅga* with a painted human face on it. A wooden pyramid has been constructed above the *mukha-liṅga*. On the nearby hill is a rock with an inscription from the year 1050 commemorating the erection of a *liṅga* by a Cham prince.

The Kate New Year is celebrated at the towers in the seventh month of the Cham calendar (around October). The festival commemorates ancestors, Cham national heroes and gods such as goddess Po Ino Nagar who assisted the Chams with their farming. On the eve of the festival, a procession guarded by the mountain people of Tay Nguyen carries king Po Kloong Garai's clothing with the accompaniment of traditional music. The procession lasts until mid-night. The following morning the garments are carried to the tower, once again accompanied by music along with banners, flags, singing and dancing. Notables, dignitaries and village elders follow the procession. This colourful ceremony continues till afternoon. The Cham's New Year celebrations then carry on for the rest of the month as they attend parties and visit friends and relatives. The Cham also uses this time to pray for good fortune.

*Hindu Gods in Po Nagar Cham Tower:* The Cham towers of Po Nagar, also known as Thap Ba (the Lady of the City), were built between the seventh and twelfth centuries. The site was used for Hindu worship as early as second century CE. Today, both ethnic Chinese and ethnic Buddhists come to Po Nagar to pray and make offering according to their respective traditions.

There are many stone slabs found throughout the complexes, most of which are related to history or religion proving great insight into the spiritual life and social structure of the Chams. Originally the complex covered an area of 5,000 sq. m and there were seven or eight towers, four of which still remain. All the temples face east, as do the original entrance to the complex, which are to the right as one ascends the hillock. In centuries past, a person coming to pray passed through

*fig*. 3.12: The Yang Mum Śiva: in high relief against an ogival stele was found in the early 1930s at Yang Mum. Lord Śiva, with *triśūla* in his hand, was regarded as the founder and protector of the Champa dynasties

the pillared *maṇḍapa* (meditation hall), ten pillars of which can still be seen, before proceeding up the staircase to the towers.

The 23 m high North Tower (Thap Chinh), with its terraced pyramidal roof, vaulted interior masonry and vestibule, is a superb example of Cham architecture. One of the tallest Cham towers, it was built in CE 817 by Pangra, a minister of king Harivarman I, after the original temples here were sacked and burned. The raiders also carried off a *liṅga* made of precious metal. In CE 918 king Indravaraman III placed a gold *mukha-liṅga* in the North Tower, but it too was taken, this time by the Khmers. This pattern of statues being destroyed or stolen and then replaced continued for sometime until CE 965 when king Jaya Indravarman I replaced the gold *mukha-liṅga* with a stone figure of Umā — *śakti* or feminine manifestation of Śiva — which remains to this day.

Above the entrance to the North Tower, two musicians flank a dancing four-armed Śiva, one of whose feet is on the head of the bull Nandī. The sandstone door-posts covered with inscriptions are parts of the walls of the vestibule. A gong and a drum stand under the pyramid-shaped ceiling of the antechamber. In the 28 m high pyramidal main chamber there is a black stone statue of the goddess Umā (in the shape of Bhagavatī) with ten arms; two of which are hidden under her vest. She is seated leaning back against some sort of monstrous animal.

The Central Tower (Thap Nam) was built partly of recycled bricks in the twelfth century on the site of a structure dating the seventh century. It is less finely constructed than the other towers and has little ornamentation; the pyramidal roof lacks terracing or pilasters. The interior altars were once covered with silver. There is a *liṅga* inside the main chamber.

The South Tower (Mieu Dong Nam), at one time dedicated to Śiva, still shelters a *liṅga*. The richly ornamented North-West Tower (Thap Tay Bac) was originally dedicated to Gaṇeśa. The pyramid-shaped summit of the roof of the North-West Tower has disappeared. The West Tower, of which almost nothing remains, was constructed by king Vikrāntavarman during the first half of the ninth century.

*My Son Sanctuary:* My Son was the site of the most important Cham intellectual and religious centre, and also may have served as a burial place for Cham monarchs. My Son is considered to be Champa's counterpart to the grand cities of South-East Asia's other Indian-influenced civilizations: Angkor (Cambodia), Bagan (Myanmar), Ayuthaya (Thailand) and Borobudur (Java).

My Son was a centre of spirituality and worship during the reign of the Champa kingdom. The My Son Sanctuary, which exemplifies the height of Cham architectural achievement, is a large complex of religious monuments originally comprised of more than 70 structures; the vestiges of 25 of these structures remain today. The builders of My Son were the nobility of the Champa kingdom who derived their cultural and spiritual influences almost exclusively from India. The Cham people worshipped the trinity of Brahmā, Viṣṇu and Śiva, although Śiva was the central figure of worship for most people. Śiva was usually portrayed in one of two forms: as the figure of a man, and very often in his symbolic manifestation, the *liṅgam*, which was usually a stone embellished with incisions placed on a stone slab. The *liṅgam* represented both Śaivism and the divine authority Śiva bestowed upon the king. The Cham people erected monumental towers — the main component of Cham architectural design — to house the *liṅgam*. My Son was once a veritable forest of towers, many of which were destroyed by the ravages of time and war.

All of the Cham towers at My Son were built on square or rectangular foundations and were comprised of three parts; the tower base representing the world of humans, the tower body representing the world of spirits, and the tower head — usually built in the shape of a lotus — representing the realm between the two worlds. The structures were usually built of baked bricks and sandstone.

*Buddhism in Champa*

As there are so many things we can say in this part, I would rather mention only one masterpiece of Buddhist art in Champa, which is Dong Duong Buddhist monastery.

*Dong Duong Buddhist Monastery in Imperial Capital — Champa Ancient Towers:* In "Dai Nam Historical Book" of Nguyen dynasty, in section "about Quang Nam province" there is a mention about Dong Duong relics which is as follows:

> There exist two towers at Dong Duong Commune, Le Duong district. The two brick towers, 15 m away from each other have square base and octagonal body of 1-m side. Forty meters away are traces of an old base.

However, only after discovery and announcement of L. Finot in 1901 and especially after the excavation of H. Parmentier in 1902, Dong Duong complex (at Dong Duong Commune, Thang Binh District, Quang Nam-Da Nang Province) became one of the most important relics of Champa.

According to the announcement of L. Finot in 1901, he discovered in Dong Duong 229 artefacts, among which was the famous bronze Buddhist statue of 1 m high. (This statue is now presented at History Museum of Ho Chi Minh City.) Right after the discovery, Dong Duong Buddhist statue turned into a subject for study of many famous scientists such as R. Rougier, A. Foucher, V. Goloubew, P. Dupont and H. Parmentier. In the opinion of these famous scientists, Dong Duong Buddhist statue represents one of the most beautiful and ancient statues in South-East Asia. The statue of 1.08 m high (without pedestal) displays Buddha standing with two hands sticking symmetrically forward. Buddha wears a long frock over the left shoulder and has a small tumour (*ūrṇa*) in the middle of his forehead.

Dong Duong statue, like any other Buddhist statue discovered in South-East Asia such a as Korat statue (Thai country), Sikendung statue (Selebes, Indonesia), Jember statue (Java, Indonesia), Angkor Borei statue (Cambodia), imitates the style of Amarāvatī Buddhist statue of India. However, it on the other hand resembles too much Amarāvatī and Anurādhapura Buddhist statue (Sri Lanka). This is the reason why some scientists presumed that Champa statue dated back to the third–fourth century and was imported from India. Although he did not affirm the Indian origin of Dong Duong statue, J. Boisselier, a famous French researcher, had to recognize: "this statue, if not imported artefacts, must have so close relation with Indian traditional style that we could not detect any figure of local characters".

However, being an imported or locally made artefact, the statue proves the strong influence of Indian Amarāvatī Buddhist on Champa kingdom in general and Dong Duong in particular. It is no mean a coincidence that north area of Champa kingdom (now known as Quang Nam-Da Nang Province) was named Amarāvatī.

One year after the discovery of the famous Buddhist statue in 1902, H. Parmentier excavated Dong Duong. Thanks to this excavation, he discovered one of the biggest and most original complexes of architecture of the Champa kingdom in South-East Asia. The relics include many complex stretching in a distance of 1.330 m from west to east. The sanctuary is located within a brick fence of 326 m long and 155 m wide. From this sanctuary, a wide road of 763 m long runs westward to a valley (300 m long and 240 m wide).

If taking overall view, the sanctuary lies in centre of the relics and represents the only complex that still maintains vestige of stone and bronze temples. Therefore, according to scientists, Dong Duong was the capital city of the 4th Champa dynasty (Indrapura dynasty) created by King Indravarman II in 875 (the period of Dong Duong stele). Dong Duong stele also praised Indrapura capital city "to be decorated magnificently as the capital city of god Indra in paradise" and to be formulated by Bhr̥gu ancestor long ago. The stele revealed that the creator of this new dynasty, King Indravarman II, "inherited the throne by his good luck and good acts from previous lives rather than by blood relation".

In Dong Duong epitaph, Indravarman II not only stated his three-generation genealogy (his grandfather Rudravarman, his father Bhudravarman and himself but also took Bhr̥gu the legendary ancestor of Bharat in *Mahābhārata* as his ancestor. According to scientists, this statement testified for the fact that Indrapura dynasty was the development of a local clan or regional leader and that Indrapura might be the central area of Indravarman II clan before turning into imperial capital.

Possibly, before he took sovereign over the whole Champa, Indravarman II and his clan followed Buddhism. So that after becoming king of Champa, he promoted the development of this religion in north Champa. As a result, a period of Buddhist art flourished in Champa over half a century (from CE 875 to 915) and lelf many original Buddhist artefacts and monuments. Most of these famous monuments and artefacts have Dong Duong origin. Therefore, scientists simply call this style or period of Champa art as Dong Duong style or Dong Duong period. Dong Duong stele and others of the same period also emphasize the leading role of Buddhism to Indrapura dynasty.

Dong Duong stele declared that in 875, "because of his belief in Buddha, the king built a Buddhist monastery (*vihāra*) and a temple dedicated to Lakṣmīndra Lokeśvara Svabhayada". The stele also mentioned "paradise" (*svargapura*) or "liberated capital" (*mokṣapura*) — the shelter saved by Buddha (*buddhapada*) for honest persons and "eight hells" for vicious persons. According to the stele, upon building completion, the king "offered country, slaves, gold, silver and many other things to Lokeśa" (or Lokeśvara or Lakṣmīndra-Bhumīśvara

Grāmasvāmin). When he died, the king was named Paramabuddhaloka. The above-mentioned facts showed that King Indravarman II had been united with Buddha under the form of god Lokeśvara both when he was alive and when he was dead. That means Buddhism in Dong Duong period was Mahāyāna Buddhism.

Other stelae discovered outside Dong Duong also emphasized Mahāyāna characteristics of Champa Buddhism under Indrapura dynasty. Ron stele (near Deo Ngang) (also known as Bac Ha stele), which was erected by King Indravarman II in CE 889, mentioned the building of a Buddhist monastery dedicated to god Avalokiteśvara. The stele started with respective sentence to god Lokeśvara in Damareśvara term: "Veneration to Glorious Damaras" (*namaḥ tasmai bhagavate śrīsanabhadreśvara, 'damareśvarāya'*).

A Thai stele (discovered in Quang Nam-Da Nang province), which was erected by a *maṇḍārin* under the name of Sthavira Nāgapuṣpa in CE 902, was completely inspired by Mahāyāna Buddhism. The stele erection aimed to commemorate the building of a statue (*lokanātha*) for Pramudita Lokeśvara monastery. In the third epitaph of the stele, Avalokiteśvara appeared as Great Benevolence who saved all convicts from punishment in hell and thus helped Vajrapāṇi in liberating them and leading them to Buddhism. In epitaph VIII and X, philosophic idealism of Mahāyāna Buddhism was summarized as follows: from the will of three gods, namely Śākyamuni, Amitābha and Vairocana come into being three Buddhism worlds (Buddhamahālaya): Vajradhātu, Padmadhātu and Sakradhātu. These Buddhism worlds were distinctive with none (*śūnya*): Vajradhātu none (*śūnya*), Padmadhātu no big (*mahāśūnya*) and Sakradhātu no supernatural (*śūnyātīta*). There were three gods to lead people from misery into Buddhism worlds, namely Vajradhara, Avalokiteśvara and Vajrasava.

The Mahāyāna Buddhist characteristics were also shown clearly in architecture and sculpture of Buddhist monasteries in Dong Duong. We twice visited Dong Duong in 1977 and 1987. Unfortunately, the unique complex of Buddhist temples in Champa and South-East Asia was completely destroyed by wars, time, nature and also human beings. Therefore, to depict a picture of Dong Duong architecture, we have to rely on the detailed description of H. Parmentier from the beginning of the last century.

According to the survey and excavation of H. Parmentier, Dong Duong relics (326 m long and 155 m wide) had three complex separating from each other by brick fence and locating in west–east direction. Of three complexes, only the one to far west (complex I) and the one to far east (complex III) retain several vestiges of architecture and sculpture.

The complex to the far west (complex I) included a sanctuary; subsidiary towers and small sanctuaries near the surrounding fence. The sanctuary was the traditional tower of Champa, which had the base, the body and the storey. The base was quite large and included two steps: the under steps forming the base for sanctuary and subsidiary towers and the upper step forming actual base of the sanctuary. The base was decorated by figures of tower and elephant's head. In the middle of the east side, was a staircase of two parts: the under and the upper matching with two steps of the base. The under part consisted three steps and had stone handrail in the figure of seven *nāga* snakes. The upper part consisted two steps and had stone handrail in the figure of two elephants heading aside.

On two-step base were a square, solid and somewhat rudiment brick tower. On the exterior of west, south and north walls were four projected pilasters and false doors in-between. The foot of pilasters was decorated with an oblong motif. The storey was destroyed but the remaining south wall resembles outlay of Hoa Lai Tower (see for further details at Hoa Lai Tower). The entrance door projected strongly to form a pavilion, which had one-storey pyramidal roof just like that of the sanctuary.

Inner space of the tower had square shape and included two big niches in north and south side. There were six niches for candles to enlighten the chapel (two below the big niche and four in the pavilion). In the chapel, there was a big stone altar — one of the big, beautiful and valuable artefacts about Buddhism (we will mention this structure in detail later). Above the alter, was a big stone pedestal. On the basis of its layout, H. Parmentier thought that it might have carried a *liṅga* or a box of relics (Parmentier 1904: 805-96). Later, when studying Dong Duong sculpture, J. Boisselier believed it would be a more reasonable presumption that the pedestal used to support a Lokeśvara statue (the key statue of the sanctuary).

In 1978, local inhabitants happened to find a bronze goddess statue of 1.14 m height. The goddess stands upright with her hands sticking symmetrically forward, her right hand holding a lotus and left hand a water jug. The upper part of her body is naked, showing big breasts and fat belly. The under part of her body wears two-layer gown: a long dress to her ankle and a covering cloth with two endings jammed at front belly. To display the softness of covering cloth, the unknown artist did carve relief parallel bent. The upright posture with the hands sticking symmetrically forward and the technique to display relief folds (which is unrealistic because gravity would naturally prevent these folds) remind us of the style of Dong Duong bronze statue (referred to above). However, the face full of Cham typical features as the head a little big over the body, square and grave face, big and curved eyebrow, big nose and mouth, etc. follows Dong Duong style and thus, the period should be Dong Duong period (CE 875). The goddess's hair is wind high up into a big knot and pin with the figure of god Amitābha. Based on the specific straits, stylized signs of the lotus and the figure of god Amitābha in hair knot, we have identified Dong Duong period and style for this statue and defined it as the Lokeśvara statue since 1978. Also in 1979 articles, we affirmed that Lokeśvara statue discovered in 1978 was the key statue of Dong Duong sanctuary and was put on the pedestal, which used to raise many presumptions. The reason for this affirmation was that the hilt of the statue and the whole pedestal coincided.

Based on the remaining traces, H. Parmentier believed that the temple was ravaged and burned badly. The inner was dug, destroyed then burned. He found a lot of ash in a pit (evidence of the digging), an *apsarā* statue burned into lime, etc. Also in 1902, he was told by village's old men that the sanctuary collapsed completely in 1820.

According to H. Parmentier's description, apart from the sanctuary, there were traces of other monuments in complex I as south tower, north tower, south-west tower, north-west tower, sanctuary, little sanctuaries near the brick fence, oblong house, gateway tower, etc.

What used to be complex II, are now traces of walls and the base? One of its most important structures was the oblong house. The house ran in east–west direction and had two doors in east and west walls. The house was lightened by windows in the longer walls. The remaining traces as the walls thin and far away from each other, broken tiles, etc. made H. Parmentier think of a tile roof house rather than a pyramidal roof tower. Although the remained vestiges of architecture and sculpture of complex II could not be compared with those of complex I in terms of numbers, some of its stone god statues (*dvārapāla*) were considered as the most beautiful and impressive not only in Dong Duong relics but also in Champa art history.

While complex I functioned as the sanctuary, complex III was, in reality, a Buddhist monastery. In complex III, apart from the oblong house, there was no trace of any sanctuary. The oblong house was supported by two rows of eight pillars. Along the central house, there were small side rooms, which were supported by the big pillars and smaller, lower ones outside. These square pillars were made from brick. There were rectangular holes in the exterior of big pillars, which lied in parallel with top of the smaller ones. It was obvious that the house used to have a wood frame to carry the tile roof above (broken tiles could be found anywhere).

The back wall of this house had a row of pillars rather than doors, where a big altar similar to that of the sanctuary in shape, structure and decoration was found. The excavation of H. Parmentier in 1902 had added many beautiful and valuable stone artefacts to Da Nang Art Museum. Dong Duong artefacts are abundant but could be divided into two groups: the relief carved group and the statue group. Among the relief carved group, the most valuable are two stone altars: one of the sanctuary and the other of monastery.

The altar of sanctuary is a structure of three parts: the rear, the big pedestal and small pedestal. The rear props on the west wall are the places to display various statues. The big pedestal has narrow staircase leading to a small plane. The smaller pedestal is decorated with four steps and carries Lokeśvara statue (as mentioned above). Around the big pedestal are relief-carved scenes of Buddha life. Parmentier described several scenes as follows: queen Māyā (mother of Buddha) in Lumbinī garden, arrow-shooting contest between a god and people who wants to marry lady Gopā, Buddha cut his hair and exchange cloths with the hunter to take the vow, servant Caṇḍaka return with Kaṇṭhaka horse after Buddha goes into the forest to take the vow, Māra troops and his daughters trouble Buddha when he's taking vow.

In fundamental aspects, *vihāra* altar resembles that of the sanctuary. Although the relief-carved scenes of *vihāra* altar are clearer and more beautiful than those of the sanctuary altar, up to now no one has ever been able to specify the content of these scenes. While the altar of central sanctuary carries the statue of Laṣmīndra-Lokeśvara, that *vihāra* altar is placed with Śākyamuni statue. In the front of the pedestal, there is a personality with four heads and eight hands, who in Boisselier's opinion might be Rāvaṇa devil shaking Kailāsa mountain (Rāvaṇānugrahamūrti). On the pedestal is Śākyamuni sitting with dangled legs, his hands putting on the knee.

This posture of Śākyamuni is rarely seen in Champa and South-East Asia but quite Prevalent in China. Around the statue are little statues of monks standing or kneeling and *arhant*. The most beautiful and valuable artefacts found in Dong Duong are statues of Dharmapāla (the god who protect Buddhist laws) and Dvārapāla (member god). Dharmapāla (1.14 m high) stand with extended legs in a solid posture, one of his hand hold a kind of weapon (had been destroyed) along the hip and the other fold and put on the thigh. Two statues of *vihāra* altar are sculpted symmetrically, one holding the weapon in the right

*fig*. 3.13: The principal temple in Dong Duong

*fig*. 3.14: Bronze statue of a bodhisattva. (The second life-size bronze statue of a *bodhisattva*, found at Dong Dzuong in 1978. She may be named as Lakṣmīndra-Lokeśvara (?!), the name of *vihāra* was mentioned in the inscription of king Indravarman erected at the site)

hand and the other in the left hand. Dharmapāla statues wear a dress of sampot style up to the ankle, their upper bodies are naked. They wear big rings at the neck, biceps and around the chest; a crown of three big flowers and a pyramidal, multi-storey hat to cover the hair (*mukuṭa*).

The statues of Dong Duong member gods are not only the biggest (2.15 m in height) but also the most successful artefacts in terms of techniques and aesthetics in Champa sculpture history. Couples of member gods in lively and strong postures are put symmetrically near entrance doors. The member gods stand with the legs extended and put on some animals. Each of its body bends a little forward, the head direction is in accordance with the posture. Some gods hold above the head a weapon in the left hand, the others in the right hand to create symmetry. The other hand is put in front of the chest. The body looks quite clumsy and unpolished while the face is carved in details to express aggressiveness. For example, a big and curved moustache, big tooth with two tooth pointing outward, big nostril, eyes projected as if they were about to fall out, long hair, tendon showing clearly on the neck. The aggressiveness of these statues is strengthened by the animals that the god put his legs on. These animals spurt out a little fighter, who hold a shield in one hand and wave a sword on the other hand and look up at the hostile god.

All member gods wear the same cloths: a dress of sampot style up to the ankle, big rings of three-head *nāga* snake at the neck, biceps and around the chest; a crown of three big flowers and a pyramidal, multi-storey had to cover the hair (*mukuṭa*). The devastated towers and many artefacts found in Dong Duong have created one of the most special styles of Champa architecture and sculpture. Although the towers are difference in shape and the sculpted scenes prove various, the typical characteristics of Dong Duong style are "the afraid of space, mystical and blossomed flowers and leaves", "strong vitality of indigenous personality", "anthropology traits of Cham people in sculpted figures", "the mystical, the strength and the portliness". As a result, Dong Duong monuments and artefacts carved for themselves an outstanding and special position in Cham art history and that of South-East Asia in general.

## IV. Conclusion

The concept of the Indianized kingdoms, first described by George Coedès, is based on Hindu and Buddhist cultural and economic influences in South-East Asia.[44] Butuan, Champa, Dvāravatī, Funan, Gangga Negara, Kadaram, Kalingga, Kutai, Langkasuka, Pagan, Pan Pan, Po-ni, Tarumanagara and Tondo were among the earliest Hindu kingdoms in South-East Asia, established around the first to fourth centuries CE. Despite being culturally akin to Hindu cultures, these kingdoms were indigenous and independent of the Indian mainland. States such as Srivijaya, Majapahit and the Khmer empire developed territories and economies that rivalled those in India itself. Borobudur in Java, for example, is the largest Buddhist monument ever built.[45] Coedès has been criticized for understating the South-East Asian element of these kingdoms, in an unconscious echo of the European "civilizing mission".[46] From the above article, we can withdraw some conclusions as follows:

- Champa was an Indic civilization that flourished along the

44 Coedès 1968.

45 Lukas 2003: 82-107.

46 Keyes 1995: 106.

coasts of what is now central and southern Vietnam for roughly 1,200-year period between CE 500 and 1700. The cities were ports of call on important trade routes linking India, China and the Indonesian islands.

- The artistic legacy in Champa consists primarily of sandstone sculptures — both sculpture in the round and relief sculpture — and brick buildings.
- Some metal statues and decorative items have also survived.
- Much of the remaining art expresses religious themes, and though some pieces would have been purely decorative, others would have served important functions in the religious life of the Chams, which synthesized elements of Hinduism (especially Saivism), Buddhism and indigenous cults.
- Heritage of Champa kingdom in central Vietnam was the evidence of the interaction of the trade and the religion between India and Vietnam in the past.

## References

Boisselier, Jean, 1963, *La statuaire du Champa*, Paris: École Française d'Extrême-Orient.

Branch, Jordan Nathaniel, 2011, "Mapping the Sovereign State: Catographic Technology, Political Authority and Systemic Change", Ph.D. thesis, University of California, Berkeley, doi: 10.1017/S0020818310000299, retrieved on 5 March 2012.

Coedès, George, 1968, *The Indianized States of Southeast Asia*, ed. Walter F. Vella, tr. Susan Brown Cowing, Canberra: Australian National University Press.

Davies, N., 2005, *God's Playground*, Oxford: Oxford University Press, vol. I.

Dellios, Rosita, 2003, *Mandala: From Sacred Origins to Sovereign Affairs in Tradtional Southeast Asia*, Bond University, Australia, retrieved on 11 December 2011.

Gould, Stephen, 1986, "Evolution and the Triumph of Homology', *American Scientist*, **70**: 64.

Hagesteyn, Renee Regina, ev van Kessel (Renee Regina Hagesteijn ev van Kessel), 1985, *Circles of Kings: Political Dynamics in Early Continental Southeast Asia*, Dissertation, Rijksuniv., Proefschr.—Leiden, Edition/Format: English, Database: WorldCat.

Keyes, Charles F., 1995, *The Golden Peninsula: Culture and Adaptation in Mainland Southeast Asia*, SHAPS Library of Asian Studies, University of Hawai'i Press.

Kulke, Hermann, 1986, "The Early and Imperial Kingdom in Southeast Asian History", in David Marr and A.C. Milner, *Southeast Asia in the 9th to 14th Centuries*, Singapore: ISEAS; Canberra RSPacS, ANU.

Lê Thành Khôi, 1990, *Histoire du Vietnam des origines à 1858* (in French), Paris: Sudestasie.

Lieberman, 2003, *Strange Parallels: Southeast Asia in Global Context c. 800–1830*, Cambridge: Cambridge University Press.

Lukas, Helmut, 2003, Theories of Indianization Exemplified by Selected Case Studies from Indonesia (Insular Southeast Asia), in Proceedings of Papers. "Sanskrit in Southeast Asia: The Harmonizing Factor of Cultures", International Sanskrit Conference, 21-23 May 2001. Sanskrit Studies Centre and Department of Oriental Languages, Silpakorn University, Bangkok: Mahachulalongkornrajavidyalaya Press, pp. 82-107.

Mabbett, Ian, 1978, "Kingship in Angkor", *Journal of the Siam Society*, (July), **66**(2): 29.

Maspero, G., 1928, *Le royaume de Champa*, Paris et Bruxelles, Les edition Van Oest, in-8, VII- 278, pp.ill; See Louis Finot, *Bulletin de l'Ecole française d'Extrême-Orient*, Année 1928, vol. 28, Numéro 28-1, pp. 285-92.

Moertono, Soemarsaid, 1968, *State and Statecraft in Old Java*, Ithaca: Cornell University.

National Library of Australia (January 1996), *Asia's French Connection: George Coedes and the Coedes Collection*, vol. 6(4).

Ngô Văn Doanh, 2005, *My Son Relics*, Hanoi: The Gioi Publishers.

———, 2006, *Champa: Ancient Towers*, Hanoi: The Gioi Publishers.

———, 2012, *Chămpa*, Hanoi: National Government Publication, Thê Giói Publishers.

Noordholt, H. Schulte, 1986, *Bali: Colonial Concepts and Political Change, 1700-1940*, Rotterdam: Erasmus University.

Parmentier, M. Henri, 1904, "Les Monuments du Cirque de My Son", in *BEFEO* **4:** 805-96. Available online at BEFEO's website.

Ricklefs, M., 1992, "Unity and Disunity in Javanese Political and Religious Thought of the Eighteenth Century", *Modern Asian Studies* (May), **26**(2): 665.

Rutherford, Scott (ed.), 2006, *Insight Guide-Vietnam*.

Stuart-Fox, Martin, 1998, *The Lao Kingdom of Lan Xang: Rise and Decline*, Bagkok: White Lotus Press.

Tambiah, Stanley Jeyaraja, 1976, *World Conqueror and World Renouncer: A Study of Buddhism and Polity in Thailand against a Historical Background* (Cambridge

Studies in Social and Cultural Anthropology), Cambridge: Cambridge University Press, 1976.

Taus-Bolstad, Stacy, 2003, *Vietnam in Pictures*, Twenty-First Century Books, p. 21.

Vickery, Michael, 2005, "Champa Revised" ARI Working Paper, No. 37, www.nus.ari.edu.sg/pub/wps.htm p. 4ff.

Wolters, O.W., 1982 (1999), *History, Culture and Region in Southeast Asian Perspectives*, Singapore: ISEAS, 1982, pp. 16-19; revised edition, Ithaca: SEAP; Singapore: ISEAS, 1999, pp. 27-9.

Wolters, O.W., 1982, *History, Culture and Region in Southeast Asian Perspectives*, Institute of Southeast Asian Studies.

# 4

# Colonial, Modern, or Traditional?

## How to Read the Indo-Saracenic Architecture of South and South-East Asia*

***Hawon Ku***

MANY introductions to modern architecture of South Asia generally divide the architecture of the nineteenth and early twentieth-century South Asia into three periods: a period of the earliest European settlements including the Neo-Classical architecture of the East India Company up to 1857, a second period from 1858, mostly comprised of Indo-Saracenic style architecture, and finally a period of the "Imperial style", after 1911 (Dehejia 1997: 380). On the other hand, while it is difficult to generalize the development of Western architecture in South-East Asia due to its historical and regional complexity, the beginning of colonial architecture is usually dated to the sixteenth century. One of the earliest examples is St. Paul's Church, Melaka, built in 1521 by the Portuguese. However, one of the popular architectural styles in South-East Asia was an eclectic style mixing traditional and Western forms, which is often termed "Mughal/ Moghul", "North Indian", "Indo-Islamic", or "Indo-Saracenic" style (O'Neill 1994: 225-26; Rasdi and Utaberta 2006: 50; O'Neill 1995: 153). This paper examines the origin and history of the "Indo-Saracenic" style, as well as its stylistic features and reception through two representative examples in South and South-East Asia.

---

* Parts of this article have been published previously in Korean.as "Indigenous Architecture of Colonial India: The Lakshmi Vilas Palace, Vadodara", in *Journal of Indian Studies* vol. 15 no. 1 (2010): 1-31, and "Tradition and Islam: The Architectural Styles of the Modern Indonesian Mosque", *East Asian Studies,* 30 (1) (2011): 223-59.

## The Rise of the Indo-Saracenic Style

Indo-Saracenic architecture was not always the preferred style for European buildings in South and South-East Asia. The earliest buildings of the new Western rulers in South Asia and South-East Asia were mostly administrative buildings or residences needed by the European community. Due to the lack of skilled architects in the colony, they were usually built by officers who copied existing plans of English houses (Tillotson 1989: 4). One famous example, the Government House of Calcutta (1798–1803), was commissioned by Lord Wellesley. We know well when criticized of the enormous amount of money spent on building the residence, Lord Valentia argued that India ought "to be ruled from a palace, not from a country house; with the ideas of a prince, not those of a retail-dealer in muslins and indigo" (Davies 1985: 68). The Government House was placed within large surrounding gardens, and the building itself was closely modelled on Kedleston Hall in Derbyshire. Such stately English homes were mostly neo-classical or "Palladian", an architectural style named after sixteenth-century Italian architect Palladio. Neo-classical architecture, popular in England and France, is well known for drawing its inspiration from the architecture of the Greeks and Romans; restrained and symmetrical, it is mostly recognized through the temple-like porticoes and the use of low decorative spherical domes. Similarly in South-East Asia, we can see that the earliest buildings built by the Europeans closely resembled those of their homelands.

However, the Great Uprising of 1857 in northern India changed a variety of policies, including those regarding architecture. As the Governor-General was replaced by the Viceroy to rule as direct representative of the Crown and Queen Victoria assumed title of Empress of India, British rule in India shifted from policies of aggressive Anglicization and Westernization to an emphasis on indigenous rule. As successors of Mughal rule in South Asia, the British were keen to express this new approach to rule in architecture (Metcalf 1989: 56). Particularly in administrative and official buildings such as revenue board buildings, post offices, railway stations, and schools, a search for a new appropriate style was started. At the same time in England, a "battle of styles" was fought, in which architecture was regarded as linked both to the mind of a nation and its landscape; for example, Ruskin believed that "architecture was the expressive locus of this conjunction" (Crinson 1996: 49). This was not simply a debate on style, but also a debate on the conceptions of national identity and purpose, as well as the "vision of an empire" (Metcalf 1984). As a result, Western architecture shifted from neo-classicism to a style that more freely incorporated non-European architectural elements. Similar changes are also found in South-East Asia, especially Malaysia, Indonesia, or Thailand, where the British were exerting much political influence.

This period, the late nineteenth century, roughly coincided with the rise of interest and systematic study of India and South-East Asia's monuments, including architectural surveys led by Alexander Cunningham, James Fergusson and James Burgess. These surveys culminated in the publication of James Fergusson's seminal work, *History of Indian and Eastern Architecture*, a book spanning the regions of South Asia, South-East Asia, up to China and Japan, two volumes which were published respectively in 1876 and 1891 (Fergusson 1876). Such studies of Buddhist, Hindu and Islamic architecture in Asia, as well as the censuses and various other studies of South Asian society of the nineteenth century, led to a clear distinction between Hindu and Islamic architecture; the British-linked Hindu architecture with domestic use, while Islamic architecture, due to its relationship with early Christiandom, was deemed more suitable for the display of power. In addition, according to nineteenth-century European aesthetics which were considered universally valid, a small number of Islamic monuments in northern India won much appreciation; for example, one of the most famous monuments in India, the Taj Mahal (Metcalf 1989: 46-47).

Thus it was finally decided that the most appropriate architectural style for British architecture in South and South-East Asia was a modern Western building, made familiar to the "native" peoples with the addition of local architectural elements, particularly those that had been aesthetically sanctioned by the British, i.e. Mughal. This architectural style came to be known as the Indo-Saracenic style.

### The Indo-Saracenic Style and Its Reception

One of the first buildings to be built in this new style was Mayo College in Ajmer (1875). Mayo College was conceived as the Eton of

India, in which the Rājpūt kings could send their sons for Western-style education. At the time of conception, Viceroy Lord Mayo preferred a classical design, which would represent the reason and enlightenment of Western civilization. However, it was finally built in the Indo-Saracenic style, so that the school would feel more familiar to the princes (Metcalf 1984: 45-46). Planned by Major Charles Mant, Mayo College is usually considered one of the earliest examples of Indo-Saracenic architecture, which include others such as the Revenue Board Building, Madras (1871, Robert Chisholm); Husainabad Clocktower, Lucknow (1880), Sultan Abdul Samad Building, Kuala Lumpur (A.C. Norman, 1897) and the Gateway to India, Bombay (George Wittet, 1910) among many other examples.

The most significant features of Indo-Saracenic style are Mughal architectural forms. Bulbous domes, cusped arches, *chajjā*s (straight eaves) creating shade on the buildings, and the *chattrī*s (small pavilions) are the most significant Mughal features of Indo-Saracenic buildings. The *baṅgalādāras* (curved roofs) were also found in Mughal palatial architecture dating from the period of Shahjahan. *Jālī*s (stone panels), pierced to make windows, are also commonly found in north Indian Islamic architecture. However, there are many features that are alien to north Indian Mughal architecture or even to Islamic architecture. In addition to *śikhara*-type superstructures found in Hindu or Jaina temples, balconies or window structures which are reminiscent of Gujarātī or Rājasthānī woodwork are found in many Indo-Saracenic buildings. Islamic architectural features not usually common in South Asia or South-East Asia are also found easily in Indo-Saracenic architecture: for example, the square tower, commonly found in minarets of northern Africa but rarely in South Asia, the use of the key-hole or horse-shoe-shaped arch, arches formed with alternating red and white stone are all features that are commonly found in Islamic architecture of north Africa or Spain, particularly in Mamluk palaces and mosques of Cairo or Kairouan, or mosques of Cordoba or the Alhambra Palace. It is likely that British architects freely incorporated these elements with which they were more familiar. Finally we can see in most Indo-Saracenic architecture the clock tower as a dominant feature. The clock tower represented modernity to the British, a reflection of a discipline and orderliness that defined one idea of the modern time (Metcalf 1989: 78-80).

Within the context of Indian art history, Indo-Saracenic has neither gained much architectural significance nor been critically appreciated; rather, it has been scorned for its amalgamation of various architectural styles. The British were "repeating the pattern established by their imperial predecessors, the Mughals", but scholars such as Tillotson also argue that the Indo-Saracenic style did not prove a satisfactory synthesis, only a mixture since "Indian design principles differed fundamentally" (Tillotson 1989: 54). As Ernest Havell had already pointed out in the early twentieth century, the fundamental flaw of Indo-Saracenic architecture was that it was a colonial style masquerading as a "national" one (Havell 1915: 218).

In spite of its questionable origins and loaded meanings, Indo-Saracenic is now accepted as the architectural style which incorporated Indian and Islamic features into the architecture of the British in South and South-East Asia (Tillotson 1989: 46). During the nineteenth century and early twentieth century it was widely adopted as the architectural style of colonial buildings in both regions. According to Tillotson, Indo-Saracenic style was preferred for several reasons, including the climate, cost and most significantly, the expression of political role. Thus the British, self-proclaimed masters of India's cultures, believed they could shape a harmony that the Indians themselves, communally, regionally, ethnically divided, could not achieve. Indo-Saracenic thus found its widest application in buildings meant for Indians, but where the content and meaning of the structure were defined by the colonial ruler and embodied British definitions of appropriate behaviour (Metcalf 1984: 50).

### A New Reading of Indo-Saracenic Style: Lakshmi Vilas Palace, Vadodara

Indo-Saracenic style was swiftly adopted by the Indian princes, nationalists, and even for religious purposes in South-East Asia, since it was possible to incorporate traditional architectural elements on the surface and acknowledge one's roots at the same time. Thus by using the Indo-Saracenic style, i.e. an imperial style comprised of a Western architectural grammar sanctioned by the British, the people of South and South-East Asia were able to create a "traditional *and* progressive" image.

For example, we may look at the Lakshmi Vilas Palace, Vadodara

*fig*. 4.1: Laxmi Vilas Palace, Vadodara

(*fig*. 4.1) Commissioned in 1875, the palace was for the newly-installed Mahārājā Sayaji Rao Gaekwad III, the twelve-year old ruler of the princely state of Baroda. This task was conferred to Major Charles Mant, the British engineer who had built Mayo College. After Mant's untimely death in 1881, Robert Fellowe Chisholm completed most of Mant's original plans with his own interior designs. Costing over £ 180,000 at its completion, it is known to be the most expensive private building to be built by a private individual at that time (Davies 1985: 202).

Set in a landscaped garden of 720 acres, the result was a tripartite palace comprised of a *durbār* hall (public audience hall), the *mahārājā*'s private quarters and the *zenānā* (ladies' quarters), forming a single structure. According to Chisholm, these three sections were designed to emulate respectively a Mughal audience hall, Rājpūt palace architecture and local Gujarātī forms (Chisholm 1896: 422). However, numerous other Indian architectural elements, such as curved *baṅgalādāra* eaves, foliated arches, *jālī*s, and moldings were liberally incorporated into the façade, creating a picturesque view. While the original plan of Mant included a clock tower, at final construction the clock was omitted, due to Chisholm's argument that it would give the building a public rather than palatial appearance (Chisholm 1896: 424).

The interior of the *durbār* hall contains imported stained glass windows depicting Rāma and Kr̥ṣṇa, and originally held twelve large paintings of Indian mythological subjects painted by a contemporary Indian artist, Raja Ravi Varma. While some of the work was accomplished by local craftsmen, sculptors and craftsmen, in addition to paintings, furniture and ornaments were brought in from Venice or England to finish interior details. In 1896, Chisholm introduced Lakshmi Vilas Palace to the general meeting of the Royal Institute of British architects in London, as an example of later "Hindu-Saracenic" style (Chisholm 1896: 421-33, 445-49). Chisholm (1896: 422) argued that

> it must be kept in view that the native *rājā*s and chiefs of India are passing through a transitional period; that an old palace like that at Ambur would be about as useless to the present Gaekwar of Baroda as to an ordinary English gentleman.

The alignment of a progressive ruler to an English gentleman is a clear reflection of the British ideas about indigenous India, i.e. an entity in a transitional phase heading from the backwardness to the enlightened modern era, through the leadership of colonial overlords and English-educated progressive rulers. Thus the Lakshmi Vilas Palace itself, to its British commissioners and architects, was a visual representation of such progress and subjugation.

As a result, not only in the building itself, but also in its source of power, the integrity of Lakshmi Vilas Palace was dependent on the colonial. Without the power of the colonizer, such buildings could not exist; through the affirmation of power by the British only, the native princes could have authority over their subjects, peace between neighbours, and thus the financial resources to produce such structures. Thus the Lakshmi Vilas Palace can also be read as a means of affirming a puppet authority, represented through the aid of Western, modern aesthetics of the colonial rulers.

The "native *rājā*" of Lakshmi Vilas Palace, Sayaji Rao III, had been adopted by the widow of the former *mahārājā* of Baroda with British approval, after the British disposed of the ruling *mahārājā* under the accusation of trying to poison a British resident. From his adoption and installation to the seat of *mahārājā* in 1875, to the actual investiture of power in 1881, his education was undertaken by an Anglicized, pro-Residency minister, Sir T. Madhav Rao, and British officials such as F.A.S. Elliott, son of a former Acting Governor of Madras, two of the administrative Regents who actually commissioned the Lakshmi Vilas Palace. Through these five years of education, a modernized

Western ruler was created out of a village boy with no prior formal education. During his reign, Sayaji Rao III was renowned for commissioning railroads and modern institutions such as colleges, and pursuing compulsory education and improvement of women's rights; in other words, he was regarded as a "perfect blend" of Indian and Englishman by his colonial observers (Codell 1998: 14). Thus the Lakshmi Vilas Palace itself, to its British commissioners and architects, was a visual representation of such progress, "a distinct advance on most modern Indian buildings, as a successful attempt to combine native details with the ordinary requirements of a modern palace" (Chisholm 1896: 422).

The Lakshmi Vilas Palace asserts progressiveness through the aesthetic features of the colonizers, thus represents a modernity of colonial domination. Not only in its layout or location, but also in its source of power, the integrity of Lakshmi Vilas Palace is dependent on the colonial.

However, the reading of the Lakshmi Vilas Palace becomes much more complex with the biographical details of Sayaji Rao himself. The reign of Sayaji Rao was "a conflicting and vacillating combination of imperatives" where he openly co-operated and admired Britain, whilst simultaneously participating in the modern Indian nationalistic movement during the first decades of the twentieth century (Codell 1998: 6). During his reign, Sayaji Rao commissioned several biographies of his life to be published in English and Gujarati. Codell argues that these biographies project Sayaji Rao not only as an idealized, post-Enlightenment reformer, but also as an Orientalized, luxurious, exotic *rājā*, as well as a nationalistic resister against British power. Through the creation of multiple identities by way of such biographies, complete with photographs of himself dressed either bejewelled in traditional Indian garb or Western garb, thus enforcing this splitting of the colonized subject, he endeavoured to negotiate his authority and power between the colonizers and the colonized. These multiple identities essentially "destabilized" the role the British expected of him (Codell 1998: 14).

The role of the *mahārājā* expected by the colonizer was the "ordinary English gentleman" of Chisholm, enlightened and guiding his subjects towards modernity, but not one who would mimic the British identity so much as to threaten it. The ruling class of India was specifically targeted by the colonial power, which reconstructed them in a favourable way to the British rule through Anglicized education such as that of the *mahārājā*. However, the controlled biographies of Sayaji Rao prove that rather than being a one-dimensional character such as the progressive English gentleman or the incompetent *rājā* dependent on the power of the colonizers, Sayaji Rao III was a person with multiple selves, moving within and determined by frameworks of the continuously shifting political configurations of the Raj. Just as the discourse on multiple identities self-created by Sayaji Rao III arise, the Lakshmi Vilas Palace acquired a new dimension, in which the readings of a single structure may have multiple readings which are not stable, but constantly modified. During his early reign, Lakshmi Vilas Palace would have reminded the ruler of his political limits, and subversively, to the viewers, the power of the British who made this building possible. However, with the rise of the popular nationalist image of Sayaji Rao, the reading of the palace has changed, from a colonial structure to one representing a pride of cultural heritage and sense of autonomy. Now the palace is currently one of the most beloved buildings of Vadodara, with its gardens opened to the public.

### "Indo-Saracenic" Style in South-East Asia: Mesjid Raya, Banda Aceh

The shift of meanings in architectural forms can be seen in another example from South-East Asia. The Great Mosque at Banda Aceh, (*fig*. 4.2) also known as Mesjid Raya or the Masjid Baituraachman (Abode of the Merciful One), was first built by Sultan Iskandar Muda (r. 1607-36) who brought about the "Golden Age of Aceh". According to Peter Mundy (1600-67), an English traveller who visited Aceh in 1637 and left detailed descriptions and sketches, the original mosque was a traditional South-East Asian type wooden building, with a flared pyramidal roof (Bouwsema-Raap 2009: 29). Even after several reconstructions, the mosque seems to have retained this form until 1873, when the Dutch attacked the city and burnt down the mosque which was being used as a military fortification. However, after the conquest of Aceh, in 1879, the Dutch Indies government announced that they would rebuild the mosque "to show that the religion of the Acehnese was respected by the Dutch authorities and that they were

*fig.* 4.2: The Great Mosque at Banda Aceh

willing to co-operate" (ibid.: 46). The new mosque was commissioned to be built by Bruins, an architect of the Department of Public Works, in consultation with a Muslim religious leader from Java (ibid.: 47).

The new mosque had a cruciform plan, commonly found in European churches and in contemporary country houses. The placement of a central dome on the second storey was reminiscent of neo-classical country houses; however, the dome of the Banda Aceh Mosque was not the classical hemispherical dome, but rather, onion-shaped, one of the most distinctive features of Mughal imperial architecture. Yet when compared with the Jama Masjid in Delhi (1656), which has beautiful domes on top of high drums, the Banda Aceh Great Mosque has an open verandah on the second storey, with the dome itself underlined with a wide cornice. Scholars suggest also that the interior stucco work was similar to those at the Alhambra Palace in Spain, with window and pillar ornaments comparable to the Great Mosque of Kairouan or the Mosque of Ibn Tulun in Cairo. Most likely these were copied from a pattern book of Islamic ornaments that was published a couple of years before the construction.[1] At the time of construction, the mosque was known to have been painted in light pink, brown, sky blue with blue mouldings. These were colours

[1] Bouwsema-Raap suggests that these colours and patterns were taken from E. Prisse d'Avennes' *Arab Art (L'Art arabe d'après les monuments du Kaire)*, Paris: Vve A. Morel, 1877 (Bouwsema-Raap 2009: 57).

that had not been used customarily in religious architecture in South-East Asia. According to scholars, the completed mosque was considered by the religious leaders to be alien and inappropriate for regular use (O'Neill 1994: 225), probably due to such exaggeratedly foreign features.

Just like Indo-Saracenic architecture of South Asia, this structure was built by the colonial rulers, the Dutch. However, while Indo-Saracenic architecture of South Asia were mostly administrative buildings for the British or palaces for the Indian princes, the Banda Aceh Mosque significantly differs from Indo-Saracenic architecture in India in that it was a religious structure, built to pacify the Muslim leadership while gaining political and economic control of northern Sumatra. At the time of building, the Dutch, apparently aware of traditional South-East Asian architecture, still chose to build the new mosque in a completely alien style. The colonial rulers were most likely aware that the mosque, particularly the *masjid agung* of Aceh and Islamic South-East Asia was closely related to the traditional power structure of South-East Asia. For example, the Sultan of Aceh gained power through "political claims upon genealogical descent from past rulers, Buddhist consecration, and Islam", and "Islam was the principle which legitimized and defined the organization of the state" (Lapidus 1988: 475). The great mosque in the capital (*negarī*) was usually built next to the central square (*alun-alun*) and was a symbol of the power of the ruler. In other earlier examples, the South-East Asian mosque acted as a symbol of the religious community centred on the king, who was sometimes symbolized by a huge central pillar in the middle of the mosque, as well as the *walī*s (holy men), the elite and the lay worshippers. In this sense, it may have been possible that the Dutch East Indies government refused to build a new mosque in a traditional style, which may reflect such symbolic political power. Rather, an Indo-Saracenic architectural style, appropriated from the architectural style of the British Raj, was selected as an alternative to the traditional mosque architecture of South-East Asia. As a result, the Great Mosque of Banda Aceh can be read as "an imperialistic imposition by the Dutch, constantly reminding the Acehnese who was in charge" (Bouwsema-Raap 2009: 63-64).

Nevertheless, in spite of the early disapproval, the Great Mosque of Banda Aceh started to gain approval in the community. There may be two reasons why the Banda Aceh Mosque and other mosques of the late nineteenth and early twentieth century were able to gain its current appeal in South-East Asia. First, the Muslims of South-East Asia, including those of the Aceh Sultanate, may have accepted the "Indo-Saracenic" architecture as "Indo-Islamic", i.e. the Mughal imperial style of South Asia. The Aceh Sultanate actively embraced Mughal culture from the reign of Sultan Iskandar Muda, who adopted the Mughal emperors' titles and attire, palace and garden architecture as well as the notion of kingship based on "Insan-i Kamil" (Milner 1983: 39-40). Even after the Mughal empire lost its political authority over the bulk of South Asia, imperial Mughal architecture, particularly the ornate Mughal style of northern India, remained a symbol of authority as well as piety, Islam and ironically, the old social order (Asher 1994). Thus the Acehnese could have come to accept Indo-Saracenic style architecture of the nineteenth century as representative of Islam itself, particularly the Islam of the great Mughal rulers.

A second hypothesis, somewhat linked with the first, is the effect of the rise of Islamic scripturalism during the nineteenth century in South-East Asia. According to Raffles, there already was tension arising between those adhering to old Malay traditions, and the religious leaders and *hajjīs* who wanted to introduce Arab law to South-East Asia by the 1810s (Raffles 1830: 80). Especially after the mid-nineteenth century, South-East Asian Muslims communicated actively with Muslims of other regions, with a significant number of the elite and *hajjīs* visiting and/or studying in Mecca or centres of the Ottoman caliphate. Aceh itself was called the "Serambi to Mecca", due to the large number of *hajjīs* leaving through the harbour. As a result, Islamic scripturalism was introduced with the ideas and culture of mainstream Islam, which led to a reformist movement in the religion in many areas. By the early twentieth century, traditional customs and rituals were rejected as they were deemed not appropriate in the context of the *sharia'*; histories were re-written so that South-East Asia's past was more conformed to a "pure" Islamic society (Milner 1983: 48). As South-East Asian Muslims encountered religious architecture of the Islamic heartland, with arches, domes and minarets, they could have provided new meanings to the colonial Indo-Saracenic architecture. Thus while the Great Mosque was built to symbolize a replacement of traditional power by the colonial rulers, its architectural features rather became associated with visual symbols of Arabia, Turkey and Central Asia; the centre of the Islamic world. This led to several enlargements starting in the early twentieth century. In 1936, two wings were added on each side of the central dome, closely copying the shape of the original dome and façade; it was enlarged towards the back in 1965. In 1992, two more domes and four minarets were added; currently it is a huge complex that includes a tower and a reflecting pool in front of the mosque.[2]

## Conclusion

Thus the colonial desire to impose their own models of architecture was rather unsuccessful, as South Asians and South-East Asians appropriated this new architecture of dominance, subjugation and control. Indo-Saracenic style structures, which were not welcomed at the beginning, were ultimately transformed into national symbols of the new states for several reasons. For example, the Lakshmi Vilas Palace acquired new meanings of national and regional pride, following the shift in the role of Mahārājā Sayaji Rao III. The Aceh Mosque became representative of Islam itself, following the rise of Islamic scripturalism and reformism of the nineteenth century in South-East Asia.

Meanings of buildings shift continuously throughout time. Therefore it is imperative to conduct an anthropological study of architecture, in which the current meanings of the buildings must be considered alongside the original ones. While the Indo-Saracenic was more of an architectural style inheriting Mughal architecture, reflecting British or Dutch ability and superiority in understanding and integrating diverse indigenous cultures, it was later accepted as a symbol of progress as well as nationalist aspirations towards a modern state, or representations of a modern pan-Islamic community. Rather than fix such architectural styles into categories such as colonial,

---

2 Several mosques were built in this "new style" during the late nineteenth and early twentieth century; for example, the Mesjid Raya of Medan, built across the Sultan's palace in 1906. In Malaysia we can find several mosques built in this manner: for example, Masjid Kapitan Keling, Penang; Jama Masjid, Kuala Lumpur; and Zahir Mosque, Alor Setar in Kedah.

modern, or traditional, one should be aware of the shifting meanings of architecture in our present world.

## References

Asher, Catherine B., 1994, "The Later Mughals and Mughal Successor States: Architecture in Oudh, Murshidabad and Rampur", in C.W. London (ed.) *Architecture in Victorian and Edwardian India*, pp. 85-98, Bombay: Marg Publications.

Bouwsema-Raap, Wilhelmina, 2009, *The Great Mosque of Banda Aceh: Its History, Architecture and Relationship to the Development of Islam in Sumatra*, Bangkok: White Lotus Press.

Chisholm, R.F., 1896, "Baroda Palace: The Town Residence of H.H. Sir Sayaji Rao", *Journal of the Royal Institute of British Architects*, 3rd series, **3**: 421-33, 445-49.

Codell, Julie F., 1998, "Resistance and Performance: Native Informant Discourse in the Biographies of Maharaja Sayaji Rao III (1863-1939)", in Julie F. Codell and Dianne Sachko Macleod (eds.) *Orientalism Transposed: The Impact of the Colonies on British Culture*, pp. 13-45, Hants/Brookfield: Ashgate.

Cohn, B.S., 1992, "The Transformation of Objects into Artifacts, Antiquities and Art in Nineteenth-Century India", in B.S. Miller (ed.) *The Powers of Art: Patronage in Indian Culture*, pp. 301-29, Delhi/Oxford: Oxford University Press.

Copland, Ian, 1999, *The Princes of India in the Endgame of Empire 1917-1947*, New Delhi: Cambridge University Press.

Crinson, Mark, 1996, *Empire Building: Orientalism and Victorian Architecture*, London/ New York: Routledge.

Davies, Philip, 1985, *Splendours of the Raj: British Architecture in India, 1660 to 1947*, London: Murray.

Dehejia, Vidya, 1997, *Indian Art*, London: Phaidon Press.

Fergusson, James, 1876 (repr. 1910), *History of Indian and Eastern Architecture*, 2 vols., London: John Murray.

Gaekwad, Fatesinhrao and Virginia Fass, 1980, *The Palaces of India*, New York: Vendome Press.

Havell, E.B., 1915, *The Ancient and Medieval Architecture of India: A Study of Indo-Aryan Civilisation*. London: John Murray.

Lapidus, Ira M., 1988, *A History of Islamic Societies*, Cambridge, New York: Cambridge University Press.

Metcalf, Thomas R., 1984, "Architecture and the Representation of Empire: India 1860–1910", *Representations*, **6**: 37-65.

———, 1989, *An Imperial Vision: Indian Architecture and Britain's Raj*, Berkeley: University of California Press.

———, 1995, *Ideologies of the Raj*, Cambridge: Cambridge University Press.

Michell, G. and A. Martinelli, 1994, *The Royal Palaces of India*, London: Thames and Hudson.

Milner, A.C., 1983, "Islam and the Muslim State", in M.B. Hooker ed. *Islam in South-East Asia*, pp. 23-49, Leiden: Brill.

O'Neill, Hugh, 1994, "[The Mosque:] South-East Asia", in Martin Frishman and Hasan-Uddin Khan eds. *The Mosque: History, Architectural Development & Regional Diversity*, pp. 224-50, New York: Thames and Hudson.

———, 1995, "Islamic Architecture under the New Order", in Virginia Matheson Hooker (ed) *Culture and Society in New Order Indonesia*, pp. 150-165, Kuala Lumpur: Oxford University Press.

Raffles, Thomas Stamford, 1830, *The History of Java*, 2 vols., London: Black.

Ramusack, Barbara, 2004, *The Indian Princes and Their States*, Cambridge: Cambridge University Press.

Rasdi, Mohamad T.M. and Nangkula Utaberta, 2006, "Mosque Architecture from Malaysia: Classification of Styles and Possible Influences", *Journal of Southeast Asian Architecture*, **9**: 43-63.

Tillotson, G.H.R., 1989, *The Tradition of Indian Architecture: Continuity, Controversy, and Change since 1850*, New Haven: Yale University Press.

———, 1994, "Orientalising the Raj: Indo-Saracenic Fantasies", in Christopher London (ed.) *Architecture in Victorian and Edwardian India*, Bombay: Marg Publications.

# 5

# Cultural Relationship between India and South-East Asia

*Tran Phuoc Phuong Thao*

**Preamble**

SOUTH-EAST Asia denotes a region belonging to Indo-China or the Indo-Chinese peninsula that locates approximately the east of India and south of China. When we study the culture of South-East Asia, we come to know that ancient India played an indispensable role in forming the culture of this region in prehistoric era. What is India's relationship with this land and how it was possible? Is it correct to say that South-East Asian countries called "Indianized states"? We know that China had a close connection with India and South-East Asia in early times. *Mahābhārata* tells the story of Pāṇḍava brothers crossing the country of the Cīnas (China) during their treking through the ranges of Himalayas to reach the land of the Kirāta king Subāhu. At the same time, we can observe that though South-East Asia has historical contact with China, why was this region strongly influenced by Indian culture but a little by China? As for Vietnam, some deny the theory of Indianization towards the South-East Asia because, according to them, Vietnam was mainly influenced by Chinese culture, except Champa, an ancient Hindu area conquered by Vietnamese over the span of land expansion. I will try to show in reverse that in prehistory, Vietnam accepted openly all the economic and cultural relations with India. I am convinced that even though Vietnamese culture was mainly dominated by the Chinese by force, it is undeniable that Vietnamese culture must be peacefully influenced by Indian civilization long before the first century CE.

In this presentation I will focus on the cultural relationship between India and South-East Asia, namely, Laos, Cambodia, Thailand and Vietnam, and try to show how the process of Indianized states in these regions took place at the beginning of the historic era. First, I will bring about some influence of Indian culture and art in Laos, Cambodia and Thailand in general. Then I will show the important factor normally ignored by scholars, that Giao Chau (in Vietnam) was the necessary station where Indian tradesmen had frequently used as the stopover before they arrived in China. Besides I will also evaluate the wrong view that Zen school in Vietnam came from China by elucidating the fact that Khuong Tang Hoi, whose father was an Indian man married a native nobility, was the first Zen Master in Giao Chau. Later he took the meditation technique to China. My intention here is that though China started dominating Vietnam in the first century, the Vietnamese accepted Buddhism as the path of peace from Indian monks who travelled along with tradesmen by sea route. I will add another evidence that Aśoka's missionaries perhaps reached Giao Chau during the Hung Vuong dynasty to introduce Buddhism. In other words, the purpose of Indian tradesmen and religious missionaries set off to the South-East Asia was not compelled by the political invasion, however, by a peaceful way. They came here for a purpose and gradually settled down in a new land. The cultural transmission got started. This appears more clearly in the case of Champa, the ancient kingdom of Hindus.

My conclusion is that so far as culture is concerned, religion is the basic factor that has rooted in a new soil and reflected in art, literature and lifestyle harmoniously and peacefully. This proves that the interrelation between India and South-East Asia embalmed the religious intentions during the trading journey rather than political invasion. Though China had the long contact with this region, Indian culture has mixed with local belief and become a part and parcel of life with its intrinsic values. Keep this in mind I would proceed to brief the bird's eye view of India's cultural relationship with Thailand, Cambodia, Laos and Vietnam.

## Indian Cultural Relations

### THAILAND

Archaeological findings showed stone beads and glass in Korat and

Dong Son, some similar beads and Sanskrit inscription in Oc Eo, Vietnam that suggested the frequent contact between this region and India in the first century BCE (Mishra 2001: 106). India's cultural relationship with Thailand dates back to the first century CE onwards when the trading relation between the two regions became more frequently involved with marine routes. The voyage to the South East required a long period of time and needed some certain stopovers, including the Thailand peninsula to complete the journey. It was likely that Indian tradesmen took the road from Menam to Mekong through Khorat plateau via Sri Tep and Mun Valley after passing Laos, Cambodia to reach Champa (ibid.: 108). This means that Thailand was one of the important lands where ancient Indian tradesmen reached the South-East Asia. Eventually, the ancient Indians brought Hindu and Buddhism to the new lands.

More than 1,000 years ago, Thailand came under the influence of the Hinduized Mon-speaking people of Dvāravatī (CE 457–657) and Khmer empires (957–1257) (Rajadhon 1950: 4). By these periods, there was a race immigration from southern China to the Indo-Chinese peninsula. However, the prominent characteristics of Thai culture were powerfully influenced by Indian culture rather than China because the migrants to the new land encountered an obstacle of different language. Many Thai words were also borrowed from Pāli, Sankrit, Cambodia, while Chinese is completely an alien kind of pictorial language. For example, the Sanskrit word *guru* (teacher) has become *kroo* in Thai, *mānuṣa* (human) in Sanskrit is *manuhs* in Khmer. Many statues found in religious sites show the great impact of Indian culture. For example, the deities with many hands, or human figures wearing jewellery and hairstyle strikingly resembles the Hindu architecture found in India. The kingdom of Srivijaya in southern Thailand was the blending of Hinduism and Buddhism. Many figures of *bodhisattva* with many arms and god Viṣṇu have shown the artistic styles of Indian tradition.

Though Hinduism was the stronghold during cultural interaction, Buddhism was favourably accepted as the main religion over the course of time. Buddhism was introduced to the Thai due to the race immigration from south China to Indo-China peninsula and trading interaction between India and South-East during this period. Many Buddhist figures reflect the beliefs of Indian people during the Gupta period. The Buddha statues and *bodhisattva* with facial expression and long earlobes were the style of ancient Indian robes. These religious figures was normally accompanied by mythical animals like *nāga* (snake) in Indian beasts of mythology. Though Buddhist literature inspires Thai folklore, it is important to notice that the two great epics of India, *Mahābhārata* and *Rāmāyaṇa*, have become Thai traditional genre. Especially *Rāmāyaṇa* has been translated into Thai version though radically different from the original version of Vālmīki. This indicates that during the course of interrelation with India, Thai people adopted the Indian culture, however, mingling with the local belief in making their own style of oriental adaptation.

## LAOS

Now let's go to Laos and Cambodia. From Mukdahan station at north-eastern Thailand, you can take a bus to Savannakhet. Laos is a locked land surrounded by Thailand, Vietnam, Cambodia and Myanmar in the north. Unlike the ancient powerful countries such as Cambodia and Thailand, Laos has the modest and turbulent history under the domination of neighbours that caused the decline of many ancient artworks. However, we could not deny the the strong impact of Indian culture on Lao culture. Many archaeological artefacts found scattered in Laos depicted the worship of Lord Śiva. The remaining of the Wat Phou built in the fifth century on the Liṅgaparvata (Liṅga mountain) in south Laos indicates the worship of Śiva and shows the cultural links with India in ancient times. Though the temple nowadays is used as a Buddhist temple, one could not deny the Hindu impact upon every aspect of the temple's architecture. The Phou Lokhon inscription (Laos) in Sanskrit also depicts the Liṅga Śiva erected by the King Mahendravarman on the hill Phou Lokhon. Many figures of gods, temples bear the stronghold of Indian art and Khmer art and a little Chinese art that reflects the mixture of the cultural influences from time to time. Customs, religious festivals and rituals also hold the Hindu belief. Like Thailand, Pha Lak Pha Lam in the Laos version is originally the epic *Rāmāyaṇa* and the most influential literature in Lao culture. Laos has introduced this Indian epic into its own style of literature, different from Thailand's *Ramakien* and India's *Rāmāyaṇa*. This traditional epic was also handled over in the form of oral version. Laotian dances, like those of Thailand, are based on Indian epics. The archaeological findings in Laos show the inscription from the time of the king Devānīka, who desired to build a *mahātīrtha*, known as Kurukṣetra. In addition, the Prah Vihar inscription belonging to CE 1037-38 mentions the village Vibedha renamed as Kurukṣetra after a native of the man who has done a great service for the Royal (Haryana Gazetteers 2009: 44-45). This strongly indicates that Laos and India had a long relationship in early days. Even lifestyles, traditions, food — all are so much close to those of the surrounding lands with its essence from Buddhism and Hinduism.

Similar to Thai culture, though influenced by Hinduism through Angkor periods, Laotians accepted Buddhism as the main religion. Many Jātaka stories have been depicted in the *wat*s, Buddhist temples. It is recorded that 547 Jātaka stories about the past lives of the Buddha in Pāli were written down in Lao, being faithful to the original version written in Sri Lanka (Austin et al. 2011: 54). According to legend, the relationship between India and Laos dates back to the time of the Buddha and king Aśoka. It is traditionally believed that the Buddha himself visited some areas of Vientiane and predicted the place for the *stūpa*. Later, some emissaries sent by king Aśoka brought to Laos the Buddha's relic now worshipped in the *stūpa* at That Luang temple in Vientiane. It is the centre of festivals every year for the Laos to perform rituals and merit as the living force of life:

> Worshipping the Buddha's relics was a way to renovate their power and consequently, the power of the king, kingdom and its people.
>
> — ibid.: 81

This indicates that both Buddhism and Hinduism have become integral to the culture and life of Laos. Like Thai language, Laos has many words borrowed from Pāli and Sanskrit in literary forms.

## CAMBODIA

From Savannakhet, you can continue riding the bus to Cambodia, the land of ancient glory. While Laos was strongly influenced by Indian culture from CE 800s onwards, Cambodia was the oldest Indianized state of Indo-Chinese peninsula with the Angkor Wat regarded as one of the most majestic monuments in the world. Kingdom of Funan and Angkor Wat was the most powerful eras of ancient Cambodia. Kingdom of Funan located near Mekong Delta River in CE 100s was the first fabulously Indianized state of Cambodia that marks the rich culture of Hinduism. In early days, Funan was a prosperous soil where Indian traders from Kaliṅga, Orissa now, arrived for trading. It is said that the market of Funan was the meeting point of many foreign traders, including those coming from China and Afghanistan. It is believed that the ancestors of Funan, namely the Khmer nowadays ware Indian *ṛṣis*. According to Chinese sources, the word Funan means mountain, and it is believed that ancestor of Funan, Khmer was an Indian *ṛṣi* who had the wisdom in making the Khmers civilized (Patra 2011: 33). The Khmers studied Sanskrit texts widely and adopted Hindu customs to rule the kingdom of Funan in accordance with *Arthaśāstra*. The entire Funan was Hinduized. Numerous inscriptions of Sanskrit are found, indicating that they had the knowledge of Veda and Brāhmanical texts as well. The history of the southern Ch'i state is that during the reign of Jayavarman (CE 500), Funan worshipped the god Maheśvara (Śiva) who descends on Mount Motan, an abode similar to Mahendragiri of Śiva in Orissa (ibid.: 34). Furthermore, the worshipping of Mahendra in Kaliṅga and Maheśvara in Funan belongs to the same time. This suggests that Funan was Indianized by the Kaliṅga traders and missionaries. The influence of Indian culture on Cambodia reflects on the religious belief.

The glory of Angkor grew in replacing the decline of Funan in CE 500. Angkor in Khmer is *nokor*, derived from Sanskrit word *nagara* (city) and *wat* comes from Pāli word *vatta* (temple). It is the largest Hindu temple complex with high classical style of Khmer architecture and the greatest religious monument in the world. The temple was built by king Sūryavarman II in the preliminary twelfth century in Yaśodharapura.[1] While Funan worshipped Śaivism, Angkor Wat, a symbol of Cambodia nowadays, was dedicated to Viṣṇu, however, later worshipping Buddhism. The architecture of Angkor Wat was based on early Draviḍian architecture, designed to represent Mount Meru, home of the *deva*s in Hindu mythology. The walls with stone carving depict the Hindu epics *Rāmāyaṇa* and *Mahābhārata*. In Cambodia, the alphabet was derived from south Indian script. Sanskrit was absorbed into the life of the people and most of the names were derived from Sanskrit names. In short, compared to Thailand, and

---

1 http://en.wikipedia.org/wiki/Angkor_Wat.

Laos, Cambodia is the unique country that has the unexcelled greatness of Hindu culture that results in the glory of Funan and Angkor. Needless to say, the marvellous architecture and art of these unsurpassed temples manifest a glorious time of Hinduism in the past and the indispensable interrelation of India and these regions. Though Cambodia had a link with China in early days, the impact of Hinduism still took over to reach the zenith of fabulous civilization.

Now, from Cambodia, you can set foot in the land of Vietnam. Vietnam is surrounded by China in the north, Laos and Cambodia in the west and south. This geographical position implies that Vietnam can act as the stopover to enter China. It is popularly known that Vietnam was dominated by China over 1,000 years, one may question the cultural value of India on this land. Next section will be dedicated to prove this fact.

## VIETNAM

When you enter the south of Vietnam from Cambodia, one can encounter here and there some small Indian communities, especially south Indian Tamils. They worship at Mariamman Hindu temple. This cultural link of Vietnam with India dates back to the pre-history of Vietnam. First, Giao Chi near Hanoi was a key region serving as a meeting point of all foreign traders who came from different places during the Chinese invasion from 200 BCE to CE 938. Luy Lau, the centre of Giao Chi located around the Red River Delta was the most important Buddhist centre during the Han period. Many Indian monks came here to propagate Buddhism, eventually they went to Loyang and Pengcheng:

> Official Chinese records do not mention the Buddhist situation here at the time because this region was considered to be a remote and barbaric area on the southern border, not worthy of attention. However, it was here that one of the earliest Buddhist Chinese works appeared. It was *Ly Hoac Luan,* which was written by Mau Tu in the second century CE. From here some famous monks such as Khuong Tang Hoi went to China to spread Buddhism. It is said the Luy Lau Buddhist centre was founded earlier than those two centres, and that Buddhism was spread from Luy Lau to Pengcheng and then to Luoyang. This seems credible. From various sources, it is possible to understand the Buddhist development in Luy Lau in the early common era. — Nguyen Tai Thu 2008: 17

History records that many talented Buddhist monks were educated here and learnt Sanskrit, Chinese to translate Sūtra to spread the knowledge to China. Thuyen Uyen Tap Anh Ngu Luc (CE 11-13) complied during the Ly dynasty reports that Giao Chau has routes to India and famous Indian monks such as Kaudra and Mahājīvaka went to China to propagate Buddhism. When Buddhism initially came to China, Giao Chau already had many temples and hundreds of monks, 15 Buddhist books translated in Luy Lau (ibid.: 19). Another important argument has currently been creating the controversy is the question of the citadel Nele where the Aśoka pillar was built in Do Son, Hai Phong, where it exactly located because the old time has washed away many crucial traces unable to be found out. What we can know about this is merely from historical reports. Aśoka (304–232 BCE) sent nine groups of Buddhist missionaries to spread Buddhism to all directions within India and overseas. The eighth one was guided by Sona and Uttara towards Myanmar, Indo-China and Malaysia. They reached Nele, Do Son, a geographical region suitable for tying the trade between Giao Chau and overseas. It was here that Chu Dong Tu (Hung Vuong dynasty of the third century BCE) met the foreign monk named Phat Quang, who eventually taught Buddhism to him. This Buddhist group later built Aśoka pillar in Do Son. King Ly Thanh Tong in eleventh century visited Do Son and came to know this pillar. He ordered to build a new tower (Tuong Long tower) on this site. This important event was mentioned in the poem "Do Son Bat Vinh" by Mien Trai (Dong Hong Hoang and Trinh Minh Hien 2008: 56).[2] Luu Han Ky in his Giao Chau Ky (360–420) also reported:

> Citadel Nele in Southeast Dinh An, 7 miles far from the river, and the tower and the house of worship built by king Aśoka have still remained, which are called Kim Tuong by woodcutters. — ibid.: 45

Though the theory that Buddhism began in Vietnam during the time of Aśoka needs more archaeological findings to prove the fact, it is hardly deniable that Buddhism was first introduced into Vietnam before entering China. This conclusion is powerfully intensified by the fact that Chinese literature popularly credited that the signal of

---

[2] http://www.hids.hochiminhcity.gov.vn/c/document_library/get_file?uuid=7afe4958-03e6-4bc5-81f1-de229f642e11&groupId=13025.

Buddhism was first appeared in China through the dream of Emperor Ming (CE 58-75). Compared to the time that Buddhism reached Giao Chau and China, we can claim certainly that Buddhism arrived in Giao Chau before it was introduced in China. In Vietnam, people believed in *karma* and rebirth, doing good deeds and avoiding bad deeds. These all moral values become an initial education almost in every Vietnamese family where parents teach their children how to be a good human being. Here we can conclude that though China ruled Vietnam for 1,000 years, it is undeniable that Vietnamese have absorbed the Buddhist teachings into daily life to become the pattern of thought, reflection and religious activities. A traditional Vietnamese proverb says: "Buddhism is the religion of ancestors". This reflects the family values in accordance with the Buddha's teachings as the indispensable principle in daily life. This process of cultural localization as the convergence of India and Giao Chau as such happened even before CE. This influence becomes more dominant when we study the cultural relation between India and Champa, an expanded region of Vietnam.

The ancient kingdom of Champa was situated in several places from south to north Vietnam. This Hindu kingdom appeared around Da Nang during the late second century. Later, it spread to Nha Trang, and Phang Rang and reached its apogee in eleventh century. With the geographical position suitable for trading from all over directions, Champa was influenced by foreign cultures such as Cambodia, China, Java and India. Champa was the main route for spice trading between Persian Gulf and southern China. It was also the well-known land of sandalwood. However, when Champa acquired the territory of Hinduized Funan in the fourth century, Indian culture started overwhelmingly infusing into the life of Champa society and mixing with the local religious belief. Hinduism became main religion with several temples and festivals dedicated to Śiva and the *liṅgam, mukha-liṅga*, the *jaṭāliṅga* mainly worshipped. In addition, Sanskrit was accepted as a scholarly language. The oldest inscription found in Champa was in Sanskrit and "up to the tenth century the Champa thoroughly studied the classical Sanskrit literature" (Sharma 2009: 35). Some dominant states got their names after Hindu gods such as Indrapura, Pāṇḍuraṅga, Vijaya. Even the word Champa came from Purāṇic mythology and was mentioned in Sanskrit and Pāli as Campā,

Campāpurī, Campā Nāga, Campā Mālinī. King Bimbisāra (544–493 BCE) established his Magadha empire from Champa to Vanarasi, and Champa was also the principal city of Magadha. Champa is also the son of Pṛthulakṣa, a descendant of Anu. The architecture of Hindu temples in Vietnam so much resembles those of Kaliṅga (Orissa) and south India. Several archaeological artefacts such as deities, gods and sculptures unearthed were similar to the architectural style of Mathura, Gandhāra and Amarāvatī (ibid.: 27). Champa festivals, and celebrations of marriage, funeral, dance, music deeply carry the Hindu elements and resemble those of India very closely, though the Cham have become Vietnamized, and the influences of local beliefs are unavoidable.

The Chams nowadays have become one of 54 ethnic groups of Vietnam. They live peacefully with the Vietnamese, who have the sense of respect to the Cham and the Hindu temples. This way of life perhaps reflects the ancient time when Indian traders reached Vietnam not like warriors, but like enterprising traders who ventured to a new land on purpose, willing to settle down in this far-reaching region to be localized as in the case of Mau Tu's father. It is convincing to conclude rationally that ancient Indians arrived in Vietnam not only as traders or elites but as immigrants (ibid.: 26) who brought the values of Indian culture in a new land and took roots into it for centuries to submerge into the cultural localization. It is not surprising that this Cham ethnic group now in Vietnam claim their ancestors are the Hindus from India (ibid.: 45) and one can observe that many Hindu temples, existing near Buddhist temples, are visited by many non-Hindus without any bias and bloodshed.

In sum, the process of Indianization towards the South-East Asian countries, e.g. Thailand, Laos, Cambodia and Vietnam, to borrow the statement of Geetesh Sharma, was "an intellectual conquest through peaceful means" (ibid.: 25) in denying the theory of colonial exploitation in a new land. This cultural infusion of Indian values in these far-reaching regions results in the intriguing mixture of Buddhism and Hinduism that plays an essential role in spreading Indian culture in the South-East Asia. In other words, India in prehistoric times was a land of highly spiritual civilization, in which the sixty-two religious philosophies had originated in search of the path leading to the redemption of human beings. Consequently, art, music, architecture, literature as a part and parcel of life in South-East Asia serve and nurture this religious purpose. This process of Indianization in these lands can be regarded as that of religious dispersion and spiritual sowing.

## References

Bush, Austin, Mark Elliot and Nick Ray, 2011, *Laos* (7th edn.), London: Lonely Planet.

Dồng Hồng Hoàn, Triịh Minh Hiên, 2009, *Thành Nêlê - Dò* Son Thòi *Asoka*, available at http://donghonghoan.wordpress.com/2009/11/15/16/or http://www.hids.hochiminhcity.gov.vn/c/document_library/get_file?uuid=7afe4958-03e6-4bc5-81f1-de229f642e11&groupId=13025.

http://www.eth.mpg.de/cms/en/people/d/ladwig/pdf/Ladwig_Relics_Representation_Power_2002.pdf.

http://www.hids.hochiminhcity.gov.vn/c/document_library/get_file?uuid=7afe4958-03e6-4bc5-81f1-de229f642e11&groupId=13025.

http://revenueharyana.gov.in/html/gazeteers/kurukshetra_2009/Chapter_II.pdf.

Mishra, Patit Paban, 2001, "India–Southeast Asian Relations: An Overview", *An Internet Journal of Pedagogy*, **I**(1), Winter 2001, USA: South Dakota State University, available at http://www.sdstate.edu/projectsouthasia/Resources/loader.cfm?csModule=security/getfile&pageid=909519

Nguyen Tai Thu, 2008, *The History of Buddhism in Vietnam: Cultural Heritage and Contemporary Change, Series III D, South East Aisa*, vol. 5, Washington: Library of Congress Cataloging-in-Publication.

Patra, Benudha, 2011, " Kalinga and Funan: A Study in Ancient Relations", *Orissa Review*, available at http://orissa.gov.in/e-magazine/Orissareview/2011/Nov/engpdf/32-38.pdf.

Sharma, Geetesh, 2009, *Traces of Indian Culture in Vietnam* , New Delhi: Banyan Tree Books.

# 6

# Indian Trade Textiles for Thai Market

***Prapassorn Posrithong***

THAILAND has a long history of textile production that traces its origin back to the prehistoric period. Textile fragments were found along with bronze ornaments at Ban Chiang archaeological site in Udon Thani Province. They date from about 3,000 years ago and reveal that early inhabitants living in north-eastern Thailand used cloth made of hemp and cotton.[1] Stone bark beaters found at archaeological sites in Chumphon and Surat Thani provinces in the southern peninsula and numbers of terracotta spindle whorls discovered at many Dvāravatī sites in central and north-eastern regions are significant evidences of local production of textiles during prehistoric to early historic periods in Thailand.[2] While the spindle whorls show their connection with Chinese textile production technique, the clothing style depicted in figural stuccos that decorated early historic monuments in Nakhon Pathom and Suphan Buri provinces show Indian inspiration of wearing *dhotī*-like lower garments. Though evidence of Indian clothing style had influenced traditional costumes of people in Thailand since early historic period (seventh century onwards), evidence of Indian trade textiles were found in Thailand only during the Ayutthaya period (1350–1767).

Ayutthaya was a major trade centre in South-East Asia from early sixteenth century. Trade between India and Siam of Ayutthaya was well established before the arrival of the European traders. Though there are no records of how and when Indian textiles were first

---

1 Aranyanak 1991: 51-62.

2 Ibid.: 62-64.

introduced to the royal court of Ayutthaya. Historical accounts of English and Dutch East India Company record that Indian goods predominantly consisting of piece goods were the most important products imported into Ayutthaya. The trade was dominated by Muslim merchants who sailed from various ports in western and eastern India to the ports on the west coast of the peninsula like Mergui and Tenasserim in lower Myanmar, which at that time were under the control of Ayutthaya. On these ports, a variety of Indian textiles were unloaded and carried overland across the peninsula to Ayutthaya. There they traded their goods for Thai products including elephants and then returned to India by the same route.[3]

At the court of Ayutthaya Indian textiles were highly rated and formalized into royal monopolies on particular export goods. The distribution of these imported textiles was closely controlled by the royal court. The finest Indian textiles were reserved for the use of royalties and courtiers and distributed to courtiers according to their

*fig.* 6.1: The court scene of early Bangkok mural at Wat Suwannaram in Bangkok shows the king distributing various Indian textiles to courtiers. Early nineteenth century. (photo credit: Wat Suwannaram, Bangkok)

[3] Smith 1977: 85.

rank in Thai social order.[4] These textiles were also used as royal gifts for visiting dignitaries and for granting of favours in recognition of service to the king (*fig*. 6.1). Simone de La Loubere, a French diplomat resident at Ayutthaya in 1687-88, recorded that silk was less popular than cotton in Ayutthaya.[5] Paintings on manuscript of the period depict Indian painted and printed cottons worn by characters in Buddha's story or the court scenes.[6]

However demand for silk textiles from India is mentioned in an official letter of the English East India Company in Ayutthaya to the office in Surat, dated 2 December 1662, asking for commissioning of *paṭolā* for the king:

> The king of Siam expects those *puttelaes* to be made according to those patterns Mr. Bladwell carried to Surat; if not to be procured, those patterns to be returned.[7]

*Puttelaes* is a old Dutch word of *paṭolā* (Na Pompejra) or silk double *ikat* mainly produced at Pathan district in north of Gujarat.

Muslim merchants from India and Persia also played an important role in introducing some Islamic traditions including use of various textiles and style of stitched costumes to the royal court of Ayutthaya. Some of them were appointed as the court officials and governors of port cities which gave them power to support Muslim traders in textile business in the kingdom of Ayutthaya. After the arrival of European traders in Ayutthaya in early seventeenth century, Indian textiles trade which was previously the monopoly of Muslim merchants was shared with the European agents. However the Europeans found stiff competition from Indian merchants who had lower investment cost in textiles and were even willing to sell Indian textiles at a loss in order to buy elephants which they could then sell in India at a higher profit.[8] Dutch records of different years have shown that about 15,000 pieces of various Indian cloths was the limit of the Ayutthaya's local

---

4 Chongkol 1982: 125.

5 La Loubere 1986: 15.

6 Na Paknam and Kanokphongchai 1985: 58.

7 India Office Records, 1915-21: 2.

8 Smith 1977: 91.

demand. The overall expansion of trade during the reign of king Narai (1656-88) was apparently more a result of the increased re-export trade of Chinese and Japanese wares than of the increased consumption by the Thais.[9]

After Ayutthaya was sacked and destroyed by the Burmese in 1767, Thonburi and Bangkok were established as new political centres of Thailand. The royal court in Bangkok continued traditions practised during Ayutthaya period including the prohibition of using Indian textiles outside the royal court. The early Bangkok revised code of 1805, commonly known as the Law of Three Seals, saying that such prohibition was neglected due to uncertain situation after the war with Burma. So the law was reissued and indicating particular types and designs of textiles that were reserved for high-ranking officials or should not be used without the permission of the king.[10]

Mural paintings of early Bangkok period dating to early nineteenth century depict Indian textiles worn by royalties, courtiers and used as décor like curtain, wall hangings, wall partitions, throne and floor covers and to drape royal vehicles. They were also made for religious

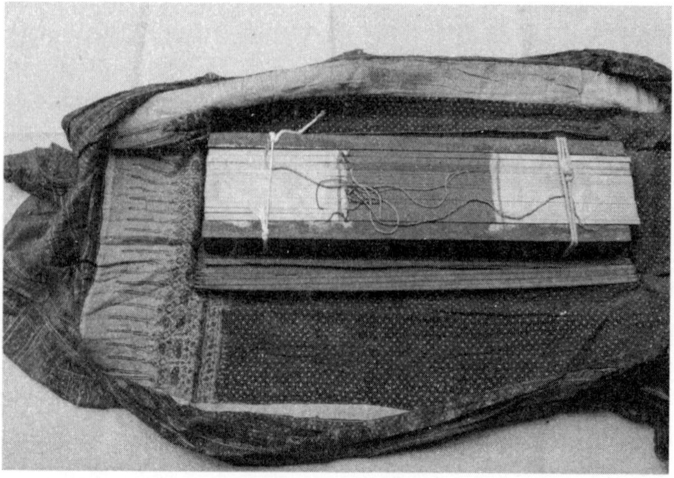

*fig.* 6.2: Indian block-printed mordant-dyed cotton from Gujarat along with silk *ikat* are used as Buddhist manuscript wrapper. (photo credit: Wat Kongkaram Museum, Ratchaburi)

9 Smith 1977: 92.

10 Chongkol 1982: 124-31.

*fig*. 6.3: Mural shows a courtier putting on *sompak lai* or Indian printed and painted cotton in the Indian *dhotī*-like style called *phanung chong kraben* at the palace gate. The cloth was used as the court uniform before European fashion introduced to the Thai royal court by mid-nineteenth century. (photo credit: Wat Matchimawas, Songkhla)

offerings such as monk's shoulder bag, alms-bowl covers and manuscript wrappers (*fig*. 6.2).

Before European fashion arrived by mid-nineteenth century the ordinary dress of the Siamese was an untailored long piece of cotton printed cloth, passed round the waist between the thigh and the ends of the cloth being stuck in behind in the Indian *dhotī*-like style called *phanung chong kraben*. Sometimes the cloth was simply worn around the hip like *sarong*. Women could wear with pleated fold in front called *phanung na nang* with a separate cloth used as breast-cloth called *sabai*. The cloth is about 3.5 yards long which is made of cotton, linen, silk, embroidered or decorated according to the taste and wealth of the wearers. Two types of textiles were used as uniform for royal court officials. One is called *sompak poom* which means silk *ikat* from Cambodia and another is *sompak lai* (*fig*. 6.3) which means Indian painted or printed cotton. The word *sompak* probably derives from Khmer word meaning cloth worn as lower garment. Old photographs taken during the reign of king Mongkut or Rāma IV (r. 1851-68) show

*fig*. 6.4: Indian textiles for Thai Royal court exhibited at Textiles Gallery at National Museum Bangkok before gallery renovation in 2007. (photo credit: National Museum, Bangkok)

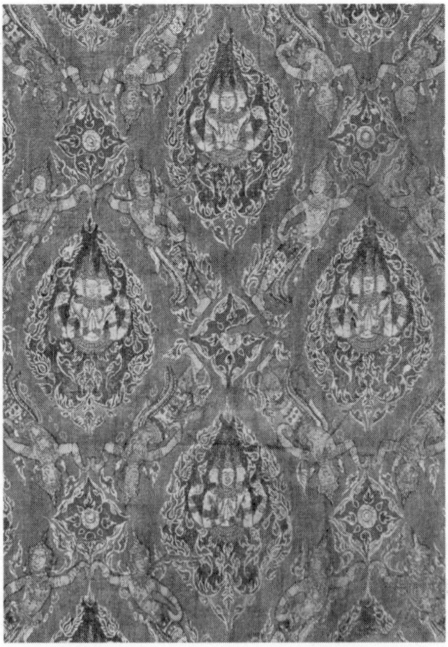

*fig*. 6.5: *Pha lai yang* with figurative repeat patterns of four-faced Brahmā flanked by dancing deities. Coromandel Coast, Cotton, painted mordant- and resist-dyed, and painted. (photo credit: National Museum, Bangkok)

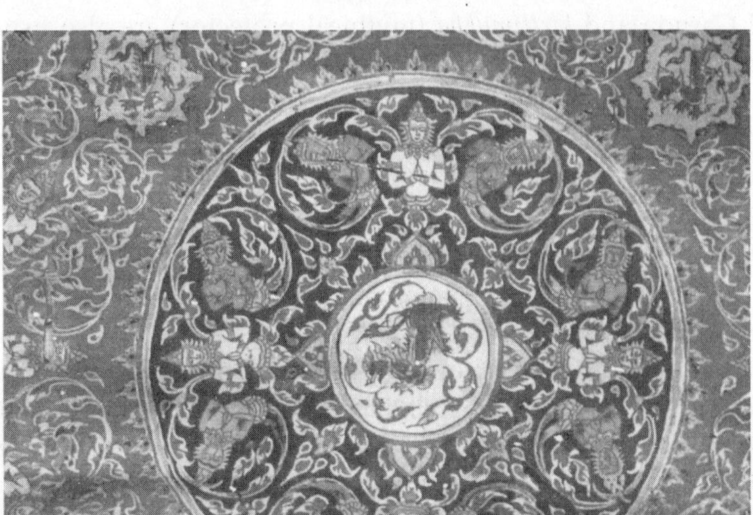

*fig*. 6.6: Freely drawn *pha lai yang* with distinctive typical Thai design of deity in respect gesture called *thepanom*. Coromandel Coast, Cotton, painted mordant- and resist-dyed, and painted. (photo credit: Chaiya National Museum, Suratthani)

that Indian textiles were also made as tailored garment for both men and women of the royal court.[11] Number of Indian textiles used by the royalties and courtiers of Bangkok period are now kept and exhibited at the National Museum in Bangkok and other branches in the regions (*fig*. 6.4).[12] Many temple museums particularly those located in the central plain of Thailand such as Ban Muang and Wat Kongkaram Museum in Ratchaburi province also possess Indian trade textiles in their collections which are mostly used as manuscript wrappers. These are mostly colourful printed and painted cotton known in Thai as *pha lai,* literally meaning cloth with design, as well as various types of brocade with Thai names given according to the richness of designs such as *attalat*, *yirrabab* and *khamkhab*. Indian textiles made for Thai market have centrefield (*tong pha*) dominated with vegetal or figurative patterns and narrow longitudinal borders called *krob pha* and elaborate end borders called *cherng*. Among them are the *pha lai yang* or Indian printed and painted textiles with distinctive Thai designs of geometric, floral and figurative repeat patterns (*fig*. 6.5). Typical figurative motifs of deities or angels in different gestures such as deity in *añjalī* gesture of respect with palms joined) called *thepanom* (*fig*. 6.6) or in dancing gesture called *theparam*. Mythical figurative motifs such as mythical bird Garuḍa and *kīrttimukha* (mythical protector) are also usually found. Geometric forms are *rajawat* (stepped square), *pracham yam* (four-petalled) diamond shape, *kan yang* (trellis), *kanok* (flame-like leaf motifs). They are mainly of freely drawn motifs similar to the *kalamkārī* produced in Coromandel Coast.

After Ayutthaya was destroyed in 1767 the Thai control over the ports in lower Myanmar declined. Route of Indian textile trade was then shifted to the ports in southern peninsula instead. An official letter written in 1812 by the royal court of Bangkok to the southern governor of Nakhon Si Thammarat with orders to send an official to Penang to negotiate with the Ship Master from Surat to continue trading in Bangkok as he did before.[13] The year after 1813, letters were again sent to the governor to ask Chinese textile agent in Penang for

---

11 Krouethong 2004: 64, 66.

12 Posrithong 1993: 183.

13 King Rama II 1776: 1.

commission of fifty *kulies* of chintz from Pulicut, Coromandel Coast, India for use in the royal procession in Bangkok.[14]

John Crawford, who led an embassy from the governor-general of India, reported on his visit to the royal court of Siam in 1823. He noted about foreign products which the Siamese take in exchange with India that

> the cotton piece goods of India, especially the chintzes of Surat and the Coromandel Coast, appear from time immemorial to have been articles of considerable demand. About the capital (Bangkok) especially a very large proportion is clothed with these articles. I have been informed that the annual quantity either imported direct by European vessels, brought by junks from Batavia and the Straits of Malacca, or across the peninsula, does not fall short of 500 bales.[15]

*fig*. 6.7: Chao Phraya Phichaiyat or Dan Bunnag (r. 1875–1946), the Secretariat of the Cabinet during the reign of King Rāma VII (r. 1925-35), wearing a Thai courtier's traditional uniform. (photo credit: National Archive, Bangkok)

---

14 King Rama II 1776: 1.

15 Crawfurd 1915: 115.

He also mentions that

> the trade with British India is conducted principally from Surat and Bombay, and occasionally from Bengal. During the long war with France, when every other branch of this trade ceased, the Surat ships, generally from two to three annually, continued to frequent the port of Bangkok. The supercargoes of these vessels have generally been Parsees or Mohamedans [Muslim]. They have commonly imported gold and silver, silk tissues, and printed cloth, the manufacture of western India.[16]

European attire was introduced to Thai royal court in the reign of king Mongkut (Rāma IV, 1851-68). It became more accepted in the later reigns of king Chulalongkorn (Rāma V, 1853–1910) who made state visits to European colonies in Asia, i.e. Batavia in Indonesia, Singapore and India, and later made royal visits to Europe twice. The traditional royal court costume was changed to uniform long-sleeved shirt known as *rajapattern* (royal pattern shirt) which was introduced in the court after king Mongkut's royal visit to India in 1872. Together with the shirt the plain long silk called *pha muang* had replaced *sompak poom* and *sompak lai* used as uniform of the Thai royal court for centuries. The European fashion gradually gained acceptance in Thailand since

*fig.* 6.8: Sample books of *pha lai* design sent by Indian textile agents in Bangkok are still kept by Maneklal T. Gujjar, a block maker whose family had been commissioning textiles for Thailand since mid-nineteenth century for a century before its decline during Second World War. (photo credit: Boumick Suprata)

[16] Crawfurd 1915: 119.

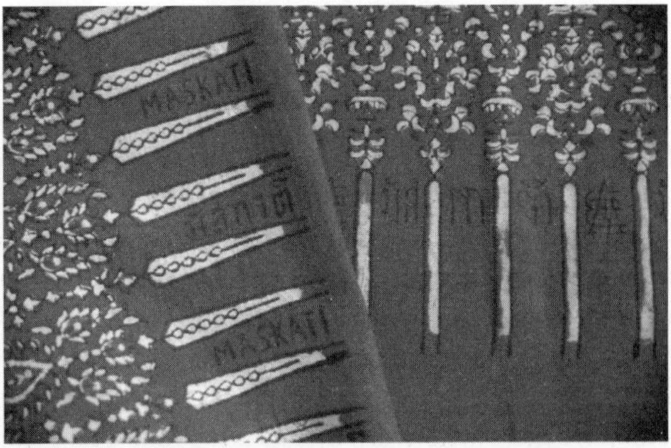


*fig.* 6.9: *Pha lai* with trademark in Thai and English of Maskati which was the most successful Indian textile agent in Bangkok for a century. Pha Maskati, block-printing mordant-dyed, resist-dyed, Chawangwan Family's legacy, Bangkok. (photo credit: Chawangwan Family)

then. However Indian trade textiles were still in demand for the royal court ceremonies for different occasions such as coronation, royal funeral and Buddhist ceremonies[17] (*fig.* 6.7).

The restriction of using Indian textiles by common people was lifted after the European fashion became more popular in the Thai royal court. Indian textiles then became available to and fashionable with common people. An official letter written in 1884 by Chao Phraya Paskornwongse, the then director of custom house headquarter in Bangkok, to king Chulalongkorn saying that there are two Muslim Indian traders who do *pha lai* business. One is Sītā shop that sells fine quality *pha lai* and another is Nakhoda Abdultyeb Esmailji who owns a big shop and sells lower quality of *pha lai* which were mostly sent out to the countryside markets.[18] Nakhoda Abdultyeb Esmailji was the founder of Maskati Company, the most famous Indian textiles agent in Bangkok. Sample books of *pha lai* design for Thai market sent by Maskati and other indian textile agencies in Bangkok like Mulbary and Vasi are still kept by Maneklal T. Gujjar, a block maker whose family had been commissioning textiles for Maskati Company since the founding of the company by mid-nineteenth century[19] (*figs.*

---

17 Thanapradit 1993.

18 Paskornwongse 1884.

19 Gajjar 1995.

6.8 and 6.9). These *pha lai* or printed cottons for Thai market was known produced as *saudāgirī* which means trade textiles in Gujarat even today.[20]

*Pha lai* were popular among people in Thailand as well as in Cambodia during mid-nineteenth to mid-twentieth century. Maskati company owned a textile factory in Astodia area of Ahmedabad and textile shops in Ahmedabad and Bangkok as well as in Phnom Penh and Phra Tambong in Cambodia. The process of making *pha lai* started when the greys cloths were sent from a company in Bombay to Ahmedabad. There the cloth was washed and bleached before printing by the factory workers who were mostly Muslims. The printed cloths were then allowed to dry on the sand basin of the river believed to absorb colours very well. After the finishing process of starching, the finished products were then sent back to Bombay for exporting to Bangkok. During the peak time of the company in early twentieth century about 600 workers had worked in the *pha lai* business.[21]

There were other Indian trade textiles agents in Bangkok who started at the same time with Maskati such as Malbary and Vasi. Both the agents were also from Gujarat but they stopped the business in Bangkok during the Second World War and returned to India. Maskati is now the only company in business in Thailand though no longer in *pha lai* manufacture business. Indian textile agents in Bangkok were mostly Dawoodi Bohras, who came from Gujarat in western India. They are Shiite Muslims well known for their trading activities all over the world.[22] These Indian textile traders first came to Thailand under the status of British citizen, to seek their fortune in Thailand. They started their textiles business in the Indian community area in Thonburi district of Bangkok known as Indian Market (*talad khaek*). After the Treaty of Friendship and Commerce between the Kingdom of Siam and the British Empire, known as the "Bowring Treaty" dated 18 April 1855, was signed they were allowed to own land. They bought land to build a mosque and lived nearby the Indian Market. Later when the business expanded they moved across the Chao Phraya

[20] Archambault 1989: 71.

[21] Maskati 2001.

[22] Leli 2007.

River to Rajawongse area where many Indian textiles shops like Maskati, Malbary and Vasi were located.

During the period when Indian textiles were in demand from mid-nineteenth to mid-twentieth centuries, *pha lai* were the most popular in Thai market. They were of good quality and expensive with special designs made to order for Thai market as well as foreign designs.[23] The materials used were both fine and crude cotton with the size of 1 yard by 3.2 to 3.2 yards sold in the market in *bales* or *kuli*, one *kuli* is twenty pieces. The Thai preferred to buy the whole *kuli* and give to family members or friends on special occasions like Thai New Year.

The Indian trade textile business was struggling during the Second World War and began to decline after the war due to many reasons. One of the causes was beginning of the Thai design printed cotton called *pha lai thai* which started in 1932 by a Chinese named Ak Seng. He was good at dyeing and had good knowledge of industrial chemistry. He had first experimented the textile printing with brass block which was successful. Then he was supported by the German dye agent of Windsor Company in Bangkok and set up a small factory on Surawongse Road to make printed cotton using brass blocks. The dyes used were of naphthols and indanthrenes which were the best

*fig.* 6.10: *Pha lai thai* or *thai* design printed cotton of Praneet Industries which started business in 1939 and replaced imported Indian trade textiles since the Second World War. (photo credit: Praneet Industries)

[23] Posrithong 2007.

synthetic dyes available after the First World War. The result was so superb with better quality, bright colours and distinctive Thai designs. After two years of success, the factory began to use screen printing machine to replace hand-printed block printing which was more time-consuming and not suitable to the market demand of the time. The factory then got support from Holland Siam Company in providing Holland white cloth for production in exchange of being agent of *pha lai thai* under the brand *ramasur-mekhala.*

In 1939, another factory named Praneet Industries was founded to produce *pha lai thai.* At the beginning, the factory produced four-coloured hand-printed cottons under the brand Sawitri. When market demand increased the factory started using screen printing by inventing printing machines of its own. In 1941, the Second World War affected Thailand which led to economic crisis and shortage of materials for machine production of textiles. The factory returned to hand printed production which helped the business to survive while the first factory founded by Ak Seng was affected a lot by the war and finally sold business to Praneet Industries. After the War, Thai government under Field Marshall Plaek Piboonsongkram (1941-44; 1949-57) announced nationalism regime which led to fashion change from wearing traditional lower garment of *phanung chong kraben* to *pha thung* (tubular skirt) instead. Therefore Praneet Industries which expanded the business during the crisis brought down their production cost by changing to *pha thung,* to suit the market demand. The European cotton fabric which had been used for printing since the business started was replaced by cheap Japanese white cotton. The company also produced two-coloured printed cotton under the brand *viranaree.* The good quality with low price printed cottons sold well during the war time. After Second World War, the factory then was back to good quality printed cottons again. An artist named Plang Maneerat was hired as designer and his designs have been used as prototype of *pha lai thai* until today (*fig.* 6.10).[24]

The emergence of Thai *pha lai,* though the price was almost double of Indian imported printed cottons, which were more popular among the Thai and also more machine-made printed cottons from Japan flooded the Thai market after the Second World War caused Indian

[24] Rakwitthayasart 1984: 105.

trade textiles, which played an important role in Thai history for centuries was gradually, wiped out from the Thai market.

## Glossary of Thai Terms

| | |
|---|---|
| *phanung chong kraben* | Method of wearing a long fabric about 1 m wide by 3½ m long wrapped around the waist and tied at the front. The excess fabric at the front is twisted or folded and passed through the legs and tucked into the waist at the back. A belt is worn to secure the folds. |
| *phanung na nang* | A style of wearing a long fabric about 1 m wide by 3½ m long wrapped around the waist and make large pleated folds at the front. A belt is worn to secure the skirt. |
| *sabai* | A long narrow cloth for women to wrap around the breasts with the ends draped over one shoulder and hanging down the front and back. |
| *sompak poom* | A long cloth made in weft *ikat* and used as Thai royal court officials' uniform. |
| *sompak lai* | Indian chintz used as Thai royal court officials' uniform. |
| *cherng* | A motif representing tassels place at the edge of textile. |
| *thepanom* | A motif depicting a celestial being with hands in the *añjalī* gesture. |
| *theparam* | A motif depicting a celestial being in a dancing posture. |
| *rajawat* | A twelve-stepped square motif. |
| *kanok* | A flame-like motif. |
| *rajapattern* | A shirt made of high-quality white fabric for official wear with high round collar, five buttons down the front, long sleeves and three pockets. Designed by King Chulalong-korn after his royal visit to India in 1871. |
| *pha muang* | Plain or twisted woven long silk fabric used as *phanung chong kraben* worn with *rajapattern* shirt. |
| *pha lai* | Indian chintz of painted or printed cottons imported for Thai royal court since Ayutthaya kingdom until the Second World War. |

| | |
|---|---|
| *pha lai thai* | Thai-design printed cottons made by Thai producers since around the Second World War. |
| *talad khaek* | Indian market. |
| *pha thung* | A woman's tubular skirt. |

## References


Aranyanak, C., 1991, *Textiles from Archaeological Sites in Thailand*, Bangkok: Fine Arts Department.

Archambault , Michele, 1989, "Block Printed Fabrics of Gujarat for Export to Siam: An Encounter with Mr. Maneklal T. Gajjar", *Journal of Siam Society*, **77**(2): 71-73.

Chongkol, Chira, 1982, "Textiles and Costume in Thailand", *Art of Asia*, **12**(6): 124-31.

Crawfurd, J., 1915, *The Crawfurd Papers: A Collection of Official Records Relating to the Mission of Dr. John Crawfurd Sent to Siam by the Government of India in the Year 1821*, England: Gregg International.

Gajjar, Maneklal T., 1995, "Interview by Author", Pethapur, Gujarat, India, 19 April.

India Office Record, 1915-21, *Records of the Relations between Siam and Foreign Countries in the 17th Century copied from papers preserved at the India Office*, vol. 2: *1607–1700*, Bangkok.

Krouethong, Poraminthra, 2004, *King Mongkut: Photographs from the Reign of King Mongkut*, Bangkok: Matichon.

La Loubere, S. de, 1986, *A New Historical Relation of the Kingdom of Siam* (1691), Bangkok (tr. of Du royaume de Siam, Paris, 1691).

Leli, Marucha, 2007, "Interview by Author", Bangkok, Thailand, 24 June.

Maskati, Rasheed, 2001, "Interview by Author", Bangkok, Thailand, 25 December.

Na Paknam, No, and Saeng'arun Kanokphongchai, 1985, *Khoi Manuscript Paintings of the Ayutthaya*, Bangkok: Muang Boran.

Posrithong, Prapassorn, 1993, "Textiles", in *Heritage of Thai Culture*, Bangkok: Fine Arts Department, pp. 180-207.

———, 2007, "Muslim Indian and Textiles Trade in Thai History", *Aksornsart Journal*, 36, v.1. Bangkok: Chulalongkorn University.

Rakwitthayasart, Mana, 1984, *Brief History of Thai Printed Textiles (Cremation Volume for Praneet Rukwitthayasart)*, Bangkok: Graphic Art.

Paskornwongse, Chao Phraya, 1884, *Taxation on Indian Textiles*, Bangkok: Custom Office.

Smith, G.V., 1977, *The Dutch in Seventeen Century Thailand* (Special Report No. 16), Northern Illinois University: Center for Southeast Asian Studies.

Thanapradit, Sawet, 1993, "Interview by Author", Bangkok,Thailand, 28 April.

7

# Hindu–Buddhist Syncretism in the Trans-Himalaya and South-East Asia
## An Attempt at a Comparative Study of Religious Literature of Tibet and Bali

*Alexander Zorin*

**Abstract**

In this paper I will try to examine the ways Hindu–Buddhist Religious Syncretism was reflected in ritualistic literature of Tibet and Bali, first of all in hymns and prayers which are especially clear in their approach to the deities worshipped. The Tibetan Buddhist Canon consists of a gigantic number of texts belonging to various stages of the development of Buddhism as a religious and ideological system. While some ancient hymns are sharply apologetic in nature and criticize Hindu gods and teachers of Orthodox *darśana*s cruelly there are some other texts belonging to the later period that treat some Hindu deities such as Gaṇapati or Kubera as incarnations of Buddhist deities. Moreover, in an unique Tibetan scroll of the thirteenth century kept at the Institute of Oriental Manuscripts of the Russian Academy of Sciences there are several texts on the cult of Viṣṇu Narasiṁha whose cult was obviously spread to some extent in Tibet, too. Nevertheless, those syncretic features which never prevailed in the practice of Tibetan Buddhism and Hindu deities were only included into the Buddhist pantheon as secondary and subjugated figures. Balenese religion, on the contrary, incorporated the figure of the Buddha as an omnipotent deity whose features resemble very much those of Śiva or Viṣṇu. Hymns to them are very much similar in respect of stylistics and religious approaches to the Buddha, Śiva and Viṣṇu. By the comparison of Tibetan and Balinese syncretic texts we can conclude that modes of development of Indian culture in the trans-Himalayan and south-eastern countries were basically the same, but that the process could result in strikingly different forms depending on local conditions and prevailing of one religion over the other.

THE approximately 5,000 km lying between central Tibet and Bali indicate the remotest points of the area strongly influenced by classical Indian culture, especially Indian religious spirit. Basically, the furthest points of the lines coming from the common centre towards the opposite directions often prove important to understand the potential of their source and the ways they have to take to keep it alive, adapting according to the changing conditions. In this sense, Tibetan and Balinese religions are perfect counterparts for the purpose of comparative study of Hindu–Buddhist religious syncretism.

The former combines the ideological and ritualistic institutions and practices borrowed from the great Indian monastic centres such as Śrī Nālandā, Vikramaśīla, Odantapurī, Somapurī, and a wide variety of local beliefs of animistic and shamanic nature. The latter is a splint of the pre-Muslim Indonesian culture based on both Hindu and Buddhist cults. Buddhism was finally absorbed there into Hindu practices, the antagonism of the two having being effectively removed on the basis of eliminating theoretical distinctions within the religion, predominating in day-to-day rites of mostly vernacular character.

Nevertheless, over several centuries, most actively in the early second millennium CE, Buddhist centres in Indonesia exercised significant influence within the Buddhist world, and some traces of this fact are still found in Tibetan scriptures. It suffices to mention one case. We know that the famous eleventh-century *ācārya* Atīśa, who later played a crucial role in the second spread of Buddhism in Tibet, had to go to Suvarṇadvīpa, i.e. Sumatra, to study "the non-tāntric Mahāyāna teachings, by then largely superseded by Vajrayāna in India itself",[1] with Master Dharmakīrti named in Tibetan Gser gling pa chos kyi grags pa (Dharmakīrti from Sumatra) whose name is attested in *Bstan 'gyur*. The second part of the Tibetan Buddhist canon contains three texts ascribed to Gser gling pa (Suvarṇadvīpa) and

[1] M. Willson, 1996, *In Praise of Tārā: Songs to the Saviouress — Source Texts from India and Tibet on Buddhism's Great Goddess*, Boston: Wisdom Publications, p. 289.

Gser gling rgyal po dpal ldan chos skyong (Suvarṇadvīpa-rāja Śrī Dharmapāla), two of which were translated by Atīśa (one along with Dbang phyug rgyal po, the other with Tshul khrims rgyal ba), while the name of the translator of the other text is not mentioned. Since Dharmakīrti may have been of royal origin, all the texts can in fact belong to him. It is important enough for the subject of this paper that one of the texts is a *sādhanā* of Gaṇapati, a form of Gaṇeśa supposed to be an emanation of Avalokiteśvara.[2]

The Tibetan Buddhist canon consists of a gigantic number of texts belonging to various stages of the development of Buddhism as a religious and ideological system. Thus, the ancient apologetic hymns by the brothers Udbhaṭasiddhasvāmin and Śaṅkarasvāmin are sharply anti-Hindu with a special emphasis on critics of Śiva since they belonged to the brāhmaṇa Śaivite family and their conversion into Buddhism was sure to sharpen their sensitivity towards this god. The anti-Śaivite motifs are expressed especially manifestly in Udbhaṭasiddhasvāmin's *The Hymn to the Omniscient Maheshvara*, in which various names and mythological plots related to Śiva refer in fact to the figure of the Buddha, so that the latter, not Śiva, turns out to be the true Maheśvara, the Great Lord.[3] The other Hindu gods are criticized, too, though less sharply. They are shown to be full of aggression, lusty desires, anger, envy, etc. The concept of the Buddha as an emanation of Viṣṇu is labelled by Śaṅkarasvāmin in his *The Hymn to the One Who Overpasses the Gods* as a conjecture of foolish people, on the basis of comparison of the Buddha and Viṣṇu. He argues that

2 (1) *'Phags pa mi g.yo ba'i sgrub thabs zhes bya ba / Āryācalasādhana-nāma*, by Suvarṇadvīpa; in *Bstan 'gyur*, Beijing edn.: P.3883, rgyud 'grel, tu, ff. 130a4-133b3, Derge edn.: D.3059, rgyud 'grel, pu, ff. 113a6-116a4; (2) *Tshogs kyi bdag po khro bo'i sgrub thabs / Krodhagaṇapatisādhana*, by Suvarṇadvīpa; in *Bstan 'gyur*, Beijing edn.: P.4994, rgyud 'grel, 'u, ff. 104b6-106a3; (3) *Bslab pa kun las btus pa'i mngon par rtogs pa zhes bya ba / Śikṣāsamuccayābhisamaya-nāma*, by Suvarṇadvīpa-rāja Śrī Dharmapāla; in *Bstan 'gyur*, Beijing edn.: P.5338, dbu ma, ki, ff. 226b1-227a6, and P.5464, dbu ma, gi, ff. 211a2-211b8, Derge edn.: D.3942, dbu ma, khi, ff. 195b2-196a5, and D.4550, jo bo'i chos chung, gi, ff. 178a4-178b6.

3 J. Schneider, 1995, "Der Buddha als der wahre Śiva (Udbhaṭasiddhasvāmins Sarvajñamaheśvarastotra)", in *Berliner Indologische Studien*, Band 8, Reinbek s. 153-87.

while the latter, as a dwarf, stole the whole universe from the hands of the *asura* Bali who had promised to give him as much earth as he could cover in three steps, this being supposed to show Viṣṇu's greed and lack of gratitude, the Buddha is said to have predicted a boy who once offered him but a handful of dust to become an universal monarch, the boy being no one else but the former incarnation of the great Indian king Aśoka.[4] Indra, Skanda, Gaṇeśa, Umā, etc. are pictured as objects hardly worth worshipping to the contrast of the Buddha. Śrī Harṣadeva, the author of the later *The Hymn to the Bright [like] the Dawn*, derides at them as being constantly drowsy while the Buddha is always as bright and clear as the dawn. The drowsiness of the gods is shown as being rooted in the *sāṁsārika* passions and longings, e.g. Gaṇeśa, the elephant-faced lord of obstacles, streaming ruttish liquid from both of his cheeks, is said to be drunken with wine and thus deep in sleep.[5]

While the early apologetic hymns blame Śiva for having the frightful appearance and abiding in the charnel grounds and covering himself with ash, the later Buddhist tāntric texts did not find it inappropriate for their *yidam* deities and *dharma* protectors to have terrible forms and enjoy the inauspicious places such as the charnel grounds. Much was discovered in respect of the relation between Buddhist and Śaivite Tantras since 1990s, mostly by R.A. Sanderson, H. Isaakson and R. Davidson. It seems clear that the Maheśvara subjugation myth was used by the Buddhists to ascertain predominance of their doctrine, even in the new tāntric appearance, over the popular Śaivite cults. Śiva, again, was blamed by the Buddhists as an aggressive deity only clinging to power while the Buddhist ideal was praised for surpassing this worldly passion, although now it was permitted to use any wrathful means to subjugate the enemy of both *dharma* and even humankind, and so transform Śiva and his

---

4 Losang Norbu Shastri, 1990, *Supra-Divine Praise of Ācārya Śaṅkaraswāmipāda*, tr. and critically edited with annotations in Tibetan, Sarnath: Pandita; M. Hahn, 2000, "Śaṅkarasvāmin's Devatāvimarśastuti", in *Vividharatnākarāṣṭaka, Festgabe für Adelheid Mette*, Hrsg. von Ch. Chojnacki, J.-U. Hartmann und V.M. Tschannerl. Indica et Tibetica Verlag, Swisttal-Odendorf, s. 313-29.

5 F.W. Thomas, 1903, "Notes from the Tanjur", *Journal of Royal Asiatic Society*, pp. 703-22.

retinue into its faithful servants.[6] The idea of the "liberation" (viz. slaying aimed at eliminating the bad *karma* and taking the better rebirth) of the enemy of the Buddhists was later canonized by the Buddhist tradition and a great number of fierce rites were included into the major Buddhist Tantras found mostly now in Tibetan translations (the enemy can be well interpreted as the inner obstructions of a *yogī*, but some cases are known for certain in which the fierce rites were directed against some concrete people).

The iconography of many tāntric deities includes the idea of subjugation of Hindu gods. The above-mentioned subjugation myth is reflected in the iconography of Cakrasaṁvara who tramples on Śiva and his divine consort Umā. Another example relates to the Six-Handed Wisdom Protector, the most popular form of Mahākāla, who tramples on Vināyaka (Gaṇeśa) who symbolizes hindrances on the path to the enlightenment. It is well known from the Indian mythology that Gaṇeśa was nicknamed Vighneśa (king of hindrances) after he was appointed by the gods to make various hindrances so as people could not obtain heaven so easily.[7]

On the other hand, the Buddhist relationship to some Hindu gods such as Gaṇeśa, Kubera (often identified with Vaiśravaṇa, one of the most popular worldly Dharmapālas in Buddhism whose function is to bestow the Buddhists with riches), Viṣṇu, etc., seems to be rather ambivalent. I have mentioned above a *sādhanā* of Gaṇapati by Master Dharmakīrti from Sumatra. There are some other texts on this deity in *Bstan 'gyur* including five hymns,[8] one of them by Atīśa. Another

---

[6] R. Davidson, 1991, "Reflections on the Maheśvara Subjugation Myth (Indic materials, Sa-skya-pa apologetics, and the birth of Heruka)", *Journal of the International Association of Buddhist Studies*, **14** (2): 197-235.

[7] Gaṇeśa, or Vināyaka, or Vighneśa, is closely related to some malevolent beings such as the eight demonic Mothers transformed into Mother Goddesses, or Śaktis of Hindu gods. They got interpreted *to be created by Śiva to aid him in his fight against the demon Andhaka. They personify (in the order of their names given above): pride; desire; illusion; attachment; greed; envy; fault-finding; and tale-bearing. Vināyaka is both an embodiment of these evil forces and their lord, Vighneśvara* [ J. Krishan, 1981-82, "The Origins of Gaṇeśa", *Artibus Asiae*, **43**(4): 289].

[8] (1) *'Phags pa tshogs kyi bdag po chags pa rdo rje'i dam tshig gi bstod pa zhes bya ba*

→

hymn, by Amoghavajra, mentions the famous story of his birth by Śiva, in its first stanza:

*Abiding in Tuṣita, the realm of thirty-three gods,*
*The chief of gods Gaṇapati,*

*Born to Mahādeva by request of the host [of gods],*
*Mercifully bestows [all] with blessings, commanding over the four continents.*[9]

This quotation clearly indicates Gaṇapati as a form of Gaṇeśa, though both Atīśa and Amoghavajra call him a monkey-faced deity. The other hymns describe him in a more standard way, as an elephant-faced one. His function is that of a worldly Dharmapāla who gives money and wealth as is formulated in the following request from Amoghavajra's hymn:

> Gather all the riches of the world with the rays of light from your body as if with a hook and stream them on me, the one invoking you.[10]

Another author, Kr̥ṣṇapāda, treats him as the Lord of Mantras, Great Hero, the Defeater of Māra, who expelled all the defilements and destroy all the malevolent asuras, etc.[11]

The Tibetan Buddhist canon obviously does not include all the translations of tāntric texts applying the Hindu gods to their own

← / *Āryagaṇapatirāga-vajrasamaya-stotra-nāma*, by Dīpaṁkaraśrījñāna; in *Bstan 'gyur*, Beijing edn.: P.4561, rgyud 'grel, nu, ff. 289b4-290a4, Derge edn.: D.3739, rgyud 'grel, tshu, ff. 74b5-75a4; (2) *'Phags pa tshogs kyi bdag po la bstod pa / Āryagaṇapatistuti*, by Kr̥ṣṇapāda; in *Bstan 'gyur*, Beijing edn.: P.4977, rgyud 'grel, 'u, ff. 88b6-89a3; (3) *'Phags pa tshogs kyi bdag po la bstod pa / Āryagaṇapatistuti*, by Kr̥ṣṇapāda (another version of the previous text); in *Bstan 'gyur*, Beijing edn.: P.4989, rgyud 'grel, 'u, ff. 100a6-100b5; (4) *Tshogs kyi bdag po la bstod pa / Gaṇapatistotra*, by Amoghavajra; in *Bstan 'gyur*, Beijing edn.: P.4991, rgyud 'grel, 'u, ff. 102a5-102b8; (5) *'Dod pa'i dbang phyug gi bstod pa / Kāmeśvarastotra*, by Candrapāda; in *Bstan 'gyur*, Beijing edn.: P.4993, rgyud 'gtel, 'u, ff. 104a8-104b5.

9 *Tshogs kyi bdag po la bstod pa / Gaṇapatistotra* (P.4991): f. 102a6-7.

10 Ibid., f. 102b5-6.

11 *'Phags pa tshogs kyi bdag po la bstod pa / Āryagaṇapatistuti* (P.4989): f. 88b8 and 89a2.

goals that ever existed or exist in Tibet. In this respect an unique manuscript scroll, Dx-178, kept at the Institute of Oriental Manuscripts of the Russian Academy of Sciences (St. Petersburg) is of a great importance because it contains a group of texts on the cult of Viṣṇu Narasiṁha of whose spread in Tibet no data was known before. Having studied this manuscript for several years, I would like to present a brief description of the relevant texts treating Viṣṇu Narasiṁha as a Dharmapāla who can be invoked for the fierce rites aimed at the suppression of one's enemy.

1. *Khyab 'jug mi'i seng ge 'dod pa'i lha na ra sing ha,*[12] (Viṣṇu Narasiṁha as the personal deity), containing a general description of his appearance and the rite of his worship aimed at the cure of a disease caused by *gdon* demons. His appearance is depicted in more or less the same way as in the text no. 3 the entire translation of which is supplied in the Appendix.
2. A rite of worship of Viṣṇu Narasiṁha and his invocation to perform protective actions against enemies, demons, hail, diseases, etc. It contains also an hymn to the deity in which outer features are intertwined with characteristics of his divine deeds thus expressing implicitly a request to continue them.
3. A narrative fragment rendering the story of the killing of the *asura* Hiraṇyakaśipu by Narasiṁha who came to help the *asura*'s son Prahlāda, called in Tibetan Thub rgyal nag po (The Black King of the Sages), that can hardly be a translation of Prahlāda's name. The entire transcription and translation of the text are available in the Appendix. It seems rather strange that this text was included into a collection of Buddhist texts though it is concluded with the list of several Buddhist authors to whom some instructions on the cult of Viṣṇu Narasiṁha are attributed.
4. *Khyab 'jug mi'i 'og gtor gyi cho ga* (The Rite of Torma Offering to Viṣṇu with the Human Body [and the Lion's Head]), a very short instruction containing the *mantra* of *torma* offering and a prayer to Narasiṁha such as

---

12 The original title had *dad pa* instead of *'dod pa'i,* and my correction is to correspond with the Sanskrit *iṣṭa*.

*The Protector of the World, Viṣṇu, the Lord,*
*Of a wrathful form, with the grinning fangs*
*And the rampant hair,*
*Beautiful, with a shirt of the tiger's skin,*
*With the human body and the lion's head,*
*Your emanations are meaningful.*
*At whatever I look — [I utter] your name,*
*At whatever I look — [I] see you.*
*If I look at the ornaments and attributes (?),*
*I invoke Viṣṇu, the tamer of* nāgas.
*If I look at the* rākṣasas,
*I invoke Viṣṇu, the tamer of* rākṣasas.
*If I look at the charnel grounds,*
*I invoke Viṣṇu, the tamer of worldly* ḍākinīs.

5. *Khyab 'jug gi dgra'i gsod pa'i thabs* (the Method of the Killing of an Enemy via Viṣṇu), an instruction on the yogic self-generation as Viṣṇu Narasiṁha and the fierce rite aimed at the suppression of an enemy by means of the burning of offerings with a special *mantra* to be recited 108 times.
6. *Khyab 'jug mi'i seng ge'i ser khri dbab thabs kyi cho ga* (The Rite of Imposing of Viṣṇu Narasiṁha on the Golden Throne), containing a description of the appearance of Viṣṇu Narasiṁha, the list of *mantras* and spells, substances to be used during the rite, and magical operation with them, finally signs of the success of the rite.
7. A rite for the invocation of Narasiṁha to perform a fierce action, with the method of the making and application of the *liṅga* (effigy figure) of en enemy. The rite must result in death of the enemy from an epidemic disease, etc. If the result is not achieved, the additional actions are mentioned.
8. A *homa pūjā*, with the list of substances to be burnt, description of the offerings supplied with *mantras*, a praise of the god of fire and a long *mantra* with invocations aimed at the killing of an enemy.

It is worth mentioning that nos. 1, 5, 6 start with a subtitle *In Sanskrit* but it is hard to ascertain their Indian titles. In the first case it is rendered with Tibetan letters as *na ra sing* $^{b(?)}$*ha* $_{ra(?)}$ *yi skan kra ni* which is obviously corrupted. I would suggest its tentative edition as *Narasiṁha-iṣṭa-tantra* — in correspondence with its Tibetan translation (given above). In the other two cases simply the name *Narasiṁha* is given as a title. Nevertheless, the Indian origins of the texts on the cult of Viṣṇu Narasiṁha are clear. Though we cannot exclude a chance for these texts to have been kept by some local Tibetan tradition it is more probable that our scroll is the only one containing them. Their insufficient validity as authentic Buddhist texts was surely the reason for their not being given a canonical status. In the Tibetan Buddhist canon there are no texts of this kind. There only are two small *sādhanā*s of Avalokiteśvara riding a lion, a bird and Viṣṇu[13] (in the Sanskrit title, all the three are named *hari* so it would be not so easy to understand the pun if we did not have its Tibetan translation) but, although the role of Viṣṇu in the context is not explained, his being a *vāhana* reminds me rather of the subjugation myth than of his independent status within the Buddhist pantheon.

In this way, Tibetan translations of Buddhist texts reflect various approaches to the Hindu gods developed over ages of the existence of Buddhism in India and its fight with the orthodox religious traditions, from (a) strongly apologetic and sarcastic criticism of them on the basis of strict moral principles embodied by the Buddha himself, via (b) the tāntric subjugation myths with application of wrathful deities who suppress Śiva and other gods, take away their powers and direct them according to the *bodhicitta* vow towards the aim of final Enlightenment of all the sentient beings, and, finally, to (c) the limited use of the Hindu gods as Buddhist *dharma* protectors, often supposed to be emanations of some *buddha*s and *bodhisattva*s, particularly Avalokiteśvara, although the texts of especially manifested

---

13 The authors are not specified, both texts (the first one is exceptionally brief, the second one a little bit more detailed) have the same title: (1) *Seng ge dang bya khyung dang khyab 'jug la bzhugs pa'i sgrub thabs / Harihariharivāhanasādhana*, Peking edn.: P. 3983, rgyud 'grel, thu, ff. 223b3-223b8; Derge edn.: No. 3162, rgyud, phu, ff. 181a7-181b4; Narthang edn.: rgyud, thu, ff. 211b6-212a4; (2) *Seng ge dang bya khyung dang khyab 'jug la bzhugs pa'i sgrub thabs / Harihariharivāhanasādhana*. Peking edn.: No. 3984, rgyud 'grel, thu, ff. 223b8-224b8; Derge edn.: No. 3163, rgyud, phu, ff. 181b4-182b2; Narthang edn.: rgyud, thu, ff. 212a4-213a4.

syncretism such as those on Viṣṇu Narasiṁha preserved in the St. Petersburg scroll were rejected from the canon as having uncertain authenticity.

We can carefully assume that all the three approaches should have been well known in the Buddhist centres of the pre-Muslim Indonesia because their teachers had direct access to the texts and spiritual traditions spread in the continent. Tāntric teachings could be though less important there as it follows from the fact that Atīśa went to Sumatra to study the Pāramitāyāna teachings. The gradual conquest of Indonesia by Islam brought about the decay of all the Buddhist educational centres there. After Islam obtained dominance over Java, by the end of the sixteenth century, Bali remained the only place where the Hindu and Buddhist cults could flourish. Loss of intellectual connections with the continent and the existential threat from the common outer enemy certainly loosened tensions between the two branches of Indian religious culture and finally produced the distinct Balinese religion with clear predominance of Hinduism and but tiny fragments of Buddhism. It should be noticed though that several centuries earlier in Sumatra there was already a tendency to syncretism as witnessed in a twelfth-century text claiming:

> The one substance is called two, that is, the Buddha and Śiva. They say they are different but how can they be divided? Despite differences there is oneness.[14]

It is quite clear then that the almost total dissemination of Buddhism within Balinese Hinduism was preceded with the stage when an highly heterodox form of Buddhism was professed as is stated by the Dutch scholar Moens:

> A strongly Viṣṇuitic-coloured Buddhism could blend with the Javanese Śaivism and only so, because the latter possessed similar tendencies. Namely by the influence of Bhāgavatism on Śaivism as well as on Buddhism the distinction between the two doctrines of salvation had become small. So for a devotee there needed exist no difference between the two "ways" leading to a final liberation. This

[14] Ven. S. Dhammika, 2013, *Buddhism in Bali*, in http://www.buddhanet.net/e-learning/buddhistworld/bali.htm [2013/11/14].

> was a union with Śiva who was Buddha, actually Śiva-Buddha.
>
> — quoted by J. Hooykaas[15]

Sanskrit texts found in Bali and edited by T. Goudriaan and C. Hooykaas[16] are quite eloquent in showing no clear difference between the images of Śiva and Buddha. Sometimes, both are even treated as superheroes, having the universal might and ability to help their worshippers. Some of the texts were obviously borrowed from India while others bear distinctively Indonesian features such as no. 775 that is a salutation to tāntric Buddhist teachers whose names are listed. This text vividly recalls the Tibetan genre of *gsol 'debs* prayers to teachers of various spiritual traditions. The Tibetans probably borrowed the idea of the genre from India since their canon has a text of this kind devoted to the eighty-four Indian *mahāsiddha*s but they developed it to a greater extent and produced hundreds if not thousands of pieces of *gsol 'debs* literature.

It is obvious then that the Indonesian Buddhists used to have highly elaborate literary and intellectual traditions of which but a faint echo has come down to us. Hooykaas, in his paper on Bauddha brāhmaṇas in Bali, states that of this special kind of Balinese priests:

> only seventeen representatives could be found in 1959 all over Bali and adjacent Lombok (ruled by Balinese princes, 1744–1894). Thus they were largely out-numbered by their gaivite colleagues — not to mention the non-brāhmaṇa *pamangku*, part-time temple or village priest, of which kind there may be thousands.[17]

Almost all the difference between these Balinese Bauddha and Hindu brāhmaṇas is now to be found in respect of conducting rituals such as that of water consecration described by Hooykaas. Although the Bauddha priests use the standard Buddhist formulae of homage to

---

15 J. Hooykaas, 1959, "A Yantra of Speech Magic in Balinese Folklore and Religion", in *Bijdragen tot de Taal-, Land- en Volkenkunde*, Deel 115, 2de Afl., pp. 187-88.

16 T. Goudriaan, C. Hooykaas, 1971, *Stuti and Stava (Bauddha, Śaiva and Vaiṣṇava) of Balinese Brahman priests*, Amsterdam, London: North-Holland Publishing Co.

17 C. Hooykaas, 1963, "Bauddha Brahmins in Bali", *Bulletin of the School of Oriental and African Studies*, University of London, **26**(3): 544.

the Buddha, the natural purity and emptiness of oneself and all the *dharmas*, the eightfolded offering supplied with special *mudrās* and *mantras*, they are no way any experts in the profound theoretical tradition lying behind them, although they do try to call upon the pristine powers. Their audience, the local people, pay no attention to the theory at all:

> they are only interested in the holy water being prepared by this brāhmaṇa priest and are not aware of the Powers of Macrocosmos and Microcosmos, of Evil and Good, to whom in perfect concentration he addresses himself.[18]

It is an attracting attention though that, unlike India, in this small part of Indonesia at least the minor forms of Buddhist practice were saved although they became a fragment of the Balinese Religion predominated with Hindu cults and ideology. In India, Buddhism lost its positions totally, being constantly violated by the nomadic conquerors who followed Islam in a rigorous way at that time. It is no surprise — we know that even Hinduism rooted deeply into vernacular religious consciousness had to undergo severe oppressions. So it is quite probable that the only way for Buddhism to keep existence at all in the areas threatened by the then Islamic fanatics was to find a minor place within the Hindu predominated society. It is totally unlike the Tibetan situation which never seriously included the Islamic factor. To the contrary, the ideological fighting between Buddhism and Hinduism of the classical period was reflected widely in the monastic educational system, literature and religious practice of Tibet. Any texts of suspected authenticity including those of manifestly syncretic character were radically excluded from the mainstream tradition although some texts could be kept at minor local traditions. Thus, the absence of both the real Islamic threaten and a serious ideological counterpart such as Hinduism made it possible for the Tibetans to save the institutions of Northern Indian Buddhism and continue developing them over time.

## APPENDIX

The untitled text on the killing of the *asura* Hiraṇyakaśipu by Viṣṇu Narasiṁha from the thirteenth-century Tibetan scroll kept at the Institute of

[18] Hooykaas, 1963: 546.

Oriental Manuscripts, RAS (St. Petersburg). The edited transliteration (according to the Wiley system, with old orthographic features rendered and a few corrections of clear mistakes, as well as conjectures on obscure places, underlined) and the tentative English translation, are given first and supplied then with a sign-to-sign rendering of the original text with all its features reflected.

The text seems to have no beginning since it starts with the middle of an introductory phrase.

brtsam par ma nus nas I yi shi zug ches nas khyab du song ba dang I khyab 'jug mi'i seng 'ge dang 'phrad pas I khyod su yin gar 'gro zer ba la kho sngags skrag ste I nga ni srin po ha ru na bya'i bu thub rgyal nag po bya ba yin I nga las phas ngà rang la phyag 'tshal dang bstod pa tshigs su bcad pa myi 'dra ba rang gyis zer de ma byas nas khyod ngas bsad nas za zer bas pha la ni zad pa myed bstod pa tshigs su bcad pa brtsam ma nus nas I bdag bsad kyis dogs nas 'khyams su 'gro ba yin zer I kho la khyab 'jug myi'i 'go khyod kyi pha ngas bsad na myi dga' myi byed dam byas pas thub rgyal na re I khong gang gis kyang bsad par myi nus ste I kho la rdzas rnam pa brgyad dang dngos grub brgyad yod pa'i phyir ro I de tsho gang yin zhes dris pas I rdzas brgyad myi bstan I dngos grub rnam pa brgyad ni I nyi ma myi sod I mtshan mo myi sod I [nang la myi sod I] sgo 'i phyi rol du myi sod I myis mi [sod] yin I myi ma yin bas mi sod I mtshon chas myi sod I mtshon chas ma yin bas myi sod pa dang brgyad do I de la khyab 'jug gis nga la thabs yod kyis zer nas kho la bstod pa bslabs pa ni I

. . . Having failed to compose [a salutation], [a youth] wandered everywhere in great sadness and met Viṣṇu Narasiṁha. "Who are you and where are you going?" — [Viṣṇu] scared him suddenly. "I am a son of the *asura* Hiraṇyakaśipu named Thupgyel Nakpo. My father told me – 'If you don't do homage and praise me variously I will kill you and eat'. I failed to compose verses of unex-hausted praise to the father and am wondering now, being assured that I am going to be killed". Viṣṇu Nara-siṁha said: "If I kill your father can it displease you?". Thupgyel replied: "Nobody can kill him. The thing is that he has eight kinds of attributes and eight *siddhi*s." When answered by [Viṣṇu] "What are they like?" — [he said:] "The eight attributes are never shown. The eight *siddhi*s are as follows: [he] can be killed during the day, can't be killed at night, [can't be killed inside the doors], can't be killed outside the doors, a human can't kill [him], a non-human can't kill [him], [he] can't be killed with a weapon, can't be killed with something that is not a weapon". Viṣṇu uttered: "I know a way [to avoid them all]", — and taught him the words of a salutation such as:

*lha rnams lha rnams nam ka'i dag la gnas |*
*ri bo ri bo kun la drang srong gnas |*
*chu klu chu klu kun la klu rnams gnas |*
*thams cad kun gnas khyab 'jug yin |*

*The gods, the gods abide in the purity of the heaven,*
*The sages abide in the mountains, in the mountains,*
*The* nāgas *live in the streams, in the streams, All, all abodes are Viṣṇu.*

byas nas phyag 'tshal ba dang | kho 'i bstod pa ma byung khyab 'jug gi bstod pa byung bas | 'o na 'di na yang khyab 'jug gnas sam zer nas rin po che'i sgo skyes la lcags brgyab pa dang | 'di na los 'dug zer nas sgo skyes rtsa nas byung ba ni | sku bdog kar po myi 'i lus la seng 'ge 'og can spyan sum pa | ral par dmar ser gyen du 'bar ba | zhal gcig phyag bzhi pa' g.yas kyi dang pa nas lcags kyi beng snams pa | g.yon pa bgregs kyi ske nas brtsir ba | phyag 'og ma gnyis kyis ro 'phre[ng] du bzung nas gsus pa bar la[ngs] te rgyu ma za ba'i tshul du byed pa' | rus pa'i rgyan gyi rgyan pa ro 'i steng na bgye ba'i 'go bo de | 'di nas los 'dug zer nas bsad pa dang | rdzas rnam pa brgyad kyang phrogs | dngos grub rnam pa brgyad kyang thob pa | bu thub rgyal nag po la byin |

[The youth came to his father] and paid homage and praised not him but he praised Viṣṇu. "Well then, is here an abode of Viṣṇu, either?" — [the father] asked shutting the precious door frame with an iron door. "Of course, here too" – [the son] replied and in the frame the Protector [Narasiṁha] appeared having a white human body and the lion's head, three eyes, rampant orange mane ablaze, one face, four hands, holding with the first right hand an iron stick, with the left one grasping the demon's neck, with the lower two hands holding a garland of corpses at his waist, devouring the bowels, adorned with the bone ornaments, trampling on a corpse. "Of course, here too" — [he] said and killed [Hiraṇyakaśipu], took his eight attributes and obtained his eight *siddhi*s and passed them all to the son Thupgyel Nakpo.

mu stegs thub rgyal nag po des na ra sing ha'i sgrub thabs mdzad pa lags skad | slob dpon a rya de bas | phyis sangs rgyas pa'i bstan pa la bcug nas | mtshan gyi rnam grangs kyang mang du btags | slob dpon chen po rta dbyangs | sdig pa bshags pa'i ched du sman dpyad yan lag brgyad

They say the *tīrthika* Thupgyel Nakpo composed a *sādhana* of Narasiṁha. They say, the teacher Ārya-Deva who later converted to the Buddha's Teaching added many lists of names while the great teacher Aśvaghoṣa composed, for the sake of redemption of his crimes, *The Medicine in Eight*

pa mdzad | bstod pa brgya' lnga bcu la sogs pa mang du mdzad pa de lags skad | ma khol | pha khol | sangs rgyas skyabs | dkon mchog 'bangs | na ra sing ha'i byung tshul | brjed byang du bkod pas | snyan na snyan na thugs na thugs na | zhal na zhal du brjed |

aṭi |rdzogs s+ho||

*Parts*,[19] *The Hymn in One Hundred and Fifty Stanzas*[20] and many other texts. Mātr̥ceṭa, Pitr̥ceṭa,[21] Buddhapālita, Ratnadāsa exposed the methods of Narasiṁha's invocation, [their texts] were passed from the ears to the ears, from the hearts to the hearts, from the mouths to the mouths.

ATI! The end.

(5b18) brtsam par ma nus nas | yi shi sug ches nas khyab du song ba dang | khyab 'jug (19) ma'i sing 'ge dang 'phrad pas | khyod su yin gar 'gro zer ba la kho sngags skrags+ste | nga ni srin po ha ru na bya'i bu chub rgyal (20) nag po bya ba yin | nga las phas nang raM la phyag gsum dang bstod pa tshigs su bcad pa myi ~~'dra~~ 'dra ba raM gyis zer de ma (21) byas nas khyod ngas bsad nas za zer bas nas la ni zad pa myed bstod pa tshigs su bcad ~~ba~~ pa brtsam ma nus nas | (22) bdag bsad kyIs dogs nas 'khyams su 'gro ba yin zer | kho la khyab 'jug myi'i 'go khyod kyi pha ngas bsad na myi (23) rga myi byed dam byas pas phul rgyal na re | khong gang gis kyang bsad par myi

---

[19] Probably, *Yan lag brgyad pa'i snying po zhes bya ba'i sman dpyad kyi bshad pa / Aṣṭāṅgahr̥dayanāma-vaiḍūryakabhāṣya*, ascribed to Sman pa chen po pha khol, i.e. the great physician Pitr̥ceṭa (see n. 21); in *Bstan 'gyur*,Beijing edn.: P.5799, gso ba rig pa, se, f. 322b5 - he, f. 467a6, Derge edn.: D.4311, gso rig pa, he, f. 335b1 - e, f. 421a7.

[20] *Brgya lnga bcu pa zhes bya ba'i bstod pa / Śatapañcāśatka-nāma-stotra*, by Mātr̥ceṭa though ascribed to Aśvaghoṣa by the Tibetan tradition (see n. 21); in *Bstan 'gyur*, Beijing edn.: P.2038, bstod tshogs, ka, ff. 129a3-136b1, Derge edn.: D.1147, bstod tshogs, ka, f. 110a3-116a5. This famous hymn was edited, studied and translated into English by D.R. Shackleton Bailey, *The Śatapañcāśatka of Mātr̥ceṭa*. "Sanskrit text, Tibetan translation and Chinese translation" ed. D.R. Shackleton Bailey, with an introduction, English translation and notes, Cambridge, 1951.

[21] In fact, the three names included into the list such as Aśvaghoṣa, Mātr̥ceṭa and Pitr̥ceṭa are considered by the Tibetans as the names of the same person although it is very dubious in respect of Aśvaghoṣa and Mātr̥ceṭa whom the modern academics tend to treat as two different poets while Pitr̥ceṭa may be indeed another name of Mātr̥ceṭa. Anyway, the whole passage is not clear enough though we can assume that it was necessary to put the manifestly Hindu narrative into Buddhist context.

nus ste | kho la rdzas rnam pa brgyad dang (24) dngos grub brgyad yod pa'i phyir ro | de tsho gang yin zhes dris pas | rdzas brgyad kyi myi bstan | dngos grub rnam pa (25) brgyad ni | nyi mo myi sod | mtshan mo myi sod | sgo 'i phyi rol du myi sod | myis(?) mi yin | myi ma yin bas (26) myi sod | mtshon chas myi sod | mtshon chas ma yin bas myi sod pa dang brgyad do | de la khyab 'jug gis ngal (27) thabs yod kyis zer nas kho la bstod pa bslabs pa ni | lha rnams lha rnams nam ka'i dag la gnas | (28) ri bo ri bo kun la drang srong gnas | chu klu chu klu kun la klu rnams gnas | {thams cad} kun gnas khyab 'jug (29) yin | byas nas phyag 'tshal ba dang | kho 'i bstod pa ma byung khyab 'jug yi bstod pa byung bas | 'o nas (30) 'di nas yang khyab 'jug gnas sam zer nas rin po che'I sgo skyes la lcags brgyab pa dang | 'di nas los ~~sus~~(?) 'dug zer (31) nas sgo skyes rtsa nas byung ba ni | sku bdog kar po myi 'i lus la seng 'ge 'og can spyan sum pa | ral par dmar (32) ser gyen du 'bar ba | zhal 1 phyag bzhi pa' g.yas kyi dang pa nas lcags kyi beng snams pa | g.yon pa bgreg (33) kyi ske nas brtsir ba | phyag 'og ma 2 kyis ro 'phre du bzung nas gsus pa bar la te rgyu ma za ba'i tshul du byed pa' (34) | rus pa'i rgyan gyi rgyan pa ro 'i sting na bgye ba'i 'go po de | 'di nas los 'dug zer nas bsad pa dang | rdzas rnam (35) pa brgyad kyang phrogs | dngos grub rnam pa brgyad kyang thob pa | bu thub rgyal nag po la byin | mu stigs (36) thub rgyal nag po des nasra sing ha'i sgrub thabs bdzad pa lags skad | slob dpon a rgya de bas | (37) phyis sangs rgyas pa'i bstan pa la bcud nas | mtshan gyi rnam krangs kyang mang du btags | slob dpon (38) chen po rta dbyangs | sdig pa bshags pa'i ched du sman dpad yan lag brgyad pa mdzad | bstod pa brgya' lnga (39) bcu la sogs pa mang du mdzad pa de lags skad | ma go la | pha go la | sangs rgyas skyabs | dkon (40) mchog 'bangs | na ra sing ha'i byung tshul | brjed byang du bkod pas | snyan na snyan na thugs na thugs na | (41) | zhal na zhal du brjed | {aTi} |rdzogs s+ho||

## References

### ADDITIONAL TIBETAN TEXTS

*Brgya lnga bcu pa zhes bya ba'i bstod pa / Śatapañcāśatka-nāma-stotra*, by Mātṛceṭa though ascribed to Aśvaghoṣa by the Tibetan tradition; in *Bstan 'gyur*, Beijing edn.: P.2038, bstod tshogs, ka, ff. 129 a3-136b1, Derge ed.: D.1147, bstod tshogs, ka, f. 110a3-116a5.

*Bslab pa kun las btus pa'i mngon par rtogs pa zhes bya ba / Śik?āsamuccayābhisamaya-nāma*, by Suvarṇadvīpa-rāja Śrī Dharmapāla; in *Bstan 'gyur*, Beijing edn.: P.5338, dbu ma, ki, ff. 226 b1-227a6, and P.5464, dbu ma, gi, ff. 211a2-211b8, Derge edn.: D.3942, dbu ma, khi, ff. 195b2-196a5, and D.4550, jo bo'i chos chung, gi, ff. 178a4-178b6.

*'Dod pa'i dbang phyug gi bstod pa/Kāmeśvarastotra*, by Candrapāda; in *Bstan'gyur*,

Beijing edn.: P.4993, rgyud 'gtel, 'u, ff. 104a8-104b5.

*'Phags pa mi g.yo ba'i sgrub thabs zhes bya ba / Āryācalasādhana-nāma*, by Suvarṇadvīpa; in *Bstan 'gyur*, Beijing edn.: P.3883, rgyud 'grel, tu, ff. 130a4-133b3, Derge edn.: D.3059, rgyud 'grel, pu, ff. 113a6-116a4.

*'Phags pa tshogs kyi bdag po chags pa rdo rje'i dam tshig gi bstod pa zhes bya ba / Āryagaṇapatirāga-vajrasamay-astotra-nāma*, by Dīpaṅkaraśrījñāna; in *Bstan 'gyur*, Beijing edn.: P.4561, rgyud 'grel, nu, ff. 289b4-290a4, Derge edn.: D.3739, rgyud 'grel, tshu, ff. 74b5-75a4.

*'Phags pa tshogs kyi bdag po la bstod pa / Āryagaṇapatistuti*, by Kṛṣṇapāda; in *Bstan 'gyur*, Beijing edn.: P.4977, rgyud 'grel, 'u, ff. 88b6-89a3.

*'Phags pa tshogs kyi bdag po la bstod pa / Āryagaṇapatistuti*, by Kṛṣṇapāda (another version of the previous text); in *Bstan 'gyur*, Beijing edn.: P.4989, rgyud 'grel, 'u, ff. 100a6-100b5.

*Seng ge dang bya khyung dang khyab 'jug la bzhugs pa'i sgrub thabs / Harihariharivāhanasādhana*, Peking edn.: P. 3983, rgyud 'grel, thu, ff. 223b3-223b8; Derge edn.: No. 3162, rgyud, phu, ff. 181a7-181b4; Narthang edn.: rgyud, thu, ff. 211b6-212a4.

*Seng ge dang bya khyung dang khyab 'jug la bzhugs pa'i sgrub thabs / Harihariharivāhanasādhana*, Peking edn.: No. 3984, rgyud 'grel, thu, ff. 223b8-224b8; Derge edn.: No. 3163, rgyud, phu, ff. 181b4-182b2; Narthang edn.: rgyud, thu, ff. 212a4-213a4.

*Tshogs kyi bdag po khro bo'i sgrub thabs / Krodhagaṇapatisādhana*, by Suvarṇadvāpa; in Bstan 'gyur, Beijing ed.: P.4994, rgyud 'grel, 'u, ff. 104b6-106a3.

*Tshogs kyi bdag po la bstod pa / Gaṇapatistotra*, by Amoghavajra; in *Bstan 'gyur*, Beijing ed.: P.4991, rgyud 'grel, 'u, ff. 102a5-102b8.

*Yan lag brgyad pa'i snying po zhes bya ba'i sman dpyad kyi bshad pa / Aṣṭāṅgahṛdayanāma-vaiḍūryakabhāṣya*, by the great physician Pitṛceṭa; in Bstan 'gyur, Beijing edn.: P.5799, gso ba rig pa, se, f. 322b5 - he, f. 467a6, Derge edn.: D.4311, gso rig pa, he, f. 335b1 – e, f. 421a7.

## RESEARCHES AND TRANSLATIONS

Davidson, R., 1991, "Reflections on the Maheśara Subjugation Myth (Indic Materials, Sa-skya-pa apologetics, and the birth of Heruka)", *Journal of the International Association o f Buddhist Studies*, **14**(2): 197-235.

Ven. S. Dhammika, 2013, *Buddhism in Bali*, in http://www.buddhanet.net/e-learning/buddhistworld/bali.htm [2013/11/14]

Goudriaan, T. and C. Hooykaas, 1971, *Stuti and Stava (Bauddha, Śaiva and Vaiṣṇava) of Balinese Brahman Priests*, Amsterdam, London: North-Holland Publishing Co.

Hahn, M., 2000, "Śaṅkarasvāmin's Devatāvimarśastuti", in *Vividharatnakaraṣṭaka. Festgabe für Adelheid Mette*. Hrsg. von Ch. Chojnacki, J.-U. Hartmann und V. M. Tschannerl. Indica et Tibetica Verlag, Swisttal-Odendorf: s. 313-29.

Hooykaas, C., 1963, "Bauddha Brahmins in Bali", *Bulletin of the School of Oriental and African Studies*, University of London, **26**(3): 544.

Hooykaas, J., 1959, "A Yantra of Speech Magic in Balinese Folklore and Religion", in *Bijdragen tot de Taal-, Land- en Volkenkunde*, Deel 115, 2de Afl. : 187-88.

Shastri, Losang Norbu, 1990, *Supra-Divine Praise of Ācārya Śankaraswamipāda*, tr. and critically ed. with annotations in Tibetan, Sarnath: Pandita.

Schneider, J., 1995, "Der Buddha als der wahre Śiva (Udbhaṭasiddhasvāmins Sarvajñamaheśvarastotra)", in *Berliner Indologische Studien*, Band 8. Reinbek: s. 153-87.

*The Śatapañcāśatka of Mātṛceṭa: Sanskrit Text, Tibetan Translation and Chinese Translation*, ed. D.R. Shackleton Bailey, with an introduction, English tr. and notes, Cambridge, 1951.

Thomas, F.W., 1903, "Notes from the Tanjur", *Journal of Royal Asiatic Society*, 703-22.

Willson, M., 1996, *In Praise of Tārā: Songs to the Saviouress — Source Texts from India and Tibet on Buddhism's Great Goddess*, Boston: Wisdom Publications.

# 8

# Beyond the Horizon of Culture-Spectrum

***Kakali Ghoshal***

HUMAN civilization wanders along the route of varied developmental phases — geographical, societal, cultural, moral, religious, traditional, technological, scientific, aesthetic and philosophical. Accordingly, civilization after civilization exhibits a multicoloured range of traditions that individuates oneself as well as demarcates oneself from the other. In this way, the story of civilization spins its fabric gradually, as standing witness to different civilization-cults, with different formulations and modifications. These formulating features are the mark or identity of each individual civilization-cult. They collectively go on to create, what might be termed, the "culture-spectrum" of any cult. Though each spectrum is unique in itself, each emerges in coagulation with the other, i.e. there is always an intermingling and exchange of cultures to enhance their resources to enrich themselves. As such, historically it cannot be claimed that the culture-spectrums of any region, so to say, South Asia and South-East Asian regions, are purely geographical or territorial. Specifically they reflect the philosophical and aesthetic aspirations of the human mind in general. And, once the philosophizing mind takes its aesthetic flight beyond the realm of these culture-spectrums, it itself evolves as a cosmic mind, transcending all barriers of regional culture, tradition, art, philosophy. This might sound, somewhat, impractical or far from the worldly affairs. Nevertheless, reality does encompass within it a spirit of emotion where theories give way to a unified creative vision. This paper is an attempt to search for, within a very limited sphere, the emotional spirit, here, a unifying philosophical outlook that can elevate the mind beyond the existing varied culture-spectrums of South Asia and South-East Asia to a common podium. It is not an expert's outlook, nor the technical study of an art historian, but merely a layman's vision trying to take a holistic approach towards an understanding of the so-called "Asian Mind".

The culture-spectrum of South Asia and South-East Asian regions is an amalgamation of thoughts and practices of varied cultures and philosophies. Be it the influence of India or that of China or to some extent the indirect effect of the Greco-Roman cultural traits, South-East Asian culture has developed its own heritage-identity. It is not merely following the footsteps of some other region's culture or philosophy. Rather, the different Asian culture-spectrums stand as the interwoven pattern of cultural and artistic heritage in their own right, which reveal their own signature mark. The aesthetic upheaval of human emotion and creativity reflected through their various cultural and artistic formations bring forth their novel philosophical outlook towards individual life and society. Thereby it becomes historically impossible to consider the cultural and societal growth of any of the Asian neighbours as truly of its own. They are the breeds of so-called "inter-culture-marriages", i.e. coagulation of one culture with the other. It is just like the child who, when born, is neither the mother nor the father, but simply a new creation. Though its existence is rooted down to its parents, yet it has now its own existence in its own right.

Limiting the discussion to South-East Asia and India, we can specify this point by citing examples from some of the cultural practices and artistic grandeurs of these regions. As well known, South-East Asia, sometimes abbreviated to SEA, is a sub-region of Asia, consisting of the countries south of China, east of India and north of Australia. South-East Asia mainly consists of two geographic regions: the Asian mainland and island arcs, and archipelagos to the east and south-east. The mainland section consists of Cambodia, Laos, Myanmar, Thailand and Vietnam. The maritime region consists of Brunei, East Timor, Indonesia, Malaysia, the Philippines and Singapore (New World Encyclopedia). Now, the cultural flavour of a region is reflected through its tradition of art and architecture, religious beliefs, social performances, etc. If one takes into consideration the majestic temple structures and the underlying philosophy therein, one can easily feel the Indian pulse beating therein. Still, they cannot be claimed to be truly Indian. For example, the various decorative motifs on the panels of these structures are the classical Indian art motifs. Some of them are — the *nāga* (crowned snake with various forms standing for the fertility cult), *makara* (sea-creature in Hindu mythology signifying power and regarded as the mount of the goddess Gaṅgā), *kāla* monster face mask, the *garuḍa* bird (mount of God Viṣṇu), peacocks, lotus, the *pūrṇa kalaśa* (vase of plenty) and many others. They appear on South-East Asian architectures as well as on their textiles, not in their original "Indianized" form but in the garb of their own style. The animal motifs of Javanese art, for example, are mostly of the dragon form depicting strength and vigour, and remind one of the Chinese forms of art. Further, the personified deity of Time in Hindu mythology, Kāla, is the god of death, and features as a recurring motif in Javanese temples. Nature with animals, plants, human figures as depicted there, is closely related to the lives of Javanese; some of them such as the leaves of the Aren palm or the fruit from the *kapok* tree are very common motifs. Then there is the famous *batik* art that is supposed to have arrived with Indian merchants in Indonesia in the fourth or fifth century. Of the various patterns, one very interesting pattern is the *sido mukti*, a *garuḍa* bird pattern. *Garuḍa* stands as Indonesia's national symbol and that of Thailand, signifying prosperity. Now, in the classical Indian epic *Mahābhārata*, *garuḍa* is projected throughout as a symbol of instinctive violent force, speed and strength. Simultaneously, in Buddhist mythology, the icon of *garuḍa* (in Pāli *garuḷā*) gets represented as a symbol of enormous intellectual bird with immense coherent civic power to harmonize the social pattern. Then there is also the tradition of sun worship with varied cultural interpretations. Actually, South-East Asian art is the harmonious blending of the realistic aspects of life with fantasy, the joyous creation of human mind — thus making life worth living amidst all its adversaries.

Further, one can cite the instances of Borobudur or Barabudur Temple, Prambanan Temple and Angkor Wat Temple, to name a few, that are much talked about in the history of art and architecture of South-East Asia. The Borobudur Temple is a ninth-century creation of the Mahāyāna Buddhist trend in Magelang, Central Java, Indonesia. The architectural features of this Temple display close affinity to Indian aesthetic pattern. The Prambanam Temple, also constructed in the ninth century in Java, is the creation of such an architectural elegance that reflects the holy Indian spirit. Taking into consideration the Vedic concept of the three phases of creation as a whole, i.e. creation, destruction and preservation, the first temple is dedicated to Lord Brahmā (the Creator), the second and largest to Lord Śiva (the Destroyer) and the third to Lord Viṣṇu (the Preserver). Another famous temple of great artistic grandeur and endowed with Indian mythological themes is Angkor Wat of Cambodia. It was built during the Khmer empire in the early twelfth century and was dedicated to Lord Viṣṇu. Highly enriched in cultural, religious and symbolic values, the temple is of great artistic significance; shaking off its Indian influence, it evolved to be a classical style of Khmer art and architecture. The mounting towers (*śikhara* in Sanskrit) of the temples are highly symbolic. Etymologically *śikhara* means "mountain peak", and it is the classical feature of Indian temples. Now, taken philosophically, *śikhara* is significant of the human craving for the highest, the aspiration of the ailing mind for the sacred as fulfilling the cherished desire for attaining divinity. As the tower soars high towards the sky, it is as if the desire of the human to merge with the divine. Thus, it is the heart-felt emotion of the human mind irrespective of caste, creed and culture. It is said that the outstanding quality of Indian temples is their spiritual content. The Indian mind is preoccupied with religious, philosophical and metaphysical intonations of a piece of art. This is reflected in the Indian temple architecture more clearly than in any other form of Indian art. But, such thought has spread its wings beyond the regional culture and it is no more the Indian mind, rather it has now evolved to be the "Asian Mind" that has its own philosophical outlook towards life.

Another interesting step towards the evolution of the "Asian Mind" is the intermingling of cultures and religious beliefs of Hinduism, Buddhism, etc. as depicted in these temple architectures. The temple structures of South-East Asia consist of three realms that are highly significant of the three realms of the universe as believed in both Indian philosophy and Buddhism. They are: the Indian concept of *bhūrloka*, which is referred to as *kāmadhātu* in Buddhism, is the lowest realm of the mortals in the pangs of desire; the *bhūvarloka* referred to as *rūpadhātu* in Buddhism, is the next realm of sacred enlightened beings; the highest realm *svarloka*, *arūpadhātu* in Buddhism, is the realm of divinity, that of gods. The base part of a temple signifies *bhūrloka*, the body of temple signifies *bhūvarloka* and the top of the temple signifies the *svarloka*. It also reflects the evolution as well as the elevation of the human mind towards a higher form of existence. Indeed, one can claim that the culture-spectrum of South-East Asia has its own unique philosophy.

If one pays attention to the decorative artistic forms on the temple walls, this will be more prominent. The reliefs of temple Angkor Wat of Cambodia, for example, bear the mark of Indian aesthetic tone, but they are not Indian. If one looks at the following images: one from Karnataka (*fig*. 8.1), India and the other from Angkor Wat (*fig*. 8.2), one finds in both of them the rhythmic depiction of *śṛṅgāra rasa*, the flow of passion and love, and *lāsya-mudrā*, i.e. soft gestures evoking the passion of love.

The bodily curves and gestures of the figures (*apsaras*es) carry the message of grace, charming beauty and fertility. They highly suggest the same emotions and their revelation, yet they do not give up their own traditional identity, i.e. their cultural heritage. Their stylizations in their headgears, ornaments and costumes and their facial outlook bear the impression of their regional expression. Both these pieces of sculpture, thus, have their individual artistic grandeur that identifies them with their specific culture and tradition.

*fig*. 8.1: *Apsaras*es, Halebidu Temple, Karnataka, India

*fig.* 8.2: *Apsarases*, bas-relief from Angkor Wat

Again, one can also feel the pulse of the "Asian Mind" when the seeds of philosophical thoughts germinate and flourish going beyond their culture horizons. As these thoughts get reflected through various artistic creations, the transition of thought is very prominent. One can cite here the instance of Buddhist philosophy. For example, one can see the three sculptures of the Buddha from Gandhāra (*fig.* 8.3), Mathurā (*fig.* 8.4) (India's art style) and from Nanchao (*fig.* 8.5), an ancient Tai kingdom, now in Yunnan province, China.

Now, here, one can readily identify the Gāndhāra style as influenced by the Greco-Roman tradition of art. The Buddha image evolved in several regions independently and sometimes simultaneously as well. The images of Buddha as shown in different postures (*figs.* 8.3-5) reflect the serenity and peace of mind far from the maddening crowd. But, the seated posture of meditating Buddha with thick drapery of large and bold fold lines, conceal the body features, thus adding volume to the image. This one is realistic in its appearance and without any grandeur. Whereas, the standing image

*fig*. 8.3: Gāndhāra Buddha

*fig*. 8.4: Standing Buddha, Mathurā

*fig.* 8.5: Bodhisattva from Nanchao

of the Buddha in Mathurā style shows the transparency of robe that reveals fineness of the bodylines along with realistic folds of the robe. The artistic decorations of the disk behind the head represent the hustle and bustle of life, i.e. signify motion. Amidst that, the image reflects a supra-mundane satisfaction of the mind. Lastly, the image of Buddha from Nanchao completely outmarks the other two images of Gandhāra and Mathurā in style and tradition. In spite of all the grandeur in its ornamentation, it depicts the meditative state with a divine and yet realistic expression. Indeed, the image does not bear any Indian traditional look; but it signifies none other than the Buddha, the enlightened one, carrying the common message of Buddhism — compassion, kindness and love. Thus, Buddhism that flourished in India took its wings to fly over the Indian territory and settled down in the various regions of the South-East Asia with their own flavour, in the garb of their own culture and tradition. With this, Buddhist art redefined its identity in different ways in different regions, though belonging to the same root. There one finds amalgamation of thoughts and practices, taking a new shape but keeping the structure of Indian minds. This marks the journey towards the evolution of the "Asian

Mind" and influences the scenario of the beautification of civilization with its aesthetic outcome.

Some other artistic creations also beautifully bring out this intermingling of various culture-spectrums. Carved into the stone wall of Angkor Wat, this scene is from the Indian mythology depicting the theme of cosmic creation through *samudra-manthana* (churning of the Cosmic Ocean) to procure *amṛta* (ambrosia), the nectar of immortality (*fig* 8.6).

Though Indian in theme, it is an outstanding example of the monumental Khmer sculpture of Cambodia. It shows the serpent

*fig*. 8.6: *Samudra-manthana*, depicted in bas-relief on the south of the east wall of Angkor Wat

*fig.* 8.7: *Samudra-manthana*, depicted on the stone slab of Virupākṣa Temple, Pattadakal, Karnataka, India

Vāsuki as the churning cord, Lord Viṣṇu in the centre, the Kūrma *avatāra* (a divine form of Viṣṇu as the turtle) below, *asuras* (demons) and *devas* (gods) to left and right and *apsarases* (heavenly damsels) and Indra above. The same theme when depicted within the cultural framework of India, it receives a different artistic treatment (*fig.* 8.7).

The postures and patterns of the figures, their dress ornamentation and the motifs carved evoke a different bend of the mind. Both the sculptural works show a common thread of religious belief that links one with the other, though each one displays its own individuating cultural mark. Even the various images of gods and goddesses also bear the mark of tradition and culture of these particular regions. For example, the images of Lord Śiva with Umā from both Cambodia (*fig*. 8.8) and India (*fig*. 8.9) very clearly illustrate this point.

The sculpture from Banteay Srei has a robust structure and does not bear any Indian mythological touch. It is very much humanly and as if, featuring characters belonging to one's daily life. Whereas, the other one from India has its typical Indian ornamentation and aesthetic features embedded with a religious belief. Its depiction reflects something mystic, not belonging to the physical realm.

In not only art and architecture but in the social performances of South-East Asian regions also, one finds evidence to these facts. Certain examples from the epics *Rāmāyaṇa* and *Mahābhārata* will provide a glimpse of this blending of the aesthetic mind and thought of Indian art and culture with South-East Asian sectors. If one sees the aesthetic ingredients of various traditional and artistic interpretations of these Indian epics in different South-East Asian versions, one receives an all-Asian intonation beyond their Indian identity. The *Vālmīki Rāmāyaṇa* was translated in the local South-East Asian dialects during the early Christian era. It is interesting to note the different names in different South-East Asian versions of this Indian epic. For example,

| | |
|---|---|
| India | *Rāmāyaṇa* |
| Cambodia | *Ramaker* or *Reamker* |
| Laos | *Phra Lak Phra Ram* |
| Malaysia | *Hikayat Seri Rama* |
| Indonesia (Bali) | *Ramakavacha* |
| Thailand | *Ramakien* |

The general theme remains the same in all these versions except for few exceptions. For instance, in the Thai version of the story of *Rāmāyaṇa*, Hanumān is married, whereas in the Indian version, Hanumān is a bachelor. Thus, the versions adopt the variations according to their cultural, social and political treatment. Further, in the Malaysian depiction, Rāvaṇa is described as receiving boon not from Brahmā (as the original theme goes), but from Allāh. Even Daśaratha is shown as a great grandson of Prophet Adam. These

*fig.* 8.8: Śiva and Umā, sandstone, from Banteay Srei, Angkor, Cambodia, late tenth century. (National Museum, Phnom Penh, Cambodia)

*fig.* 8.9: Śiva and Umā, Śiva Temple, Bhojpur, India

indicated a step towards a newborn culture. Further, when Rāvaṇa abducted Sītā and Lord Rāma approached monkey king Sugrīva for help to find out Sītā, Sugrīva dispatched his men in search of Sītā to Yavadvīpa, which actually is the island of Java or Sumatra.

Similarly, in *Mahābhārata* also some variations are available: a drift from the original Vedavyāsa's *Mahābhārata*. For example, in the Indonesian edition Draupadī is married to only Dharma or Yudhiṣṭhira, the eldest of the five Pāṇḍava brothers. Whereas, in the Indian origin of the epic Draupadī is the common wife of the five Pāṇḍava brothers. The traditional dance and shadow-puppet theatres in many South-East Asian regions, such as Thailand, Malaya and Java still present the themes of *Rāmāyaṇa* and *Mahābhārata* in their own artistic grandeur through puppet-shadow plays such as Wyang Kulit or Wayuang Kulit and the Wayang Purwa. Thus, these epics have received an Asian intonation beyond their Indian identity and evolved to be an immortal creation crossing all spatio-temporal barriers.

In conclusion, it might be said that the "Asian Mind" is the coloured canvas of varied cultures that intermingled with each other to create a novel colour-band of unique culture. The shared knowledge systems of the different sectors have their own aesthetic appeal and yet one reminds us of the other. For example, as discussed above the Angkor Wat Temple in Cambodia and the Prambanan Temple in Java clearly reflect the Vedic philosophy of India. Today the so-called "culture-demarcating" walls of these sectors have evolved themselves into an interwoven pattern of cultural and artistic heritage. But, as the aesthetic mind takes its flight beyond the realm of these individual culture-spectrums, the boundaries seem to wither away leaving behind a grey area without any specific regional hue. It is not the fragmented South Asia or South-East Asia in particular, nor is it the India, but the Asia as a whole that emerges as the culminating centre of the sedimented aesthetic values and culture.

Further, some of the temple architectures of South-East Asia bring out the Indian philosophical thoughts in their most grandeur and aesthetic versions, so much so that they transcend all barriers of religion, society and geo-cultural formations. This paper does not attempt to propose any theory. It is, rather, an effort to explore the various arenas of the aesthetic venture of the human mind to find out a common thread that takes in its fold the myriad cultures, simultaneously going beyond the existing domain. Indeed, it is the earnest craving for a unified neo-culture-spectrum — where the mind resides in harmony with nature, where our culture-spirit gets re-united with the universal world-spirit.

## References

Ministry of Trade of the Republic of Indonesia, 2008, *Indonesian Batik: A Cultural Beauty*.

Mishra, Patit Paban, 2001, "India-Southeast Asian Relations: An Overview", *Teaching South Asia* (An Internet Journal of Pedagogy), **I**(1), Winter.

Sukla, Ananta Ch. (ed.), 2001, *Art and Representation: Contributions to Contemporary Aesthetics*, Westport: Praeger.

# 9

# Far from the Mother's Womb

*Madhu Kapoor*

WHEN one talks about the cultures of South-East Asian countries, the idea that immediately flashes into one's mind is that of an Indian joint family, where a large number of members of different ages reside as wrapped in different relationships. The South-East Asian scenario is also like that of a joint family where each individual country has its own identity but that too bound by a cultural legacy. The concept "South-East Asia" can be taken to represent a vast family organization under the umbrella of Buddhism. In this paper I propose to talk about this common thread which is rooted in the teachings of Lord Buddha. However, the word "Buddhism" has often been rendered with a Hindu touch and in spite of its some anti-Vedic teachings it has many similarities with Hinduism. Though interpreted in so many different ways, one can feel the intangible influence thereby. Such wider connotation in the present scenario of South-East Asian countries will clearly pave the path for an open dialogue highlighting the fact that though different, these cultures are inclusive as well.

This paper attempts to establish that the bond of relationship between the two individuals vis-à-vis two countries depends upon their certain basic needs. As the relationship matures it may take the turn in two ways. Either the relationship remains a formal relationship (*sāmayika*), or it becomes an informal, one of natal type. We may call it a natural relationship (*anādi*). If it is of the former type, the relationship no longer exists once the need is over. But, if it is of the latter type the relationship exists even if there is no such need except that of emotional bond. In the later case, the relationship no longer diffused even if the umbilical cord is cut off. Since the pang of separation is felt so deeply that the relationship somehow remains. Just as the child, when, no longer depends on its mother still it feels a kind of emotional bond with her. I will use this metaphor in order to accomplish my point regarding the relationship between India and South-East Asian countries. No doubt there was a historical relationship between the two countries; they used to share trade, art, culture, religion and social pattern of life, etc. But now they have established their own individuality, they have their own problems, they have their own mode of operations to handle them, they no longer require the assistant to guide them, still there remains that pang of separation which an adult also feels when in crisis. However, the genetic lines remain the same; they have adopted the different styles, behaviour, manner and everything. The South-East Asian countries have close affinity vis-à-vis "family resemblance" in their dance forms, music, rituals and mythology, etc. They have defined themselves differently, so, there is now a rare possibility of uniting them together. Yet one may rise above this unique character and wish to raise the voice of Upaniṣadic text:

*yatra viśvam bhavati ekanīḍam*

The example I will cite is that of Cambodia, yet it will be applicable for other South-East Asian countries too. I will narrate a small history of that relationship before I enter into the major focus of this paper.

Along with Vietnam and Laos, Cambodia is one of the three states of Indo-China region. The first point to be noted is that the name "Cambodia" which is an English name for Khmer word *Kamuchea* derived from a Sanskrit term *Kamboja.*

Missionaries of king Aśoka introduced Buddhism into South-East Asia in the third century BCE but the strong influence of Hindu rituals, idolatry and mythology were there with a strong amalgamation of Buddhism too. Hindu style of temples are visible in Angkor Wat on which the script written is, in Khmer, a derivation of Sanskrit and Pāli scripts of south India as mentioned in the previous para. And, thus historically speaking, Indo–Cambodia relationship goes back to fourth-sixth century CE when merchants, priests and princes visited Cambodia. They propagated Indian language, religion, philosophy, customs, manners, etc. which cut a deep mark, visible even today.

Right from the beginning of Funan dynasty in the first century CE there were powerful states like Champa, Chenla, Angkor, Kambuja absolutely influenced by India until the end of the thirteenth century. The Funan society and its political system had flavour of Indian contacts. Sanskrit became the literary and ritual language of Cambodia. The reflection and the manifestation of Indian culture were palpably visible in every sphere of Cambodian life and in the field of political and social organizations of that time.

When Funan kingdom was conquered, the foundation was laid for the establishment of Khmer empire (Kambuja). At the beginning of the eighth century, Khmer kingdom was divided into land Chenla and water Chenla which was again united by Joyvarman II, founder of the Angkor dynasty. In this period, one can see both Hindu and Buddhist styles of architect and art, which were reflected in every aspect of Cambodian life. This happens because of the patronization of the ruler. Every aspect of Indian culture and its society was spread in a peaceful manner. One can see a kind of unique record of cultural colonialism which was totally devoid of any imperialistic aspiration. There was no religious conflict but a kind of harmonious and mutual respect for each others' religion. The debate and dialogue was, of course, seen and shown at theoretical level in philosophical discussions only. The Buddhists used the metaphor of Vajrapāṇi, killing Śiva in order to bring him back to life, but there is not a single piece of evidence that such acts ever occurred in real life. Healthy exchange of ideas, images, styles in realms of art and literature were continued for 1,000 of years which was mainly pursued silently and in a peaceful manner which was unique in South-East Asia. This unique flavour sets it apart from all other geographical areas.

For the first 1,000 years of Khmer history, Cambodia was ruled by a series of Hindu kings with an occasional Buddhist kings such as Joyvarman I. A variety of Buddhist traditions coexisted peacefully throughout Cambodian lands under the tolerant rule of Hindu kings and neighbouring *Mon Theravādins* kingdom.

The presence and growing influence of Buddhism continued as the Angkor empire increased in power. King Yaśovarman built many Buddhist temples in 887-89 representing the Maṇḍala of Mount Meru, the mythical axis of the world. The largest of these temples is in Phnom Kandal or "Central Mountain" which lies near the heart of Angkor complex. King Rājendravarman II studied Buddhism intensely but he decided to remain Śaiva. Joyvarman V, son of Rājendravarman also remained a devotee of Śiva. Joyvarman VII withdrew his devotion from the old gods and began to identify more openly with Buddhist traditions. His regime marked a clear dividing line with the old Hindu past. Before CE 1200 scenes from the Hindu art were portrayed in the temples but gradually the Buddhist scenes began to appear as standard motifs. Thus the period brought a kind of co-mingling of the two forms of art and architect. Monuments were dedicated to both Hinduism and Buddhism, for example, Angkor Wat and Bayon in Cambodia.

Sūryavarman's posthumous title of *nirvāṇapāda* (the king who has gone to *nirvāṇa*) is the strongest evidence that he was a Buddhist. This shows that there was no religious biasness and prejudice among the rulers. Whatever seemed to be the natural demand of mind for them, they used to adopt without any prior commitment.

After the fifteenth century, contacts between India and Cambodia were significantly weakened under the onslaught of European powers seeking colonies in South Asia. But, this bilateral relationship is revived after India got Independence in 1947. With Non-Aligned Movement (NAM) coming into force, the relationship is strengthened between India and Cambodia.

In India the conflict between the two religions were seen when Buddhist and Jaina attacked on Vedic rites and rituals. And thus, though Buddhism was founded in India as a reaction against certain aspects of pre-existing Vedic religion, it flourished under the umbrella of South-East Asian countries. The reason is still unknown and inexplicable to the scholars. One may guess here that the root of Hinduism was so deep in India that Buddhism failed to overthrow it and gradually took its root to neighbouring countries. Whatever be the reason one cannot overlook the intimate relationship between the two religions, sharing many aspects of life — social and cultural as well.

In China there was no impact of Hinduism but South-East Asia upheld the torch of two religions for accomplishing their mark on more or less equal terms for about 1,000 years. This was true in India too but in India the struggle was eventually decided in favour of Hinduism, in South-East Asia the result was the opposite. In India there was a deep antagonism between the two religions but both religions used the same substratum of artistic vocabulary to convey their philosophies yet differing in their attitudes and identity.

This borderline inner conflict or dilemma with Hinduism and Buddhism revealed the evolving concept within the society. The conflict is not perceived as two opposite forces trying to demolish each other, but somehow reconciling and absorbing and making space for each other.

Cambodia as it stands now is a Buddhist nation. Though Indian Buddhism underwent a massive process of missionary diffusion throughout the Asian world, assimilating new values and undergoing major changes in doctrinal principles, it has maintained its "signature mark". Under the impact of conflicting ideologies of science and technology, Buddhism passed through various internal changes.

Theravāda, the official mark of Cambodia, as it exists today, represents the sole survivor of the numerous ancient Indian schools. It has a fixed body of canonical literature, a relatively unified orthodox teaching, a clearly structured institutional distinction between monistic order and laity.

Cambodian people have officially professed to Theravāda Buddhism since the late thirteenth century and then it has become a way of life and cultural foundation among them. It serves Khmer society in a variety of functions such as cultural, moral, educational ones. One can find that Cambodian's national Trinity is Nature, Religion and King. This suggests that Buddhism is so much essential for Khmer society since it is deeply embedded in Khmer beliefs and has become a part of Khmer identity.

Following the third Buddhist Council 218 years after Buddha's death, king Aśoka sent two Theras — Preah Sonathera and Uttarathera — to Suvvannabhūmi to propagate Buddhism. It is interesting to learn that merchants used to carry images from India to avoid bad luck.

After fifteenth century, Buddhism finally established itself and set its foot permanently there at Cambodia. The form of Mahāyāna and Brāhmanism gradually lost their followers and their credibility also. The core teaching of Lord Buddha emphasizing the good deeds, accumulation of merits and peacemaking, deeply put its mark on the Khmer traditional society. It remained as a guiding principle for the

Cambodian society. For reason that a tree cannot survive without its roots, so Theravāda Buddhism the official hallmark of Cambodian people draw its teaching from the main teacher Lord Buddha.

There are two sects of Theravāda — Mahanikata and Dhmmayuta. The word *theravāda* is derived from the Sanskrit word *sthaviravāda* — the teachings of the elders and is the oldest surviving Buddhist branch. After unsuccessfully trying to modify the Vinaya, a small group of elderly members broke away from Mahāsaṅgha during the Second Council giving rise to Sthaviravāda which derived their teaching from Vibhajjavāda (the doctrine of analysis). It promotes the teaching of analysis (*vibhajja*). It systematizes the Buddhist teaching with perfect accuracy and critical analysis and not with blind faith. It shows that their adoption of Buddhism was not based on blind faith but was accepted after undergoing a critical reflection. According to them *arhant* has an "incorruptible nature" but our understanding may corrupt, so the undergoing of deep critical analysis is required. The progress in understanding comes all on a sudden in "insight" (*abhisamaya*) and not gradually (*anapūrva*) through logical steps. One may recall here the famous slogan of Buddhist philosophy, *appa dīpo bhavaḥ*. One has to enlighten one's own lamp. The three characteristics of Buddhist path are *aniccā* (impermanent), *dukkha* (suffering) and *anattā* (no soul). A living being is composite of *pañcaskandha*. Theravādin believe that we are responsible for our own deeds and also for our self awakening.

The Cambodian Buddhist Saṅgha was virtually annihilated by the communist Khmer Rouge regime in the 1979. Destruction of Buddhism was almost complete in that period. The quality and standard of the Cambodians Saṅgha have remained low given the loss of an entire generation of learned monks. After UN brokered peace plan in 1991 and election in 1993, the partial recovery was performed.

Cambodian society has began a process of opening up and democratization in part through the prodding of an international community still operating for the most part on European time, reason and logic. Bereft of the moral and cultural leadership base of the Saṅgha, it is difficult to imagine the Khmer people overcoming that inner and outer conflicts and charting a peaceful tolerant course for rebuilding the country. Today Buddhism is struggling to re-establish itself although political instability, social, cultural changes are making it difficult.

In conclusion we may say that in spite of undergoing so much changes and turmoil, the teaching of Lord Buddha remains the common thread revered as a human teacher. It redefines the meaning of existence and the nature of man and society within a more universal transcendent framework which becomes the basis for new cultural reconstruction. Although the present situation provokes a deep spiritual malaise and intensifies earlier, innovating speculations about the meaning of the self and the world, the improvisation by time and environment brings out the best with unparallel sharpness. It values all worldly activities of life and questions them with all practical relevance.

Cambodian Buddhism was instrumental in fomenting Khmer national identity and the freedom movement in the twentieth century leading to Cambodian independence as a sovereign state became the birthplace of Cambodian nationalism. Cambodian Buddhism is organized nationally in accordance with regulations formulated in 1943 and modified in 1948.

The present conflict of the Cambodian society is the radical devaluation of the phenomenal world on the one hand and simultaneous affirmation of the other world, i.e. the realm of absolute transcendence. To resolve this conflict the only goal of all human beings is to strive for absolute peace that can be obtained through Buddhist teachings. The existential problem of modern human beings can be handled with the same innovative spirit as in the earlier time, deriving its main inspiration from the natal root. Buddhism is now represented as first councillor concerned with the analytical understanding of the human mind and the need for innovation and progress. The principles of love and non-injury are extracted as the basic axioms for organized social action and reform. The value of mere making metaphysics has been refocused and restructured on the need for support of national ideology, and now economic and technological goals. It is not the metaphysics as understood previously, but the metaphysics that underlines human situations. The deeper layer of human existence is revealed with novel interpretations of the meaning of existence. The mass conversion of Khmer society to

Theravāda Buddhism amounts to non-violent revolution at every level of Cambodian society. As mentioned before, scholars struggle to account for this sudden and inexplicable transformation of Khmer civilization. It is true that the transformation remains "inexplicable" in logical and conceptual pattern, but as I always like to go beyond the logical framework and try to hold the situation in somewhat different emotional way, I can say that this transformation should be seen as the passionate human urge to meet the combative forces within the self. The conflicting forces are within; we have to cope up with them with an inclusive and universal approach. And where does one find this perspective of looking back? The justification of the title of the paper lies here — where one is separated from the mother yet looks back to the mother for support and coherence, keeping intact one's own identity. One may consider it as the presence of spiritual revival and meta-call of human beings, which continues to speak therapeutically to the human situation even as one seeks to recreate and improvise oneself to meet one's own identity.

**References**

The material provided, while writing this paper, is taken from various websites. Some of these are mentioned below:

- en.wikipedia.org/wiki/History_of_Cambodia.
- www.britanica.com/Ebekhecked/topic 90523/cambodia/129475/history.
- www.fauna-flora.org> publication & multimedia
- www.civilservicesindia.com/Subject/History/prelims/funan
- welcome2cambodia.blogspot.com/2009104/history of cambodia
- www.everyculture.com/Bo-co/cambodia. html
- www.cambodia_travel.com/khmer-civilisation.htm.
- www.boloji.com/index.efon?md= concepts & sol= articles & article
- www.encyclopedia.com/topic/cambodia.aspx.
- www.amazon.co.historycambodia-David-Pchandler/dp1

BOOKS

- *Cambodia/Facts and History* by Kollie Szczepanski
- *A Short History of Cambodia* by Tim Lambert.

# 10

# Thailand and Karnataka

*G. Kavyashree*
*P. Nagabhushanagoud*

## Introduction

THAILAND is 2,400 km away from Karnataka, a south Indian state. Thailand's clocks also forward by 1.5 hours. But there are more similarities in culture, customs, festivals, sports and other things between both Karnataka and Thailand. Both Karnataka and Thailand have same number of population. Climate is also little bit equal. So in this research we try to highlight the interconnection between India and Thailand with special reference to Karnataka state.

India and Thailand have enjoyed a close and mutually enriching relationship for over a millennium and the friendship seems to be growing by leaps and bounds even to this present day. The close relationship between India and Thailand is rooted in centuries of continuous interaction. Thailand's relationship with India spans over 1,000 years and understandably this resulted in an adaptation of Indian culture to suit the Thai environment.

The most significant cultural contribution of India, for which Thailand is greatly indebted, is "Buddhism". Propagated in Thailand in the third century BCE by Buddhist *bikkhus* (monks), especially Sona and Uttara sent by Indian king Aśoka, it was adopted as the state religion of Thailand and has ruled the hearts and minds of the Thais ever since. Due to king Aśoka's missionary zeal Buddhism quickly spread through out the length and breadth of Asia particularly to Laos, Cambodia, Vietnam and Thailand.[1]

---

1 Summary of speech by Wanna Sudjit, "Cultural Attached to the Thai Consulate Mumbai", Talk was made to the members of "Somvar Mandla" on 18 November 2002.

In the Buddhist country Thailand, Christmas is a huge celebration; foreigners specially the Western people arrive in Thailand to celebrate Christmas and New Year. Thailand also like Western countries celebrate New Year on 1 January. On these special occasions Thailand enjoys a lot. The people observe the festival with fervour. The country shines with Christmas tree, huge banners, cakes, candles and varieties of recipe.

Thailand's 514,000 sq. km landscape lies in the middle of the mainland South-East Asia. It is six times smaller to India. Thailand's population equals with Karnataka's 65,000,000. Among these 94 per cent are Buddhists, 4.5 per cent are Muslims and rest are Christians and others. Like Karnataka, the temperature in Thailand also ranges from 19 to 38 °C. Generally speaking the best time to visit Thailand is from November to February when the north-east monsoon is blowing cool, dry air which serves as a respite from the heat. Nights can be particularly chilly and at high altitudes the temperatures drop below the freezing point. Basically it is an agricultural country. But in the recent past it achieved progress in the field of industry. Rice, rubber, maize and palm oil are the main exports. Products like computers, electronic goods, television and ornaments are also exported from Thailand. Resembling Karnataka in size, population and climate achievement of 95 per cent literacy by Thailand is appreciable.[2]

Thai is the language of Thailand. As Sanskrit and Prākr̥t languages influenced Kannada, the official language of Karnataka, Thai is influenced by Sanskrit and Pāli. Some Sanskrit inscriptions are also found in Thailand. It can also be noted that Malay and Chinese languages also have influenced Thai. Both Kannada and Thai have their own script and literature. Even though the use of English dominate in the cities, medium of instruction is in the mother tongue Thai only. Importance is given to Thai in almost all shops and sign boards. In Karnataka it is compulsory to write Kannada on the top of all the name boards of commercial shops. And medium of instruction is the mother tongue Kannada.

In Thailand we can see the mixture of Indian and Thai culture. In the names of the towns also one can see the influence of Indian culture.

---

[2] Sudha Murthy, 2005, *Kaveriyinda Mekangige* (Kannada), Bengaluru: IBH Prakashan, pp. 89-90.

Now the entire Thai people are the followers of Buddhism. Buddhism — born in India — reached some parts of Thailand through Sri Lanka and reached some regions via China. But the Thai culture reflects Indian culture.

Mekong River is one among the twelve world famous rivers. Mekong and its tributaries bring fertile soil while flowing and made Thailand a fertile land. It changed the future of Thailand. Mekong joins South China Sea in Cambodia. Laos lies on the left bank and Thailand on the right bank. Nāgā culture of India and dragon of China also existed here. We can also see the influence of India in the names of villages and towns. For instance Viyeya as Vijaya, Danong as Amarāvatī, Pāṇḍraṅga as Pāṇḍuraṅga, Ayutthaya as Ayodhyā, Dungdaavng as Siṁhapurī. We can also see the shadow of Karnataka culture in this.[3]

Like Indians for their livilihood, Thai people depended on *Rāmāyaṇa*. Based on India's *Rāmāyaṇa* story, a famous epic *Ramkiyan* is also written in Thai language. But their *Rāmāyaṇa* is different from ours. Local episodes are also included in *Ramkiyan*. In Karnataka also apart from original *Vālmīki Rāmāyaṇa*, Kuvempu (CE 1904-94) wrote *Rāmāyaṇa Darśanam*, Veerappa Moili (former minister in government of India) has written *Rāmāyaṇa Mahanveṣane*, Ponna, a Jain poet lived in Karnataka in 10th century (CE 950), wrote *Bhuvanaikya Rāmābhyudaya*, Kanakadasa (CE 1550) wrote *Rāmādhyanacarite*, Devachandra (CE 1800) wrote *Rāmakathāvatāra*, Nagachandra (CE 1100) known as Abhinava Pampa wrote *Rāmacandra Carita Purāṇa*, Nandalike Laxminarayanappa known as Muddanna (CE 1900) wrote three books on *Rāmāyaṇa*, viz. *Rāma Paṭṭābhiṣeka*, *Adbhuta Rāmāyaṇa* and *Rāmāśvamedha* in which all these writers describe *Rāmāyaṇa* in their own way.

**Traditional Similarities**

The traditional Thai greeting, the *wai* has close similarities with the centuries old *namaskāra* system of Karnataka. We see the method of giving respect with *namaskāra* in the inscriptions of Karnataka. In the northern part of Karnataka, the people used to say *śaraṇu śaraṇārthī*. Even today the All India Radio begins its farm and house (agricultural

---

3 Sudha Murthy, 2005: 92.

programme) programme by saying *śaraṇu śaraṇārthī* to the listeners. Generally this is offered first by the younger of the two people meeting, with their hands pressed together, fingertips pointing upwards as the head is bowed to touch their face with the hands. The elder then is to respond afterwards in the same way. When children go to school, they are taught to *wai* to their parents to show their respect for them. The *wai* is a sign of respect and reverence for another, similar to the *namaskāra* greeting of India in general and Karnataka in particular.

Like most Asian cultures, respect towards ancestors is an essential part of Thai spiritual practice. Thais have a strong sense of hospitality and generosity, but also a strong sense of social hierarchy. Seniority is an important concept in both Karnataka culture of "Hiriyara Habba" and the Thai culture. Elders, by tradition have a greater role in family decisions or ceremonies. Older siblings have duties towards younger ones.

Touching someone's head or pointing with the feet are considered as taboos in Thailand and Karnataka alike. Head is considered the most sacred and the foot as the dirtiest part of the body. If unknowingly a foot touches another person immediately the person will beg apology by touching the latter's upper body, i.e. hand, arm or shoulder with his right hand, and will put that hand to his chest in Karnataka.

In the field of art, literature, architecture and music also Karnataka's culture is blended with that of Thailand. In dance too Karnataka culture has crept in. Garuḍa (Phra Khrut Phah) has become Thailand's national animal. In Karnataka during the Cāḷukya rule there was a military wing called Garuḍa. The Garuḍas were the elite bodyguards of kings and queens. They were known as *leṅkā*s (heroes) or *jolavali*s (indebted to the king for food) and *velavali*s (those who stood by the king at all times). They served the king the way the mythical eagle Garuḍa served Lord Viṣṇu and committed suicide upon the demise of their master. Hero stones (*virgal*) erected in memory of such heroes are called Garuḍa pillars. The Garuḍa pillar at the Hoysaḷeśvara Temple built by Hoysaḷa rulers in Halebidu depicts heroes brandishing knives and others cutting their own heads. Kuvara Lakshma, a minister and bodyguard of king Vīra Ballāla II, took his own life and that of his wife and other bodyguards upon the death of his master. The details of his loyalty are etched on this inscription (*śāsana*).[4]

Even today the Buddhist monks from Thailand visit Nālandā in Bihar state. They also visit the Buddhavihāra of Gulbarga in Karnataka state. The main attraction of Buddhavihāra in Karnataka is a gold-coated 8.5 ft tall *pañcaloha* statue of the seated Buddha. This is supposed to be the tallest Buddha statue in the south. Interestingly it was imported from Thailand.

North part of Thailand has many mountains. Four main rivers flow here and join sea. Islands like Pukheta, Chang and Samuya, cities like Bangkok and Pattaya are tourist centres. Thailand's ninety per cent of income comes from tourism. Tourism has become a systematic industry. It has made a strong platform for the nation's employment also. The tourists are eager to visit Buddhist *vihāra*s. Thousands of tourists from Karnataka also can be seen here but it is said that many of the tourists visit Bangkok with some motivations. The most important motivations are to have fun, followed by the desire to enjoy the beautiful environment, scenery, and beaches, four core types of Indian tourists are novelty seeking, stress busting/fun, achievement and family oriented/education. It is also said that people go to Thailand with an intention to have an entry into massage parlours of Thailand. Like all tourist centres of the universe, in Thailand also there is organized fun but its extent is little more in Thailand. But it is accepted as a part and parcel of the tourism business. To meet the demands of the travellers and to facilitate them all entertainment facilities available are. It can be recalled that foreign travellers Paes and Nunez who visited Karnataka mentioned that in the Vijayanagara Empire (1336–1565) of Karnataka in the capital city Hampī there was a street called *sūli bazaar* (prostitutes lane). Another visitor, Abdur Razzak of Herat, came to Vijayanagara during the reign of Devarāya II in 1443. He corroborates the observations of Alberuni saying prostitution was under state control and served as a source of revenue.[5]

---

4 S. Settar, "Hoysala Heritage", *Frontline*, **20**(8), 12-25 April 2003.

5 Robert Sewell, 1900, *A Forgotten Empire*, S. Sonnenschein & Co., repr. (1 June 2004) Kessinger Publishing.

Thailand is known as an important commercial establishment in the Indo-China. So it is also described as gateway of Indo-China. Earlier Thailand was a mild country now that character is vanished and now they were turned to a kind that is cruel to cruel. The kind character of the Thai people as Kannadigas, was mentioned in the Bādāmī inscription of Kappe Arabhaṭṭa which reads as below:

*Sādhuṅge sādhu, mādhuryaṅge mādhurya*
*bādippa kalige kaliyuga viparītan*
*mādhavanītan peranalla*[6]

*Kind to the kind,*
*Sweet to the sweet,*
*Very cruel to the cruel*
*He was nothing but god Viṣṇu in this regard.*

Thailand also is a democratic country like India. People are also ever smiling, industrious, and loyal like Kannadigas. They like flower a lot. They have grown arched gardens. Capital city of Karnataka is also described as garden city. And Lal Bagh of the city is famous for its flower exhibition.

Hindu culture influenced Thailand in a large scale. Whatever be the king's name, the name Rāma should be suffixed with it, the state is run by the name Rāma which can be termed that they had the dream of *rāmā-rājya* like India. For instance 9th ruler Bhūmilāl Atyulya Devarāma's dynasty is Chakri. Priest performed his coronation according to the Hindu rituals.

One interesting thing to be noted about Thailand is that unlike the neighbouring countries Burma (Myanmar), Laos and Cambodia it was never a colony of any Western country. Thailand remained an independent country all through the colonical era.

In Thailand there are many attractive sites, e.g. Golden Buddha, Sleeping Buddha, China Town, King's Palace, etc. Thai people like gold. Good quality of gold, stones, readymade garments is, specially designed *sayyam* silk are in great demand. Indians are also very fond of gold. In Karnataka Kolar Gold Field is mining gold. Now a *huṭṭī*

[6] Translation by Karnataka Sahitya Akademi, Government of Karnataka, Bengaluru.

gold mine is also producing gold. There are some ancient towns' Suvarṇagiri, Kanakagiri depicting gold.

Mysore silk of Karnataka and *sayyam* silk of Thailand are in great demand. Ritual methods of Kālī Temple of Bangkok are as same as those in Mysore Cāmuṇḍī Temple. There are some pagodas with Buddha statues formed in the sixteenth century. Sleeping Buddha under a snake, sitting Buddha and other Buddha *stūpa*s attract the visitors.

Sculptures also shine with their beauty. Like the Hindu shrines, the pagodas reflect the natural beauty. In the full-moon light and also with illumination pagodas and *stūpa*s look like *devanagarī*s. In the Buddha *stūpa*s Śivaliṅga, Brahmā, Viṣṇu and Nandī idols are also sculptured.[7] This binds one with the Nandī idols of Cāmuṇḍī hills, Kuravatti Malllikārjuna Temple and Pattadakallu temples.

When Hinduism was in its peak in Thailand, Cāmbodia, Malaya Java, Sumatra and Bali, Buddhism stepped in there. The simple teaching methods of the new religion influenced the common people. When Hiuen Tsang visited Karnataka in CE 641 there were 10,000 Buddhists living in the state. When it got support from the rulers it spread out to many countries.

As discussed earlier Buddhism did not enter into Thailand directly from India but it came from Sri Lanka and China. But Hinduism transferred its culture to Thailand. The Hindu temples, statues of Hindu gods and goddesses were errected. Brāhmanical ritual systems directly influenced in the life of Thai people. The people believed that Buddha was the incarnation of Lord Viṣṇu. Thus mixture of Hindu–Buddhist customs is embedded in the Thai culture. Buddha's life story is carved out on the temple walls as described in the Jātaka stories.

The sculptors in Thai temples were made of gold, pearls and precious stones. The Thai people perform *namaskāra* with folded hands and also perform *dīrghadaṇḍa namaskāra.* There is a method of praying by sitting with closed eyes in the temples. There is importance for lotus in the *pūjā* system. Sprinkling water with lotus flower on the deities is considered as holy. Around the temples one can hear the sound of the Feng Sui gongs.

---

[7] Venkatesh Machakanur, 2005, *Agneyadangalalli* (Kannada), Bellary: Lohia Prakashana, pp. 11-12.

Gautama Buddha, the founder of Buddhism, did not say anything about the existence of god or spirit of god. He showed the simple living and high thinking. But contrary to this the same Buddha has become god in the minds of his followers. Different types of Buddha statues are being prayed. In Karnataka also in the twelfth-century philanthropist Lord Basaveśvara opposed the idol prayer but his followers considered him as a god and they are installing Basaveśvara statues everywhere in Karnataka.

**Folk Dance**

Thai folklore is based on the folk beliefs of Thai people that have a regional background, for they originated in the rural countryside of Thailand. With the passing of time, and through the influence of the media, Thai folklore has become part of the wider popular Thai culture.

There are some art villages developed in Thailand. One among them is Nung Nooch nearby Pattaya city. An individual artist developed this village artistically. A garden and an auditorium have been constructed here. Regular cultural events are organized here. Maximum number of Thai folk dance is contested here. About thirty to forty artists perform different types of dance. They take the spectators to a new healm by their artistic dances and costumes.

Elephant fight is very much appreciated by the audience of the world. Next to South Africa and India, Thailand stands third in number of elephants. They train elephants and make them to perform entertainment activities. Programme starts with elephants' march past.[8]

"Karnataka Loka", a folklore museum established by Mrs. and Mr. Dr H.L. Nagegowda in Karnataka is such type of a village in which all varieties of folk items are kept and explain the folk culture of Karnataka.

Apart from folk and regional dances (Indian-influenced Manohara dance), the two major forms of Thai classical dance-drama are Khon and Lakon Nai. Khon is a genre of dance-drama from Thailand. It is traditionally performed solely in the royal court, by men in masks accompanied by narrators and a traditional piphat ensemble. Hanumān role in the play is well versed. Interestingly it is said that Hanumān is born in Kiṣkindhā of Karnataka. In the beginning both were exclusively court entertainments and it was not until much later that a popular

[8] Venkatesh Machakanur, 2005, op. cit., p. 28.

style of dance theatre, Likay, evolved as a diversion for the common folk who had no access to royal performances. The *wai* is an annual ceremony performed by Thai classical dance groups to honour their artistic ancestors.[9]

In Karnataka also, apart from *yakṣagāna*, in the folk arts like *gigi, gondaligara pada, sannata, doddata,* the same process can be seen.

World famous Alcazar show is organized in Thailand. Along with Thai folk dance, songs in English and Chinese are sung. Stage decoration here is very attractive. Special attention is given to Thai folk dance in this cultural exhibition.

**Festivals**

Festivals, of many types, serve to meet specific needs, as well as to provide entertainment are observed in Thailand. These celebrations offer a sense of belongingness among religious, social, or geographical groups. Modern festivals that focus on cultural or ethnic topics seek to remind members of their traditions.

Hindu belief in death, heaven and hell is also prevailed in the minds and hearts of the Thai people. On the walls of the temples Yamarāja, the deity of death sitting on his vehicle water buffalo giving justice with the assistance of Citragupta and Dharma, scenes of menace in the hell, punishment methods are carved. The battle between Vāli–Sugrīva (brothers), Kurukṣetra scenes, Rāmāyaṇa warfare, Kṛṣṇa holding Govardhana mountain, Hanumān bringing mountain Sañjīvanī are carved out in the walls of temples.[10] Deity Hanumān is lovable for Thailand people. In Karnataka also people celebrate Hanumān Jayantī with fun and fervour. Every Saturday is considered as the day of Hanumān in the state. Many of the Thai festivals are based on Hindu festivals. Some of them are discussed here.

HOLI AND SONGKRAN

Holi is a very popular festival of India. Bagalkoṭ district of Karnataka is widely known for its celebration of Holi. Thai people also celebrate the same festival in the name, Songkran. The word *songkran* is derived from the Indian official language Hindi. *Soṅg* means fancy dress. Great

[9] John Hoskin, 2006, Thailand, p. 26.

[10] Venkatesh Machakanur, op. cit., p. 12.

excitement can be seen in people on the next day when it is actually the time for the play of colours. Shops and offices remain closed for the day and people get all the time to go crazy and whacky. Bright colours of *gulāla* and *abīra* fill the air and people take turns in pouring colour water over each other. Children take special delight in spraying colours on one another with their *picakārī*s and throwing water balloons on passers-by. Women and senior citizens form groups called *ṭolī*s and move in colonies applying colours and exchanging greetings. Songs, dance on the rhythm of *ḍholak* and mouth-watering Holi delicacies are the other highlights of the day. In the same way Thailand people celebrate the Songkran.

In the both Holi and Songkran the enemies also become friends. All people, irrespective of caste, creed, age and sex, participate in the festivals. The children and youth go to each home of the village/area and collect contributions in the form of money and spend it for refreshments in group. This brings the people united.

Songkran is in fact the celebration of the vernal equinox similar to those of the Indian Holi festival, the Chinese Ching Ming and the Christian festival of Easter. The Songkran festival is in a certain sense like April Fool's Day, when the maids of the village play pranks on any gallant who happens to pass by their way. He will be caught and bound by the maids and they will daub him with black colour.

## LOI KRATHONG

Loi Krathong is a well-known festival in Thailand. It is held on the 12th full moon of the Thai Lunar calendar. It is an auspicious day in Thai culture, in which the people *loi* meaning "to float" a *krathong* a small raft traditionally made of a section of banana tree, decorated with elaborately — folded banana leaves, flowers, candles, incense sticks, etc. Karnataka people, specially who live on the banks of rivers, celebrate the similar festival called Teppotsava or Dīpotsava but instead of candle people here use cotton thread dipping in the edible oil in the *hanate* (disc) made of mud. The act of floating away the candle raft is symbolic of letting go of all one's grudge, anger and defilements, so that one can start life afresh on a better foot.[11]

---

[11] Interview with Mr Panduranga, a resident of Hole Mutkur village in H.B. Halli Taluk, Karnataka.

## SAVASDĪ

Savasdī is a festival of greeting. As discussed earlier, in traditional Thai greeting, the *wai* is generally offered first by the younger of the two people meet, with their hands upwards as the head bowed to touch their face to the hands, usually coinciding with the spoken word *sawasdee khrap* for male speakers and *sawasde ka* for females. The elder then is to respond afterward in the same way. When children go to school they are taught to *wai* to their parents to show respect for them.

In India during the sankramana on 14-15 January every year and on *ugādi* (new year starting for the people of Andhra Pradesh, Karnataka, etc.) Indians greet each other by hugging with brotherly affection. Even the birthdays of king–queens, saints, *swāmijīs*, are celebrated. The *wai* is a sign of respect and reverence for another in Thailand, similar to the *namaste* greeting of India.

Point to be noted in this connection is that till ten years of marriage king Biday (Vijay) did not get a child. Then he visited Bangla Sahib Gurdwara of Delhi, and prayed for a child. It is believed that after this prayer he got a male baby. So Thailand people, even today, believe Indian gods. If they meet any Indian they happily say that "your god is very strong". The VIPs and members of the Thai royal family visit Delhi and pray for a child till today.[12]

## KITE FESTIVAL

Another widely enjoyed pastime, and once a competitive sport, is kite flying in Thailand and India. Kite festivals are a popular form of entertainment throughout the world. They include large local events, traditional festivals which have been held for hundreds of years. They are usually small, flat, flattened diamond-shaped kites made of paper and bamboo. Children and youth enjoy the kite festival a lot. This is a natural training for the children to grow with friendly, entertainment and joyful environment. In Karnataka people in rural areas start flying kites after the rainy season specially after Makara Saṁkrānti. In locally arranged kite competitions participants try to snag each other's kites or cut other's kites down and even tease the loser, and shout aloud in joy.

---

12 Sudha Murthy, 2005, op. cit., p. 93.

## Palace Decorum

Thailand's Palace decorum is peculiar. Present king's palace is a separate one. The old palace is kept open for visitors. King's thrones, religious prayers and political meeting halls attract the visitors. Campus is called as palace ground. There is a dress code for everyone of long pants or demure skirts, and shirts with sleeves (short sleeves OK, but no tube tops or tank tops, no bare bellies).

Though the Mysore Palace stands tall in its beauty and legacy, Thailand's palace has its own beauty. Like Mysore kings Thailand rulers also have their respect in the religious rituals and other functions. In Mysore Daśaharā and Vijayanagara (Hampi) Brahma-rathotsava, the involvement of the members of Mysore royal family is very much expected by the public.[13]

## Social Conditions and Customs

### NEW BORN

There are some similarities in customs when a baby is born. The tradition includes making offerings at a temple on the third day after the baby is born and obtain blessings from a *swāmijī* (monk in Thailand).

In Thailand fire-shaving ceremony takes place when the child reaches the age of one month and one day. But in Karnataka on fifth day people perform *aidesi* function in which they worship grinder (made of stone) and pestle and threshold. It is also believed that *śetavī* will write the baby's destiny on fifth day. So the brother-in-law of baby should sleep across the threshold and request *śetavī* to write a good thing for new baby. On the same day baby is temporarily called with god's name or ancestors (grand grandfather or grand grand-mother) name. But fire-shaving ceremony in Karnataka differs from one district to the other, generally it takes place after nine months of the birth. On that day as a mark, a priest cut the baby hair with betel leaf.

### MARRIAGES

In Thailand and Karnataka the monk (*swāmī*) present may say a few

---

[13] Philip Cornwell-Smith, 2005, *Very Thai*, River Books, pp. 180-82.

words to the newly-married couple offering advice or encouragement to lead a good life. They also begin a series of recitations from Sanskrit scriptures (Pāli scriptures in Thailand) intended to bring merit and blessings to the new couple. The couple may then make offerings of flowers and gifts to the *swāmī*/monk.

DOWRY SYSTEM

The Thai dowry system is known as *sin sodt*. Traditionally, the groom will be expected to pay a sum of money to the family to compensate them and to demonstrate that the groom is financially capable of taking care of their daughter. Sometimes, this sum is purely symbolic, and will be returned to the bride and groom after the wedding has taken place.

In Karnataka dowry system is prevailed and in some groups of people *teru* system is also in practice in which a groom should pay money to the bride's parents.[14]

Among the Thai Muslims the *imām* of the local mosque, the groom, the father of the bride, men in the immediate family and important men in the community sit in a circle during the ceremony, conducted by the *imām*. All the women, including the bride sit in a separate room and do not have any direct participation in the ceremony. The Thai Muslims frequently, though not always, also follow the conventions of the Thai dowry system.

**Food Habits**

Thai people are used to eat rice as their meal. Most Thai people can't have sandwiches as their meal. They call sandwiches a snack. Also, most Thai people do not sit down to eat a proper meal because they usually eat when they are hungry, especially kids and teenagers. If you know some Thai persons, you might hear them say *gin khao yung* every time you meet them. It means "have you eaten yet?" or more precise "have you eaten rice yet". Karnataka people also give importance to meals. Whenever two persons meet each other they ask *oota aayta*, which means "had you have your meals"?

---

[14] Nadoja Geetha Nagabhushana (ed.), 2010, *Sanskruthi Mahilaa Maalike*, Karnataka Sahitya Akademi, Bengaluru vide an article "Duraga Mururagi Sanskrutiyalli Mahile" by G. Kavyashree, pp. 180-81.

Ninety-nine per cent of Thai people are non-vegetarians. They eat almost all type of non-veg. In the hotel menu we can see elephant soup, crocodile soup, shark soup, etc. Rice and vermicelli can also be seen everywhere. They use plenty of coconut water for preparing food even in the *caṭanī* and *dāl*. In the coastal areas of Karnataka and Kerala people use coconut oil as edible oil for preparing food.

Thailand is also producing varieties of fruits. Guava fruit, at time weighing 1 kg, is very tasty.

**Women**

Women, both in India and Thailand have voting power. However they are still underrepresented in the society and politics. Females in India and Thailand marry at an earlier age than male. The role of women in Thailand's national development has not yet been fully established. Factors that affect women's participation in the socio-economic field include "inadequate gender awareness in the policy and planning process" and social stereotyping. *Sāṛī* (a single piece of a long cloth worn around the body) and *salwār kamīẓ* are worn by women all over India. *Bindī* is part of the women's make-up. Unlike common belief, the *bindī* on the forehead does not signify marital status, however the *ṣindūra* does. *Raṅgolī* (or *kolam*) is a traditional art very popular among Indian women. In rural India, agriculture and allied industrial sectors employ as much as 89.5 per cent of the total female labour. In the realm of entrepreneurship, Thailand's female population comprised 47 per cent of the country's workforce, which makes up the highest percentage of working women in the region of the Asia-Pacific. However, these women are also subjected to high discrimination and gender inequality when it comes to wages and of being "concentrated in low-paying jobs".[15]

**Funerals**

In Thailand, funerals last for at least one week. Crying is discouraged during the funeral, so as not to worry the spirit of the deceased. Many activities surrounding the funeral are intended to make merit for the deceased. Copies of Buddhist scriptures may be printed and

15 Human Development Report, 2011, *Sustainability and Equity*, United Nations Development Programme, pp. 137-39.

distributed in the name of the deceased, and gifts are usually given to a local temple. Monks are invited to chant prayers that are intended to provide merit for the deceased, as well as to provide protection against the possibility of the dead returning as a malicious spirit. Pictures of the deceased from his/her best days will often are displayed next to the coffin.

## Recent Developments

Abhisit Vejjajiva, the Prime Minister of Thailand, paid a state visit to India during 4–5 April 2011 at the invitation of Manmohan Singh, the Prime Minister of India. Both leaders agreed to increase the cultural interaction, connectivity and enhancement of trade and economic through the bilateral and regional frameworks, viz. ASEAN-India, BIMSTEC and MGC. It was also decided to increase the trade between two countries from its 2010 figure of $6.7 billion to its double in 2014.

Prime Minister Yingluck Shinawatra paid a state visit in January 2012 as the chief guest of Indian Republic Day. This is a significant sign of good relationship between the two countries. As the result of this visit, there were six bilateral agreements signed, including treaty of transfer of sentenced persons.

## Glossary

*caṭanī:* spicy paste made of coconut, etc.

*dīrghadaṇḍa namaskāra*: type of praying crawling the body around the temple.

*doddata*: plays which all the night.

*gigi pada*: type of folk song explains a Purāṇic story.

*gondaligara pada*: Gondaliga community people perform this show in which they describe the victory of goddesses over the evil.

Kālī: a goddess.

*kāmadahana*: a symbolic setting fire to effigy of Manmatha during Holī festival in India.

*kannadiga*: a person whose mother tounge is Kannada, generally lives in Karnataka.

*nāga:* snake.

Nandī: bull, vehicle of god Śiva.

*pañcaloha:* as an alloy of gold (Au), silver (Ag), copper (Cu), iron (Fe) and lead (Pb) as the major constituents.

*picakārīs*: syringe to spray colours.

*sannata*: small play on the stage with less duration.

*sūli bazaar*: a street during Vijayanagara Empire in Karnataka where the prostitutes were living.

*ṭolī:* a group of some individuals.

# 11

# Global Ancient India and Suvarṇabhūmi (South-East Asia)

## A Historical Perspective

*Shiva G. Bajpai*

THE historic relationship between Global Ancient India and Suvarṇabhūmi, Suvarṇadvīpa, or Suvarṇanagara (the Land, Island or City of Gold) South-East Asia is indeed woven with golden threads. While the geographic identification of the Land of Gold with any particular country at a given time is problematic, it meant always a distant region across the seas beyond the eastern shores of traditional Bhārata — India. It came to denote virtually the entire region of modern South-East Asia during the classical ages in India through the eighth century CE. Obviously it had economic importance and was the destination of the sea voyages of bold and adventurous persons wanting to acquire fabulous wealth and get rich quick. The stereotyped image of historic India as a world apart, isolated and self-sufficient is as misleading as the nationalist emphasis in certain aspect of South-East Asian historiography that the interrelationship between India and South-East Asia was created entirely by the South-East Asian rulers and people themselves. The process, however, was complex and the role of indigenous as well as India agents varied over time and place. Closer to the truth is the position that it was the product of mutually co-operative agents in which the role of warriors in initiating, sustaining and promoting diverse aspects of the relationship was negligible. The traders, adventurers and missionaries were the more important agents and the prime movers of the early globalization phenomenon and international cultural relationships.

While India's global connections through trade and commerce

began in prehistory, these entered a critical phase since the first century CE when India emerged as the central node of an international system of maritime trade, commerce and culture. India's trade relations extended to the Red Sea areas, Egypt and across the Mediterranean to Roman Europe in the West and to the South-East Asian regions within the expansive south-eastern Indian Ocean and China in the East. Many historians have viewed this as the first appearance of what is called "World System . . . the economic integration by trade of most of the inhabited globe". While the annual gold drain of the Roman empire to the tune of 55 million Roman gold coins to India has been ruefully recorded by Pliny the Elder in the mid-first century, we have no way to estimate the gold that flowed into India both in metal and other preciosities including spices from Suvarṇadvīpa. It is fair to estimate, however, that it was substantial and kept on growing for about 1,000 years through the entire classical and early medieval ages of Indian history (i.e. first and twelfth century). India indeed had become the lynchpin of the global trade and culture, a development that accelerated movement of goods and ideas and culture primarily because India did not aspire for overseas political empire and Indian culture was not exclusionary, promoting as it did an integration of the enduring indigenous beliefs and customs.

While "a beckoning eldorado beyond the ocean" enticed the Indian merchants and adventurers, the rulers and elites of Suvarṇabhūmi were irresistibly drawn to the high culture and religions of the land of *dharma* and took the initiative to adopt and promote it in their realms. The rulers sent emissaries to various courts in India to request them to send brāhmaṇas with ideological and cultural package for the transference of the traditional classical culture to their kingdoms. They were motivated by their need to legitimate their polity among their subjects and raise their status by showing how closely their courts resembled those in India. The amicable and close cultural ties between the Dharmabhūmi (India) and Suvarṇabhūmi often called "Indianization" of the latter are rather unique in world history. Despite the debate over whether indigenous rulers and elites or Indian agents, brāhmaṇa priests, Buddhist missionaries and master artists played the determining role in transferring Indian culture to South-East Asia, it is evident that the people of South-East Asia have been the recipient of Indian dhārmic culture and religions, Sanskrit language and literature, art and architecture. The vast scope of borrowings was more in the nature of acculturation and appropriation of Indian ideologies and institutions, culture and religion apart from material and economic exchanges. The entire course of reinforcing "the marriage of interests" was largely apolitical and non-violent in nature with the exception of the Coḷa military expedition and temporary occupation of parts of the Srivijaya empire in the eleventh century. The immensity of Indian cultural impact on countries of modern South-East Asia has led historians to describe the process as "Indianization" that went on for over millennia. The Sanskritists led by Sheldon Pollock include entire South-East Asia as part of the realm of Sanskrit cosmopolis. Certainly people of South-East Asian countries have practised Hinduism and Buddhism and integrated various aspects of Indic culture and spiritual value system for over 2,000 years. Despite the spread of Islam, Muslims in Indonesia and Malaysia and elsewhere in the region people still exhibit their Hindu/Buddhist imprints on their behaviour and psyche. Much of South-East Asia remains culturally much closer to India than any other country. The best-known monuments are Angkor and Borobodur that daily attract throngs of visitors, as does the Hindu culture of Bali. The language of Indonesia is called "Bhāṣā" which means speech or language in Sanskrit. The ruler of Thailand still assumes the name Rāma and the International Airport at Bangkok is named Suvarṇabhūmi.

The historic affinity of the Dharmabhūmi (India) and Suvarṇa-bhūmi (South-East Asia) is poised to enter a very significant phase again in the years ahead. Dharma/Dhamma that is the spiritual light of Asia will again show us the path of mutually rewarding enterprises and of promotion of our collective well-being that embraces the entire humanity.

This conference itself is a tribute to our mutually beneficial historic relationship and holds a promise of our future progress in the evolving global age.

# 12

# The Interconnection between India and South-East Asia

## Especially Indonesia in Art, Culture and Architecture

*Komang Santhi Arsa*

### Introduction

INDIA and Indonesia are known for their diversity. No wonder, this has resulted in these two countries having a myriad of cultural pluralism. When did their bilateral relationship start and how is it going, these need to be analysed from the historical and current perspectives. Also, we have to address the question: how did the construction of cultural assimilation take place between Indonesia and India? Was it just a natural development?

This paper is an attempt to find answers to these questions. The origin of Indonesia–India relationship started with their trade links in ancient times. Indonesia's spices were world famous and they found greater demand in the entire European continent and its populace, be it the English, Portuguese, Spanish, Dutch or the French. The Europeans used spices as a food preservative as well as a flavour enhancer of the processed foods, but spices' most important function for them was to keep their body temperature warm. For a Westerner, who stays most of his days in the cold climate, spices are a must for him to keep himself warm. As part of their international trade, the Indonesians used boats, called *perahu bercadik,* to ferry their products. Their products first came to India and from there they were directed to different destinations in Europe. And Kolkata (Calcutta) was a favoured Indian destination for the Indonesians. So, the producer–distributor–consumer pattern of trade was prevailed among Indonesia as the producer, India as the distributor and the Europe as the consumer in spice trade. On the other hand, there was a reciprocal to this, i.e. the reverse trade flow. Along with many other products, the Indian *sāṛī* fabric was a highly sought-after product in Indonesia.

With such regular and high-value trade relationship, there was a regular inflow of religio-cultural essence from India to Indonesia through the men involved in trade. This has influenced significantly the thought-pattern and the cultural affinities of the people in both the countries.

**Construction Arguments**

These relationships, of late, took clear-cut forms in culture, art and architecture. While deliberating on all these aspects, this paper will delve deep into how India's religions got deployed in Indonesia, and how they grew and widely spread across the country, until the onset of Islam. India contributed significantly in changing the ancient Indonesian civilization to a civilization based on the beliefs of a known religion. Before their contact with Hinduism, the Indonesian people lived in traditional beliefs such as respect for ancestral spirits, the forces of the universe and certain objects (animism and dynamism). Influence of Hinduism made Indonesian people began to worship the gods and goddesses that were similar to those in India. Not only Hinduism, Buddhism also made inroads into Indonesia through the Indian people.

Buddhists in Indonesia (also Thailand, Cambodia, Vietnam, Myanmar, Laos) follow Hīnayāna Buddhism, whereas Mahāyāna is more accepted in China, Korea, Taiwan and Japan. The development of early Buddhism in Indonesia is evidenced by the findings of the Buddhist inscriptions, belonging to second century CE in Sikendeng, South Sulawesi. Another example is the kingdom of Srivijaya that existed in the sixth century CE in Sumatra. Buddhism's rapid development in South-East Asia in the early centuries of CE was mainly due to the political factors.

When Buddhism reached its golden age in Asia, particularly in India and China, many kings and monarchs made Buddhism as their official religion. However, Buddhism lost its glory when a number of Buddhist kingdoms experienced their downfall. Instead, Hinduism became the official religion of the kingdoms where this downfall took place.

Though Hinduism and Buddhism could make strong inroads into Indonesia, Hinduism got prominence in many ways. Many of the kings were practising Hindus, thus the whole kingdom got an image of a Hindu state, though there were sizeable Buddhists among them. But the most striking fact is that there was a syncretic religion, which was a fusion of Hindu Śaivism and Buddhism. Śaiva–Buddhist religion began to grow rapidly during the reign of the Singasari rulers in east Java to the civilization of the kingdom in Bali. During this period the Javanese created works of art and architecture where the Java elements were more prominent than the India elements; this is a form of assimilation that took place during the period. When it comes to the theological front, Hindus absorb local culture in presenting the concept of god, especially in arts and architecture. Given the central tenet of Hinduism — philosophy, ethics and rituals as the basic framework of the Hindu religion — the first two are based and developed on the precincts of scriptures, i.e. the Vedas. Whereas the third factor, i.e. ritual, is flexible and incorporates the local, indigenous traditions. Therefore, we find some differences in the practices of Hindus in India and Indonesia, when it comes to rituals. Similarly, among the Hindu community, there are area-wise differences in conducting rituals. This is one reason why we consider Hinduism as a flexible religion. Following the writings in the books "where we step on the earth, there we must honour the sky", Singasari kings like Kertanegara and Wisnuwardhana, adherents of the new religion, built up temples.

Keeping in mind the fact that art becomes an icon in the spread of the religion, the rulers promoted arts and architecture in many ways and the last in the artistic heritage was puppetry. Wayang, a classical Javanese puppet drama (*fig.* 12.1), is an Indonesian cultural heritages recognized by UNESCO in 2003. Puppet as "Masterpieces of World Culture" UNESCO recognized not just puppets of Java, but the Indonesian Wayang puppets which include Balinese, Sundanese puppet show, puppet Lombok and others. The stories played are about gods, romance and heroism, especially stories from Indian epics, *Mahābhārata* and *Rāmāyaṇa*.

In temple building, there is a lot of similarity between India and Indonesia in terms of site selection, structure and form. Even though there are architectural affinities, the presentation of deities has a local influence in Indonesia. However, these similarities do not repeat in

*fig*. 12.1: Indonesian Wayang

matters like worship. In India, temples are believed as the abode of gods and goddesses and they are primarily the places of worship or in other words, they are *devagṛhas*. However, there is a difference in the usage of temples in Indonesia. Indonesian temples are more used as the places for ancestor worship or as a burial place; in other words, they are places used for *ātmapratiṣṭhā*. *Fig*. 12.2 shows the spread of temples across Indonesia. *Fig*. 12.3 depicts a typical temple structure in Indonesia.

The process and time of the entry of Hinduism and Buddhism to Indonesia are still a debatable topic among historians. There are at

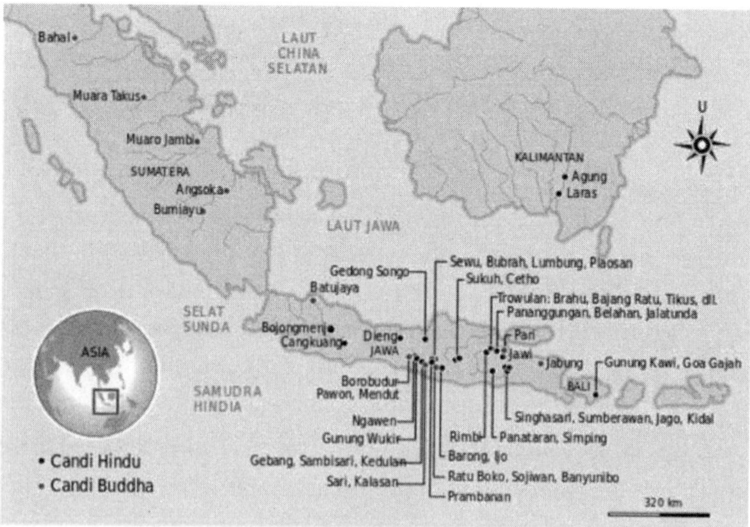


*fig.* 12.2: The spread of temples in Indonesia

*fig.* 12.3: One of Indonesian temples

least four opinions, each of which is actually re-enforcing. The following are the opinions about the entry of Hinduism and Buddhism to Indonesia.

1. **Brāhmaṇa Theory:** It says that the ownership of bringing Hinduism to Indonesia belongs to brāhmaṇas. The brāhmaṇas who came to Indonesia were invitees of the kings of the traditional religious practices in Indonesia. When they arrived in Indonesia, they became catalysts in spreading Hinduism there. Van Leur is one of such scientists who believe in this theory.
2. **Vaiśya Theory:** According to this theory, Hinduism was brought to Indonesia by vaiśyas, especially the traders. Many traders had exercised a strong relationship with the kings who were the rulers of the archipelago. Their regular visits and long staying in Indonesia gradually influenced the local people and the rulers alike. They were keen in keeping the local people and the native rulers happy for the smooth working of their business and gave them gifts, which were mostly in the form of foreign commodities. This situation paved the way for the penetration of Hindu faith into the Indonesian archipelago. N.J. Chrome is the propagator of this theory.
3. **Theory of the Knights:** This theory advocates that the arrival of Hinduism in Indonesia was heralded by the knights, namely the nobility and warriors. According to this theory, Indian knights arrived in Indonesia mainly due to two developments. One, knights shifted their base because of the political developments in India. Two, those knights who were defeated in wars took asylum in Indonesia. Scientists who advocate this theory are C.C. Berg and Mookerji.
4. **Reverse Flow Theory:** This theory stipulates that those who were instrumental in spreading Hinduism in Indonesia are the Indonesian people themselves. These are people who had been to India to study Hinduism and Buddhism. In their travelling across India, they found an organization called *saṅgha*. Once back in Indonesia, they eventually adopted the tradition they got used to while in India. This has resulted in the migration of Indian religions to Indonesia. This opinion is due to F.D.K. Bosch.

The arrival of brāhmaṇas from India happened at the behest of many local groups or indigenous merchant chiefs who wanted to highlight their social status and position in the society by engaging brāhmaṇas in their religious rites. With the approval and blessings of the brāhmaṇas, they crowned the political rulers (kings). The rulers also liked such developments because the new religious order gave them a new status of god-king (*deva-rāja*) so that they could exercise more power in the society. This new status made them more respectable among all sections of the society and they could build up a strong army for their safety and the expansion of their territory. Monarchy thus became more powerful and confident as the kings enjoyed more internal security and a centralized power system.

This in a way resulted in the establishment of an empire state, where the feudal system enjoyed terrific validity and status. Feudalism per se is a "social or political system that gives greater power to the nobility" (KBBI 2002). Thus, the king had to determine the direction in which the kingdom would roll on. The practice of feudalism was quite developed in the kingdoms of the Hindus and Buddhists, particularly in Java. The society, who are based on feudalistic *kasta* made their relationship (in group) stronger. Feudalism guaranteed the political stability necessary for the survival of a ruler's kingdom.

Actually there is no caste system among Hindus. It is very clear from the book Pañcam Veda, *Bhagavad-Gītā*. The society is divided into four groups based on the division of labour — its skill sets and expertise. It should not cause segmentations that are rigid. But the nature of this teaching is flexible, people can easily switch from one profile to the other. While caste is a political product, just to keep the descendants of the Arya in the highest stratum.

The caste system divides people into four categories such as:

1. Brāhmaṇas who acted as chaplains and religious educators.
2. Kṣatriyas. Knights who formed the monarchy, ruled the society and defended their country (the king, the king's servants, soldiers) belonged to this group.
3. Vaiśya who acted as merchants, craftsmen, farmers, fishermen and performers.
4. Śūdra, who belonged to the category of unskilled workers, labourers, slaves, servants and so on.

However, one has to note that in the Buddhist kingdoms, *pengkastaan* did not play because Buddhism does not recognize and approve the caste system. Therefore, the Buddhist society is more democratic and egalitarian in structure. Thus, the more developed feudal system in the Hindu kingdoms functioned normally in a particular pattern. In determining important policies, the king was assisted by the head priest (pastor) and a group of brāhmaṇas as the king's spiritual and policy advisors. They were a group of people who knew the content of scriptures, which are written in Sanskrit. As a result, the general public could not understand the contents of the scriptures without the interpretation of brāhmaṇas, who were adept in them. Brāhmaṇas had the absolute right to organize a religious ceremony, such as fixation of holy days, the coronation of the king, the inauguration of plaques or inscriptions, or blessing the marriages of the nobility. They also pioneered in developing schools and dormitories in the Buddhist community. Their position can be compared to the powers and responsibilities of clerics and scholars of the present time.

Over a period of time, the Hindu–Buddhist civilization of Indonesia was ousted and replaced by Muslim civilization of the Middle East. However, Islam got into Indonesia through India, by the trading activities especially from Gujarat as the transit point (Turkey–India–Indonesia) at that time. Now Indonesia, in spite of the largest Muslim population among all countries in the world, still keeps up some of the ancient cultural practices in the day-to-day life of the people.

## Conclusion

In this chapter, I have tried to outline India's influence on Indonesian culture and civilization in the historic period. With India's influence, Indonesia got two organized religions — Hinduism and Buddhism. These religions replaced the old religious faiths of Indonesia and a large number of temples were erected across Indonesia with the patronage of the local rulers. Though those temples were akin in structure and architect to Indian temples, they had imbibed the local perceptions in sculpturing the deities. Also the purposes of Indian and Indonesian temples varied.

We have also dealt with another point that an Indonesian is

basically a friendly person who believes in long-lasting relationship. This character basically leads to an exchange of civilization. This enables us to absorb good things from others, of course, not blindly. One has to apply logic to what he is absorbing and understand why it is done. We have to filter many a value that come across us.

We should take the good, and prune whatever is not needed for our national culture and interest. Keeping our local and national interests in tact, we should think global and transmit our values for the benefit of others too. We should equip ourselves to live in the world, facing the new challenges that crop up with the developments in science and culture. The limits of space and time are no more existent. All can be connected easily and quickly. So what is the foundation of our national identity? Here is the answer: the genius of local traditions and culture, and local wisdom. We still come across terms like globalization, modernization, but not necessarily lost in the storm. We have to make our own culture as a permanent identity, distinguish it from the rest, and make it competitive. We have to filter the outcomes that globalization throws at us and absorb things that are compatible with our local culture, according to the needs of our nation. I believe that Eastern countries are capable to compete with the West if we practise all these points in life.

**References**

Hindu Association, "Hindu Religious History". http://www.parisada.org/index.php?option=com_content&task=view&id=37&Itemid=29 (accessed on 24 November 2012)

Siswoyo, Agus, "History of Hinduism Spread to Indonesia". http://agussiswoyo.net/sosial-budaya/5-teori-cara-penyebaran-agama-hindu-dan-buddha-di-indonesia/ (accessed on 24 November 2012)

726.143 Ari p Ariswara Prambanan/Ariswara; english translation by Lenah Matius Ed. 4 Jakarta Intermasa 1994 56 hlm. 10077/PN/96 [1] Matius, Lenah Prambanan (candi).

726.143 Dim c Dimarcan, Jaques Candi Sewu dan arsitektur bangunan agama Budha di Jawa Tengah/Jaques Dumarcay; diterjemahkan kedalam bahasa Indonesia oleh Winarsih Arifin dan Henry Chambert-Loir Cet. 1 Jakarta Proyek Penelitian Purbakala, Departemen Pendidikan dan Kebudayaan 1986 xx, 148 hlm. 7787/PN/96 (1) Arifin, Winarsih.

# 13

# "Interculturality" in South Asia
## With Special Reference to Dissemination of Rāmakatha

*Avadhesh Kumar Singh*

### South Asia Studies

SOUTH Asia is now an established category as an area study with support and acceptance by American academia in particular.[1] It is a geographical category like India. It refers to many sovereign states of

1 I have my reservations against the category South Asia, as it is less naturally formed and more imposed by the academic hegemony of the US.

Let me hasten to add that I have been extremely sceptical to the category called "area studies", as it is primarily a Pentagon category that came into existence in the post-Second World War period. Toby Valkman who was a Ford Foundation Program Officer has brought it out in her pamphlet published in 1999. Area studies were considered indispensable for American interests. The US wanted to control the world after the Second World War by dividing it into knowable categories because knowing is controlling and having too, in the end. The office of Secretary of State had departments after these areas, and accordingly the funding for research projects in area studies in universities was provided. However, it was later realized that areas like the South-East Asia, West Asia, Middle East, among others, were not self-contained, as was assumed. Hence they were followed by intercultural studies and multiculturalism. It is necessary to know the inherent politics and economics of areas so that the area studies in India can move in a meaningful direction of dialogue among cultures. Only then we who subscribe to the notion of the entire world as a family (*vasudhaivakuṭumbakam*) would contribute to the area of intercultural studies, and give a positive dimension to area studies. →

diverse demographical and geographical measures like Bangladesh, Bhutan, India, the Maldives, Nepal, Pakistan, and Sri Lanka, and even Myanmar (which known earlier as Brahmadeśa or Burma) like so many provinces of British India till 1935 (Bose and Jalal 1999: 3).

South Asia has been a site of civilizational, religious, intellectual and cultural confluences in different periods, marked by interlinguality, interliterariness and interculturality. Since cultural and geographical contiguities are not handcuffed to categories, South Asia does not get limited by the political boundaries or passports to me. Intercultural relations are more porous than they are thought, hence I use the term South Asia for region that is known as South and South-East Asia that due to trades, travellers, religious movements among others became a sphere of circulation of cultural ideas during the period of Sanskrit cosmopolis and continues to be so even now to a good measure. This paper would discuss salient issues pertaining to intercularality which I prefer to interculturalism, for interculturality is a state of mind and the latter a restrictive "ism" to which a true culture never adheres.[2]

---

← Admittedly, South Asia is a neutral category which suited the post-Second World War US strategy of dividing the world in knowable areas in order to understand, know and control the world. It was more than a mere coincidence that the Pentagon areas and area studies followed the same trajectory and support — financial and academic by the US institutions. Though South Asia has been accepted now as a category in the academic world, the fact is that it amounts to Indian subcontinent or what is known as the SAARC countries. Hence the superimposition of a new category like South Asia on Indian subcontinent or SAARC appears to be a ploy to deny India any centrality to India or categories that centralize it even symbolically. Moreover, the term India, to go by the Greek usage for the land of people inhabiting beyond the Indus River, is at least 3,500 years old, against the term South Asia which is about six decades old.

[2] I prefer the terms interlinguality and interculturality to interlingualism and interculturalism, for the latter stand for "isms" whereas they are cultural states, rather than fixed "schools" or approach. Also interculturality is different from multiculturalism, for multiculturalism accepts the existence of other cultures but sees them vertically situated without interaction among them. In practice too, multiculturalism →

**Contactuality**

Interculturality is a consequence of "contactuality", to use a term of comparative literature by various agencies, institutions and individuals. Human history informs us that the movement of humanity (individual or collective) due to natural (droughts, famines), religious (discrimination, persecution), political (war, partitions, exile due non-subscription to ideologies), economic (business, employment) have led to construction to major political discourses, e.g. diaspora discourse, identity discourse, war/partition discourse, regional/community/identity discourse. It is no surprise that travel has been one of the most important means of contactuality and has contributed to all major discourses. It would be no exaggeration to say that travel is among the governing principles of human existence.

Travel permeates all spheres of life. Life without travel gathers moss and becomes a corpse. The sages and seers of the Upaniṣads have realized it and underscored its significance when they pronounced:

> *caraṇbai madhu vindati caraṇtsvādu mudambram* ।
> *sūrsya pāśya śrīmān yo na tandrāyate caraṇa* ।
> *caraiveti caraiveti* । — *Aitareya Upaniṣad*
>
> The honey bee, by its motion gathers honey, and birds enjoy succulent fruits by constant movement. The sun is revered by virtue of its constant shining movement. Therefore one should be constantly in motion. Keep moving; Keep moving on.

Travel permeates the universe. Human existence in moon is travel. Travel sums up the essence of human existence. Travelling is seeing. Life is a present continuous tense. When "life" which is a noun becomes verb, travel discourse comes in existence, as the new definition of home begins with its quest. In terms of civilizational paradigms in terms of human history, even at the risk of being reductionist, the following stages may be considered:

1. "I am because I exist and think about existence." (Meta/physical discourse)

---

← remains a slogan, for in it the entire discourse takes place in a state of linguistic/cultural hegemony, as it is dominated by English.

2. "I am because I believe." (Theological discourse)
3. "I am because I think." (Modernist discourse)
4. "I am because I revolt." ["I revolt; therefore we are." (Albert Camus)] (Existential discourse, non-Sartrean)
5. "I am because/what I consume." (Post-modernist discourse)
6. "I am where I think not." (Neo-psychological Lacanian discourse)
7. "For we are where we are not." (Pierre-Jean Jouve, *Lyrique*, p. 59.) It is true because only after leaving a place or a home or a set of people, the true worth of things and people is realized. Similarly, only the absence reveals the worth of presence of what is absent now
8. "I am because I travel." It might be worded differently, "I travel therefore I am."

The space constraints do not permit elaboration of these paradigmatic pronouncements here. However, it deserves to be stated that the last is the overarching paradigmatic statement covering all periods and discourses. Whenever a small-or large-scale movement of human beings has taken place for various reasons — natural, political, religious, economic or cultural — for a short or long period, willingly or otherwise, individually or collectively, a rich body of knowledge discourse has come into existence along with discourses. These discourses have given new directions to human civilization in different parts and periods.

A traveller does not create the world that s/he travels. Rather s/he lives the way s/he travels. Or s/he creates a new world within the world s/he travels or sees it. Travelling and seeing are integral. The difference between the seeing of a traveller and a tourist is that a traveller sees what the new world offers her/him, and a tourist sees what s/he wants or had already decided. Touring is a choice but travelling is a compulsion. Therefore, two different kinds of seeing are involved in them. Travellers see beyond what is visible to the naked eye, whereas a tourist may remain trapped in surfaces. A traveller sees, sees being seen, and sees her/his seeing being seen by others. A traveller is wherever s/he is. S/he erases the difference between self and other. On the other hand, a tourist maintains the binaries, as s/he has to return home, sooner or a little later. Travelling and seeing are the means of knowing. Buddha, a rapacious traveller that he was, ended his discourses with the words, *jñānmi ca, paśyāmi ca* (I know, and I see too).

I'll try to explain interculturality in South Asia by focusing on a traveller (Ibn Battuta) and circulation of the narrative of Rāmakathā (*Rāmāyaṇa*).

## II

Travel, trade, translation and circulation of cultural texts are interrelated activities. Takṣaśilā, one of the earliest established centres of learning, was at the confluence of Uttarpatha, Dakṣiṇāpatha and the Silk Route. Pāli was the language used by Buddha but he knew Sanskrit, and had no problems with translation, unlike many monotheistic religious sects that considered it profane. Buddhism travelled within India and out of India in Sanskrit which was the language of learned composition, and thus found new homes for it. Travellers like Megasthenese, Al-Beruni, Ibn Battuta, the Bhakti movement poets and sūfīs, and a host of Europeans travelled across for trade and colonization (exploitation of resources — natural, human, economic and intellectual), and subsequent struggles for freedom from colonial yoke contributed to travel discourses. In a way all of them represented human spirit for new lands, people and their culture that went into making their homes. Travel as a means of cultural voyeurism was a means of peeping into other homes and refashion their own in the process.

All travellers in different parts of the world chose homelessness as their fate. Some of the traces of their fated lives went into making of travel discourse.

Ibn Battuta (25 February 1304-68 or 1369), who was Petrarch's[3] contemporary, travelled about 75,000 km in the fourteenth century. Known for his travels — published in the *Rihlā* (Journey) — he is considered one among the great travellers of all time.

He left for India and arrived at the Indus River on 12 September 1333. He said:

---

[3] Francesco Petrarca is his Italian name.

> I set out alone, finding no companion to cheer the way with friendly intercourse, and no party of travellers with whom to associate myself. Swayed by an overmastering impulse within me, and a long-cherished desire to visit those glorious sanctuaries, I resolved to quit all my friends and tear myself away from my home. As my parents were still alive, it weighed grievously upon me to part from them, and both they and I were afflicted with sorrow. — Gibb 1929: 43

After spending another year in Mecca, Ibn Battuta decided to seek employment with Muhammad-bin-Tughluq, the Sultan of Delhi. In 1330 (or 1332), in need of a guide and a translator for his journey, he set off for the Seljuk-controlled territory of Anatolia to join one of the caravans that went from there to India.

Tughluq was a patron of various scholars, and sūfīs, and other functionaries. On the strength of his years of study in Mecca, he was appointed as a *qādī* or qaẓī (judge) by the sultan. He found it difficult to enforce Islamic laws beyond the sultan's court in Delhi (Bently 1993: 121) In the Sultanate of Delhi, Ibn Battuta swerved between living the high-profile life of a trusted subordinate and falling under suspicion of treason for a variety of offences. His plan to leave on the pretext of taking another *haj* was stymied by the sultan, who asked him instead to become his ambassador to Yuan Dynasty China. The traveller in him willed to visit new lands that saw in it an opportunity to get away from the sultan, he enthusiastically consented to the proposal.

During his travel to China, Ibn Battuta and his party were attacked by a group of bandits (http://en.wikipedia.org/wiki/Ibn_Battuta - cite_note-44). He was robbed and nearly lost his life (Dunn 2005: 215). Despite all hindrances, he continued on to Khambat (earlier known as Cambay) in the present Gujarat and later sailed to Kozhikode (Calicut). He did not return to Delhi as he was seen as a failure, and stayed for a while in south India under the protection of Jamal-ud-Din, ruler of the small but powerful Nawayath Sultanate on the banks of the Śaravathī River next to the Arabian Sea, known as Hosapattana of the northern Karnataka. Since this sultanate was soon overthrown, Ibn Battuta had to leave India. Determined to continue his journey to China, he first took a detour to visit the Maldive Island, and spent nine months on the islands as the chief *qādī*. He worked his way back to the Madurai kingdom in India in the court of the short-lived Madurai Sultanate under Ghiyas-ud-Din Muhammad Damghani, from where he returned to the Maldives and boarded a Chinese junk, still intending to reach China and take up his ambassadorial post.

He reached the port of Chittagong in Bangladesh intending to travel to Sylhet to meet Shah Jalal, who became so renowned that Ibn Battuta, then in Chittagong, made a one-month journey through the mountains of Kamaru near Sylhet to meet him. On his way to Sylhet, Ibn Battuta was greeted by several of Shah Jalal's disciples who had come to assist him on his journey many days before he had arrived. At the meeting in 1345, Ibn Battuta noted that Shah Jalal was tall and lean, fair in complexion and lived by the mosque in a cave, where his only possession was a goat he kept for milk, butter and yogurt. He observed that the companions of Shah Jalal were foreigners and known for their strength and bravery. He also mentions that many people used to visit Shah Jalal to seek guidance. Ibn Battuta went further north to Assam, then returned to continue with his original plan.

After returning to Quanzhou in 1346, Ibn Battuta began his journey back to Morocco (Dunn 2005: 261). In Kozhikode, he once again considered throwing himself at the mercy of Muhammad-bin-Tughluq, but thought better of it and decided to carry on to Mecca and went to Granada through Valencia. Thus, his travels became a cartography of his time and the regions in which he journeyed in South Asia and beyond. The route of Ibn Battuta is an exercise of cultural mapping of South Asia before the category was even imagined.

## III

Before considering the circulation of Rāmakathā in South Asia, let me briefly discuss movements in the region which were consequences of contactuality facilitated by various eco-socio-political factors that created intercultural space in the region.

Different periods witnessed emergence and descent of different movements in the region that might be seen in the following manner.

### Stage I: The Sanskrit Empire

It was a period what Sheldon Pollock called Sanskrit Cosmopolis, as the influence of Sanskrit as the language of learned composition, and also of communication extended from the Central Asia to South and South-East Asia, and continues to hold its influence even now.

## Stage II: The Buddhist Religious/Cultural Empire in South Asia

Buddha ushered a new logic of love, truth and compassion in the natural language of people, i.e. Pāli. The Sanskrit empire in a major way was jolted by questioning by Lord Buddha who for the first time used Pāli as the language of communication with his followers, though later on Sanskrit was used for composition and preservation of Buddhist discourses. Along with trade, Buddhism moved along with the Silk Route and extended to Afghanistan, Tibet, China, Korea and Japan. It had earlier taken the eastern and southern direction, as it spread to Burma, Vietnam, Combodia and Sri Lanka among others.[4]

## Stage III: The Bhakti Movement

The movement was marked by advent of Sūfism paralleled by the logic of sword from the Western frontiers of India, and the Bhakti movement that had started much earlier in south India by saints and *ācāryas* with a few attempts of synthesis of religions in the form of the *Deen-e-Ilahi* of Akbar.[5] With the advent of Sūfism and invaders, Sanskrit and Prākr̥ts were joined by Arabic and Persian and later by Turkish which was the language of the Mughals. Amir Khusaro came from Turkey and settled in Delhi which has been a witness to many emperors and kingdoms. Its ruinscape tells volumes about its history. But the protector of Delhi is Hazart Nizamuddin Aulia, a sūfī saint who was the teacher of Amir Khusaro. When Nizamuddin Aulia died in Delhi, Khusaro was shattered and composed the following couplet:

> *gorī soye sez̧ par, sar par ḍāre keśa* ।
> *chal khusaro ghar āpne, sānz bhai chahu deśa* ॥

In the couplet, the supreme authority or spiritual *guru* becomes the beloved (*gorī*) which is not possible in the mainstream Turkish tradition. Khusaro's poetic sensibility is not shaped by his Turkish

---

4 For discussion please see Avadhesh Kumar Singh (2014).

5 For a discussion of *bhakti*, its origin, expansion and influence, please see Avadhesh Kumar Singh (2008).

ancestry but by the Brij cultural landscape that he lived and cherished. The term *gorī* is Brij, and is alien to Turkish culture. He synthesized the Persian and Hindavī/Brij traditions in the same song with one line in Persian and the other by Hindavī/Brij.

The Sūfism came as a fresh whiff of air for stifling stratified Indian society. Bulle Shah, Shah Hussain, Guru Nanak, Lal Dêd in the northern, and Narsī and Nāmdev in the western Indian region, Āṇḍāl, Akkā Mahādevī and saints and *ācārya*s in the south, Caitanya Mahāprabhu and Śaṅkaradeva in the eastern parts of India, Kabīr, Mīrā, Tulsīdās, Sūrdās, Raidās, Malik Mohammad Jāyasī among others in the central and northern India contributed to it. The movement from the western Asia to other parts of India was accentuated by the Bhakti movement that took the entire Indian subcontinent in its fold and beyond.

The influence of *bhakti* poets did not remain confined to land or region in which they had physically moved. The charm of Kabīr's ideas went beyond the Hindi heartland to different parts of India up to Gujarat and is cherished still in Pakistan. The movement lent a new dimension to interculturality in Indian and South Asian region. With the decline of the Mughal Empire in the nineteenth century, Bahadur Shah Zafar, the last Mughal emperor, was interned in Rangoon (Burma, now Myanmar) due to colonial connections. Though his last wish remained unrealized, it became one of the earliest manifestations of death in diasporic due to colonial compulsions.

*itnā thā badnasīb ki dafn ke liye,*
*do gaẓ ẓamīṅ nā mil sakī kuc-e-yār meiṅ* ।

### Stage IV: The Colonial Interaction: Confluence or Clash of Knowledge Civilizations

Colonization that pervaded India and South Asia in the nineteenth century provided a cultural linkage of connections in South Asia. It was an encounter of knowledge civilizations. To say that there was no clash of civilizations would amount to glossing over the eco-socio-political and cultural realities of colonization; and to state that there was only clash would also be untrue. The fact is that colonization as a trope for exploitation of human, natural, economic and intellectual resources of the region in South Asia connected the geo-political entities and their predicaments together.[6] Also it brought a new cluster of European languages like English, French and German among others to the region, adding to the linguistic scenario, and changing the linguistic hierarchies as well.

With the colonization, English joined the fray in the eighteenth century, and being the language of master, it enjoyed social prestige as the language of administration and communication. It brought with it a new world of literature, a new stage and poetics to consider, compare and measure literary works with William Shakespeare as the crown of poetic and dramatic achievement. The same period saw the reception of the classical Sanskrit works, e.g. Kālidāsa's *Abhijñāna-Śākuntalam*, *Gītā*, Vedas and Upaniṣads, *Rāmāyaṇa*, *Mahābhārata*, *Manu-Smṛti*, among others to name a few. It is a different story that when the West raved about them, they were being driven out from Indian academic world. The entire South Asia went through as a series of changes with varying degrees.

The colonization systematically de-systematized judicial, bureaucratic/revenue, educational and religious institutions, depending on their convenience.

**Stage V: The Post-Colonial Post/Modernism (in the South Asia)**

Interlinguality is discernible in linguistic density in the South Asia in which languages change after every 4 *kos* (1 *kos* is equal to 3 km). The layers of languages are sedimented in the regions.

Initially the region witnessed the supremacy of Sanskrit which was a language of learned discourse and composition. It coexisted with Prākṛts or natural languages.

With travellers, traders and translators its influence extended from West Asia to South Asia which Sheldon Pollock terms as Sanskrit Cosmopolis.

It lost its centrality by the eleventh century, as it was replaced by *lokbhāṣā*s. The Bhakti movement democratized knowledge by making learned, abstract, abstruse, complex, Śāstric/scriptural knowledge contained in the "sacred" texts and discourse available in the languages

---

6 For the discussion of colonization and its impact in India in particular, please see Avadhesh Kumar Singh (2012).

of the people. Consequently, the discursive practices and institutions — social, political, religious and cultural — were beyond the access of the common people.

The region was the site of the earliest literary compositions in the form of Vedic discourses and epics like *Rāmāyaṇa*, *Mahābhārata* and *Śilapadikāram*. The region received the best from all parts of the world, and gave it their own orientation. For instance, it received new languages in its ambit like Arabic, Persian, Turkish with the Moghals.

The institution of democracy tried to have moorings in the South Asian societies. With it, secularism became the principle of democracy. Democracy and secularism have been modelled in their own way in different countries. The reasons are not far to find. The monotheistic societies chose different political systems and experimented with democracy too. In a society like India, secularism attained different connotation. It did not mean absolute abandoning of one's own faith and religion but to be rooted in one's own with equal respect. Mahatma Gandhi defined it thus:

> The State is bound to be wholly secular. . . . All subjects will thus be equal in the eyes of the law. But every single individual will be free to pursue a religion without let or hindrance so long as it does not transgress the common law. — *Harijan*, 31-8-1947, p. 297

He further added:

> The key to the solution of [communal] tangle lies in everyone following the best in his own religion and entertaining equal regard for the other religions and their followers.
>
> — *Harijan*, 4-1-1948, p. 497

It would be congruous for me to note that Gandhi did not consider nationalism to be an evil, as did Tagore.

> Nationalism is greater than sectarianism. And that sense, we are Indians first and Hindus, Mussalmaans, Parsis and Christians after.
>
> — *Young India*, 26-1-1922, p. 62

To others, it may appear an apologetic secularism or secularism that is attended by an adjective or a "disclaimer" of one sort or another, in practice at least in India. The basic reason for bringing in the discussion of nationalism is that nationalism of Sri Aurobindo or Gandhi does not limit itself to India but in consonance with true Indian ideals attains cosmopolitan connotations.

Incidentally, languages came to be associated with castes or communities. Sanskrit with brāhmaṇas, Urdu with Muslims, Hindi with Hindus, Gujarati with Gujaratis, Marathi with Maharashtrians, Tamil with people of Tamil Nadu and so on. The fact, however, such associations were multilayered and intersectioned in many ways than defy the present national boundaries and definitions. However, these languages and their literatures were not insulated and compartmentalized along the boundaries of states or nations. The intercultural and interliterary multilayered horizontality defies religious and geographical configurations in South Asia in different ways, presenting it as a more complex site of different "altermodernities". Post-modernism tried to replace the grand narrative with little narratives. But the project had its location elsewhere because at least in South Asia little narratives were always ever present, though not recognized or venerated as the grand narratives were. The grand epics like *Rāmāyaṇa*, *Mahābhārata* and *Śilapadikāram* were clusters of little narratives, and traces of other versions too waiting to be told or told on the margins after post-modernist consciousness.[7]

## III

As a metonymic text, *Rāmāyaṇa* branched out in different forms of literature and various art forms, and its tradition in varied versions proliferated within and beyond India. Like *Rāmāyaṇa*, the multimedia text of *Mahābhārata* had it in the form of *Rāmopākhyāna* within the Sanātana Dharma tradition.[8] Buddhism that branched out of the Sanātana Dharma tradition wove its version in the form of *Daśaratha*

---

[7] Here I am using the term post-colonial for the state of mind or consciousness when the colonial ways are understood and the colonized begins to resist them. Since the external colonization and its agencies are physically absent, the attention is diverted to internal colonization which was discussed and resisted in the colonial period but not discussed in an upfront manner.

[8] For a discussion of *Ramopākhyāna* in *Mahābhārata*, see Avadhesh Kumar Singh (2006: 32-38).

*Jātaka* with Rāma as *bodhisattva* in the pre-Christian era — its versions with Rāma as a martial hero into a spiritual protagonist. Jainism constructed its own version of *Rāmāyaṇa* in the form of Jaina monk Vimalasūri's *Paumacarīya* in which Rāma appeared as one of the 63 *śalākāpuruṣas*. He, like a practising devout Jaina, was a believer in non-violence. Accordingly he performed no sacrifice involving killing of animals. It is not Rāma but Lakṣmaṇa who kills Rāvaṇa in the end. Hemcandra Sūri who wrote the grammar of Prākr̥t in the twelfth century composed *Jaina Rāmāyaṇa,* followed by another Jaina version by *Rāmacandracarita Purāṇa* of Nāgacandra. By the Bhakti period, different versions of Rāmakathās were available in the native traditions — Budhhist, Jaina and Purāṇic traditions among others. The Muslim rulers contributed to it in different parts of the country including Bengal, to take a case from D.C. Sen:

> The Pathans occupied Bengal early in the thirteenth century. . . . The Pathan emperors learned Bengali and lived in close touch with the teeming Hindu population. . . . The emperors heard of the far-reaching fame of the Sanskrit epics, *Rāmāyaṇa* and *Mahābhārata,* and observed the wonderful influence they exercised in moulding the religious and domestic lives of the Hindus, and they naturally felt the desire to be acquainted with the contents of those poems. . . . They appointed scholars to translate the works into Bengali which they now spoke and understood. The first Bengali translation of *Mahābhārata* of which we hear was undertaken at the order of Nasira Saha, the emperor of Gauḍa [in Bengali] who ruled for 40 years till CE 1325. . . . The name of the emperor of Gauḍa who appointed Kr̥ttivāsa to translate *Rāmāyaṇa* is not known with certainty. He might be Rājā-Kaṁsanārāyaṇa or a Moslem emperor, but even if he was a Hindu king, there are abundant proofs to show that his court was stamped with Muslim influence. — Sen, 1999: 11-12

With the establishment of the Mughal dynasty of rulers in northern India by sixteenth century, the linguistic scenario changed in India. Since the Mughals were Turkish, so Turkish was added to the existing plethora of languages. Babur, who established the empire after the conquest of Delhi in 1526 wrote *Baburnāmā* which was translated into Persian and later in other languages including English. Since Persian Sūfism had already found many followers in India, it (Persian) shared many features with the Bhakti movement in India. Persian found a place of eminence as a new language which was followed by Arabic, a language of religion of the rulers. Akbar's *Deen-e-Ilahi* which was a synthesis of different religions, e.g. Islam, Hinduism, Jainism, Christianity and Zoroastrianism among others saw translation as a mode of bridge building among different denominations. Akbar, the Great, ordered Vālmīki's *Rāmāyaṇa* to be translated into Persian along with other Sanskrit classics. Mullah Abdul Qadir Badayuni reluctantly translated it under royal pressure into Persian, the language of the elite and court during the Mughal period. Mullah Badayuni showed initial hesitation when he was asked to translate Vālmīki's *Rāmāyaṇa*, for it was not acceptable to the Mullah from monotheistic religion. Yet he had to do a part of it unwillingly. It is not a compilation of Islamic knowledge on Hinduism. It was how a scholar and politically powerful person as a victor would receive the plethora of Hindu knowledge, and its world. He had himself suggested it in the beginning:

> *nānāpurānanigamāgamasammatam yat*
> *rāmāyaṇe nigaditam kvacitoanyatopi* ।
> *svāntaḥsukhāya tulsī raghunāthagāthā*
> *bhāṣānibandhamatimañjulamatanoti* ॥
> — Tulsīdās's *Rāmacaritamānasa*, Bālakāṇḍa, *śloka* 7

> Whatever is supported by different Purāṇas, Vedas and Śāstras and is described in the *Rāmāyaṇa*, and what I learnt from others (sources, traditions and texts pertaining to various versions of Rāmakathā) I extend it in an extremely sweet language for the satisfaction of my own self.

Tulsīdās's *śloka* is significant for understanding the tradition, its reception, internalization and modification, and also the tradition of translation. Tulsīdās was composing the *Rāmacaritamānasa* in a period of transition from oral to written and from Sanskrit to *lokbhāṣās*, Awadhī to be precise in the case of Tulsī. His acceptance of the accordance to Śāstras was not unnatural in his case because of the choice of the theme made by him for the epic and the class he came from. Moreover, within the Brāhmanical structure, he belonged to the priestly class which has its own compulsions to maintain the sanctity of the Śāstras. He accepted the centrality of *Rāmāyaṇa* in Rāmakathā tradition, and acknowledged it. But along with it, the term *kvacidoanyatoapi* refers to a large number of texts that the oral tradition would have contributed to his creativity. In Indian tradition, *bahuśruta* (much-heard) is privileged over "well-read". Tulsīdās was *bahuśruta,* and he used what he received in his compositions. The critics and scholars have studied and proved that there are traces of at least 72 texts in *Rāmāyaṇa.*[9]

---

[9] Mandakrata Bose, editor of *The Rāmāyaṇa Revisited* (2004) has studied transformation of *Rāmāyaṇa* in terms of its "re-formation" with and without hyphen. She saw three distinct movements in the process of transformation:

1. from righteous man to living legend;
2. from moral emulation to surrender; and
3. from elite to popular audience (Bose 2005: 2-3).

The study needs modification by adding a few missing links. First, it is not *Rāmāyaṇa* but the Rāmakathā that underwent various stages of transformation. *Vālmīki Rāmāyaṇa* is a milestone, the first and most momentous, of course, but not the ultimate destination. From a living person (though some may be sceptical about his Rāma's historicity), I believe till definitive facts are found that he was born as a human being, not as a god but he was elevated to the level of god by the collective eternal psyche of people that at a later period paid tribute to his life and strict adherence to the principles of *dharma* and *puruṣārtha.* Rāmakathā, a means of this process of apotheosization, flourished in many tongues. The shift from collective to individual creativity needed a comprehensive sublime soul, and had to wait for *Vālmīki.* His *Rāmāyaṇa* marked the stage of transformation from oral to composed written form that earned the sobriquet of the *ādi-kāvya* (primordial poetic composition) for the poem and the *ādi-kavi* (primordial poet) for *Vālmīki. Vālmīki Rāmāyaṇa* coexisted with other oral versions. With the development and currency of other languages, various other versions came to be composed. Two traditions were developed in the process: *Bhakti* that was based on surrender of self to the godhead and further elevated Rāma to a level of his incarnation as a god or as *maryādāpuruṣottama,* as in the case of Tulsīdās's *Rāmacaritamānasa.* The other tradition was constituted by sceptics who could not remain indifferent to the sway of the narrative but made irreverential changes, as in the Jaina and Buddhist traditions. The Buddhist and later on Bhakti period witnessed these versions in different Indian languages. The trend continued in different segments of societies which preserved

→

Moreover, having lived and being exposed to the oral traditions Tulsīdās subscribed to the practice of self-effacement too. He claimed no credit for originality of the theme or its treatment. Therefore, he mentioned that he wrote the epic for *svāntaḥsukhāya* (for the satisfaction of his inner self). The extract has been taken rather literally. The poets speak in the language of metaphors, and it might be dangerous to take a poet's words literally. The problem is not with *sukha* but with *svāntaḥ*. A poet's *antaḥ* is inclusive and ever-expanding. Hence, he was the conscience of the entire society and humanity, though it does not mean that he was free from newness of the period or class. Then he states that he wishes to extend *Rāmāyaṇa* in an extremely sweet language, and thereby he suggests the shift from Sanskrit to Awadhī. In fact, after this *śloka* he begins the *Rāmacarita* in Awadhī. The *Rāmacaritamānasa* becomes a site of confluence of different traditions — oral and written, Śāstric and *laukika*, *śloka* and *loka*, and *devabhāṣā* and *lokabhāṣā*. Moreover, he said that he did not claim to say anything new but to extend the already existing Rāmakathā. The extension is modification of the Rāmakathā tradition through his approximation and appropriation verging on translation.

Among others, Tulsī had received *Gītā* as a part of the tradition, and internalized it too. The pattern that emerges is that the *bhakta* poets received their tradition in Sanskrit and natural languages, and internalized it. They digested and took whatever was useful to them and used it for their purposes. For instance, *Gītā* has the famous *śloka*:

---

← their fluid oral versions, and also in written and printed versions in modern Indian languages. The folk versions in *Rāmalīlā* used hybrid versions — Rāmakathā relying on the core of the *Vālmīki Rāmāyaṇa*, but heavily on Tulsīdās's *Rāmacaritamānasa*, and using generously the couplets from folk Radheshyam *Rāmāyaṇa*.

The *kathā* tradition combines various elements from different oral, written and printed versions and even local interpretations with interpretations that people see and hear on the TV and in the virtual world too. Different *kathākāra*s have added to the tradition, as the oral form dominates among others. Hybridity and fluidity characterize the oral *kathā* rendition traditions. Fluidity is possible due to freedom that the *kathākāra*s take for their purpose of imparting education through instruction. It adds an element of novelty to Rāmakathā (Bose 2005: 1-11).

*yadā yadā hi dharmasya glānir bhavati bhārata* ।
*abhyutthānam adharmasya tadātmānaṁ sr̥sjāmyaham* ॥
— IV.7

O Arjuna! whenever there is decline of *dharma*, I create myself then for the protection and furtherance of *dharma*.

Tulsīdās's version in the *Rāmacaritamānasa*, Bālakāṇḍa (120: 3-4) runs thus:

*jab jab hoi dharma ki hāni* । *baḍahiṅ asur adhama abhimāni* ॥
*tab tab dharī prabhu manuj śarīrā* । *harahiṅ niśācara santan pīṛā* ॥

The important thing to be borne in mind is that Indian tradition valued idea (*vicāra*). It used *dr̥ṣṭānta* (illustration) as the means of communicating *vicāra* to *loka* (common people). Language as the vehicle of *vicāra* is inconsequential. The *bhakta* poets made deliberate choice of writing in *lokbhāṣā*s (language of people). Here the idea of reincarnation for elimination of the cause of evil is important for sustaining rudderless people and their faith in the good in an age of chaos. Therefore, *bhāvānuvāda* (sense translation) was a kind of translation suitable for the *bhakta* poets. *Bhāva* was the structure for them, which they sincerely adhered to and used the texture, i.e. illustrative mode and devices — metrical, prosodic, images, myths and symbols among others, as suited their purposes.

Apart from *Rāmacaritamānasa* in Awadhī/Hindi, many translations of *Rāmāyaṇa* were attempted in the following period. Here translation of this epic as *Ramayan-e-Masih*, by Sheikh Sadullah Masih Panipati, who was a contemporary of Jehangir and Shahjahan, deserves special mention. It was published in 1899 by Munshi Naval Kishor Press, Lucknow. It is not a translation in strict sense of the term but re-telling in Persian. Since *Ramayan-e-Masih* was written during Jehangir's reign when Muslim readers' interest in Hindu scriptures waned in comparison to Akbar's, it did not earn their attention. Rather Masih came under criticism of orthodox Muslims for translating/composing *Rāmāyaṇa*. He justified his stance in the beginning of his work, and wrote against his unnecessary criticism by the orthodox fanatics under the heading *Dar Mazammat-e-Hussad*, i.e. condemning the jealous. He had to prove his credentials as a staunch follower and propagator of the Islamic faith by mentioning that his critics note the two *nāt*s in praise of the Prophet Mohammad written in the beginning of the epic, and *Paighambarnāmā*, his other epic poem which dealt with the life and achievements of the Prophet. Masih based his *Rāmāyaṇa* mainly on the *Vālmīki Rāmāyaṇa*. However, not even once did he mention the name of Ādikavi Vālmīki. He composed it on the basis of his reading of Badayuni's version. It led to the speculation that perhaps he did not know Sanskrit or could not read it. He wrote it in Persian *masnavī* style, resembling the heroic couplet of English, and did not divide his *Rāmāyaṇa* into *kāṇḍas*, as in the original epic poem. He gave separate headings to all events or episodes. His diction was Persian and devoid of Sanskrit words. He used the term *zāhid* for Ṛṣi Vālmīki when Sītā after her exile went for shelter to the *āśrama* of first poet Vālmīki.

The other rendition that deserves our attention is by S. Mohar Singh. He was from a village named Ram Nagar in Gujranwala district of Pakistan. He served in the army of Mahārājā Ranjit Singh. He could not complete *Rāmāyaṇa* in his life so it was his close friend Hiranand "Lal" who completed the small residual part of it dealing with Rāma's fight with his sons Lava and Kuśa and the subsequent reconciliation with Sītā and their return to Ayodhyā. Hiranand "Lal" followed the same metre and style, adopted by Mohar Singh. This *Rāmāyaṇa* also could not get much response, as after the occupation of Punjab by the British, Persian lost the prestige and currency that it enjoyed earlier.

Mohar Singh's rendition in Persian had influence of the Persian, as he did not divide his *Rāmāyaṇa* into the traditional cantos but dealt with incidents under various headings in the manner of *masanvī* writers. Unlike Masih, he adhered to Vālmīki rigorously and mentioned the name of the sage-poet Vālmīki frequently with reverence. It can be inferred from his rendition that he had studied *Vālmīki Rāmāyaṇa* and followed it closely leaving no space either for anachronisms or for changing the tone of the epic into a romantic tale. Masih and Mohar Singh came from the undivided Punjab, but none of them mentioned Tulsīdās's *Rāmacaritamānasa* thereby suggesting that the Hindi/Awadhī had not attained circulation and currency in the then western part of India.

Both the *Rāmāyaṇas* in Persian are not translations of *Vālmīki Rāmāyaṇa* but the poets' own creations. Unlike Masih, Mohar Singh used Sanskrit words liberally: *as-śīsa* (head), *rājā* (king), *mātā* (mother), *nāga* (serpent), *yuga* (age), *surpat* (king of gods), *cāṇḍāla* (a low-born cruel person) and *rūpa* (beauty). These two poets not only enriched the epic tradition related to Rāma but also paved the way for communal amity. One has painted Rāma as a human being with divine qualities and other has depicted him as a divine being with human characteristics.

Rāmakathā (narrative of Rāma) attained the acceptance of the people of India that all Indian languages came to have their versions/ translations. Purāṇas changed the stature of Rāma from a warrior against a selfish culture in the *Vālmīki Rāmāyaṇa* to the status of incarnation of Viṣṇu as in *Bhāgavata Purāṇa* and *Viṣṇu Purāṇa*. In *Śiva Purāṇa* Rāma appears as a devotee of Śiva, thus bringing a synthesis of the Vaiṣṇavism and Śaivism. *Adhyātma Rāmāyaṇa*, a late fourteenth-century text, engaged with Rāmakathā to communicate the non-dualist (Advaita) perspective. In the similar vein, different versions of *Rāmāyaṇa* in Indian languages were prepared in different periods. In sixteenth-century Narahari's *Torave Rāmāyaṇa* in Kannaḍa, Balarāma Dās's *Oriyā Rāmāyaṇa,* Thunchathu Ramanujan Ezhuthachan *Malayālam Rāmāyaṇam* are worth mentioning. In the seventeenth century, Premanand wrote *Rāmāyaṇa* in Gujarati, and in the eighteenth century Śrīdhar composed *Rāmāyaṇa* in Marathi. *Rāmāyaṇa* did not remain confined to Malayalam and Hindus only, and the Muslims of Kerala and Lakshdweep islands rendered it in Mappillapattu, a popular song genre among the Muslims in which some changes have been made, e.g. the story of Rāma becomes the story of a Sultan who is many times referred to as "Laman". The rest of the characters remain the same. These songs pertaining to *Rāmāyaṇa* put together constitute *Mappilla Rāmāyaṇa*.

All these versions of *Rāmāyaṇa* are creative renditions of Rāmakathā, and cannot be called translation in the strict sense of the term, as there are additions and deletions in consonance with the requirements of the individual, community or society. This tradition beggars traditional term translation, as it is too vast and rich to be captured in translation. We may use the term re-co-creation (*punarsahasrajana*) for it. It is a part of the Indian tradition that may be understood by using Pandit Hazari Prasad Dwivedi's term *punarnavā* which is the renewal mechanism, like a tree renews by throwing off the old leaves in autumn and then having new ones in spring. *Rāmāyaṇa* tradition in a new spring season reappears in its renewed forms in different places in different linguistic garbs.

With the movement of people beyond Indian shore, *Rāmāyaṇa* was transmitted to different parts, particularly to South-East Asian countries which came in trade and cultural contacts with India. The sapling of *Rāmāyaṇa* was planted in geographically contiguous countries like Myanmar, Malaysia, Cambodia, Vietnam, Thailand and Laos, and it grew in the new land and habitation. Though the kernel remained the same, it underwent changes depending on the character of the new elements. Rāmakathā journey to the South-East Asia via the land route from the eastern part of India, particularly from Bengal to Burma (now Myanmar), Thailand and Laos, and the other through the sea route from the western coast of Gujarat and the southern coast of India to Java, Sumatra and Malaya.

The old Javanese has one of the earliest versions in the ninth century in which Rāmakathā is rendered in 2,774 stanzas in the *maṇipravāla* style having assortment of Sanskrit and Kawi languages. Bhaṭṭi's *Rāvaṇavadham* which is known as *Bhaṭṭikāvya* also exercised its influence on the Javanese and Indonesian versions of Rāmakathā. A *Rāmakavaca* of 22 stanzas in Sanskrit has also been found in Bali in which some of the stanzas are similar to, in a way taken from, *Vālmīki Rāmāyaṇa* (Aveling 2012: 25-43). The Vietnamese and Cambodian versions were influenced by the Javanese Rāmakathā (Desai 1980: 5-20). Hindu and Buddhist traditions of Rāmakathā were transmitted through trade routes (Cowell 1894: 78-82). [Cowell had speculated in the beginning of the twentieth century that the *Daśaratha Jātaka* could be dated earlier than *Vālmīki Rāmāyaṇa*.] The Cambodian Val Kantel inscriptions that are traced to the seventh century refer frequently to recitals and Purāṇic legends.

The only surviving text, the Javanese *Kākawin Rāmāyaṇa,* dates back to CE 930. It is deeply influenced by the *Rāvana-Vadha*, a seventh-century south Indian text, as has been discussed by Hooykaas (1958: 5). Haji Muhammad Salleh remarked about the impact of *Vālmīki Rāmāyaṇa* thus:

> This epical work of Vālmīki branched out to become scores of prose and poetic versions that were relatively shorter. These versions then branched further when they were brought to South-East Asia. Among

> the earliest was the *Rāmāyaṇa Kākawin*, which according to Eva Vanicknova (Prusek 133) is the oldest manuscript of an epic ever discovered, i.e. *c*. ninth century, and possibly written during the reign of Rājā Dyah Balitung. — Salleh 2009: 5

The Javanese *Kākawin Rāmāyaṇa* is significant for subscription to and also deviation from the Rāmakathā in *Vālmīki Rāmāyaṇa*. Nearly the first half of the *Kākawin Rāmāyaṇa* is similar to the original Sanskrit version. The subsequent part departs radically from the source. The new addition to the latter part was in the form of the all powerful Javanese deity Dhayana who is the guardian god of Java Semar that is known as Twalen in Balinese literature. The guardian god has deformed sons named Gareng, Petruk and Bagong who become clowns that would light up the performance of *Rāmāyaṇa*. It is illustrative of the accommodative ability of *Rāmāyaṇa* to allow space to the local cultures in its fold. The standardized text of *Vālmīki Rāmāyaṇa* was oral, though not totally indeterminate, but did not come in the way of appropriation and even domestication of the tradition of the Rāmakathā in India and beyond its shores. *Hikāyat-Seri-Rāma* is the Malaysian version of Rāmakathā.

It is yet another instance of localization and aculturation of Rāmakathā. Haji Muhammad Salleh has commented on the changes due to these processes:

> The influence of *Rāmāyaṇa* in Malaysia was and is not as strong as on the Javanese. The Malay story, called *Hikāyat-Seri-Rāma*, as found today, is far removed from its Hindu source. In general, it is truncated or enhanced by the new religion of the Malays, Islam, and censorship against its pre-Islamic beliefs and elements. As it is, only the love story between Siti Dewi and Seri Rāma is foregrounded.
>
> — Salleh 2009: 5

The Malay *Hikāyat-Seri-Rāma* makes changes in the original version according to the local needs of Islamic religion. In the very beginning this shift is discernible. Its Malay version runs thus:

> *Ini hikayat yang terlalu indah-indah termasyhur diperkatakan orang di ats angin and di bawah angin nyata kepada segala sastera perkataan Maharaja Rawana yang sepuluh kepalanya and dua puluh tangannya. Raja itu terlalu besar ia beroleh kerajaannya, empat tempat neggeri dianugerahkan Allah Taala.*

> This is the story of great magnificence, renowned and mentioned in all quarters by people above and below the wind, to all writers who the words that concern Mahārāja Rāvaṇa with the ten heads, and twenty hands. Great was his empire, four sites were there for his empire, given by Allāh Tālā. — Shellabear 1964: 1

This version of Rāmakathā earns our attention for different reasons. The new religion, i.e. Islam being monotheistic could not accept Rāmakathā as it is. However, such was the charm of Rāmakathā that it had become the part of the collective unconscious and cerebral system of the people that they cannot part with it too. The *kathā* is domesticated in consonance with the new local religious and cultural requirements. Consequently, a religiously hybrid new version comes into existence in which Rāma descends from the prophet Adam. Allah desired that Rāvaṇa should be born through Nabi Adam. Equally significant is pronouncement regarding the acceptance of grandeur of Rāmakathā among people in different parts of the world, and the description of Rāvaṇa in the beginning as the Mahārāja. Moreover, in the incident of Sītā's kidnapping by Rāvaṇa, Jaṭāyu of *Rāmāyaṇa* becomes Catayu Kisubrisu who reminds Rāvaṇa of his relationship with Adam (Rajantheran 1995: 239).

The Cambodian version of Rāmakathā in the form of *Ramakerti* follows *Vālmīki Rāmāyaṇa.* Under the Khmer influence, names were changed. Rāma becomes Preah Ream, an incarnation of Viṣṇu. Preah Ream is married to Neang Seda who mothers two children but experiences no happiness, as she has to go through the trial of fire. Lakṣmaṇa is Preah Leak and Rāvaṇa is Krong Reap. Preah Leak helps his brother Preah Ream in the fight against Krong Reap, the king of Langka (Laṅkā) and in the rescue of Neang Seda. Sopphanakhā, the sister of Krong Reap wanted to seduce Preah Leak, but failed in her attempt and lost her nose and ear in the process.

*Rāmakerti* follows most of the narrative of *Rāmāyaṇa*:

> Preah Reap (Rāma) is sent to the forest according to the plan of one of the queen mothers. In the forest he is joined by his wife Neang Seda who is a rare combination of beauty and fidelity. He had won her in a fight. Preah Leak (Lakṣmaṇa) is worried about the welfare of his elder brother and joins his brother and sister-in-law. They meet Sopphanakhā who strives to seduce the elder brother first and later

on the younger one. Infuriated by her actions Preah Leak chops off her nose and ear. Sopphanakhā goes to her brother Krong Reap (Rāvaṇa), the king of Langka. Krong Reap plans to take revenge against the perpetrators of humiliation on his sister Sopphanakhā.

To take revenge he goes to the forest secretly and sees Neang Seda, a woman of divine beauty. He tricks Preah Ream and Preah Leak with a ruse and kidnaps Neang Seda by disguising himself as a saint. Both the brothers go out in search of Neang Seda; and help Sukreep (Sugrīva) in defeating his rival Pali Thirat (Bāli) and re-attain his kingdom. Sukreep is the king of monkeys, and sends Hanumān, the son of the wind, to help Preah Ream. Hanumān finds out that Krong Reap had held Neang Seda as a captive on the island of Langka. He asks his soldiers to build a bridge of stones and thereby connecting the mainland with the island. There were many mermaids that used to steal stones to disrupt the construction of the bridge. He decides to imprison Princess Sovanna Maccha, also known as Neang Maccha, for she had tried to blight the plan of Hanumān but both of them fall in love. The completion of the bridge led to war between Preah Ream and Krong Reap. Preah Ream becomes triumphant in it, and returns to Ayodhyā as the king. Neang Seda undergoes the test of fire to prove her purity. Once again the people spread canard about her, and she is forced to leave the palace, and finds refuge in the *āśrama* of *Vālmīki* where she mothers two sons. They meet their father who recognizes and accepts them as his sons. He was agreeable to having Neang Seda in the palace if she agreed to prove her purity. Frustrated Seda asks her mother the goddess of earth to bear out her purity, and passes the test.

Thus there are not many changes in the main narrative of *Rāmāyaṇa* in *Ramakerti*. The names have been considerably indigenized, but the obvious onomastic relations make it possible to identify the characters. Commenting on the alterations in *Rāmakerti*, Saveros Pou has mentioned that Cambodian *Rāmāyaṇa* version, known as *Rāmakerti*,

> reveals a variety of instances of indigenization. Agni rides a rhinoceros instead of a ram, for example, and the portrayal of Rāma's character and behaviour is moulded to fit the Theravāda ideal of a hero who is an image of the Buddha; also, the lives led by *Rāmakerti* are those of saintly paragons of virtue. To deal with the problem for Cambodian sensibilities posed by the major role played in *Rāmāyaṇa*

> by the monkeys, Khmer authors devised ways to portray also their unattractive, repugnant features. — Saveros Pou 1992: 89-102

The Theravāda Buddhist influence in the new land is echoed in *Ramakerti* in the conduct and nature of Rāma. Rāma is transformed from a kṣatriya noble being who remains a kṣatriya, as he kills for the sake of the *dharma*. Pou's observations are pertinent in this regards:

> If we add up these different aspects of Rāma's behaviour, we find behind them a firm and steadfast motivation made up of *metta* (friendship), *karuṇā* (compassion), *mudita* (altruistic joy), and *upekkhā* (equanimity), which together form the foremost sublime tenent of the Buddhists, called Brahmavihāra, or blissful state of mind.
>
> — Ibid.

Rāmakathā attained different art forms in India and outside as well. Along with its narrativization in the form of sculpture and murals in temples in Cambodia in particular, in Laos it was articulated in the form of dance-drama which is known as "Phalak Phalam", standing for Lakṣmaṇa and Rāma, respectively. The re-narration modifies the Rāmakathā tradition with radical changes in the core of it. The shift may be discerned in the names and birth of the major characters. Phalak is the elder twin of Phalam:

> He cleaned up the way into the world for Phalam, the incarnation of God Viṣṇu. Another easily observed difference is the Lao version of Suphanakha's goal: Suphanakha attacks Sida, but not the two brothers. She forgot the reason of her visit to help Ravaṇa in conquering Sida and to decimate the fighting energy of the two men. She was too fascinated by Phalam and Phalak and therefore she acts jealously against Sida. — Gisa Jähnichen 2009: 14

Along with it, Hanumān's character and role undergo drastic change in it. He is depicted as a son of Rāma. He assumes the form of monkey for three years after eating a fruit called *nikhot*. He lived in the company of Nang Phengsi who was a daughter of a sage. Since she loved Hanumān she too ate the fruit *nikhot* and got changed into monkey to be alike Hanumān (ibid.). Hanumān's birth as Rāma's son provides justification for his devotion for Rāma.

Dissemination of Rāmakathā in India and beyond speaks about the complex cultural ways in which the various processes and kinds of translations take place. The modifications in the source text and the consequent outcomes of various processes of reception and acculturation in the new space make the task of naming them more difficult. They may be summed up in the following manner:

1. Various folk versions of Rāmakathā in oral and written Prākr̥t.
2. Standardization and preparation of the finished product in Sanskrit.
3. Adaptations in different native sects and religions, e.g. the Buddhist *Rāmāyaṇa* and Jaina *Rāmāyaṇa* (recreation).
4. Translations in native languages in Assamese, Bengali, Kannada, Kashmiri, Gujarati, Hindi, Marathi, Oriya, Tamil, Telgu among others (co-recreation).
5. Translation in different foreignized native sects religions (adaptations through appropriation).
6. Translations in different foreignized native sects religions reversions (adaptation through domestication).
7. Translations in allied cultures (*anusrajana* or subsequent or co-creation).
8. Translations in alien foreign cultures (domestication or appropriation).
9. Translations proper in its traditional sense (*anuvāda*).

*Rāmāyaṇa* translational activities constitute a cultural project, not so much owned by certain mediated and furthered by different cultures that needed it for their cultural needs in the land of its origins and outside. It was a study into translation of a text that existed at multiple levels. Except Akbar in the Mughal period and to an extent in the colonial period, there was not much sincere interest shown by the state. The text earned interest of different creative minds and communities, as it fulfilled their multiple purposes. Against it, there was a translational project of knowledge texts of metaphysical nature like the Upaniṣads.

Rāmakathā with *Vālmīki Rāmāyaṇa* as the anchor text attracts the attention of creative writers even today in different languages, and it would keep doing so in future. In Indian languages many modern writers have written about Rāmakathā in different classical and literary forms. Among others the mention may be made of Kuvempu's epic *Rāmāyaṇa* in Kannada, and novels in Hindi by Narendra Kohali and Bhagvan Singh's novel *Apne Apne Rama* that strives to modernize the mythical part of Rāmkathā with his sceptical reading. Recently, Vayu Naidu's novel *Sītā's Ascent* sees the epic from Sītā's perspective. She returns to the earth, as her mother has died a few years ago, and she suffers from the thought of contamination by a stranger's touches and fear of her daughter's life that rendered her frail. She appears as a victim of circumstances and accepts her fate, a streak that can be traced to *Vālmīki*'s Sītā's acceptance of her torture and humiliation by the she-demons, as discussed earlier. The title page of the novel has a haunting image on it with Sītā returning to the cave in earth with her daughter in her and Rāma watches her in a contemplative mood. A couple of sages, hopefully Vasiṣṭha, his brother Lakṣmaṇa and family members, counsellors and courtiers constitute the mute spectators. Rāma leaves everything to Sītā with full faith in her, "She is central to everything. She will understand". The author sees her descent as her ascent. However, it does not prevent a twenty-first century author to make Sītā a woman of progressive thoughts who states candidly about how women always adapt to their husband's home and make it their own. The questions do persist: why does she accept wrongs committed to her? Why does she suppress her anger? They remain unanswered; and laden texts are not supposed to answer all questions. They are left unresponded so that newer creative and critical interpretations may be adumbrated by subsequent generations.

Often we consider linguistic, geographical, religious and political lines as complete and vertical but the fact is that they are highly porous. The circulation of Rāmakathā in South Asia for centuries proves it speaks about the cultural efficacy of *kathā* and its first systematization in the form of *Vālmīki Rāmāyaṇa,* the epic which knows no boundaries of religion or nation. It has taught the values of life and behaviour to men and women over centuries, across India and South-East Asia. There is no finer example in the world of a multi-religious, international culture than *Rāmāyaṇa*. Scores of generations watched performances and narrations of the great epic for more than 2,000 years and learn values of life. It has been the cornerstone of the life of India and South-East Asia. The story of *Rāmāyaṇa* is enacted more often than any other story of the world. It is performed by Hindus, Buddhists and Muslims. It constitutes the core of cultural traditions in many countries in Thailand, Cambodia, Indonesia, Laos, Myanmar, Nepal and India. It has also been widely prevalent in Singapore, Malaysia and Vietnam. *Rāmāyaṇa* as the intercultural text unites India and the countries of South-East Asia, and shapes and sustains cultural ideals, as it did thousands of years ago.

## References

Aurobindo, Sri, 1956, *Vyasa and Vālmīki,* Pondicherry: Aurobindo Ashram.

———, 1997, "Indian Literature", *The Renaissance in India and Other Essays on Culture,* Pondicherry: Sri Aurobindo Ashram.

Aveling, Harry, 2012, "Rāmāyaṇa", *Kritika Kulture,* **18**: 25-43.

Benjamin, Walter, 1999, *Illuminations,* ed. with an Introduction by Hannah Arendt, tr. Harry Zorn, London: Pimilico, Random House, first published by Jonathan Cape in 1970.

Bently, Jerry, 1993, *Old World Encounters: Cross-Cultural Contacts and Excanges in Pre-Modern Times,* New York: Oxford University Press.

Bose, Mandokrata (ed.), 2004, *The Rāmāyaṇa Revisited,* New York: Oxford University Press.

Bose, M., 2005, "Re-forming the Rāmāyaṇa: The Source Text and Its Cultural Transformation", *Translation Today,* October, **2**(2): 1-11.

Bose, Sugata and Ayesha Jalal, 1999, *Modern South Asia: History, Culture, Political Economy,* Delhi: Oxford University Press.

Cahoone, Lawrence (ed.), 1996, *From Modernism to Postmodernism: An Anthology,* Oxford: Blackwell.

Cowell, E.B., 1894, *Buddhist Mahāyāna Texts,* Part I, *The Buddha-Karita of Ashvagoṣa,* trs. from Sanskrit in the Sacred Books of the East, vol. 49, Oxford: Oxford University Press, 1894.

Desai, S.N., 1980, *Hinduism in Thai Life,* Bombay: Papular Prakashan, 1979.

Dunn, Rose E., 2005, *The Adventures of Ibn Battuta,* Oakland, CA: University of California Press.

Ganeri, J., 2011, *The Lost Age of Reason: Philosophy in Early Modern India 1450-1700,* Oxford New York: Oxford University Press.

Gibb, H.A.R. (tr. & ed.), 1929, *Ibn Battuta, Travels in Asia and Africa 1325-1354,* London: Broadway House, retrieved on 2 April 2011, Fordham University.

Gupta, Gargi and Ramanath Tripathi (eds.), 1992, *Rāmacaritamānasa ke Anuvāda,* Delhi: Bharatiya Anuvad Parishad (Hindi).

Habermas, Jurgen, 1981, "Modernity versus Postmodernity", *New German Critique*, **22**: 3-14.

Hooykaas Christian, 1958, The Old-Javanese Ramayana: An Exemplary Kakawin as to Form and Context, Amsterdam: Noord-Hollandsche Uitgevers Maatschappij.

Jähnichen, Gisa, 2009, "Re-Designing the Role of Phalak and Phatam in Modern Lao Ramayana", *Wacana Seni Journal of Arts and Discourse*, **8**: 1-42.

Pou, Saveros, 1992, "Indegenization of Ramayana in Indonesia", *Asian Fotklore Studies*, **51**: 89-102.

Rajantheran, M., 1995, *Hikayat Seri Rama,* Kula Lumpur: Dewan Bahasa dan Pustaka.

Richman, Paula (ed.), 1991, *Many Rāmāyaṇas: The Diversity of a Narrative Tradition in South Asia,* New Delhi: Oxford University Press.

———, (ed), 2003, *Questioning Rāmāyaṇas: A South Asian Tradition*, New Delhi: Oxford University Press.

Salleh, Muhammad Haji, 2009, *Asiatic*, December, **3**(2): 5.

Saran, Malini and Vinod C. Khanna, 2004, *The Rāmāyaṇa in Indonesia,* Delhi: Ravi Dayal, pp. 32-87.

Sattar, Arshia, 2011, *Lost Lives: Exploring Rama's Anguish*, Delhi: Penguin Press.

Sen, Amartya, 2005, *The Argumentative Indian*, New Delhi: Penguin.

Sen, D.C., 1999, *History of Bengali Language and Literature*, Delhi: Gyan Publishing House.

Singh, Avadhesh Kumar, 2006, "Rāmāyaṇa in the Mahābhārata", in *Textuality and Intertextuality in the Mahābhārata*, New Delhi: Sarup & Sons.

———, (ed.), 2007, *Rāmāyaṇa through Ages: Rāmakathā in Indian Languages,* New Delhi: D.K. Printworld.

———, 2008, "In Their Own Worlds and Words: Indian Bhakti Women Poets ", in *Voice of Women: Gārgī to Gaṅgāsatī,* Avadhesh Kumar Singh, (ed.), New Delhi: D.K. Printworld.

———, 2012, "Theory of Creative Process in Narratives about the Rāmāyaṇa and the Mahābhārata: Mythic Narrative as Mode of Constitution of Knowledge", in *Revisiting Literature, Criticism and Aesthetics in India,* Avadhesh Kumar Singh, New Delhi: D.K. Printworld.

———, 2014, "Constructing a Trajectory of Cultural Transaction in South Asia", *Affinities: India and Korea,* New Delhi: D.K. Printworld.

Shellabear, W. (ed.), 1964, *Hikāyat Seri Rāma*, Singapore: MPH.

Shulman, David, 2001, *The Wisdom of Poets: Studies in Tamil, Telugu and Sanskrit*, Delhi: Oxford University Press.

Srinivasan, K S., n.d., "Rāmāyaṇa Traditions in South East Asia", *CIRSW*.

Tulsīdāsa, Goswāmī, *Rāmacaritamānasa*, Gorakhpur: Gita Press, Saṁvat 2054 (Awadhī/Hindi).

Winternitz, Moritz, 1927-33, *A History of Indian Philosophy*, tr. Shilavati Ketkar, 2 vols., Calcutta: Calcutta University Press.

# 14

# Syncretism of the Cultures of India with the Cultures of South and South-East Asia

*S. Ram Mohan*

THERE is an undeniable cultural umbilical chord connecting the South and South-East Asia (which G. Coedes terms as "Farther India") and the Indian mainland especially south India. Culturally speaking:

> Farther India today is characterized by more or less deep traces of the Indianization that began long ago — the importance of the Sanskrit element in the vocabulary of the languages spoken there; the Indian origin of the alphabets with which these languages have been or still written; the influence of Indian law and administrative organization; the persistence of certain Brāhmanical traditions in the countries converted to Islam as well as those converted to Singhalese Buddhism; and the presence of ancient monuments which in architecture and sculpture are associated with the arts of India and bear inscriptions in Sanskrit.[1]

The elevating influence of the Indian impact on these states is exemplified by a simple observation by Coedes. He points out that on the basis of a somatological observation, characteristics of a Cambodian peasant scarcely differ from the Prongs or Samre of a neighbouring region but while the prongs have remained in a state of crude civilization, including the absence of a writing system, the Cambodian peasant lives in a stage of developed civilization and culture. He has coherent views of the world and the hereafter that are shared by a large part of Asian humanity; finally, he uses a system of writing that gives him access to a vast literature and enables him to

---

[1] G. Coedes, *The Indianised States of South East Asia*, Honolulu: East West Center Press, 1968, p. XIV.

communicate from a distance with his fellow men. All this he owes to India.[2] From this original Indian impact, various kingdoms like Cambodia, Champa, the small states of Malay peninsula Svarṇabhūmi and Sri Vijaya developed, as well as Burmese and Thai kingdoms received the Indian culture through the Mons and Khmer. Interesting factor here is that while the Indian cultural impact got synergized with the indigenous substratum, each of these states developed according to their own genius. A syncretism of the cultures was born and is still being maintained, each with its own interesting hallmarks but with a common thread. Each country has its own source of information on "Farther India". Cambodia has its epigraphical source, the Champas have documentation in Chinese annals, Burma on Chronicles, etc.

While the initial advent of Indians consisted of individuals or corporate enterprises, peaceful in nature, it was followed by advent of the cultivated elements of upper castes who profoundly impregnated the native cultures with elements of Indian religion and language. The cult of Śaivism started taking root. In the words of K.A. Nilakanta Sastri:

> just as in classical times, the Greek Colonists carried with them the fire from the sacred hearth of the city as token of their filial relation to the land they left in search of new abodes, so also the Hindu Colonists carried a cult with them, the cult of Śaivism in which Śiva played the role of the guardian of the state, thanks to the kind offices of his chief devotee.[3]

However the rigid social–hierarchical centre system of India had undergone profound modifications due to cross-pollination of ideas in Farther India; nature societies. August Barth observes that the brāhmaṇas of Cambodia do not appear to have been very scrupulous about racial purity.[4] There were mixed marriages, stretching the rules of endogamy. The Indians brought the native chiefs not only a complete administration but an administrative technique capable of

---

2 Coedes 1968: XVII.

3 K.A. Nilakanta Sastri, "Agastiya" quoted in *TBG*, Germany, 1936, p. 252.

4 Auguste Barth, *Inscriptions Sanscrites du Cambodge*, Paris Imprimerie Nationale, 1885, p. 159.

being adopted to new conditions in foreign countries.[5] Under the Indian impact, native chiefs did not have a ready-made administration forced upon them but were presented with a technique of administration which could be adopted to varying conditions overseas. Competent syncretism in administration evolved.[6]

It has been posited that Indian culture contained within it many pre-Aryan elements and many survivals of basic culture common to all the monsoon area of Asia.[7] Hence the people of Farther India would not have felt that they were imbibing the elements of an alien culture, which facilitated the syncretism. The sources indicate that southern India, especially the Pallava kingdom with its capital at Kāñcī played a significant role in the cross-pollination.

Inscriptions and epigraphy indicate the two main sects of Pāśupata of Śaivism and Pāñcarātra of Vaiṣṇavism coexisted in South and South-East Asia as in India itself. Both epigraphic and iconographic materials indicate how important the syncretic cult of Harihara was at this period.[8] The course of political and cultural history of the region has been influenced by forceful personalities like Aniruddha of Burma, Jayavarman of Cambodia and Ramakhamherg of Thailand. Excavations at the numerous Funanese sites in the Mekong Delta indicate that its culture seems to have been a result of the extension of the process of Brāhmanization, which had been functioning in India, to countries overseas. In the reign of Jayavarman, it was the custom to worship Lord Maheśvara, who ceaselessly discend upon Mount Mo-tan. This refers to the sacred mountains from which the country and the kings took their names. The inscription of prince Guṇavarman shows the prevalence of cultural syncretism of Vaiṣṇavism in the temple, especially in Cambodia. The style of decoration, having gradually departed more and more from the Indian models to which it had been so close in the seventh century, had reacted the points, where Indian influence, is no longer discernible. Although the type of decoration remained the

[5] Coedes, *Making of South East Asia*, Berkely and LA: University of California Press, 1962, p. 55.

[6] Ibid., p. 52.

[7] Ibid.

[8] Ibid.: 94.

same as was borrowed from Indian art, vegetable, animal and other motifs had been introduced and treated in an entirely original manner.[9] It is also evident in the "Pyu" architectural style of Burma, with semblance of an inner chamber surmounted by tapering superstructure called *śikhara* in India.

The sociologists aver that the civilizations emerged as a result of changes brought about in local cultures, by having Indian culture, grafted upon them and it envisages the process as one of the developments of the indigenous cultures in response to an Indian stimulus, and regard

> the fundamental nature of each indigenous group — its local genius — as having been the determinative factor in its particular kind of response. The syncretism typical of Indian thought is what chiefly characterized Brāhmanian and enabled it, despite its lack of centralized organization and of a programme of action, to give spiritual unity to India; and it was this, together with the tolerance of Śaivism that enabled Indian culture to assimilate, as we have seen the most diverse foreign elements when it was transplanted overseas.[10]

In Cambodia, there was a hereditary occupational system, similar to *varṇāśrama*, in a loose sense, and a governance system whose, functions were termed in Indian words. That facilitated the Khmer society to have an integrated society in Indian model.

"Farther India" of South and South-East Asia is not a result of political colonization but rather cultural dependence. The power of penetration by Indian culture in these areas is validated by the fact that even though these countries soon passed into European hands and the population getting converted to Islam later, the impact of Indian culture remained potent as ever. In Phnom Penh, the ceremony of king's coronation-day sees a brāhmaṇa priest as well Buddhist monk performing separate ceremonies. In the Buddhist countries of this region, the belief in Hindu cosmogony and the doctrine of *karma* and transmigration remain deeply implanted even in the minds of lowest classes. Even in the Islamic country of Indonesia, there exists

---

[9] Codes, 1962: 105.

[10] Ibid.: 55.

the mildness and liberal attitude to the embedding of Indian cultural traditions over centuries. There is also continued inspiration from Indian epics and books like *Harivaṁśa* for local literature. Dances and theatres in these countries still involve around themes of Indian epics and mythologies, while retaining the original character of pantomime Indian law system like "Smṛtis become the framework for ordering of local customs; the temporal governance has drawn from works like *Arthaśāstra* as observed by Coedes. There are many Sanskrit words in the South and South-East Asian language repertoire. Indian lunar calendar and Buddhist era are still in use here. India produced its definitive master works only through the activity of the foreigner or foreign soil. In architecture, it is in distant Cambodia and Java that we must seek the two marvels born of the Indian genius — Angkor and the Borobudur", thus comments Sylvain Lévi.[11]

What is the reverse impact? The influence of the native substratum on Indian art was mostly formal, external; that is why, from the very first, it is more striking than the internal ties that unite the plastic tests of Farther India to India. We know no monuments in India resembling even the Bayon of Angkor Thom or the Borobudur. And yet these monuments are pure productions of the Indian genius, the deep meanings of which are apparent only to the eyes of the Indian.

The two major countries of East Asia — India and China — both had done a form of colonization in South and South-East Asia. But there is an essential difference. Chinese led by conquest and political integration. India led by a process of cultural osmosis which allowed the individual character of each of the Indianized countries to be expressed and manifested with an Indian framework — the difference in India–China acculturations to the great civilization of Asia — perhaps qualitative rather than quantitative.[12] In Indian penetration in their region, there is the positive result of syncretism — very different from the conquests in any part of the world.

---

11 Sylvain Lévi, *L'Inde Civilisatrice,* aperçu historique, Paris: Institut de Civilisation Indienne, 1938, p. 38.

12 Paul Mus, "Borobudur" in *BEEFO* (*Bulletin de l'École Française d'Extrême Orient*), XXXII–XXXIV, 1935.

# 15

# Understanding South Asia–South-East Asia Cultural Contacts

## An Alternative Perspective

*T.S. Satyanath*

### Introduction

AREA studies like South Asia and South-East Asia are based on geographical regions that reflect an American political interest during the post-Second World War period. Furthermore, the formation of nation states during the twentieth century has increasingly created barriers within the continent. Thus, Asia that was historically a well-connected cultural region of shared religious, trade and cultural features has been turned into a fragmented region of nation states involved in conflicts and tensions. The concept of modernism, on which the nation states and their cultures have been formulated and understood, makes use of the logic of imperialism and logical oppositions, in which the self is always defined as positive and the other as negative. Making use of a conflict model and the terminology of warfare that involve concepts such as crisis, elimination, endangerment and death, modernism advocates the discourse of endangered languages and cultures thus predicting their eventual death and formation of a monogenetic and homogeneous culture.

This paper attempts to suggest an alternative model of looking at cultural contacts and the consequent changes and continuities by perceiving Asian sub-cultures as continually evolving systems. The Asian cultures are constructed on the principle of coexistence and plural epistemology and demonstrate an astonishing tendency for sustenance rather than endangerment and eventual death of languages and cultures. These cultures were a consequence of a cumulative and fine-tuned pool of human experience, spanning over long periods that involved many complex cultural interrelationships. As long as changes within such cultural systems are being seen as innovations and not as contaminations, the systems tend to remain as continually evolving ones. Such systems keep modernizing themselves constantly, implying that modernisms could be pluralistic and there could be alternative modernisms and even vernacular cosmopolitanisms. Furthermore, considering that Indian cultural representations are often scripto-centric (textual), phono-centric (orality) and body-centric (performance, painting and sculpture) in nature, a plea can be made for a comparative study of Asian literary cultures. Such a comparison could not only bring in the transmedial dimension into the study of Asian literary cultures but could also incorporate trans-regional and trans-national dimensions.

The methodology of comparison, though started as influence and reception studies, has been transformed into a highly dynamic one by the incorporation of new concepts like margino-centricism, multicultural corridors and pluralistic epistemologies. Within the theoretical and methodological issues outlined here, this paper attempts to problematize the cultural exchanges between Indian and South-East Asian writing cultures, suggests models and processes to re-evaluate studies done earlier and proposes an alternative model to overcome their limitations. The suggestions have significant implications for our understanding of Asia as a cultural region on the one hand and the agencies of cultural contact and change within the region on the other.

The area of South Asia with which the concept Comparative Indian Literature is associated and the area of East Asia to which the theme of the conference is connected pose certain conceptual problems. Asia was historically a well-connected cultural region of shared religious, trade and cultural links. On the other hand, area studies titles like South Asia regional studies, East Asia regional studies and South-East Asia regional studies are based on regions that reflect American political interest during the post-Second World War period, in particular the Cold War period. Furthermore, the formation of nation states during the twentieth century has increasingly created barriers not only within the subcontinent but has also created imagined communities with contesting identities. It is a happy occasion that these areas have started interacting among themselves, and thus an interface, which had not been developed hitherto since colonization of the region by the European expansionism, is slowly developing.

Another important issue that we need to keep in mind is our own trajectories during the twentieth century. The way modernity has affected the regions of South Asia, East Asia and South-East Asia is not only not uniform but also consists of diverse forms of colonial hegemonies. These aspects have significant implications for our own historical positioning with regard to modernity. Whereas South Asia and South-East Asia have a history of colonial domination as a consequence of modernism, their colonial histories however have different trajectories. Unlike modernism in Europe, in which modernity is confronted with realism, the Indian modernity has been confronted with tradition and classicism. On the other hand, the colonial experience of South Asia and South-East Asia has been different, marked by different colonial dominations and colonial experiences. China, Korea and Japan either did not experience a colonial past at all or experienced only a partial colonization. Consequent to the colonial intervention, Asia that was historically a well-connected cultural region of shared religious, trade and cultural features has been transformed into a fragmented region of nation states involved in mutual conflicts and tensions. This has prevented the regions in general and nation states in particular from coming closer and taking up comparative studies involving the entire region.

A majority of the comparative studies done on India and South-East Asia presume an Indian influence on South-East Asia, in terms of religious (Buddhism and Hinduism), literary (*Rāṃāyaṇa* and *Pañcatantra*), architectural (temple architecture) and sculptural aspects. Raghavan (1975), Iyengar (1983) and Saran and Khanna (2004) are some of the examples of such an approach. Hence, we need to interrogate this model and explore the possibilities of developing alternative models for undertaking comparisons. In order to do this, we need to interrogate and problematize the influence model of comparison that is central to such projects.

### Comparative Studies: The Influence Model

The history of comparative literature as an academic discipline reveals that the French school was used as an important model for comparative studies. Its characteristics could be briefly summarized as follows. First, literatures chosen for comparison are defined on the criteria of nation states (and also colonies) and studied as in a cultural contact. Second, the study implies a colonial contact and subsumes colonial domination over the colony. Third, the term "influence" itself epistemologically suggests a flow from a higher to lower level. Last, it also lists the assimilation of dominant culture's elements by the colony and thereby implies a cultural hegemony. The implications of the influence model of comparison are that it establishes a hierarchy between the two literatures and suggests a relationship of power. Accordingly, a donor–recipient relationship is conceived between the literatures involved in contact. This further implies an imperialistic relationship between the two literatures.

Two key concepts need to be discussed in order to understand the nature of cultural exchanges that are being problematized here. The first one is "pluralistic epistemology" and the second one is "margino-centricism". The nature of interrelationship among multiple versions of a text needs to be conceived as pluralistic epistemology rather than as being derivatives from an Ur text. As against a hierarchical model of understanding the relationship between a text and its versions, thereby implying an influence model in the diffusion of the text, pluralistic epistemology treats the text as well as its versions as coexisting systems and attributes an equal significance to them. As cultural dimensions take part in the production and consumption of all the multiple versions of a text, the representation categories (theme, genre, multi-mediality, etc.) and social categories (sect, region, language, gender, caste, etc.) interact with each other and transform these categories as social epistemologies. Hence, we need to read and understand the so-called versions as cultural specific dimensions of the texts. Viewed from this perspective, the multiple versions of the Rāma story, though sharing an indexical relationship with the purported text, are actually texts produced and consumed by communities and they can be re-conceptualized as cultural negotiations by these communities with the purported text's literary culture. Such a re-conceptualization not only nullifies the effects of imperialistic influence model of comparison but also takes comparative studies and translation studies into the domain of cultural studies.

Second, coming to margino-centricism, the model of influence studies also inherited the discourse of modernism in which the "self" is always the Europe (centre) and the "other" is always the colony and the subjugated (margin). In this sense, the view is always from the centre to the margins. In this sense, the colonial modernity was not just a political intervention but was also a system that advocated a dualistic system of conceiving the world, in terms of binary oppositions and logocentric constructions. On the other hand, if cultures are treated as continually evolving systems, then they could be perceived as eternally modernizing ones. Furthermore, if cultures are treated as a constellation of pluralistic epistemology, then the logic of dichotomous opposition and its imperialist discourse could be contested and countered. Such a contestation provides a pluralistic epistemology, rather pluralistic social epistemology that is organically linked to religion, language, caste, gender, etc. Viewed from the perspective of pluralistic social epistemologies, we are able to get margino-centric views, that not only reverse the dominant centre–margin singular perspective but instead also provide multiple perspectives from the margins, that are compatible with Spivak's (2003) planetary views.

By using the influence model of comparison, if we conclude that a culture got its cultural traits from some other culture, then we would be further dominating and marginalizing the locally developed and perfected knowledge systems, even if they are the borrowed ones. Moreover, in a comparison, it is the differences rather than the similarities that are equally valuable for the understanding of cultures. On the other hand, it is the cultural specificities that constitute the uniqueness of a culture. Culture as a knowledge system is a consequence of cumulative and fine-tuned pool of human experience spanning over long periods that involved many complex cultural interrelationships and innovations. Terming them as influence and borrowing actually amounts to undermining the contribution of the people in sustaining and developing them to further perfection to suit the specific requirements of the community. These changes need to be understood as contributions of the local community's knowledge system rather than as contamination of the "original" culture. As long as changes within systems are seen as innovations and not as contaminations, the systems are conceived as continually evolving ones. Such systems tend to modernize themselves constantly (Satyanath 2012). This is an altogether different way of looking at history of culture and its periodization.

It is within the context of the above discussion that we need to understand the cultural correspondences between India and South-East Asia. In order to show how looking at differences could provide an altogether different model of understanding the cultural contacts, I will take up a couple of examples. To start with, we need to take a look at the existing positions on the cultural correspondences between India and South-East Asia. The two figures given in *fig*. 15.1 provide the direction of diffusion of Buddhism from India during the first (Mahāyāna) and second (Theravāda) millennia. In any case the diffusion has been perceived to be unidirectional, implying an influence model.

However, such a model of diffusion of Buddhism in the entire Asia raises several questions. If there were such intense contacts within the region, then how is it that the South Asian studies have not recorded the movement of ideas and cultural traits in the opposite

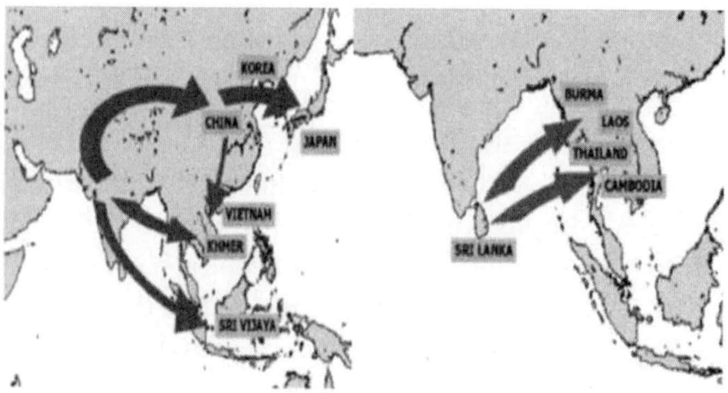


(a) (b)

*fig*. 15.1: Maps showing the diffusion of Buddhism: (a) Mahāyāna Buddhism (100–1000)[1] and (b) Theravāda Buddhism (1000 onwards)[2]

1 http://en.wikipedia.org/wiki/File:mahayanamap.gif (accessed on 13 August 2013).

2 http://en.wikipedia.org/wiki/File:theravadamap.gif (accessed on 13 August 2013).

direction. The silk and tea definitely have come from China but the studies somehow hesitate to celebrate the coming of silk and tea into India. Linguistically speaking, the category of numerical classifier, most probably diffused from one of language families of South-East Asia into the language families of India. In order to put the facts in the right perspective, we need to investigate this lack of interest in detail.

**Problematization**

Contrary to the unidirectional mode of diffusion as presumed by the influence model of comparison, research suggesting the flow of material culture in the other direction is also available, though not as conspicuous as it has been demonstrated for diffusion from India to South-East Asia. However, many of them are highly important cultural features and suggest a two-way interaction between the regions contrary to proposed unidirectional flow. Maloney (1979) suggests that several cultural artefacts such as rice, coconut and peacock are a consequence of their movement from South-East Asia. Masica (1976), in an attempt to define areal linguistic features using a cultural geography model, suggests that several linguistic features are shared commonly between South Asia and East Asia. Some of them, for instance "numerical classifiers", could as well be a case of diffusion from the Austro-Asiatic language family into the language families of India.

Masica's real interest has been in the typological convergence of languages belonging to different linguistic families in the area of South Asia and beyond, and provide possible explanations for such convergences and point out their implications for linguistic and cultural history of the region. Furthermore, Masica (1979) points out through a study of agricultural terms in Indian languages that many terms like rice and agricultural implements have moved from South-East Asia into South Asia. Scholars have suggested that presence of the technique of "resist dyeing" might be indigenous to South-East Asia, in particular to Indonesia, and might have diffused all over the world (Jett 1999). All these movements suggest that we need to treat material and cultural transactions between India and South-East Asia as a "multicultural corridor" in which intense cultural exchanges took place all along the history. In order to problematize the issue further let us consider the case of *Pañcatantra*.

The movement of *Pañcatantra* over several continents is a fascinating story of diffusion of texts and cultural elements during the precolonial period. Edgerton (1924) notes that it is the most frequently translated literary product of India and that the text has gone through many different versions and translations from the sixth century to the present day. However, it is only in terms of the themes of the stories that such diffusion appears to have taken place. If we compare the sculptural representations of *Pañcatantra* tales in India and the Persian and Arabic illuminated manuscripts from the Middle East region, then the margino-centricity that I am suggesting here becomes evident. Not only the painting conventions but also the literary versions are highly local. We need to take a careful look at the cultural details of the concept of the text here. The pre-modern texts in Asian cultures constituted manuscripts with painting as an integral part of it and were mostly narrated orally. In fact, they have to be treated as knowledge systems that were evolved locally. A thematic similarity need not reduce their cultural significance like a mechanically reproduced printed text that could easily be moved anywhere devoid of its systemic cultural knowledge.

Let us take a closer look at a recent comparative study of Pañcatantra's sculptural and literary traditions in India and Indonesia (Patil 2001). This study is a dense and meticulous comparative study that involves two levels between the sculptural and literary traditions subsuming trans-mediality on the one hand, and between India and Indonesia subsuming spatiality/nationality on the other. Though done within the influence and diffusion model of comparison, Patil's conclusions help us in the problematization that is being attempted here. Patil (2001: 89-90) notes that the Pañcatantra sculptures are conspicuous in their presence in south India, particularly in Karnataka, as compared to north India. Furthermore, he observes that whereas the north Indian sculptural versions follow the Viṣṇuśarman's literary tradition, the south Indian and the Indonesian sculptural traditions follow both Viṣṇuśarman's and Vasubhāga's literary traditions.

First of all, the two literary versions that have been conceptualized as part of Indian literary tradition could also be re-conceptualized as texts from two sectarian traditions, namely, the Brāhmanical (Viṣṇu-śarman) and the Jaina (Vasubhāga). The very fact that Durgasiṁha's

Kannada *Pañcatantra* (1031), Sanskrit *Tantropākhyāna* (*c.* 1200) and Tamil *Tantropākhyāna* (*c.* 1200) belong to the Vasubhāga's tradition, a Jaina tradition that comes from south India. Similarly, the Indonesian *Tantrī Kāmandaka* (*c.* 1400) too belongs to Vasubhāga's tradition is noteworthy. These re-conceptualizations bring together sectarian, sub-regional and medieval dynastic and trade links into focus. Hence, the comparison that is being made at the national level (India and Indonesia) actually turns out to be a comparison of sub-regions involving the political dynasties and their patronage to the poets, and their cultural and trade contacts. Treating medieval representations, be they literary or sculptural, as national representations is one of the criticisms that comparative literary studies have been increasingly confronting these days.

Second, a predetermined assumption that the sculptural representations are an outcome of literary representations also becomes a highly problematic one. I have pointed out elsewhere (Satyanath 2009) that the sculptural representations of the Kirāta Śiva and Arjuna episode of *Mahābhārata* from medieval Karnataka region not only pre-dates the literary versions but also follow a local version of the story that is radically different from the literary versions of Vyāsa, Bhāravi and many Kannada poets. On the other hand, medieval Indian representational modes, scripto-centric (manuscript), phono-centric (orality) and body-centric (performances, painting and sculpture), need to be conceived as a pluralistic epistemology that are independent and are autonomous representation systems, having a semiotic system of their own. We should note that Patil (2001: 90) observes that "most of the sculptures are earlier than the surviving literary traditions". Not only that "surviving" sculptural representations may pre-date "surviving" literary traditions but also that they may belong to an alternative and autonomous tradition of their own.

The two points discussed above have significant implications for our understanding of intercultural contacts during the medieval period. First of all, there is a need to blur the national literary traditions and instead go for specific regional traditions that are redefined in terms of medieval cultural categories rather than the modern ones. Second, re-inscribing, whether textual or sculptural, could be understood as tellings and renderings which make use of conventions from a cultural pool of signifiers consisting of plot, characters, names, geography, incidents and relations. Ramanujan (1991: 46) uses the metaphor of crystallization to capture this process and its function:

> The various texts not only relate to prior texts directly, to borrow or refute, but they relate to each other through this common code or common pool. Every author, if one may hazard a metaphor, dips into it and brings out a unique crystallization, a new text with a unique texture and a fresh context.

Scripto-centric, phono-centric and body-centric representations that are characteristic of medieval Indian literary culture are processes of such crystallization and are simultaneously trans-regional/national and culture-specific re-inscribings. Third, there is always a possibility that the body-centric tradition (sculptures and paintings) is not only older but also densely local (culture-specific) than the scripto-centric versions (literary traditions). Lastly, such re-conceptualizations create the possibility of viewing the interrelationship between cultures from a margino-centric perspective that provides a perspective from the "recipient" culture. Methodologically located in margins, such perspectives are always pluralistic and provide a "planetary view", one of the radical changes that Spivak (2003) has advocated for rejuvenating comparative literature.

I have suggested that comparative studies can get an altogether different perspective by re-conceptualizing inter-cultural relationships as pluralistic epistemology and adopting a methodology of margino-centricism. In a series of studies, dealing with *Rāmāyaṇa* and its versions in South Asia and South-East Asia, attempts have been made to demonstrate the influence of Indian texts on the South-East Asian texts, and in particular the version of Vālmīki *Rāmāyaṇa* (Raghavan 1975; Iyengar 1983). However, *Rāmāyaṇa*s within India themselves vary significantly on the axis of sects (Jaina, Buddhist and Śākta), region (vernacular traditions) and trans-medial dimensions (textual, oral, performative, sculptural and painting). Some of these studies have been either contested or re-conceptualized within the broad framework of the studies that have been noticed in recent years, particularly after Ramanujan's (1991) path-breaking paper "Three Hundred Ramayanas" appeared (cf. Richman 1991, 2001, 2008).

The studies within South-East Asia are not far different from such new developments. For example, Malay variations have a Rāma story in which Lakṣmaṇa plays a larger role, sometimes becoming more important than Rāma, much like the Lao's *Phra Lak Phra Lam.*[3] Rāma, although righteous and virtuous, was perceived to be weak and his character is often moved to the background while the younger Lakṣmaṇa is admired for his courage and willingness to react decisively. Within the context of the present paper, this deviation or development could be explained in two ways. The first one is to treat it as a local development specific to the Malay region. Alternatively, Lakṣmaṇa's prominence in these versions could be linked to the Jaina and tribal *Rāmāyaṇa* versions within India, where it is not Rāma but Lakṣmaṇa who is the dominant character. In the Jaina tradition (Vimalasūri), Rāma is an incarnation of Balabhadra, one of the sixty-three *śalākā-puruṣa*s (the revered ones), who is destined to become a liberated soul in his present birth. Obviously, he cannot commit violence by killing Rāvaṇa and his clan. Thus, the onus of killing them is on Lakṣmaṇa, an incarnation of Vāsudeva and thus it is he who is designated to kill Rāvaṇa, a Prati-Vāsudeva. In the Bhīl folk version too, it is Lakṣmaṇa who is the dominant character. Although an easy osmosis flow is possible between the folk and literary versions in Indian literary culture, it is safe to presume that the elements from the Jaina version might have been absorbed by the folk version, considering the fact that Vimalasūri's Jaina version dates back to the second century. It has been already pointed out in the case of *Pañcatantra*, it is elements of the Jaina version of Vasubhāga that are found in the Indonesian versions. Interestingly, it is the elements of the Jaina version of the Rāma story that appear conspicuously in the Indonesian versions. Medieval sectarian patronage, sectarian versions and trade contacts appear to play a crucial role in the diffusion of texts and their reception. However, there is plenty of scope for revisiting the issue of versions of Rāma story in the regions of South Asia and South-East Asia.

---

[3] This is the epic of the Lao people and is similar to some Malay versions of the *Hikayat Seri Rama*. The epic has lost its association with Hinduism and is instead considered a Jātaka story. It is also very popular in north-eastern Thailand, a region of Thailand mostly populated by ethnic Lao.

In order to take the argument further, in particular the significance of body-centric representations in the form of sculptures, we need to look at the temple architecture. The planning scheme like *tri-kūṭa* (three shrines complex) and *pañca-kūṭa* (five shrines complex), the shape of the *vimāna* (Draviḍa, Nāgara and Vesara), the decorative elements and epic themes on the walls can be considered for comparison and can be re-analysed making use of pluralistic epistemology and margino-centricism. However, if the aspect of cultural uniqueness and indigenous knowledge systems are to be understood and appreciated, the influence model of comparison needs to be abandoned and instead a margino-centric approach needs to be taken up.

Let us a look at two sculptural reliefs from the Rāma story, Rāvaṇa lifting the Kailāsa mountain. Though commonly perceived as a representation from the *Rāmāyaṇa* theme, it is possible to argue that this needs to be read more as a component of *Śiva Purāṇa*, rather than *Rāmāyaṇa* (Sharma 2012). The centrality of Rāvaṇa and the detailing given to him in both the sculptures, along with the relative proportioning of the characters, further substantiates this point. The two sculptures have a chronological order; the first one (*fig*. 15.2) is from the Virūpākṣa Temple from Pattadakal (740) in Karnataka and the latter (*fig*. 15.3) is from the temple Beantey Srei in Angkor, Cambodia (tenth century). Interestingly, the first one is a specimen of Bādāmī Cāḷukyan style, and this style has already been claimed to be one of the potential sources of influence for the sculptures in Prambanan.

Though the similarities in general establish an easy correspondence between the two sculptures (theme, posture, level, etc.), there are several technical details in which the two differ significantly: size, stone (medium), ornamentation, facial details and the paraphernalia of the sculptures, etc. The differences are located in the margins and it is such a margino-centric view that we need to take in order to understand the significance of technology and indigenous knowledge systems. It is the local conventions and the skills of the craftsmen that need to be highlighted here. What is striking between the two images is the technology and indigenous knowledge system of sculptures. Whereas the Indian sculpture is done using a single stone, in the case of Prambanan, the episode is made out of pre-sculpted smaller panels,

*fig.* 15.2: Rāvaṇa lifting Kailāsa, Virūpākaṣa Temple (740 CE), Pattadakal, Karnataka, India[4]

which have been joined together. If we fail to notice such details in an attempt to read similarities and influence, then the project of comparison becomes a hurdle in understanding cultural specificities of contacts. The two technologies of sculptural representation and indigenous knowledge systems are a part and parcel of pluralistic epistemology and their differences need to be celebrated as much as their similarities.

4 *Source*: Shyama Chatterji: http://przmn.blogspot.in/201108 01 archive.html (accessed on 18 January 2013).

*fig.* 15.3: Rāvaṇa lifting Kailāsa, temple at Banteay Srei in Angkor (tenth century CE), Cambodia[5]

## Implications for Comparative Asian Literary Cultures

Let us take a closer look at pluralistic epistemology, margino-centricism and cultural representations as indigenous knowledge systems in order to work out a model for understanding Asian literary cultures in a comparative perspective. The model of pluralistic epistemology and margino-centricism not only interconnects the representational formats and provides a holistic view of representations, but also takes societal and community orientation as social epistemologies in the understanding of cultures. They also allow us to compare Asian communities and their literary cultures. As social epistemologies tend to get mediated by community inscribings, the processes of re-mythicization, re-ritualization and re-iconization become constantly ongoing processes and keep the literary culture pluralistic and at the same time, activate a sustenance mode rather than the merger and replacement mode. It is also possible to argue that the pluralistic

[5] I thank Ms. Stuti Sharma for drawing my attention to this sculpture; *Source*: http://localhost/upload.wikimedia.org/Wikipedia/commons/0/07/Banteay_Seri_in_Angkor.jpg (accessed on 18 January 2013).

epistemology and margino-centricism could as well be a case of centrifugal (diversifying and vernacularization) rather than centripetal (unifying and cosmopolitan) process. This further suggests that pluralistic epistemology and margino-centricism could as well be a case of co-operative and coexisting systems rather than a case of hierarchical systems. As pointed out earlier, in the case of Indian literature, social aspects like sect, gender, caste and language constitute the social epistemology of cultural representations. This in turn brings in structural convergences within the representational formats. The structural similarities might prompt us to anticipate syncretism or convergence and eventually the merging of systems. This might eventually predict the elimination of pluralistic epistemology and facilitate a monogenetic form and the efficacy of the influence model. However, this may not be the case as we have already seen. At the same time, it is important to understand that pluralistic epistemology is also social epistemology and would take us to the understanding of the cultures on the one hand while on the other margino-centricism may encourage the sustenance of plurality rather than their merger. For a long time, comparative studies have been undertaken within the framework of an influence model. It is time that we start looking for alternative models that are sensitive to culture studies.

Furthermore, the argument put forward here facilitates us to suggest that as a case of pluralistic epistemology, multiple representations could also have their own independent semiotic systems rather than a unitary or composite one. Thus we can expect multiple and/or hybrid semiotic systems in operation for scripto-centric, phono-centric and body-centric representational systems. The possibility of a format-specific semiotic system would in turn provide a case for the separation of monogenetic textual context and pluralistic performative contexts that reflect divergent social epistemologies. This is only to underscore the need for an appropriate model to undertake comparative studies of literary cultures of Asia and to point out that such a model needs to incorporate comparison, trans-mediality and interdisciplinarity as its essential components. Furthermore, area studies needs to be re-conceptualized within the context of cultural areas on the one hand and mediating colonial modernity on the other hand. The twentieth century construct of national literary culture need to take a trans-national dimension to incorporate the construction of meaningful cultural areas.

**Acknowledgement**

An earlier version of the paper was presented at the "International Conference on South-East–East Asia and India" held at Bhagat Phool Chand Mahila Vishwavidyalaya, Khanpur Kalan during 18-20 January 2013. I would like to acknowledge Professor Kapil Kapoor and Dr. Daisy Nehra for inviting me to the Conference and to the editors for including my paper in the volume. I also wish to acknowledge Ms. Sakshi Soni for her suggestions and comments, most of which have been incorporated.

## References

Edgerton, Franklin, 1924, *The Panchatantra Reconstructed* (vol. 1: *Text and Critical Apparatus*, vol. 2: *Introduction and Translation*), Connecticut: American Oriental Series, vols. 2-3.

Iyengar, K.R. Srinivasa (ed.), 1983, *Asian Variations in Ramayana*, New Delhi: Sahitya Akademi.

Jett, Stephen C., 1999, "Resist-Dyeing: A Possible Ancient Transoceanic Transfer", *New England Antiquities Research Association Journal*, **33**(1): 41-55.

Maloney, Clarence, 1975, "Archaeology in South India: Accomplishments and Prospectus", in *Essays on South India*, ed. Burton Stein, pp. 1-40, Hawaii: University Press of Hawaii.

Masica, Colin P., 1976, *Defining a Linguistic Area: South Asia*, Chicago: The University of Chicago Press.

———, 1979, "Aryan and Non-Aryan Elements in North Indian Agriculture", in *Aryan and Non-Aryan in India*, ed. M.M. Deshpande and P.E. Hook, pp. 55-151, Ann Arbor: Karoma.

Patil, Chennabasappa, 2001, "Panchatantra Sculptures and Literary Traditions in India and Indonesia: A Comparative Study", in *Narrative Sculptures and Literary Traditions in South and Southeast Asia*, ed. Marijke J. Klokke, pp. 73-95, Leiden: Brill.

Raghavan, V. (ed.), 1975, *The Ramayana Tradition in Asia*, New Delhi: Sahitya Akademi.

Ramanujan, A.K., 1991, "Three Hundred Ramayanas: Five Examples and Three Thoughts on Translation", in *Many Ramayanas: The Diversity of a Narrative Tradition in South Asia*, ed. Paula Richman, pp. 22-48, Berkeley: University of California Press.

Richman, Paula (ed.), 1991, *Many Ramayanas: The Diversity of a Narrative Tradition in South Asia*, Berkeley: University of California Press.

——— (ed.), 2001, *Questioning Ramayans: A South Asian Tradition*, Berkeley: University of California Press.

——— (ed.), 2008, *Ramayana Stories in Modern South India: An Anthology*, Bloomington: Indiana University Press.

Saran, Malini and Vinod C. Khanna, 2004, *The Ramayana in Indonesia*, Delhi: Ravi Dayal and Orient Longman.

Satyanath, T.S., 2009, "Tellings and Renderings in Medieval Karnataka: The Episode of Kirata Shiva and Arjuna", in *Decentering Translation Studies: India and Beyond*, ed. Judy Wakabayashi and Rita Kothari, pp. 43-56, Amsterdam: John Benjamins.

———, 2012, "Mapping Alternative Modernity: Smallpox as a Knowledge System", in *Folklore and the Alternative Modernities*, vol. II, ed. Nandini Sahu, pp. 450-68, New Delhi: Authors Press.

Sharma, Stuti, 2012, *Mapping Myriad Faces of Ravana in Indian Representations*, Unpublished M.Phil. Dissertation, University of Delhi, Delhi.

Spivak, Gayatri Chakravorty, 2003, *Death of a Discipline*, Columbia: Columbia University Press.

# 16

# Religious Art in Cambodia
## Śaivism, Vaiṣṇavism and Buddhism

*Rajnish Kumar Mishra*

**Abstract**

This paper explores the dissemination and assimilation of Indian culture in Cambodia (the name derived from Sanskrit *Kambuja*) through art and architecture in the long history of more than a millennium. In the three successive phases, three major *dharmas* of India, Śaivism, Vaṣṇavism and finally the Theravāda Buddhism were introduced in Cambodia and got integrated with the mass culture and religious practices. The fusion of cultural elements of these *dharmas* is visible in the temple art and architecture of Angkor Vat (lit. the temple city), Mealea and Bayon. Cambodia has the attested history of Indian contact since the first century BCE when the brāhmaṇa rites and rituals were introduced and in the first century CE. The south Indian emigrants firmly established the brāhmaṇa faith, Sanskrit alphabet system and Indian customs and rituals. The paper records such shared cultural elements and illustrates them through the philosophy of religious/temple art and architecture.

### Historical Contacts and Early Settings

TOPOGRAPHICALLY South-East Asia refers to the area which is south of China and east of India which includes sovereign states like Myanmar (Burma), Thailand, Laos, Cambodia (Kampuchea) and Vietnam. From mythology to history this area has been umbilically connected to India and the historians have conceptualized this relationship as "Greater India", "Farther India" or "Indianized States".[1] These nomenclatures

---

1 Historians like R.C. Majumdar discuss this relation under the general theme "Colonial and Cultural Expansion". See Majumdar et al. 1978: 202.

→

precisely include Mynmar, southern Thailand, Cambodia, south Vietnam, coastal west Malaya, eastern Sumatra and Java's north coast.

Much before the age of empire building began, the Indian traders, scholars and saints had discovered and opened up the routes to these far off lands beyond the sea. In its long, rich and even in the millennium of invasion, bloodshed, mental subjugation and colonization, India never lived an isolated life. Politically and culturally India remained actively engaged with Far East, Western and Central Asia and major parts of the West. Around the second half of the first century a Greek trader in his minute and reliable account of experiences in a book called *The Periplus of the Erythraean Sea* has stated about India's frequent trade relations with the Arab and the Western countries. According to this record, the Indian merchants were also settled in some islands of the Arabian Sea and the island of Socortra had a colony of Indian merchants.[2] But the impact of Indian culture and religion was far deeper and sustainable than these economic ties. We learnt that Emperor Aśoka had sent Buddhist missionaries to western Asia, northern Africa and south-eastern Europe and it was claimed that the tenets of that religion were welcome in all those places. Even long after Emperor Aśoka, Alexandria exhibited interest in Buddhism. Both Buddhism and Brāhmanism were widely prevalent in the several countries of Western Asia. The advent of Islam set a new world order. Due to the political disintegration at home and troubled medieval period in the Western and Central Asia, India gradually got cut-off from Europe and slipped into mythical imagination of the West only later to be discovered by the Columbuses and the Vasco da Gamas that eventually resulted in another phase of contacts, interactions and finally physical and mental colonization.[3]

---

← Prof. Kapil Kapoor reasonably grouped the major countries of the South-East Asia into two — (i) "South-East-East Asia" comprising Laos, Thailand, Cambodia and Vietnam (which constitutes the theme of the International Conference held in January 2013 organized by the Centre for India-Asian Studies, BPS Mahila Vishwavidyalaya, Khanpur Kalan, Sonipat, Haryana) and (ii) South-South-East Asia comprising Myanmar, Singapore, Malaysia and Indonesia.

2 Ibid.: 202-03.

3 For a detailed account on this theme, see Danino 2000.

In the South-East Asia, too, both through the overland and maritime routes, Indian traders had already expanded their trade by the beginning of the Christian era. Though the Chinese trade and culture were flourishing in this region, but the Indian imprint remained more prevalent than that of the Chinese between the first to fifteenth century CE. The "Indian or Indianized States" weakened and declined by the middle of the fourteenth century CE and the Islamic influence took over the area between thirteenth to fifteenth century CE mostly through the maritime trade. The seventeenth century witnessed the consolidation and organization of these new influences followed by the European colonizers and Christian missionaries. Again a new world order was shaping and this process finally culminated into the age of imperialism and the two world wars. India due to its troubled medieval period and colonization thereafter again remained oblivious of its immediate neighbourhood or its extended cultural geography. Yavadvīpa (modern Java, Skt. literally means "the land of Millet") and the Suvarṇabhūmi (Golden Land) or Suvarṇadvīpa (Island of Gold), a general designation of the several regions in the Far East frequently mentioned in the narratives of *Jātaka*s and *Kathāsaritsāgara,* slipped again into its mythical imagination. The anonymous author, cited above, of *Periplus of the Erythraean Sea* refers to some of the Far Eastern countries as Chryse which too means Golden Land.[4]

As stated above, though some historians and Indologists have used the term "colonial expansion" to define this phenomenon of presence of India beyond its political boundaries, but the term "colonial" does not share the connotation which is constituted in the disciplines like Colonial or post-Colonial, neo-Colonial studies. These disciplines are foregrounded in the age of imperialism (political or cultural) and broadly in the context of "third world countries". In the imperial or colonial contexts official history is not meant for *bhūtārtha kathana* (stating the truth — as it has happened) as Kalhaṇa would put it,[5] but history has also been devised as a "memory eraser", an effective

[4] Majumdar 1978: 205 and a map on pp. 48-49; Majumdar 1981: 288-312. Chryse is identified with Malaya Peninsula was also known as the Land of Gold (p. 312).

[5] "That man of merit alone deserves praise whose language, like that of judge, in recounting the events of the past has discarded bias as well as prejudice," *Rājataraṅginī*, 1.7.

tool to weaken or to wipe out mass memory of a nation or community. At this juncture of forced and self-inflected cultural amnesia we need to look at India's past and its cultural and religious affinities particularly in the South-East Asia.

But before we move to our theme under discussion, we need to note a possible pitfall associated with the reference of the two names: Kambuja and Kāmboja. Though they appear phonetically similar but they denote two different geographical locations. Kāmboja was one of the sixteen *janapada*s in ancient India mentioned in early Buddhist texts and was located in south-west Kashmir and Gandhāra.[6] *Śrīmadbhāgavata* records that Śrī Kr̥ṣṇa had defeated the king of Kāmboja.[7] References to Suvarṇadvīpa are available in ancient literary accounts such as in *Jātaka-Aṭṭakathā* and *Kathāsaritsāgara*, yet it would be difficult to establish that Cambodia was once known as Kāmboja instead of Kambuja. Etymologically, both the words are derived from the Sanskrit word *kambu* (literally conch). Cambodia has not yet given up this deep historical and cultural affinity with "Greater India" as conventional the name used by the Royal Government of Cambodia is Preh-reach-ana-chak Kampuchea, a compound formed by Khmer, Sanskrit and Pāli words where *preh* means sacred, *reach* (Skt. *rājā*) means king or royalty, *chak* (Skt. *cakra*) means wheel and the name of the country Kampuchea is phonologically derived from Sanskrit Kambuja. The present Cambodia, which experienced the colonial history like India under the French got its independence in 1953, has Khmer as the state language and Theravāda Buddhism as its state religion. But this is at the end of a long glorious and troubled historical journey.

The Khmer, Mon-Khmers also known as Kambujas or Cambodians come from the Sino-Tibetan race and origin that occupied and settled in the Mekong and Menam deltas including southern Burma. Most of

---

6 Jawaharlal Nehru in his celebrated book *The Discovery of India* seems to have confused these two names: Kamboja and Kambuja: "Thus Cambodia, as it is known now, was called Kāmboja, which was a well-known town in ancient India, in Gandhara or in the Kabul Valley." (p. 202). Kālidāsa is familiar with Kāmboja as he clearly mentions: *kāmbojaḥ samaresoḍhum tasyavīryamaniśvaraḥ* / (*Raghuvaṁśam* 4.69). But he does not show any acquaintance of Kambuja. Yāska (ninth century BCE), the renowned Sanskrit semanticist and etymologist too refers to Kamboja as *śavatīrgatikarmā kāmbojeṣveva* (*Nirukta* II.23).

7 *Śrīmadbhāgavata*, 2.7.35.

the early information is derived from the Chinese sources.[8]

The mythical-legendary accounts hold that a brāhmaṇa Kauṇḍinya from south India, probably around the first century CE came to Fu-nan (Chinese name), married Somā, a Nāga princess[9] and established the kingdom in this land of Nāga worshippers. He built his capital near the Mekong River and the Soma dynasty began hereafter.[10] Around the fourth century CE we came to know another Kauṇḍinya and according to the Chinese accounts he was a brāhmaṇa from India who out of divine inspiration visited Fu-Nan[11] and Pan-Pan (south of Fu-Nan). He was elected as king and transformed the existing political and cultural practices and popularized Indian customs and rules.[12] After 300 years we hear about another Kauṇḍinya who visited Fu-Nan and established his kingdom.[13] It seems that the name Kauṇḍinya gradually got institutionalized in course of time to denote the father-founders of the Cambodian kingdom. The historical accounts also refer to a brāhmaṇa named Agastya from Āryadeśa who is also believed to have founded a royal dynasty. The queen Indradevī (of King Indravarmana) and her mother Rājendradevī was believed to be the descendants of the royal family founded by Agastya. *Brahmāṇḍa Purāṇa* refers to Kambu who was one of the ten sons of Raivata Manu.[14] Mythical-legendary accounts establish that Kambu-Svayambhū was the Manu and Khmers his descendants. The name Kambuja also

---

8 Cf. Coomaraswamy 2006: 824.

9 Cam inscription 659 also referred to the same story where the princess is designated as Nāginī.

10 Stealse Inscription of Prakāśadharmaḥ records:

. . . *kalāsībhujagendrakanyā someti sā vaśaṁkarī pṛthivyām* ı
*kauṇḍinyanāmnā dvijapuṅgavena kāryyārthapatnītvamanāyiyāpi* ıı

11 A group of kingdoms including Cambodia, Cochin-China and Southern Siam.

12 Brijen Raj Chatterji, *Indian Cultural Influence in Cabmodia* (p. 210) quoted in Vedalamkar 1999: 187.

13 Kauṇḍinya is a frequent name in the Vedic-Paurāṇic narratives. The *Śatapatha Brāhmaṇa* 14.4.5.10 mentions his as a prominent sage. The Sabhāparva of *Mahābhārata* also refers to a sage Kauṇḍinya who was born in the Kuṇḍin clan (4.14).

14 *Brahmāṇḍa Purāṇa* 2.36.64.

indicates the same as it means born of Kambu. We do intend to extend these records into the ambit of history; nevertheless, these records establish the cultural and political bonding of these two countries since the dawn of history itself. This legend is definitely of the Indian origin. Nāga cult has been popular in the Indian Śiva-Śākta mystic systems. Sage Patañjali is said to be a re-incarnation of Śeṣanāga, a great custodian of knowledge and is depicted as half human (upper part) and half serpentine (lower part). The Kauṇḍinya narrative has also the Indian origin as the Pallavas are said to be the descendants of the union of a Coḷa king and a Nāginī.[15]

It is important to note that the notion of Greater India has not been seen only as an expansion of political boundaries but as a continuity and integrity as well. An Arab traveller opined that Kambuja was a part of India and its people maintained relations with India.[16] Similarly another traveller Masuhī (CE 943) recorded that India was a big country. One of its tribes inhabited far away in Kambuja.[17] Another Arab writer observed:

> The kings and peoples of India abstain from drinking wine but they do not consider adultery as an illicit act, with the sole exception of the Khmer king who forbids both drinking and adultery.[18]

The passage clearly indicates the continuity and integrity of this vast land of South-East Asia.

Śrutavarmā (fourth century CE), bearing the patronymic — *varman* (protector cf. Varmā), however, not exclusively a Pallavas' patronymic, of the Lunar dynasty, was the first king who organized Cambodia along the assumptions of a Hindu civilization. Then we came to know the mighty empire founded by Bhavavarman at the end of the sixth century CE. Bhavavarman took the designation of *rājādhirāja* (greatest among all the kings). He was a great devotee of Śiva but at the same time was devoted to Viṣṇu — a cult of Harihara (both Viṣṇu and Śiva). Cambodia had been a witness of synthesis of many distinct cults such as Śiva, Viṣṇu, Buddha (both Theravāda and Mahāyāna),

15 Coomaraswamy, 2006: 824.

16 Quoted in Vedalamkar 1999: 215.

17 Ibid.: 215.

18 R.C. Majumdar, 2009, *The History and Culture of Indian People*, vol. IV, p. 419.

Brāhmanism and the local Nāga worshipping which was not so smoothly synthesized in the homeland (India) of these cults. However, Haihara worship is not something unknown in India.[19] Mahendravarman succeeded the throne in CE 604 was also a devotee of Śiva and an inscription from Bayon exhibits he had established Śivapada (revered feet of Śiva) which reminds us of the same religious symbols of Viṣṇupada at Bodh-Gayā (Bihar) and Buddhapada at Siam and Ceylon. His successor Īśānavarman paid equal respect to both Śaivism and Vaiṣṇavism but Śaivism was more prominent in his time.[20] He also laid the tradition of building *āśrama*s (abodes for the ascetics and saints).

By the eighth century the vast kingdom of Bhavavarman disintegrated into a number of principalities but the two of them referred in the Chinese sources are: Kambuja of Land and Kambuja of Water. The first broadly refers to the northern Cambodia and the large part of Laos. Kambuja of Water mainly refers to the lower valley of the Mekong River. This part of Kambuja is of our particular interest as here we witness the representative art pertaining to the three most prominent religions. Local inscriptions make reference to three kingdoms with their capitals at Śambhupra (modern Sambor on the Mekong) , Vyādhpura (probably the ancient kingdom of Fu-Nan) and the third Aninditapura (east of Angkor). R.C. Majumdar notes that it is the rulers of Aninditapura who claimed to the descendants of Kauṇḍinya and Somā.[21]

We have very little details about the life and role of Jayavarman I, but with the emergence of Jayavarman II and III Kambuja initiated writing of its unparallel saga of glory in the South-East Asia. The reign of Jayavarman II who ascended the throne in CE 802 and his son Jayavarman III who ruled from CE 854-77 saw again the emergence of a

---

[19] The two nomenclatures of the religious city Haridwar or Hardwar referring to the corridors to Badrinātha and Kedāranātha refer to this fact. In Sonpore of Bihar, there is a famous Śiva temple named Hariharnātha. *Rāmacaritamānasa* of Tulasīdāsa can be seen as an attempt to bring about the synthesis between Śaivism and Vaṣṇavism.

[20] In one of his Sanskrit inscriptions, Īśānavarman praises Śiva as:
*jayatīndukalāmaulirneka guṇavistaḥ* ।
*sa ādirapi bhūtānāmanādinidhanaḥ śivaḥ* ॥

[21] Majumdar, 2009, *The History and Culture of the Indian People*, vol. IV: 416.

mighty Kambuja. According to a Chinese traveller in CE 862 the whole of Laos was part of Kambuja. Jayavarman II fixed his capital at Mahendraparvata and invited the brāhmaṇa Hiraṇyadāma from India who instituted the cult of Devarāja and initiated Śivakaivayla (the royal *guru* tradition, very similar to the Indian royal dynasty). For rest of his life, Jayavarman II ruled his kingdom from his old capital Hariharālaya, some 13 miles to the south-east of Angkor.

A new dynasty was founded by King Indravarman (CE 877) after Jayavarman III who was remotely related to the family of the latter. Indravarman was a Śaiva and the founder of the city of Śivapura. After the successful reign of twelve years he passed away in 889 and his son Yaśovarman inherited the kingdom. Like his father he, too, founded the city of Kambupurī which was later known and Yaśodharapur. He was well versed in traditions of Śāstra (scholastic texts) and Kāvya (poetic compositions). Sources record that he also composed a commentary on *Mahābhāṣya* of Patañjali.[22] Though he too was an ardent devotee of Śiva, he was equally liberal to other faiths and cults like Vaṣṇavism and Buddhism. He was a brave warrior, a philosopher–scholar king and a great devotee.

After his death in CE 900 his two sons Harṣavarman and Īśānavarman succeeded the kingdom. But the struggle for succession began and Jayavarman IV overthrew Īśānavarman and became the king. After three intervening years (CE 941-43) of rule by Harṣavarman II, the son of Jayavarman IV, Rājendravarman succeeded the struggle for the monarch. He died in CE 968 was succeeded by his son Jayavarman V. During these of instability and struggle, Śaivism remained the official religion but Rājendravarman also propagated Buddhism in his kingdom. Jayavarman V died in CE 1001 and the royal lineage of Indravarman also ended with him.

This followed instability in the ruling classes till Sūryavarman I ascended the throne in CE 1010. It appears that he had embraced Buddhism as he had been posthumously designated as *nirvāṇapāda*.

22 Majumdar, vol. IV: 420. If this claim is true then Yaśovarman could be credited with defying the maxim: *mahārājāyaṁ vā pālanīyam mahābhāṣyam vā pāṭhanīyam*, i.e. either one should rule a vast country or teach/study *Mahābhāṣya*. Writing a commentary on such a text which itself is a Grand Commentary is not in any form an inferior assignment compared to teaching this text.

As the earlier kings of Kambuja represented a rare but true synthesis of various religious faiths and cults, Sūryavarman's inscriptions also exhibit the testimony to this trend as they record the invocations of Śiva and Buddha. The King Sūryavarman was a great scholar of various Indian philosophical systems, social thought and poetry. The reign of this great king was followed by political turmoil and after a series of intervening rulers such as Udayādityavarman, Harṣavarman and Jayavarman VI, again a great king Sūryavarman II ascended the throne in CE 1113. He expanded and maintained the territories and achieved the zenith of glory of the Angkor/Classic period by constructing the greatest religious temple complex and one of the wonders of the world at Angkor Vat. And after a few more rulers in between, finally the last glorious king who succeeded was Jayavarman VII whose reign continued till the twelfth century.

## Śaivism, Vaṣṇavism and Buddhism

As we have seen above that right from the inception of the empire, the rulers of Kambuja could be characterized by three elements: bravery, scholarship and religiosity. They strictly followed their *rājadharma*, leading the life of ideal kings of Indian legends and mythology. The religious life of Kambujadeśa was happily wedded with what was indigenous to Khmer and what was brought to their land by the mythical–legendary individuals like Kauṇḍinya or Agastya. The wedding of Kauṇḍnya and Nāga princess Somā is nothing alien to the Indian mind or to the Khmers. Nāga as a religious cult or race have been quite known to the Indian subcontinent. The dissemination of Śaivism and subsequently Vaiṣṇavism and Buddhism in India also got reflected in the life of Cambodia. Throughout the religious history of Kambuja, particularly till the tenth century, Śaivism remained a prominent faith among the kings and masses. But the kings themselves were liberal to other cults and faith, including the Tāntrikas, their personal or state religion never impeded the growth and dissemination of others. In fact, some records establish this liberty of religious practices and various forms of worship:

> People of Fu-Nan worship many gods and they also make the images of gods — some gods have two hands and some four hands, and some even four mouths. . . .[23]

[23] Quoted from Vedalamkar 1999: 187.

This land might have been associated with China for its politics, trade and commerce but its culture, religion, art and architecture all are essentially Indian. The metaphorical extension of the wedding of Kauṇḍinya and Somā symbolizes the peaceful reception and interaction of Indian culture with that of the Khmers. Indian thought systems have always travelled beyond the political boundaries and got assimilated into the indigenous host cultures and traditions. The dissemination of Buddhism beyond the Indian frontiers and taking new form in China, Korea, Japan, Thailand, Bhutan and Cambodia is one of such phenomena that exemplifies the adaptability and assimilative nature of Indian thought systems. We have seen that the early kings like Bhavavarman, Mahendravarman, Īśānavarman and also those who followed them were mainly devotees of Śiva but they generously protected and supported the Vaṣṇavaites and the Buddhists. In the same vein, Sūryavarman I and II were Vaiṣṇava kings but they never neglected the parallel faith systems. In all the major phases and practices of religious faiths namely, Śaivism, Vaiṣṇavism, Nāga cults and Buddhism, Kambuja remained essentially related to India. This religiosity and integrated devotions and regards for the other systems also got translated into the grand and immortal religious art and architecture of the Khmer kings and the artists.

## Religious Art: Philosophy and Expressions

All art expressions may not be necessarily religious but grand and immortal art is profoundly religious in nature. This is perhaps a world-wide phenomenon when we glance over the great examples of art and architecture created by renowned kings and anonymous artists. Great art is conceived as a humble and total submission to the desired deity whether *saguṇa-sākāra* (with attribute and form) or *nirguṇa-nirākāra* (with a specific form and attribute). Art expressions in India and in Greater India are testimony to this fact. Art experience is also that of the experience or realization of the Self.[24]

Cambodian art is an unparallel monument of human devotion and singing of the glory of the Supreme. Grand religious structure and temple cities like Angkor Vat derived its philosophy and art

[24] Here one may refer to the exposition of Bharata Muni's *rasa* theory by the great Śaivācārya Abhinavagupta, Kashmir poetician in tenth-eleventh-century.

principles mainly from India and assimilated the Khmer elements as well (*fig*. 16.1 and 16.2). The temple in its grand design is perceived as the replica of the cosmos (*brahmāṇḍa*) or the inner self of an individual (*piṇḍa*). From *pāda* (foot) to *śikhara* (top), a temple is a pulsating being, with the deity at its sanctum sanctorum (*garbhagṛha*). Leaving apart the vast physical space we move towards the narrow enclosures of a

*fig*. 16.1: Angkor Vat Temple (early 12th century CE)

*fig*. 16.2: Image of *samudra-manthana*
(the famous Paurāṇic theme of sea-churning)

temple. The gradual shrinking physical space ensures the expanding spiritual space. The moment we cross the five or three enclosures of the temple we face the deity, at first with the sense of duality and subsequently with non-dual devotion and total submission. The deity and the devotee become one and the same.

Cambodia on the whole is a temple civilization, a sacred topology. Its religious architecture is shaped by the finest fusion of Sino–Khmer–Indian elements. These architectural devices can be broadly classed as those which have pyramidal shape, i.e. a series of narrow terrace rising one above the other (Phimeanakas); those which have *meru* (*śikhara*) that is enclosed and raised terrace each rising 15-20 ft higher than the level of other (such as Angkor Vat and Bayon); those which have only three enclosures like the temples of Ta Prohm and finally those which are smaller temples — a series of three to five sanctuaries with the central one being prominent. The religious architecture of Kambuja is marked with the south Indian elements such as *śikhara*, *gopuram*, *maṇḍapam* and *garbhagṛha*.

Bayon is supposed to be a Śiva temple city. However, the inscriptional evidences indicate the presence of Viṣṇu as well. The Śiva Temple was in the middle of the city and it was the greatest building in the city. It is pyramidal in shape and has three sections each having high *śikhara*s with engraved meditating Śiva (*fig*. 16.3a, b). It seems the deity himself has come out to receive his devotee. The third eye of Śiva is also noteworthy in these images. Bayon is regarded as the excellence of Kambuja architecture.

Angkor Thom was the capital city established by Jayavarman VII, about a mile north of Angkor Vat. Once a splendid city, often compared by the historians with Rome, which in the days of Nero had suffered from both man and nature. Angkor Thom, now in ruins, is marked by the Brāhmanical and Buddhist structures (*figs*. 16.4-16.6).

Much has been written about Angkor Vat — the greatest monument in religious art. Fergusson's comment on the Coḷa artist aptly describes this magnificent Cambodian Viṣṇu Temple, now a centre of Theravāda Buddhism. Fergusson states: "The Coḷa artists conceived like giants and finished like jewellers".[25]

---

[25] Quoted by Majumdar 1978: 243.

*fig*. 16.3a: Bayon Temple (late 9th century CE)

*fig*. 16.3b: Bayon Temple's *śikhara* carved with meditating Śiva (*mukhaliṅgam*)

*fig*. 16.4: Earliest surviving mount temple of Bakong

*fig*. 16.5: Bakong, Angkor

*fig*. 16.6: The Buddha with the serpenthood

The nature of Cambodian art is deeply religious. This is one of the central characteristics of Indian art as well. No history of Asian art would ever be claimed as complete without the reference to the magnificant South-East Asian art.

## References


Basham, A.L. (ed.), 1975, *A Cultural History of India*, Delhi: Oxford University Press.

Chandler, David, 1992, *A History of Cambodia*, Boulder: Westview Press.

Coedès, George, 1968, *The Indianized States of Southeast Asia*, Honolulu: East West Center Press.

Coomaraswamy, A.K., 2006, "South-East Asian Art", *Cultural Heritage of India*, VII: pt. 1 (ed.) Kapila Vatsyayan, Kolkata: The Ramakrishna Mission.

Denino, Michel, 2000, *The Invasion That Never Was*, Delhi: Aditya Publications.

Forbes, Andrew, David Henley, 2011, *Angkor, Eighth Wonder of the World*, Chiang Mai: Cognoscenti Books.

Gode, P.K., 1961, *Studies in Indian Cultural History*, Hoshiyarpuram: Vishweshwaranad Vedic Institute.

Greene, Ronald et al. (eds.), 2012, *The Princeton Encyclopedia of Poetry and Poetics* (4th edn.), Princeton and Oxford: Princeton University Press.

Higham, Charles, 2001, *The Civilization of Angkor*, Berkeley: University of California Press.

Kalhaṇa, *Rājataraṅginī*, 1968, *The Saga of the Kings of Kaśmīr*, tr. R.S. Pandit, Delhi: Sahitya Akademi.

Majumdar, R.C., 1944, *Kambuja-Deśa*, Pennsylvania: Institute for Study of Human Issues.

———, 1953, *Inscriptions of Kambuja*, Calcutta: The Asiatic Society.

———, 1960, *The Classical Accounts of India*, Calcutta: Firma KLM.

Majumdar, R.C. et al., 1978, *An Advanced History of India*, 4th edn., Madras: Macmillan.

——— (eds.), 2001 (5th edn.), *The History and Culture of Indian People* (vol. V, *The Struggle for Empire*) Mumbai: Bharatiya Vidya Bhawan.

———, 2009 (5th edn.) *The History and Culture of Indian People*, vol. IV, Mumbai: Bharatiya Vidya Bhawan.

Nehru, Jawaharlal, 1946 (1981), *The Discovery of India*, New Delhi: Jawaharlal Nehru Memorial Fund and Oxford University Press.

Sharma, Ranaprasad, 1986, *Pauraṇika Kośa*, 2nd edn., Varanasi: Gyanamandal.

Vatsyayan, Kapila (ed.), 2006, *The Cultural Heritage of India* (vol. VII, pt. 1), Kolkata: The Ramakrishna Mission.

Vedalankara, Chandragupta, 1999, *Vr̥hattara Bhārata*, 3rd edn., Delhi: Dayanand Sansthan.

# 17

# Buddhist Engagement in South-East Asia
## A Case Study of Vietnam

*Anita Sharma*

SOUTH-EAST Asia is one of the most important emerging regions in the present-day world. The long colonial rule in this region intermingled with conflicts at different levels and the active involvement of world powers in this area have contributed towards the relative instability and backwardness of some of the countries. Though Buddhist social activism started in response to Christian interaction in many Asian countries, the term "Engaged Buddhism" was first coined in 1963 by Thich Nhat Hanh, a Vietnamese Zen Buddhist monk at a time when his country was ravaged by war. He began to seek solutions to this and other problems by applying Buddhist teachings in a more activist way than had hitherto been the case.[1] His view of symbiotic relationship between spiritual cultivation and social engagement revolves around the fact that a reformed mind is more receptive for cultivation of progressive ideas. Engaged Buddhist Reform Movement of Thich Nhat Hanh is concerned with physical, social and political as well as the mental, emotional and spiritual dimensions of human existence. His Engaged Buddhist Movement has strengthened Buddhism by giving it a new direction.

The Buddhist movements in the form of social engagement are gaining popularity in Vietnam society where many lay Buddhists along with monks are extending their hands to assist downtrodden people. Buddhists constitute the major portion of the religious population in many countries on the Asian subcontinent where Buddhists, like their

---

1 Damien Keown, 2003, *A Dictionary of Buddhism*, Oxford University Press, p. 86.

counterparts in other nations, have been making efforts to turn Buddhism into a socially relevant and useful religion. The contemporary socially-engaged monks are bringing religion to the mainstream of social life by setting up a persistent charitable organization. "Socially Engaged Buddhism" is bringing all Buddhist sects on a common platform. Keeping this in view, along with undertaking the task of maintaining monasteries and practising rituals, a large number of monks and nuns have also assumed social responsibility in the modern globalized world. The present paper is an attempt to offer holistically the origin and development of Engaged Buddhist Movement in Vietnam with a focus on the contribution of Thich Nhat Hanh.

It is imperative to note that Buddhism has already been engaged with society for 3,000 years, setting an example of coexistence with diverse cultures. Kenneth Kraft has argued that "the principles and even some of the techniques of an engaged Buddhism have been latent in the tradition since the time of its founder".[2] Buddhist social ethics, in keeping with the Buddhist Doctrine of Dependent Origination, shows that individual betterment and perfection on the one hand and social good on the other are fundamentally interrelated and interdependent. The essence of the non-self doctrine which has been repeatedly emphasized since the beginning of Buddhism is that there is in fact no difference between himself and others. It asserts the extension of one's own existence beyond the boundary of the self, to encompass that of others. Buddha's *dharma* like the social tradition itself has been ceaselessly transmitted from generation to generation, characterized by universality. The virtues embedded in the Buddhist nucleus — kindness, compassion, humanity and equality — have been truly instrumental in the promotion of social solidarity and harmony in a broad socio-cultural spectrum. Socially Engaged Buddhism aims to combine the cultivation of inner peace with active social compassion in practice and lifestyle that support and enrich both.[3] Engaged

---

[2] Christopher S. Queen, 1996, "Introduction: The Shapes and Sources of Engaged Buddhism", in *Engaged Buddhism: Buddhist Liberation Movements in Asia*, ed. Christopher S. Queen and Sallie B. King, New York: State University of New York Press, p. 33.

[3] Ken Jones, 2003, *The New Social Face of Buddhism*, Wisdom Publications, p. 173.

Buddhism is a redefinition of the nature and role of Buddha's *dharma* for the modern and pluralistic world. The engaged Buddhists have started modern social welfare work by establishing Buddhist organizations throughout the world. The leading Buddhist leaders like Thich Nhat Hanh, H.H. Dalai Lama, Master Cheng Yan, B.R. Ambedkar, A.T. Aryaratne and many more consider Socially Engaged Buddhism to be an extension of the Buddhist tradition, that is to say, its implementation is practice. Dalai Lama asserts the importance of social engagement and encourages Buddhists to participate in the society. He says that Buddhism and social activism can contribute to each other. This is a timely and potentially faithful field of enquiry. While the main emphasis of the Buddhist's teaching is an inner development that is no reason for Buddhists not to participate in the society in which they live. We are all dependent on others and so responsible to others. The phenomenon of social activism is an attempt by likeminded people to alleviate social problems through drawing attention to them and trying to change the attitudes of those in a position to affect them.[4] Master Cheng Yan of Taiwan is a good example of Engaged Buddhism, she says that we cannot ignore a single act of kindness because every small act counts and contributes to the force of compassion, which ultimately will nurture peace in the world. More importantly, the happiness that we feel in doing good deeds is immeasurable. Ambedkar who initiated deeper socio-political engagement in modern India, declared that the Buddha has a social message and answers all these questions.[5] The Sarvodaya-Shramadana Movement of Sri Lanka is an admirable example of Buddhist practice where the founder, A.T. Ariyaratne, has defined the "Shramadana" which means "sharing" of one's time, thought and energy for the welfare of all.[6]

4 Ken Jones, 1989, *The Social Face of Buddhism: An Approach to Political and Social Activism*, Wisdom Publication, p. 9.

5 Sallie B. King, 1996, "Conclusion", in *Engaged Buddhism: Buddhist Liberation Movements in Asia*, ed. Christopher S. Queen and Sallie B. King, New York: State University of New York Press, pp. 403-15.

6 Though the Sarvodaya concept of "the welfare of all" was first coined by the Mahatma Gandhi that was later spread through the India by the Acharaya Vinoba Bhave. A.T. Ariyaratne has interpreted this notion through the Buddhist concept of *dāna* (donation) and interdependence, and has been

→

Socially Engaged Buddhism is a novel interpretation of Buddhism, which bears great historical significance. A very beautiful thing happened to Asia and the world when some of Buddhism's core teachings were reinterpreted to meet the challenges posed in the face of colonialism, war, poverty, caste exploitation, environmental degradation, social inequality and political domination and other kinds of sufferings of the people. The goal of Engaged Buddhism lies in helping the people who are in trouble, affected by changing scenario and to solve the social problems engendered by their activities. It guides them towards a true and pure path for upliftment of humanity.

Modern societies all over the world are facing many problems. The question we need to ask ourselves first is: what are these problems which may be called the problems of modern societies and modern individuals. It does not imply that the traditional man as opposed to modern man did not face any problem. Of course, problems were there but they were of different types and the scale of the problem was also presumably different, the world was facing less misery and pain. Most of the problems have their genesis in the economic, scientific and technological developments. We desire to have good consequences of all these developments but the ill effects of the developments are also inbuilt with them. The biggest ever crisis that provoked humanity in an unprecedented manner and extent is the current ecological crisis. An unprecedented imbalance of nature, climate and weather system, can be seen in each and every corner of the globe. The global warming effects, water pollution due to toxic waste and chemical waste pollute the natural environment and also contaminate ground water.

Christopher S. Queen, in his introductory remark, categorizes:

---

← successfully applying to remodel the village community and rural culture by promoting collective responsibility. For basic philosophy and objectives of Sarvodaya see A.T. Ariyaratne, 1996, *Buddhism and Sarvodaya,* Sri Satguru Publication, pp. 3-15. Also see George D. Bond, 2003, "Sarvodaya Shramadana's Quest for Peace", in *Action Dharma: New Studies in Engaged Buddhism*, ed. Christopher Queen, Charles Prebish and Damien Keown, Routledge Curzon, pp. 128-35. A.T. Ariyaratne, 1999, "Sarvodaya Shramadana's Approach to Peacebuilding", in *Buddhist Peacework: Cheating Cultures of Peace,* ed. David W. Chappell, Wisdom Publications, pp. 69-77.

> The Buddhism that attracted Americans was not one of pessimism, resignation, and retreat, but a vigorous religion of optimism and activism.[7]

I think that Buddhism has reconstructed and deconstructed itself in the modern times to show a path to the society and the world that if religion has to survive, it has to relate itself to the social and economic needs of the people; if spirituality has to sustain, it will have to get itself actively involved in solving the societal requirements. It is in this context that Engaged Buddhism has surfaced before the world as an alternative social practice.

The foundation of Engaged Buddhism lies in the fact that service to society and suffering humanity is the basis of genuine spirituality. Socially Engaged Buddhism is a kind of movement which along with spiritual practice addresses issues such as violence and peace, race and gender, health, education, homelessness, prisons, environment, justice, commerce and unsustainable society in the most peaceful and compassionate ways. Queen gives three characteristics of Socially Engaged Buddhism. The first may be called awareness. The second is a deep identification of the self and the world — a sense of oneness, non-dualism, interdependence and empathy for all beings.[8] The third characteristic of Engaged Buddhism is the imperative of action.

One of the best known and most respected Zen masters in the world today, poet, and peace and human rights activist Thich Nhat Hanh has led an extraordinary life. Born in central Vietnam in 1926 he joined the monkshood at the age of sixteen. The Vietnam War confronted the monasteries with the question of whether to adhere to the contemplative life and remain meditating in the monasteries, or to help the villagers suffering under bombings and other devastation of the war. Before Thich Nhat Hanh, Buddhism's engagement with the socio-economic and political affairs of the war-ravaged Vietnamese people caught the attention of the world when a Buddhist monk Thich Quang Duc along with thirty-six other monks and a lay woman laid down their lives in fire on a Saigon street in 1963 to show

---

7 Christopher S. Queen, 1996, op. cit., p. 30.

8 Christopher S. Queen, 2000, "Introduction: A New Buddhism", in *Engaged Buddhism in the West*, ed. Christopher S. Queen, Wisdom Publications, p. 6.

their deep anguish and lodge their peaceful protest against the devastating war between the American army and the communist party of Vietnam which not only divided the country into north and south but also brought uncounted miseries to the people there and the subsequent practising of engaged Buddhism by Thich Nhat Hanh to bring relief to the people of Vietnam. Sallie B. King has concluded that Thich Nhat Hanh, along with the Dalai Lama, "tend to see themselves more as reinterpreters of tradition than as its critics, stressing continuity with the basic principles of Buddhism as they see them".[9]

Buddhist monks in Vietnam helped people built their houses, set up schools, dispensaries and orphanages. Engaged Buddhism has great potentialities in meeting not only the present-day socio-economic problems but through its compassion, love and humane attitude holds the key to solving most of the problems the world is afflicted with. Thich Nhat Hanh's life has since been dedicated to the work of inner transformation for the benefit of individuals and society. Thich Nhat Hanh strongly believes: "once there is seeing, there must be acting".

In the rush of modern life, we tend to lose touch with the peace that is available in each moment. Thich Nhat Hanh's key teaching is that, through mindfulness, we can learn to live in the present moment instead of in the past and in the future. Dwelling in the present moment is, according to Thich Nhat Hanh, the only way to truly develop peace, both in one's self and in the world.

Thich Nhat Hanh shows us how to make positive use of the very situations that usually pressurize and antagonize us. For him a ringing telephone can be a signal to call us back to our true selves. Dirty dishes, red lights, and traffic jams are spiritual friends on the path to "mindfulness" — the process of keeping our consciousness alive to our present experience and reality. The most profound satisfactions, the deepest feelings of joy and completeness lie as close at hand as our next aware breath and the smile we can form right now.

Thich Nhat Hanh provides exercises to increase our awareness of our own body and mind through conscious breathing, which can bring immediate joy and peace. Thich Nhat Hanh also shows how to be

---

9 Sallie B. King, 1996, op. cit., p. 403.

aware of relationships with others and of the world around us, its beauty and also its pollution and injustices. The deceptively simple practices of ***Peace Is Every Step*** encourage us to work for peace in the world as we continue to work on sustaining inner peace by turning the "mindless" into the mindful. He asserts:

> Meditation is not to get out of society, to escape from society, but to prepare for a re-entry into society, and we call this "Engaged Buddhism".[10]

Thich Nhat Hanh has combined traditional Zen teachings with insights from Theravāda and Mahāyāna traditions. He emphasizes social engagement and service to others. He endeavours to transform Buddhist tradition in accordance with the contemporary needs of society and progressively. Socially Engaged Buddhism of Thich Nhat Hanh is a guide towards a true and pure path for the uplifting of society and, in a greater sense, for the uplifting of all peoples of the world.

---

[10] David Arnott, 1993, "Buddhist Perceptions of Desirable Societies: The Individual and Society", in *Buddhist Perception for Desirable Societies in the Future*, ed. Sulak Sivaraksa, Thai Inter-Religious Commission for Development Sathirakoses-Nagapradipa Foundation, p. 22.

# 18

# Śaivism in Ancient Cambodia as Revealed from Sdok Kak Thom Inscription

*Bachchan Kumar*

## Introduction

THIS paper discusses the prevalence of Śaivism in ancient Cambodia based on the Sdok Kak Thom (SKT) inscription, one of the largest inscriptions of Cambodia. It also discusses the ritualistic and artistic manifestation of Śaivism in ancient Cambodia. Śaivism is a pre-Vedic religion of India. Its origin can be traced back from the time of Indus Valley Civilization. During Vedic age, the term *Rudra* was employed for God Śiva. Later, this god emerged as a benevolent as well as a destroyer deity of the Hindu pantheon. Śaivism was introduced to Cambodia (*fig*. 18.1) during the later phase of the Funan kingdom (first to fifth century CE). It is evident from the epigraphic record that second Kauṇḍinya first invocated Lord Śiva. Since then worshipping of the deity began. It is very difficult to say from which part of India Śaivism got introduced to ancient Cambodia.

*fig*. 18.1: Map of the Khmer Kingdom

The SKT. inscription is an important epigraphic record that gives a valuable account of Śaivism in ancient Cambodia. This inscription is engraved on a sandstone stele in the shape of a parallelogram (*fig*. 18.2). It stood originally at the north-eastern angle of the enclosure-wall of the temple of SKT. The inscription is on all the four faces of the stele. Faces 1 and 2 are only in Sanskrit, written in sixty and seventy-seven lines, respectively. Face 3 contains fifty-five lines in Sanskrit and twenty-nine lines in Khmer language. The fourth face of this inscription has two lines in Sanskrit and 117 lines in Khmer language. The original stele was preserved in the National Museum, Bangkok while three estampages of the original text were taken by M. Aymonier. One copy of it was preserved in Bibliotheque Nationale, (no. 32(4)), Paris and two copies in École Frainçaise d'Extrême-Orient (nos. 256 and 1191), Paris.

The text of the inscription gives history and religious foundations of a priestly family for about 250 years with dates and gives account of the various kings of this family (Jayavarman II to Udayādityavarman II) and therefore this particular inscription is considered to be the most important among all the inscriptions of Cambodia. It gives a detailed account of the prevalence of Śaivism of Tāntric nature during that period.

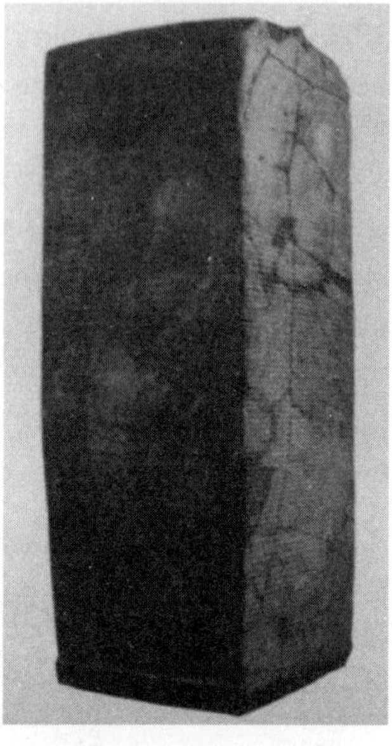

*fig*. 18.2: The Sdok Kak Thom inscription

## Date of the Inscription

It is very difficult to assign the date of this inscription as it does not give the date of its erection. It mentions the last date of Śaka 974 (CE 1052) when the Kamraten Jagat Śivaliṅga-Jayendravarmeśvara was installed at "Bhadraniketan". Based on this information George Coedes dates this stele to eleventh century.

## Early Study of the SKT Inscription

The SKT inscription was brought to light in the year 1901 by M. Aymonier who first published a resume and partial translation of the Khmer text. The study of Aymonier was also accompanied by a paraphrase of Sanskrit text by A. Barth. In 1915, Finot edited the inscription and first translated both the Sanskrit and Khmer portions and published the text. After thirty years, M. Coedes and Pierre Dupont published a vast improvised edition of the inscription. An English version of the French text of Finot was published by R.C. Majumdar in 1953. Later, the commentary on this inscription was given by Adhir Chakravarti in two volumes (1st in 1978 and 2nd in 1980) published from Sanskrit College, Calcutta.

## Śaivism in Ancient Cambodia

Śaivism has been a prominent religion of ancient Cambodia. Its first appearance in Cambodia seems to be in the later period of Funan Kingdom (first to first half of the sixth century CE). The Chinese annals discuss the prevalence of the cult of Maheśvara. Based on it, Bhattacharya opines that Śaivism was the state religion of the kingdom of Funan (Bhattacharya 1961: 16-20). Moreover, archaeological and antiquarian remains of the cult of Śiva are lacking in the lower part of Mekong Valley and its delta. It seems quite possible that this area had weak concentration of Śaivites. On the other, the inscription of Wat Luang Kao of fifth century attests the popularity of Śaivism in the Vat Phu area. It was the seat par excellence where the phallic-shaped Liṅgaparvata (*fig.* 18.3) had formed. The place later became the nucleus of the most sacred pilgrimage.

Sachchidanand Sahai opines that Śaivism spread southward from northern centre of Vat Phu and gradually established a stronghold in this region. A Śaivite wave was virtually launched by the Dangrek chiefs who in several phases annexed the territories of Funan in the

*fig*. 18.3: Liṅgaparvata

south. Though, the theory of conquest appears weak after the irreversible decline of economic and political power in the north of Cambodia (Sahai 2010: 27).

After the decline of the kingdom of Funan, Chen-la or Pre-Angkorian kingdom (sixth to eighth century CE) took its place. King Bhavavarman and his brother Citrasena-Mahendravarman emerged as a new political force in the middle of the Mekong Valley by the end of the sixth and the beginning of the seventh century. King Bhavavarman was a staunch follower of Śaivism. The inscription of Phnom Banteay Neang issued by King Bhavavarman mentions the commemoration of the establishment of a Śivaliṅga. Citrasena, the next Śaivite king, after accession to the throne, assumed the name Mahendravarman and installed a *liṅga* at the "mountain" Śiva (Girīśa) and erected the images of Nandī, the vehicle of Śiva. Since these *liṅga*s and images were set up on the occasion of "the conquest of the whole country", we can conclude that King Mahendravarman sought the blessings of Śiva for his territorial expansion as his predecessors did (Barth and Bergaigne 1885: 69).

During the reign of Jayavarman I (CE 657-81), Śaivism was a popular religion. The king paid special attention to the ancient sanctuary of Ba Phnom and Liṅgaparvata. Due to misfortune in CE 713, Queen Jayādevī made donations to the sanctuary of Śiva Tripurāntaka. This sanctuary was founded by princess Śobhājayā, a daughter of

Jayavarman I who married the Śaivite brāhmaṇa Śakrasvāmin born in India (Coedes 1967: 85).

Śaivism had its stronghold during Angkor kingdom. In CE 802, the foundation of Angkor kingdom was laid down by Jayavarman II. He was the most dominant king of ancient Cambodia. With his accession to the throne of Khmer empire, a new era began in the history of Cambodia and also a very active tradition of Śaivism. There are metaphors for Jayavarman II when he accessioned to the throne: "for the prosperity of the people, in this perfectly pure race of kings, great lotus which no longer has a stem, he rises as a new flower". He was one of the most unique kings of Cambodia though he did not issue any inscription. Fortunately, the principal episodes of his reign are related in some detail in the SKT inscription (Finot, *BEFEO*, XLIII: 53-106). He began his rule with the establishment of a city Indrapura now located in the province of Thbong Khmum, to the east of Kompong Cham.

The inscription of SKT begins with homage to Lord Śiva. It discusses that the real nature of Śiva is highly proclaimed without word by the subtle self of living beings. Śiva pervades the innermost region of the body and activates the sense-organs. It seems that the king was supposed to be a part of Śiva or his incarnation. Also the founder king had direct communication with god through the worshipping of *liṅga*.

The SKT inscription gives detailed account of Śaivism in the Angkor empire. King Jayavaraman II started ruling from Indrapura and took into his services as royal chaplain a brāhmaṇa scholar, Śivakaivalya who followed him in all his changes of residence. This brāhmaṇa became the chief priest of a new cult called as "Devarāja". Adhir Chakravarti (1980: xxi) opines that the immediate object of the inscription seems to record the installation of a *liṅga* (*fig*. 18.4) or Sarva called Kamraten Jagat Śivaliṅga or Sarva-Jayendravarmeśvara at Bhadraniketan which had earlier been known as Bhadrayogī or Bhadrayogīpura. Its founder bore the personal name of Sadāśiva and successively received the names of Jayendrapaṇḍita along with the title Kamraten An and Vrah Kamraten An and Jayendravarman with the style *dhuli jen Vrah Kamraten An*. He received a two cubit high *liṅga* (of Sarva-Jayendravarmeśvara) as a gift from King Udayādityavarman II. There is a mention in the Khmer text also of another *liṅga* of Śiva characterized as Vrah Kamraten An Śivaliṅga

*fig.* 18.4: Śivaliṅga on the pedestal in the inner gallery at Bayon Temple

for whose service slaves were specially assigned. King Udayādityavarman II might have been its founder since it was he who ordered one of his ministers to install one *liṅga* equally described as being two cubic high.

## Śaivite Cult as Revealed from SKT

SKT refers the words Īśvara, Śaṅkara, Śambhu and Bhadreśvara for Lord Śiva and exclusively gives information on the establishment of Devarāja or "God-king" cult relating to the worshipping of Śiva. It was a ritual or ceremony mainly of Tāntric in character. His Majesty (Jayavarman II, r. 802-50) installed a *liṅga* as royal god in the town of Indrapura. The king took the services as royal chaplain, a brāhmaṇa named as Śivakaivalya. Originally the family of Śivakaivalya hailed from the Sruk of Satagrama and was known as the family of Aninditapura from India. We have to establish the location of this place in India. The popularity of Kurukṣetra of *Mahābhārata* during Angkor period and depiction of scenes of Kurukṣetra on the walls of Angkor Vat (*fig.* 18.5) cannot rule out the location of this place somewhere in Haryana nearby Kurukṣetra as this area has been well known for Śaivism. I would recommend this esteemed university to begin a research project on comparative study of Śaivism in India and South-East Asia.

Later the king went to reign at Mahendrapravata and the priest Śivakaivalya followed him and served as the royal priest. Later, a brāhmaṇa named Hiraṇyadāma, adept in the magical science, came from Janapada (India) at the king's invitation to perform a ritual designed to ensure that the country of the Kambuja would no longer be dependent on Java and that there would be no more than one sovereign who was *cakravartin* (universal monarch). The brāhmaṇa performed the ritual according to the sacred Vinasika and established a Śivaliṅga as the Lord of the Universe (Devarāja). The brāhmaṇa taught the sacred Vinasika, Nayottara, Sammoha and Siraccheda. These are the Tāntric Śaivite rituals of India.

Brāhmaṇa Hiraṇyadāma recited the complete text from the beginning to end in order that they might be written down and taught to priest Śivakaivalya. The brāhmaṇa also ordained priest Śivakaivalya to perform the ritual of the Devarāja. The king and the brāhmaṇa Hiraṇyadāma took the oath to employ the family of priest Śivakaivalya to conduct the worship of Devarāja and not to allow others to conduct

*fig.* 18.5: The war of Kurukṣetra depicted on the wall of Angkor Vat

it. Śivakaivalya, the chief priest, assigned all his relatives on this cult. The cult reveals that Śiva was the main god of the king.

In 1002, Sūryavarman I ascended the throne. He was a follower of Buddhism and earned his posthumous name Nirvāṇapāda. Being a follower of Buddhism, in no way, he neglected Śaivism. The king continued the worship of Devarāja. During his reign, says SKT, the members of the priestly family officiated for the Devarāja as before. He even singled out a member of his family for the worship of the god. SKT mentions that a nephew of the great priest Śivācārya, named Sadāśiva, had quit the religious state and married to the king's one of sisters-in-law and elevated to the dignity of Kamsteng Śrī Jayendra-paṇḍita, the first step of a brilliant career.

Sūryavarman I, marked the boundary of his kingdom by setting up Śivaliṅgas. The epigraphical evidence reveals that the king founded four great *liṅga* shrines to the north, south, east and west of his capital. This was with a view to seek Śiva's protection for his empire in totality (Mabbett and Chandler 1995: 112).

After the death of Sūryavarman I, King Udayādityavarman II became the king of Angkor in 1050. The new king conferred the semi-royal title of Dhuli Jeng (dust of the feet) Vrah Kamrateng An Śrī Jayendravarman on the former chief priest of the Devarāja, the Sadāśiva-Jayendrapaṇḍita (Finot *BEFEO*, XLIII: 93). On the advice of high priest of Devarāja, King Udayādityavarman II built a new temple mountain for the royal *liṅga,* more beautiful than those of his predecessors.

> Seeing that in the middle of the Jambudvīpa, the home of the gods, rose the mountain of gold (Meru), he had constructed, as in emulation, a mountain of gold in the centre of his city. On the top of his gold mountain, in a gold temple shining with a heavenly light, he erected a Śivaliṅga in gold.

This edifice, "ornament of the three worlds", has been identified by Coedes as the temple Baphuon (Coedes: *BEFEO*, XXXI: 18).

For the maintenance of the temple and regular services of the god, the king offered surplus services of slaves from other places. Brāhmaṇa Jayendrapaṇḍita is said to have performed *karma-dharma,* i.e. obsequies of Vāgīndrapaṇḍita. He taught the king all the sciences beginning with *Arthaśāstra* and Āgama beginning with Vijaya and ending with Parameśvara. The king duly received initiation and gave magnificent honorarium to his teacher. The honorarium included ornaments like *makuṭa-veṇika, kuṇḍala, keyūra, kaṇṭhasūtra* and *ūrmika*. He also offered different types of utensils made of copper and spared time for the religious services. SKT gives a list of articles donated to the teacher that includes varieties of spices, drugs, perfumes, 1,000 horses along with charioteers and bridles, 500 cows with calves, 50 buffaloes, 100 sheep and 100 pigs. The Khmer text mentions a donation of 200 elephants to the teacher. SKT also furnishes the additional information that the king performed the ancillary ceremonies of *bhuvanāḍhya, mahotsava* and *pūjā* according to the sacred Guhya (= tantra). SKT reveals the prevalence of *guru–śiṣya paramparā* in ancient Cambodia. Brāhmaṇa Jayendrapaṇḍita had great respect for him and the teacher always performed rituals for the welfare of the state.

M.K. Sharan opines that worshipping Devarāja has been an exceptional one which can be compared with the Aśvamedha *yajña* of ancient India. The basic difference between this cult and the Indian *yajña* is that the Cambodian kings used to personify and identify themselves with the *liṅga*s and temples (Sharan 1974: 256-57). In my opinion, worshipping of Deverāja was no way different to ancient Indian *yajña*s. Before the establishment of Devarāja in Cambodia, such Tāntric practices were prevalent in Java as it is evident from the inscriptions of Changgala and Dinaya of Central Java. Jayavarman II in the beginning of his reign took shelter in Java where he had heard about such practices.

## Lord Śiva in the Art of Cambodia

Śiva is depicted in the form of images and reliefs of the temples. These art expressions of ancient Cambodia have deep similarity with the Indian art style of the Gupta period. A beautiful image of Śiva has been discovered from Phnom Bakheng Temple of early tenth century. In this image, the headdress of the god is adorned with a crescent moon. The third eye is also placed. Such image is a fine example of Angkorian art style. Śiva is depicted in various forms on the carvings of the Khmer temples (*fig*. 18.6). His ascetic forms are well depicted in the Angkorian temple. Umā (Pārvatī), the consort of Śiva, is beautifully depicted on thigh of Lord Śiva. It seems that the image of Umā is symbolized here as a part of the body of Śiva. In one relief, Rāvaṇa, the great devotee of Śiva, has been shown as shaking Mount

*fig*. 18.6: Śiva in ascetic form, relief of the Khmer Temple

Kailāsa (*fig*. 18.7), the abode of Lord Śiva. In the SKT inscription, Śiva's consort Umā is named as Bhagavatī. His carrier, Nandī, has been nicely placed in a shrine of Śiva. Śiva and his consort Umā riding on Nandī are beautifully carved a lintel on the northern tower of Muang Tam in the north-eastern Thailand (*fig*. 18.8).

Apart from Viṣṇupada (footprint of Viṣṇu), Śivapada (footprint of Śiva) was equally sacred and worshipped in ancient Cambodia. We learn from the record that a pious brāhmaṇa consecrated the representation of a footprint of Śiva and a cistern for the ablution of the god, on the top of a hillock. In the year Śaka 526 (CE 604) the representation of the divine footprint was surrounded by a brick wall. Sahai (2010: 34) opines that Śivapada was one of the essential components of the Śaiva rituals in the Khmer Kingdom. After shifting from Śaivism to Mahāyānism, the Brāhmanical divinities, including Śiva and his footprints were incorporated into the new pantheon. Śivapada was installed at Preah Khan Temple dedicated to Lokeśvara during the rule of the Buddhist king Jayavarman VII. Moreover, this sacred footprint at Preah Khan Temple had secondary position as compared to the central Buddhist figure. The worshipping of Śiva through footprints has been very popular in south India during the early centuries of the Christian

*fig*. 18.7: Rāvaṇa shaking Mount Kailāsa, relief at Banteay Srei Temple

*fig*. 18.8: Śiva and his consort riding on Nandī, carving at a lintel on the northern tower of Muang Tam in the north-eastern Thailand

era. Even, the blessings of Śiva is transferred by putting footprints at the head of the devotee at Ekāmranāth Temple in Kāñcīpuram (Kumar 2010: 13-16).

## Conclusion

We see from the inscription of SKT that Śaivism had an important place in ancient Cambodia. Buddhism flourished in Cambodia but Śaivism retained its position. Devarāja cult was a ritual connected with the worshipping of Lord Śiva. But it was a medium of communication between Śiva and the Khmer kings. Brāhmaṇa is shown as the mediator between the two. Śiva was worshipped for the protection of the kingdom and its boundary.

## References

Barth, Auguste and Bergaigne, 1885, *Inscriptions Sanscrites du Cambodge* (*ISC*), Paris: Imprimerie Nationale.

Bhattacharya, Kamleshwar, 1961, *Les Religions Brahmaniques dans l'ancien Cambodge*, Paris: EFEO.

Chakravarti, Adhir, 1980, *The Sdok Kak Thom Inscription*, part II (Text, Translation and Commentary), Calcutta: Sanskrit College.

Coedes, George 1967, *The Indianized States of Southeast Asia*, ed. Walter F. Vella, tr. Susan Brown Cowing, Honolulu: East-West Centre Press.

——, "La date du Baphuon", *BEFEO*, **XXXI**.

Coedes, George and Pierre Dupont, "Les Steles the Sdok Kak Thom, Phnom Sandak et Prah Vihar", *BEFEO*, **XLIII**.

Finot, Louis, "L'Inscription de Sdok Kak Thom", *BEFEO*, **XLIII**: 53-106.

Kumar, Bachchan, 2010, "Shiva's Sandals at Ekamranath Temple in Kanchipuram", *SEAR*, January–December, **XXXV**(1-2): 13-16.

Mabbett, Ian and David Chandler, 1995, *The Khmers*, Chiang Mai, Thailand: Silkworm Books.

Majumdar, R.C., 1953, *Inscriptions of Kambuja*, Calcutta: Asiatic Society.

Sahai, Sachchidanand, 2010, "Shiva in the Angkorian Mould", *SEAR*, **XXXV**: 23-43.

——, 2011, *Shivapada in Khmer Art: Rediscovering Angkor in the Foot Prints of Shiva*, Bangkok: White Lotus.

Sharan, Mahesh Kumar, 1974, *Studies in Sanskrit Inscriptions of Ancient Cambodia*, New Delhi: Abhinav Publications.

——, 2010, "Shiva in the Angkorean Mould", *SEAR*, January–December, **XXXV**(1-2): 23-43.

# 19

# Rammān Pāttar Performance in the Central Himalaya and Its Parallels in the Balanese and Javanese Theatre

*D.R. Purohit*

A COMPARATIVE study of the mask dance-dramas of Uttarakhand Himalaya, locally known as *pāttar*s, and the Balinese and Javanese theatre of Rāmāyaṇa brings forth interesting parallels on the grounds of dissemination of the pan-Indian myths, motifs and performative styles — keeping in view their centrifugal expansion. The comparative space is occupied by the *Rāmāyaṇa* performances of Uttarakhand Himalaya and those of the South-East Asian countries, particularly Indonesian, Thai, Laotian, Cambodian and Myanmarian.

The Rāmakathā and its artistic expressions have travelled to multiple directions and to multivocalities from a common centre (and a common text and with a common motive) — *Rāmāyaṇa* of the main subcontinent and the other mask dance-dramas from the Deccan territories.[1] The common motive is the human desire for performing *līlā*s which humans share with God's desire to manifest itself in the *līlā*s of the universe:

> . . . God in his creating and governing of the world is moved not by need or necessity but by a free and joyous creativity that is integral to his nature. He acts in a state of rapt absorption comparative to that of an artist possessed by his creative vision or to that of a child caught up in the delight of a game played for its own sake.[2]

---

[1] Harry M. Buck, 1980, "The Role of the Sacred Book in Religion, the Rāmāyaṇa", in *The Rāmāyaṇa Tradition in Asia*, New Delhi: Sahitya Akademi, p. 41.

[2] Norvin Hein, 1995, "Līlā", in *Gods at Play: Līlā in South Asia*, ed. William S. Sax, New York: Oxford University Press, pp. 13-20.

It is just not a coincidence that in the comparative texts under study, just before the narrative of *Rammān* or any other performance, the narrative of the cosmology is sung in detail in order to show that birth and *līlā*s of Rāma are also part of the *līlā*s of the creator. In the South-East Asian performances such text gets interpolated with local versions of cosmogony.

Rāmakathā in the South-East Asia, Induja Awasthi writes, lives through several variants existing in several countries and several communities. *Kākawin Rāmāyaṇa,* authored by a certain Yogeśvara, is popular in Indonesia. Indonesian rulers swear by eight principles of administration which were preached to Vibhīṣaṇa by Rāma on the occasion of the former's coronation. The Javanese Rāmāyaṇa is presented in epic style and seems to have been influenced by the Bhaṭṭikāvya.[3] *Vayangkulit* (literally, shadow puppets) is the Rāmāyaṇa of Zakarta rendered with the help of shadow puppets made out of leather. The director of the performance is called *dalaṅg* whose role in the theatre is very similar to the role of *bhāna* in Garhwal theatre. Both of them are directors as well as singers. The music orchestra of the Zakartan theatre is called *gamalan*. The narrative text and dialogue delivery come turn by turn as they do in the *Rammān* tradition of Garhwal.

*Vayanggolek,* another variant of Zakartan theatre and very similar to *vayangkulit,* is marked for the sharp features of the masks and for the brighter colours of the costumes and the props. *Vayangwang* uses human characters instead of puppets and thus becomes the successor of *vayangkulit*. However, the actors follow the make-up of the puppets. Roles of Rāma, Lakṣmaṇa and Sītā are performed by women whereas the demons and monkeys are enacted by men. The latest versions of the *vayangwang* have eliminated the text and the narrative; only the choreography makes up the entire performance. The venues of

---

3 A.B. Keith, 1928, *A History of Sanskrit Literature,* Oxford: Clarendon Press. (Bhaṭṭikāvya, or "Bhaṭṭi's Poem", is a Sanskrit-language poem dating from the seventh century CE, in the formal genre of "great poem" (Mahākāvya). It focuses on two deeply-rooted Sanskrit traditions, the *Rāmāyaṇa* and Pāṇini's grammar, while incorporating numerous other traditions, in a rich mix of science and art, poetically retelling the adventures of Rāma and a compendium of examples of grammar and rhetoric.)

performances are the temples of Prambanan and the occasion is the full moon. The performance lasts over four days. Names of the characters also change a little. Sītā is Shinta, Bāli is Subaali, and Laṅkā is Alanka (Induja Awasthi 2000).

In Bali, both the performative and narrative forms exist. Rāmakathā is performed in front of the temple which houses a formless deity called Ananta. The surviving ballet performance, as Induja Awasthi writes, continues for two hours. The other variant is the narrative singing by two groups sitting face to face. The first group sings the Sanskrit text and the other repeats it in the local version of the same.

In Thailand, the Rāmakathā theatre exists in three forms: (1) shadow puppets theatre, (2) masks dance-dramas, and (3) ballet theatre. The Thai Rāmāyaṇa text is believed to have influences from the Jaina Rāmāyaṇa, *Paumchariu* and is known as *Ramkein*. The major variations in the Thai Rāmāyaṇa are: (i) the episode of slitting Śūrpanakhā's nose. Since Lakṣmana has already slain the son of Śūrpanakhā, she wants to seduce and humiliate him to seek revenge, (ii) Śūrpanakhā's daughter who is staying as guard with Sītā in Aśoka-Vāṭikā coerces the latter to draw a picture of Rāvaṇa. This motif on the part of Sītā prompts Rāma to suspect Sītā's integrity, (iii) Hanumān is a white-coloured god and falls in love with so many women: he makes love to the slain Indrajit's wife, to the daughter of Vibhīṣaṇa and to Svarṇamatsya (to win over the entire sea fauna on the occasion of constructing Setubāndhu). One of the styles of variants of Thai Rāmāyaṇa is similar to the *Rammān* where marionettes of Nṛsiṁha and Prahlāda are held in hand by the performers.

The Malayasian Rāmāyaṇa is called *Hikayat Seri Rama*, existing both in the oral and written media. It is performed with the help of the shadows of puppets made out of leather. The occasion of performance is the wedding or the seven-day long harvest season.

The Laotian performance text of *Rāmāyaṇa* is known as *Phra Lak Phra Lam* or *Ram Jaataka*.[4] The Rāmakathā manifests itself through music, images, dance, drama and painting. The text is oral: Rāma is known as Phralam, Lakṣmaṇa as Phralak, and Sītā as Sidaa.

---

4 Sacchidanand Sahai, 1996, *Rama Jataka in Laos: A Study of the Phra Laak Phra Laam*, Delhi: n.p.

In Kambodia, *Rāmāyaṇa* is popularly known through the stone images of the Angkorvat group of temples. The tradition seems to have been borrowed distantly from *Vālmīki Rāmāyaṇa*. Again the performance media are mask dance-dramas called "Khols", shadow puppets, and the ballet (Induja Awasthi 2000).

The Myanmarian Rāmāyaṇa is known by the names of *Ramavatthu* and *Rama Jnagyin*. The context of performance is extensively Indian Rāmalīlās.

The emergence of Rāma cult in Garhwal as a deity seems to have begun in the eighth century when Ādi Śaṅkarācārya restored the shrine of Badrīnāth. Every year before the shrine of Badrīnāth opened, festivals called *dyar*s or *ausar*s were held for the entertainment of the pilgrims and the performances invariably included episodes from the life of Rāma. In the fifteenth century when the rulers from Gurjar Pradesh or quasi-historical Kannauj came to Garhwal, they also brought along the attachments of *bhakta maṇḍalī*s who became instrumental in popularizing the Rāma cult and in founding the Rāma temples. Thus in Srinagar town which was the erstwhile capital of the royal princes, the episodic enactments of Rāma's life were common happenings in the local temples and the royal court.

The texts of Uttarakhand Rāmāyaṇas selected for comparison are the *Rammān* of Painkhaṇḍa and Malla Nagpur, *Rammān* of Kedār Valley, *Aidi Rāmāyaṇa* and *Sītā Lodi* of Pauri Garhwal.[5] The *Rammān* tradition of Painkhaṇḍa which is rendered through masked characters, comes closest to the South-East Asian Rāmāyaṇa.[6] All of the texts cited here are the oral texts. The South-East Asian texts selected for comparison are *Kakawin Ramayana* (Java), *Serat Kanda, Rama Kidung* and *Ramkein* (Thailand), the *Hikayat Seri Rama* (Malayasia), and the *Ramavatthu* (Myanmar).[7] There

5 D.R. Purohit, 2006, "Rama in the Folk Performances of Garhwal", *Rāmāyaṇa Tradition in Historical Perspective*, ed. D.P. Saklani, New Delhi: Pratibha Prakashan, pp. 126-34.

6 D.R. Purohit, 1993, "Medieval English Folk Drama and Garhwali Folk Theatre: A Comparative Study", Ph.D. Dissertation, H.N.B. Garhwal University, Srinagar.

7 Pranabanand Jash, 2006, "The Rama Katha: Contact and Adjustment in Southeast Asia", *Rāmāyaṇa Tradition in Historical Perspective*, ed. D.P. Saklani, Delhi: Pratibha Prakashan, pp. 175-86.

are considerable departures in the narrative units from *Vālmīki Rāmāyaṇa* and other canonical texts. Adam, Noah and even Satan appear in the South Asian texts. However, the intermixing of the narrative and performance, rendering through dance and dialogues, use of masks and marionettes, choice of colours in costume, and use of music remains similar in both the traditions. The trend of interpolations and insertions of the local myths into the text is also a great similarity.

**Mask Dances "Pāttar"**

A mask theatre and dance form of Uttarakhand hills exists in oral form. Its songs have a fixed text while the prose dialogues are partly improvised according to the situation and as per the talent of the artistes performing the roles. The word *pāttar* is a corruption on the Sanskrit word *pātra* (character). Each mask donned by a person makes a *pāttar*. About twenty-four characters don the masks and act out their roles in the village arena. The South-East Asian Rāmalīlā is invariably enacted either in the royal court or in an arena.[8] *Pāttar* is a semi-ritualistic entertainment attendant to the main processional rituals of Jākh, Dvārī, Kaṁsa, Caṇḍikā and Kṣetrapāla deities who are on a six-month processional journey to the devotees of different villages. Everyday after the main deity of the ritual has been sent to sleep by offering a song called *dhoop chharo* (myrrh and incense), and after the supper is eaten, the villagers and the artistes gather in the yard of the deity and the team of the artistes accompanying the procession begins the show. The show has to be presented come what may, rains, snow or storm. Even if the procession is forced to stay in the jungle, some *pāttar*s have to be presented, audience or no audience.

Within the dialogic text is interwoven the song text. Burhdeva, a corruption on Bhardeva (a brāhmaṇadeva), is the folk comic version of Nārada. In the text he is alternatively addressed as Nārada. In the performance area is seated the director of the performance called *bhāna* (cf. *dalaṅg*). He is assisted by other male and female singers of his community. To the beats of drums and tunes of song enters Burhdeva, dancing around the arena. He stops and *pat* comes the

[8] Induja Awasthi, 2000 (1979), *Ramalīlā: Paramparā aur Śailiyāṅ* (Ramalīlā: Traditions and Styles), Delhi: Radhakrishna Publishers, p. 256.

question from the *bhāna* "O, Burhdeva, where did you come from?" "Straight from Tholingmath of Tibet", says Burhdeva. Then Burhdeva describes his experiences all through the route till the point where he is standing at now. The *bhāna* asks him several questions relating to directions, time and space. Then Burhdeva is directed to enact the several phases and colours of human life. Burhdeva does it mockingly, turning everything inside out, satirizing the odds and obliquities of life. He first enacts *pūjā*, then wedding, then ploughing, sowing, weeding and reaping, cooking, meeting the *sādhus* and *paṇḍitas* of the society and so on. Most of the text is orally fixed but the artiste playing as Burhdeva is free to use his ingenuity in dialogues and comic punches.

Interspersed with Burhdeva's dialogues is the text of songs which are sung to the entry of other mythical, legendary, human and animal characters who are invited by the *bhāna* at appointed intervals to the arena and to interact with *bhāna* and Burhdeva. Some characters like Vaidi Vaida, Gaṇapati-Gaṇeśa, Kananu, Kauriā Kṣetrapāla, only dance and exit and do not interact with other characters or the audience. Some of them like Īśvara Rājā, Rāma, Lakṣmaṇa, Sītā, Nṛsiṁhāvatāra, Hariṇ, Cītal and Baraha only receive *āratī* (offering light) from Burhdeva and exit. But the human characters like Latā-Latī, Lāl Borā, Nāthu Pāṇḍe, Baniyā–Baniyan and *sādhus* going to Kedārnāth make comic interaction with Burhdeva and the audience. The best feature of the text is the scope provided to Burhdeva to deal with the contemporary issues. He is free to refer to elections, or Indian parliament or the latest imbroglio of religious conversions. In the villages he refers to the local issues like the panchayat elections or the transfer of the school teachers. The most popular text for Burhdeva is the oddities of the people who meet the processional party in different villages.

The director of the performances is *bhāna*, a term probably a derivative of Sanskrit word *bhāṇa* (ballad singer). He is the in-charge of the performance supported by Ganwais in the Mandākinī Valley variant of mask dances. There are only three families of *Bhānas* surviving in the entire Chamoli district: one each at Urgam, Kandai Maṅkhi and Laṅkhi Bheṅṭi.[9]

[9] Chamoli district borders with Tibetan state of China and also is known for the famous Badrīnāth shrine.

## Rāmakathā through Mask Dance-Dramas

Another variant of *pāttar* is the annual presentation of characters from the scriptures and human world on or around Baisākhī festival (13 or 14 April) in and around Jośīmaṭh town. In Selaṅg, Barosi and Saloor Duṅgrā villages, *Rāmāyaṇa* being the main performance, the event of the mask performances is also called *Rammān* or *Rāmāyaṇa*.

The occasion of performance is also called *ausar*. The songs seem to have been long ago composed by the *bhāna* community. The lead lines are sung by the males and repeated by the female. The images, symbols and metaphors used in the songs are highly evocative. The language is poetic Garhwali, capable of evoking pertinent emotions.

The following are the major rituals which occasion the performance of *Rāmāyaṇa* or Rāmakathā:

1. Concluding week-long ritual of the Jākh processional performance.
2. Thaul festivals held in the month of Baisākha (Mandākinī Valley).
3. Caitra festival performed by the traditional entertainers like Deochellis (no more extant).
4. Mask performances held in Alaknandā and Dhauli valleys in the month of Baisākha.

## Jākh Represents the Duo of Mahābhārata and Rāmakathā Narratives

In the Rāmakathā narrative and ritual he is unambiguously the incarnation of Hanumān. He burns Laṅkā and with this event the narrative ends. In the variant of Malla Nagpur, i.e. the area around Jośīmaṭh, Jākh stands for Babruvāhana, a hero who was beheaded through conceit by Kṛṣṇa but whose trunkless head watched the entire Kurukṣetra war. For propitiation of the sin of betrayal committed by Kṛṣṇa. He himself ordered Bhīma to hoist the head of Babruvāhana on a tall tree and then to take him around on a pilgrimage to villages and shrines. Since then, the processional ritual is the re-enactment of this mythical event. There are twelve seats of Jākh on both the slopes of the upper Alaknandā Valley — Dummak, Kalaṅgoṭ, Bemru, Paldā, Pokhanī, Tapovan, Urgam, Chain, Thain, Selaṅg, Pakhi, Kujaun-Maikoṭ,

Gwār, Taṅgni, Ravigrām and few more (in common parlance they are just twelve Jākhs). Every village, on an average, takes out a Deorā (processional journey) of the deity after every twelve year.

### Jākh Processional Ritual and Rāmāyaṇa

During the six-month-long processional ritual of Jākh deity, Rāma, Lakṣmaṇa and Sītā are presented as *līlā mūrti*s on the day of Bhārātra, (night of special ritual). It is the night when the entire spectrum of masked characters is presented. On rest of the dais only a limited number of characters are presented.

During the concluding ritual, the story of Rāma is sung every night of the seven-day ritual. The narrative is sung in the following manner:

*rāvaṇa lyoṅdo bai laṅkhī dyo*
*sītā harikā bai laṅkhī dyo*
*sonā kī laṅkā bai laṅkhī dyo*
*aśok bāṭikā bai laṅkhī dyo*
*sītā dharali bai laṅkhī dyo*
*bokaran roṅdi bai laṅkhī dyo*
*rām, rām boldī bai laṅkhī dyo*
*lachman boldī bai laṅkhī dyo.*

Rāvaṇa abducts Sītā, reaches Laṅkā and places Sītā in the Aśoka-Vāṭikā, the woman Sītā calls aloud Rāma-Rāma, Lakṣmaṇa-Lakṣmaṇa and bursts into wails. She grieves how she has fallen into the hands of the demons.

But the myth current in Mandākinī Valley says that the deity of Jākh travelled to Jākhdhar in the shape of a granite stone mixed with the granules of salt purchased at Dummak and Kalaṅgoṭ by the villagers Devshal, Koṭhiyārā, Nala, Bheṭṭa, etc. The deity of Jākh, then, made an oracle that he had embodied a small granite stone mixed inside the collection of granule salt. There is no clue to the process of transformation of the form of the deity from Babruvāhana to Hanumān. The Jākhu temple at Shimala is a fortress of monkeys and most of the devotees believe that Jākhu is Hanumān. It looks the two myths have synthesized in the Jākh of Mandākinī Valley.

**Caitra Festival of Mandākinī Valley**

The tradition died out in around 1933. An interview of a villager of Temriyā (name is deliberately concealed) revealed that the festival was performed by a caste of entertainers called *deochellis*, the female attendants of gods, in about five temples of the valley.[10] As part of their repertory, which consisted of songs, dances and plays, a play called *Rāvaṇa Badh* (Slaying of Rāvaṇa), was performed and the plot showed that Sītā, and not Rāma, killed Rāvaṇa. The play lasted for about an hour. Such a motif is also found in Tamil Rāmāyaṇa *Catakanarāvanan Katai*, a prose version of Sītā's battle against the demon Śala Kaṇṭharāvaṇan episode unknown to *Vālmīki Rāmāyaṇa*.[11]

**Annual Mask Performances of Alaknandā and Dhauli Valleys**

Every year from 1st 15th of Baisākha, mask dance-dramas as parts of the central ritual of respective village deities are held in Lāṭa, Selaṅg, Saloor-Duṅgrā, Duṅgarī, Sītāpur, Bargāun, Ḍhāk, Tapoban, Subhain, Chain, Thain, Sugi, Tolmā, Jhelam and Droṇagiri villages of Alaknandā and Dhauli valleys in Chamoli district. About eighteen to twenty-four masked characters appear in the arena, present the dance and drama on the days allotted to them and then exit. *Rāmāyaṇa* or *Rammān* performance is presented as the central event of the festival, in Saloor-Duṅgrā, Duṅgarī and Selaṅg villages; while Rāma, Lakṣmaṇa, Sītā, and Hanumān appear only as tableaux in the rest of the villages.

The performances are however invariably accompanied by the singing of the narrative. *Rāmāyaṇa* characters do not don the masks; no evidence of any such practice existing earlier has been found. However, the three performances recorded by me in 1988-90 and 2003 showed that the change in the costume of the characters has occurred. In 1988 Rāma and Lakṣmaṇa wore turbans and Pahāṛī tunics; in 1990, they wore crowns and coats used in Rāmalīlā performance (see *fig*. 19.1). In 2003, Hanumān opted for wearing a plastic mask.

---

10 Late Mahanand Semwal belonged to the community of priests who donned the mask of Bhairava in the mask performance rendered by the *deochellis*. He had narrated the tradition to the writer in the year 1990.

11 David D. Shulman, 1996, "Battle as Metaphor in Tamil Folk and Classical Traditions", *Another Harmony*, ed. Stuart H. Blackbun, Barkeley: University of California Press, p. 106.

*fig*. 19.1: Śrī Rāma and Lakṣmaṇa dancing after hunting the deer

One damaging change noticed during 2003 was, no *Rāmāyaṇa* singing was performed in the village. The old singer Prem Singh Bhalla was dead; so were the old singers of Saloor-Duṅgrā village. In the year 2010, Than Singh Negi, an octogenarian of Subhain village, and probably the last authentic singer of the narrative of *Rammān*, along with his co-singer Bharat Sing Rawat of Duṅgarā village were recorded for the narrative ballad by the author. And the *Rammān* text which was about to die was thus salvaged through transcription. It was then passed on to Kushal Singh Bhandari of Saloor-Duṅgrā village. Now since 2010 the text is being used for narrative singing of *Rammān*: The text contains fine musical melodies like:

*gaṇeśa balo nyutala bolāyo,*
*gaṇeśa balo nyutala bulāyo*
*tab bolāyo bhado bāman*
*tab bolāyo bhado bāman.*
*ayodhyā naguri bhalo cha vyohār,*
*ayodhyā naguri bhalo acha vyohār*
*jankapurī bājani badhāi*
*janakapurī bājani badhaī.*

> The child Gaṇeśa was invited; then was invited Nārada, the brāhmaṇa. In Ayodhyā city is good governance; in Janakapurī city, play the auspicious drums.

The text of this variant also seems to have changed with time. The present text is, more or less, on the line of the pan-Indian story of Rāma. The main episodes sung are Sītā-Haraṇa, Laṅkā-Dahana and Rāvaṇa-Vadha. These episodes are also performed in the annual *Rammān* tradition of Saloor-Duṅgrī and Selaṅg villages. Although the singers, participants and even the audience are common (the traditions occur in a radius of 3 km), the singing style in both the traditions differs. While the narrative is the charge of a traditional *bhaldā* (ballad singer) in *Rammān* tradition, the *Rāmāyaṇa* in Jākh tradition is sung by amateurs, villagers. The flexibility of the text can be attributed to this non-professionalism.

### The Rammān Tradition

It acquires the name *Rammān* simply because the enactment of the life of Rāma is the principle structure of the whole presentation. Other theatrical or ritual performances fit into it as intervals and interludes. The entire story is danced out in eighteen *tāl*s, each *tāl* consisting of five kinds of beats and each beat completed in two to three rounds.

The most elaborate presentation of *Rammān* is found in Saloor-Duṅgrī village (near Jośīmaṭh). The date of performance is fixed in a panchayat held on the 2nd or 3rd of Baisākha. The final and grand performance generally falls on 13th or 14th of Baisākha. The ritual worship begins from the Baisākhī day and continues till the end. On the final day, the characters of Rāma, Lakṣmaṇa, Sītā and Hanumān are offered ritual worship at the opening and the close of the daylight performances. They are all the while treated as very sacred *personae.* The ballad singer, accompanied by village elders, sings the complete ballad of *Rammān*, and parallel to it is presented the mimetic dance by Rāma, Lakṣmaṇa, Sītā and Hanumān. Properties in hands, their gestures, dance steps and movements change as the ballad progresses in theme.

The other theatre and tableau performances in the *Rammān* tradition are: Kālinkā, Gaṇeśa, Īśara Rājā, Nārada, Sūraj, Rānī Rādhikā (Gopichand), Mwar-Morin, Baniyā–Baniyan, Khelwari, Chorbari, and Selbharis, Gannā–Gunnī, Pāṇḍava Dance, Purcheli, Nṛsiṁha, Prahlāda and Hiraṇkaśyapu, the *malla*s.

The four red and white wrestlers (two of each) in the *malla* show present the most exciting sport-cum-theatre of *Rammān*. They fight with guns, swords and hands for about two hours, using mimetic gestures from the folk, martial arts. There always are risks of the symbolic fight converting actual fight. Therefore, utmost care is taken to delimit it to a sport.

## Rammān, the Performed Mime

*Rammān*[12] is a term given to the annual re-enactment of the life of Rāma in Saloor-Duṅgrā, Barosi and Selaṅg villages near Jośīmaṭh in Chamoli district. The same performance has now been confined to mere tableaux in Chain (Sītāpur), Thain (Rāmpur), Bargaun, Ḍhāk, Tapoban, Sugi, Subhain and Tolmā villages in Dhauli Valley. Once upon a time the performances were as elaborate as they are now in Saloor, Barosi and Selaṅg.[13] Though all the mask-characters, similar to those of Nanda, Nr̥siṁha, Kās and Jākh cycle, appear in these villages, but owing to the dominance of *Rāmāyaṇa* ritual, the cycle is called *Rammān*. The myths, tales and legends do not refer to Rāma's sojourn in this area. They rather locate the locales of Rāma's history in the region itself.

The traditional narrators of Rāma's history, called *bhaldā*s, are invited to sing the ballad on 12th and 13th day of Baisākha (25-26 April). In their song, they are given company by the villagers too.

*Rammān* is not rendered through dialogues; the medium here is pure dance supported by the ballad. The lifetime of Rāma and his people is danced out in eighteen *tāl*s; a *tāl* is made up of five beats of drums and corresponding dance rhythms. The *tāl*s are punctuated by other mask dramas like Mwar-Morin, Banyā–Baniyan and Khelwari

---

12 *Rammān* performance of Saloor-Duṅgrā village of Jośīmaṭh region has been included in the list of the Intangible Heritage of the World by UNESCO in 2009.

13 The difference between the *Rammān* enactment of other villages around Jośīmaṭh and the *Rammān* proper exists in the following:

In *Rammān*, the story is the structural action, while in others it is only a partial tableau. Rāmakathā is still sung and enacted in the *Rammān* while in other performances it is only presented as a pageant now. Once upon a time it was also performed elaborately in Lāṭa, Bargaun, Subhain, Tolmā, etc.

at a fixture. For the purpose a person sitting by the arena goes on drawing lines to count the *tāl* and to coordinate the entry of the other characters. The sequence of *tāls* comes in the following manner:

*Seven tāls* are danced out to the beats of drums and to the narrative of the *bhaldā*, enacting the birth of Rāma and his brothers, their education and their visit to Janakapurī where auspicious drums are playing (now the Bhūmyāl, the god of Earth, comes out and dances, see *fig.* 19.2).

*Eighth tāl*: Rāma and Lakṣmaṇa dance representing their meeting with Sītā and the wedding, and thereafter, their return to Ayodhyā where they are ordered to go into exile. (Here a character half-man–half woman, called *ardhaṅga* enters and asks the audience, "Have you seen Rāma and Lakṣmaṇa here?" The audience says no to it.)

*Ninth tāl*: Rāma, Lakṣmaṇa, Sītā and Hanumān make dance enactments of some happenings in their exile. The ballad narration continues simultaneously. (Here Mwar-Morin enters and present the theatrical piece, see *fig.* 19.3.)

*Tenth and eleventh tāls*: Rāma, Lakṣmaṇa, Sītā and Hanumān dance to

*fig.* 19.2: God of the land

*fig*. 19.3: Mwar, a herdsman

the narration of Rāma's meeting with Sugrīva, etc. (Banyā–Baniyan and Khelwari present their event, see *fig*. 19.4)

*Twelfth and thirteenth tāls*: Rāma, Lakṣmaṇa, Sītā and Hanumān dance. (Seijbhāri and Chro Pāttar perform their mime.)

*Fourteenth tāl*: Rāma, Lakṣmaṇa, Sītā and Hanumān's dance and ballad in synchronization.

*Fifteenth tāl*: The same followed by the dance combat of *malla* (the fighting gallants) for about two hours and then the disrupting entry of Kurjogi, a man attacking with Kummars (briars).

*Sixteenth tāl*: Rāma, Lakṣmaṇa, Sītā and Hanumān's dance to the rhymes of the ballad. (Entry of Purcheli, the blessing goddess.)

*Seventeenth tāl*: Rāma, Lakṣmaṇa, Sītā and Hanumān. (Here the mimetic enactment of Sītā-Haraṇa (abduction of Sītā by Rāvaṇa) and Laṅkā-Dahana is presented.)

*fig.* 19.4: The merchant and his wife

*Sītā-haraṇa*: A glittering deer (a man wearing a deer mask) enters. Sītā runs after dancing, offers milk to the deer and dances. Then Rāvaṇa, a man wearing a goat hide enters and takes away Sītā.

*Laṅkā-dahana*: Hanumān comes, tramples upon a hut made of grass and burns all the grass piled up there.

*Eighteenth tāl*: Dance of Rāma, Lakṣmaṇa, Sītā and Hanumān. The ballad singer narrates how Rāvaṇa is decimated and how they return to Ayodhyā. (Nṛsiṁha, Prahlāda and Hiraṇyakaśyapu, and the ritual enactment of Nṛsiṁhāvatāra and killing of Hiraṇyakaśyapu.)

In the end, Rāma, Lakṣmaṇa, Sītā and Hanumān are shown meeting Bharata. They dance in a circle inter-locking their hands upon one another's shoulder. The following dialogue is repeated twenty-four times after each round of dance.

> "O, Bharata Bhāī, how are the characters like Raunlya and Paulya?"

Dancing, in the interlocked position, they sit down and bend forward upon a flat basket carrying *prasāda* in it. The *Rammān* ends here.

Thus expansion of Rāmakathā in Uttarakhand follows the universal pattern which we find in the South-East Asia. The meeting points in both the traditions are:

1. Universality of the structural text.
2. Local variations such as Rāma's exile on the point that he married without the consent of his father.
3. Intermixing of narrative and enactment.
4. Using trance as a histrionic device called *aṅgkiaṅg* in Balinese Rāmāyaṇa.
5. *Saliṅg enyuhin,* condition for extemporizing of the Balinese theatre, is common with the improvisations of the characters in *Rammān*.
6. Use of masks, costume, dance and music in the rendering of the text is strikingly common.

# 20

# Reflection of Indian Culture in the Kambuja Empire of South-East Asia

*Swati Raikhy*

**Abstract**

Indian traders across the seas for trade purposes eventually gained control over the territories either by conquering or by marrying the local princesses and ultimately founded empires in South-East Asia. These traders with the passage of time settled in these regions, and their influence on the culture of South-East Asian people is well reflected in the social, economic, religious sphares, and in art and architecture of these countries as well.

Empire of Kambuja, ruled by Khmers, was established during the sixth century. Funan empire which, according to a legend, was founded by a brāhmaṇa and was largely influenced by Hinduism. There was a blend of Hindu culture with the local cluture in the case of Kambuja. Similarly, the artistic structures, depicting Buddhist religious influence, do find but are rare in this part of South-East Asia. The name of rulers and the religious practice they followed were derived from the Hindu tradition. This is well established from the art form of Angkor Thom. The inscriptions engraved on the walls of temples are either in Sanskrit or in Pāli, the architecture style is a mixture of Indian art. The literary works marked by Indian influence are largely depicted in their style of writing. Even their epics bear the characters resembling to the characters of *Rāmāyaṇa* and *Mahābhārata*. The classical dance form of today's Combodia is based on *Ramaker* which is the version of Hindu *Rāmāyaṇa*. Today Angkor city, the capital of Khmer rulers, is in ruined state and is under the care of UNESCO, which has declared it as a world heritage site.

THE achievements of the Indian colonists in the South-East Asian countries were great. They introduced Indian religions, literature, philosophy, social and political institutions and art to millions of people who readily accepted whatever ancient India had to offer. This cultural conquest produced brilliant results of an abiding value. India, thus, played the role of a great civilizing force in the life of the people of South-East Asia (Nayyar 2002). The Chinese have preserved many details of its early history (Sethna 1997: 550).

Hindu kingdom named Kambuja was established in the south of Champa by the Hindus who made their way up the Mekong River there before the Christian era. The kingdom, when at its height, stretched from the valley of Menam to Sigon and from the Vientiane to the Gulf of Thailand. It included the eastern part of Thailand and southern Laos. The natives (called Khumers) believed that an Indian *r̥ṣi* (sage) was their ancestor; hence their country was called Cambuja or Cambodia (Luniya 1994: 636).

Indian culture played an important part in the history of ancient Indo-China. This was known as Kambojdeśa and consisted of two parts — Funan and Chenala. The capital of Funan was Vyādhpura and its rulers descended from Kauṇḍinya, a brāhmaṇa who came from the Indianite colony of Malay in the third century CE and married a local Nāgā princess. This kingdom ruled over the area for about five centuries and was very prosperous. More than 1,000 brāhmaṇas resided there (Varma 1973).

Early in the seventh century CE Kambuja, originally a vassal state of Funan, became very powerful and during the reign of Rudravarman the struggle was prolonged for some time and ultimately Funan was conquered (Geodes 1944).

Henceforth Kambuja became the leading power and gave the name to the whole country. Kambuja came under the influence of the Śailendras but Jayavarman II re-established its independence by revolting against foreign rule in early ninth century CE (Majumdar 1994: 480). He spent his early days in Java and became ruler of Kambuja in CE 802. He united Kambuja put it on the road to recovery and gave it stability. Even now he is regarded as one of its divine heroes. He is represented as the son of Lord Indra. The sacred sword of Kambuja which is used by its kings at the time of coronation is believed to be a relic of Jayavarman II (Nayyar 2002). In Indian mythology Indra is a warrior and Jayavarman II was greeted as his son since he had fought for the freedom of Kambujadeśa.

The religion of the Khmers was a curious mixture of the cult of Devarāja and tāntric Hinduism (Varma 1973). The cult of Devarāja, instituted by Jayavarman II (Nayyar 2002) continued to be the state religion for centuries (Chatterjee 1998: 489-501). Under the cult the king was known to be a bearer of divine entity, *devatva* (Chopra et al. 2004: 298-309), like we find among Indian kings of Mauryan and Kuṣāṇa dynasties. It was a new religious cult of king driving all sanctity and strength from Lord Śiva by designating the *liṅgam* as Devrāja (Sengupta 2005: 99). Thus there were religious formations also having influence from India as depicted in the cult founded by Jayavarman II.

King Indravarman, who succeeded Jayavarman III and founded a new royal line, was a great builder and was succeeded by Yaśovarman who occupies a pride of place in the country's history (Nayyar 2002). He ruled during CE 889–908 (Majumdar 1994: 480) and was a follower of Śaivism, but also patronized Buddhism (Nayyar 2002), set up a *saṅgatāśrama* for the Buddhist monks. His border extended up to the frontier of China (Nayyar 2002).

This dynasty lasted up to CE 1001. By the time Siam and Laos were also formed the part of Kamujadeśa (Srivastav 2007: 895-909). Indravarman, father of Yaśovarman, even claims in his record that his commands were respectfully obeyed by the rulers of China, Champa and Yavadvīpa (Majumdar 1994: 481).

Yaśovarman was the founder of a new capital city which was called at first Kambupuri (Majumdar 1994) and later Yaśodharpur (later on known as Angkor Thom, the glory and splendour of which form the most brilliant chapter in the history of Kambuja) (Luniya 1994).

He acquired proficiency in the art of music, dancing, architecture and script (ibid.). He is said to have mastered various Śāstras and Kāvyas and composed a commentary on Patañjali's *Mahābhāṣya* (Majumdar 1994: 480). The court poets of Yaśovarman adored him with the title of "Second Manu" (Vedalankar 2004: 134).

He established the institution of *āśrama*s (establishments or abodes of religious communities), homes of pious devotees, who consecrated their lives to study and mediation. Adequate endowments were provided for their maintenance. A large number of *āśrama*s were set up all over Kambuja by royal munificence and private efforts. King Yaśovarman claims to have founded no less than 100 *āśrama*s (Majumdar 1994: 491).

Detailed and definite regulations were issued by the king for the maintenance and conduct of these *āśrama*s, modelled on the lines of Hindu hermitages or *tapovana*s (Luniya 1994). This clearly depicts the influence of India.

The Siemreap River was conceived as the holy Gaṅgā and on a mount by the side of this river, Yaśovarman I erected in the ninth century the central temple of Devarāja (King-God) with the symbol of Śivaliṅga enshrined in it. The hilltop was considered as the mount Meru. Śivaliṅga was adopted in indigenous worship from the seventh century CE. Śivaliṅga of the southern Indian peninsula style and Śiva bust with a vertical crown were executed in Kambuja (Luniya 1994). In the temples of Preach Koh, not only the divine bull Nandī but also the *dvārapāla*s (guards of entrances) appear (Chatterjee 1998: 527). At Bekong, temples have the free-standing images of Śiva and his consort with the figures of lions near the doorways, which are the reminiscent of the south Indian origin. At Phnom Bakheng are five terraces with sixty-four turrets and on the highest terrace a temple with five stone towers was built on the rectangular roof of the shrine. At the temple complex of Prasat Kravan, we find a row of giant towers and bas-reliefs on walls. Viṣṇu, the supreme god, is carved on the brick walls. He is represented, riding on the shoulders of Garuḍa, his *vāhana* (vehicle). The shrines at Beantey Srei (meaning citadel) were built on a flat surface. It is 20 km north of Angkor. Beantey Srei contains a profusion of bas-reliefs of unsurpassed excellence which depict episodes from Hindu lore, particularly from Kṛṣṇa's life. One of the finest reliefs shows Kṛṣṇa slaying Kaṁsa in a vigorous relief. Other specimens of delicate and sensitive style of bas-relief at Beantey Srei is the series of lovely girls, the *apsaras*es in the niches, having moon-like breasts, attired in transparent skirts and intricate coiffeurs. The birds, the flowers, the stylized *makara*s and elephants and the panels of intricate pattern, floral and geometric, all have been delicately carved richly adding to the beauties of the paradise of the temple sculpture (Luniya 1994). The appearance of *dvārapāla*s is a feature of

Coḷa art form which justifies the Indian influence besides the decorative motifs in the form of floral patterns. And animal depictions are also the characteristic of the Indian art.

Since king Yaśovarman founded the most glorious city of Angkor Thom in the heart of Cambodia in the ninth century, which was surrounded by a high stone wall which had five gates with five great avenues each 100 ft wide and running straight from one end of the town to the other. These avenues converge on the temple of Bayon which is a masterpiece of Kambuja architecture. Fifty huge towers surrounded by 200 faces identified with Avalokiteśvara the all-merciful *bodhisattva*, still stand facing the vagaries of the weather (Varma 1973). This entire vast edifice has been chiselled into endless beautiful designs and patterns. Even the outer walls are sculptured. In the first gallery there are panels 90 or 100 yards long, depicting the stories from *Rāmāyaṇa* and *Mahābhārata*, Viṣṇu in all his incarnations reigns supreme at Angkor Vat (ibid.).

The Khmers patronized Sanskrit and their inscriptions were drafted in classical Sanskrit style. Very often these inscriptions excel in literary merits the inscriptions so far discovered from India (ibid.). More than 100 Sanskrit inscriptions have been discovered from Champa. Those in Kambuja are not only larger in number but are also of higher literary merit. They are composed in beautiful and almost flawless Kāyva style such as would do credit to any Indian *paṇḍita*. Some of these inscriptions run to great lengths. Four inscriptions of Yaśovarman contain respectively 50, 75, 93 and 108 verses each; one of Rājendravarman contains 218 and another 298 verses. One of his ministers was an expert in Horāśāstra (Majumdar 1994: 488). The influence of Kālidāsa seems to have been very great, and one inscription contains no less than four verses which are distinct echoes of four verses from *Raghuvaṁśa*, repeating sometimes the very words used by the great poet (ibid.). This clearly shows that the style of writing was largely influenced by Indian literary works.

King Jayavarman V (CE 968–1001) of Kambuja was surrounded by intellectuals, poets, writers and scholars (Luniya 1994). Like Vikramāditya of Ujjain and Bhoja of Dhar of Malwa, he was surrounded by intellectuals, poets and scholars (ibid.).

Sūryavarman I established the authority of Kambuja over northern Siam and probably even invaded lower Burma (Myanmar). From this time, Khmer art and culture were firmly established in the Menam Valley, and Khmer civilization spread in the north as far as Sukhothai in Siam. He was versed in Bhāṣyas, Kāvya, six philosophical systems and Dharmaśātras. Another king of Kambuja learnt from his priest, astronomy, mathematics, grammar, Dharmaśāstras, and all the other Śāstras (Majumdar 1994: 481).

The next powerful king was Sūryavarman II (CE 1113-45) whose dominions, according to the Chinese, included lower Burma and northern part of the Malay peninsula. He also reduced the northern part of Champa but could not retain it for long. He has earned undying fame by constructing the famous Angkor Vat, one of the veritable wonders of the world (ibid.).

Angkor Vat, the largest temple in the world, built by Sūryavarman II in CE 1125 (Srivastav 2007); a 2.5 mile long and 650 ft wide moat surrounds the temple. The broad paved avenue which runs from the western gateway to the first gallery is 1560 ft long. The first gallery measures about 800 ft from east to west and 675 ft from north to south. There are three such concentric galleries each double the preceding one in height. The central stone tower on the third stage rises to a magnificent height of 213 ft (Varma 1973).

King Sūryavarman II, under the advice of his brāhmaṇa *guru* and councillor Divākar Paṇḍit, exalted himself from Devarāja (king-god) to Viṣṇu Rājā (Supreme God King) and he began the construction of shrine in Angkor Vat mainly as an exaltation of himself to the Viṣṇu incarnation in life and death. The general plan of the temple consists of a wide moat, with "two external enclosures, the approaches, the three concentric galleries, the central mass, the large tower in the centre and the smaller towers on the corners of the two inner galleries and three still smaller ones on the west entrance of the outer enclosure — twelve in all". The dimensions of the first enclosure is 1000 x 815 m, and the second 340 x 270 m. Next to the second enclosure is the first terrace, around which runs the covered gallery of bas-reliefs. This measure 275 x 187 m. Thus the approximate length of the sculptures in this gallery is 800 m or half a mile. The second terrace measures 100 x 115 m. The third terrace has central tower, surrounded by four smaller towers. The central tower rises to a height of about 66 m above the ground. It is 22 m higher than the present pinnacle of Borobudur. The towers have been imitated to lotus-buds and pineapples. The bas-reliefs in the galleries of the temple of Angkor Vat stretch up to 800 m (Luniya 1994).

The Vaiṣṇava themes (of Rāma and Kṛṣṇa incarnations) are predominant. We find there eleven episodes from *Rāmāyaṇa* (including the pursuit of the golden deer by Rāma, the duel of Vāli and Sugrīva and the fire ordeal of Sītā), five exploits of Kṛṣṇa (including his breaking of the twin, trees and lifting of the Govardhana hill), four scenes of Viṣṇu lore (including his Śeśaśāyī form and the churning of the ocean) and three scenes of Śaiva lore (including the burning of Kāmadeva, the god of love, by Śiva, and Rāvaṇa, shaking the Kailāsa). Then, there are panels of sculptures depicting thirty-three scenes of hell and thirty-seven of heaven. The panel beings with the court of Yama (god of death and justice) attended by his registrar, Citragupta. Beside these, there are court scenes depicting kings, queens, their attendants, officials, ministers, armed chiefs, imposing royal procession, etc. Starting from the 2 ft above the ground, the bas-reliefs are 6 ft in height. Besides the scenes from *Rāmāyaṇa*, *Mahābhārata* (Sharma 1990: 237) the temple walls are adorned with birds, flowers, dancing maidens (Luniya 1994).

After the death of Sūryavarman II the war with Champa continued and in 1177 Jaya/Indravarman, king of Champa, sent a naval expedition which plundered the capital city. But the accession of Jayavarman VII, the grand monarch of Kambuja, in CE 1181, ushered in a new period of glory.

Jayavarman VII (CE 1181–1215) planned a new capital city, Angkor Thom was built in the old Yaśodharpur means Nagara Dhama or great city. The town was surrounded by a high stone wall with a ditch beyond it, 110 yd wide. The ditch, like the wall, has a total length of nearly 8½ miles, and its sides are paved with enormous blocks of stone. The enclosing wall was pierced by five grand avenues, each 100 ft wide and running straight from one end of the town to the other. Each gateway consisted of a huge arched opening, more than 30 ft high and 15 ft wide, surmounted by figures of four human heads placed back-to-back. The town was square in shape, each side measuring about 2 miles, the grand avenues converge to the temple of Bayon which occupies almost the central position of the city, and is justly regarded as a masterpiece of Kambuja architecture. To the north of Bayon is a great public square, a sort of forum, about 765 yd long and 165 yd wide, surrounded by famous structures such as the Baphuon, the Phimenakas and the Terrace of Honors, each of which forms a splendid monument by itself (Majumdar 1994: 482).

Another famous temple of Kambuja was Ta Prohm built by Jayavarman VII (http://www.vietvisiontravel.com viewer.asp?pgid=41&aid=2218).

It was dedicated to the Buddhist divinity Prajñāpāramitā of the Mahāyāna sect. This Buddhist temple now in ruins was surrounded by a double stone wall. There were three courtyards, surrounded by three galleries. The entrance pavilion was in the middle of each side. The central shrine had four corner towers (Luniya 1994). In Indian art form there is the occurrence of this deity too.

It was King Jayavarman VII (CE 1181–1215) (Luniya 1994: 504) who propagated Buddhism by his liberal patronage. He held typical Buddhist views of life, particularly the feeling of charity and compassion towards the whole universe.

Jayavarman VII was the last great king of Kambuja. From the fourteenth century CE its power and prestige rapidly declined. The chief cause of this lay in the rapid progress of the Thais who, proceeding from Yunnan, advanced towards Burma and Siam. Towards the close of the thirteenth century CE Ram Kamheng, the famous Thai king of Sukhodaya carried his victorious arms to the heart of Kambuja. The Thai kingdom of Ayodhyā (Ayuthia), which replaced that of Sukhodaya about CE 1350, made itself the master of nearly the whole of Siam and Laos. On the east, the Annamites gradually conquered nearly the whole of the kingdom of Champa by the fifteenth century. Kambuja was now hard-pressed by these two important Thai powers on two sides, which steadily encroached upon its territory.

This simultaneous pressure from the two flanks proved the ruin of Kambuja. Its weak and helpless rulers tried to save themselves by playing off their two powerful enemies against each other, but with disastrous consequences to themselves. For centuries Kambuja remained the victim of her two pitiless aggressive neighbours. At last, shorn of power and prestige, ang Duong, the king of Kambuja, now reduced to a petty state, placed himself under the protection of the French in 1854, and thus the once mighty kingdom of Kambuja, became a petty French Protectorate (Majumdar 1994: 483).

**Influence on Language and Literature**

In general character, customs and manners, the Cambodians are even today more akin to the Hindus of India than their neighbours. The letters of the Khmer language were derived from the old south Indian alphabet. A very large number of Sanskrit words in all branches of learning have been adopted by the Khmer language. Sanskrit became the official language. Several Sanskrit inscriptions discovered there was composed in beautiful and flawless Kāvya style. The engravers of the inscriptions were masters of calligraphy and were the noted craftsmen for the finish and elegance of their letters. Sanskrit was taught not only to the princes but to the people also. Some of the kings like Jayavarman II, Yaśovarman I and Sūryavarman I were sound scholars of Sanskrit. Indian religious texts, the four Vedas, the *Mānava Dharmaśāstra*, *Rāmāyaṇa* and *Mahābhārata*, Purāṇas, Darśanas (system of philosophy) and Siddhāntas (mathematics and astronomy) were studied with keen interest. Indian books of medicine and Indian method of treatment were popular. It is said that a Kambuja king Rudravarman had appointed two Indian physicians in his court. There were several *āśrama*s in the country, the heads of which were ascetics. These *āśrama*s were founded and maintained by royal charity and private munificence. These formed a salient feature of the religious and social life in Kambuja and served as radiating centers of Hindu culture and religion (Luniya 1994).

The language of the court and the polished society was Sanskrit. Several Sanskrit inscriptions of very high literary merit have been discovered in Kambuja, Champa, Malaya Peninsula and Java; about thirty inscriptions in Champa and seventy in Kambuja were discovered. This indicates a very great progress in Sanskrit and the keen interest and enthusiasm with which the people took to the study of Sanskrit (ibid.).

The earliest Sanskrit inscription in Cambodia is that of Jaya-varman, discovered at Neak-Ta-Dambeng-Dek in the Funan region. The contents of this inscription prove that Hindu religious practices followed by queens in India by that period had been in vogue in Funan at that early period (Geodes 1937: 139-48).

Ladies of the royal dynasties participated freely in learned gathering like Gārgī and Maitreyī of India. Indo–Javanese literature flourished under the profound influence of Sanskrit. It borrowed subject matter from Indian literature. Its important monumental works are the old Javanese *Rāmāyaṇa*, the prose translation of *Mahābhārata* and numerous Kāvyas and other works written on the bases of the Purāṇas (Luniya 1994). Women also served as chiefs of monasteries and held positions in the state administration and judiciary (ibid).

The Khmers had a higher and deeper spiritual view of life which is the true essence of all religions. Education was widespread in Kambuja and students went to *āśrama*s which were on the model of Indian *āśrama*s. These *āśrama*s were powerful centres of Indian culture in Kambuja (Varma 1973).

The Khmer kings were Hindus and had their names ending with varman (ibid.). In Kambuja inscriptions India is termed as "Āryadeśa" (Vajpayee 2002: 145).

**Evolution of Architectural Style with Indian Influence**

In the beginning, the art of Kambuja and Siam was directly derived from India and artists and craftsmen who built the temples and made the images of gods came from India, and from Funan the Indian art of the Gupta period spread over a wide territory in Indo-China (Luniya 1994).

Though in Kambuja the earlier series of monuments at Angkor consisted of isolated temples which showed great resemblance to Indian temples, gradually a new style was evolved in the eleventh and twelfth centuries CE, first by the introduction of gallery, and later still by pyramidal construction in several stage. The combination of these two features resulted in a series of concentric galleries, enclosing each successive stage of the pyramid, with a crowning tower at the centre of the top or the highest stage. Similar towers were added at the four corners of each stage of the pyramid, and finally we have the *gopuram*s at one or all the four faces, each consisting of a gateway with a vestibule, surmounted by an ornamental tower in the form of a stepped pyramid as we see in south India. The central and corner towers were of the north Indian *śikhara* style. The best and the complete example of this type is Angkor Vat. An innovation was introduced in Bayon, where the towers were capped by four heads facing the four directions.

The gallery, referred to above, is, in its final shapes, a long narrow running chamber with vaulted roof supported by a wall on one side and a series of pillars on the other. It has a verandah with a half-vaulted roof of lower height supported by columns of smaller dimensions. The walls of these galleries are generally covered with continuous friezes of bas-reliefs and other sculptures.

The wide ditches, surrounding the temples and cities, with paved causeways over them, form an important feature of construction, and the figures of long rows of giants pulling the body of a serpent, which serve as the balustrades to the causeway on its two sides, are justly regarded as one of the most ingenious and interesting architectural devices to be seen anywhere in the world (Majumdar 1994: 496).

There was a spirit of religious toleration and the king supported all the temples irrespective of the deity to whom they were dedicated (Varma 1973). The temples are square or rectangular in the plan with a pyramidal tower. The evolution of the temple style absorbed the Pallava shore temple style of India. There are Śaiva shrines at Preach Koh and Bekong. In the middle of the eleventh century, at Baphuon a pyramidal stone temple was built on the top of five terraces with three galleries placed one above the other. On the terraces were pavilions through which pilgrims went to the temple. These pavilions were profusely decorated with sculptural reliefs. Besides this, the whole circumference of the outside wall of the temple was carved with reliefs of Hindu myths and legends. The sacred themes, spilled over into images of everyday life, executed in dynamic manner, showing birds and animals, processions of the hunt, war and ascetics, sleeping on nailed beds (Luniya 1994).

The chief image from Beantey Srei Complex is a splendid sculpture of Śiva seated and holding his wife Umā on his left thigh (BEFEO 1961).

Thus, there was a considerable evolution of temple architecture form there are three new features — the galleries, the pyramidal construction in several stages and high central towers sometimes capped by four human heads facing the four cardinal directions (Sen 1999: 530-35).

The monumental remains in foreign lands open to us a rather unknown chapter of India's ancient glory. Shrines dedicated to Śiva on the Dieng plateau (Java) and the vast panorama of bas-reliefs on the walls in the colossal temples at Borobudur and Prambanan (central Java) as also the remarkable ruins at Angkor Vat and Angkor Thom (Kambuja) reveal the hand of Indians and show that they had migrated to the far east and spread their power and culture there (Tripathi 1999: 9).

## Influence of Indian Religious Ideas

A salient feature of religion in these countries was that beyond the external forms of religion, there was a higher and deeper spiritual view of life. There appeared "a spirit of piety and renunciation, a deep yearning for emancipation from the trammels of birth and evils of the world and longing for the attainment of the highest bliss and salvation by union with *Brahman*, the Ultimate Reality". These ideas have been the bases of Indian religious and spiritual life. A large number of inscriptions in Kambuja and Java reveal these ideas. The kings, the queens, state officials and aristocracy were inspired by these high spiritual ideals. This was partly due to the close contact with India and partly to the propagation of these ideas by pious and learned brāhmaṇas who went to Kambuja and other countries. Agastya, Divākara Bhaṭṭa, Hiraṇyadām and Sarvajñamuni were such brāhmaṇas. Divākara Bhaṭṭa, born on the banks of the Yamunā in India, went to Kambuja, and married Rāja Lakṣmī, the daughter of King Rājendravarman. Divākara Bhaṭṭa and his descendants were royal priests for 250 years. People from Kambuja visited India to acquire religious knowledge and receive spiritual instruction. One of them was Śivasoma, the preceptor of king Indravarman. He went to India and learnt the Holy Scriptures from the famous Śaṅkarācārya (Luniya 1994). Within a few years of his death in CE 820 Śivasoma spread his doctrine in Kambujadeśa (Nilkantha Shastri 1976).

Vaiṣṇavism was flourishing in Funan in early centuries of the Christian era. Later on, Śaivism became a predominant religion in Kambuja Empire (Sharma 1990: 237). Sūryavarman I and Jayavarman

II patronized Mahāyāna Buddhism. The images of Śiva and Umā, Viṣṇu and Lakṣmī, Kṛṣṇa, Gaṇeśa and Skanda having found there testify the popularity of these deities. The interesting features of the Cambodian Hinduism were the worship of Śiva's feet in the same way as Viṣṇu's in India and the association of *liṅga* (the cosmic symbol of Śiva in India) with Viṣṇu also. An inscription of Vat Prei Var refers to the installation of *liṅga* of Viṣṇu-Īśa (Majumdar 1994).

Brahmā, Viṣṇu and Śiva were worshipped together with satellite gods and goddesses. The images of these gods combined together in Trimūrti as well as the images of the composite god Śiva and Viṣṇu were found in Java and Kambuja (Luniya 1994). In India the worship of Trimūrti is popular also. Buddhism was introduced in Kambuja in the closing years the fifth century, but it was not a popular religion till the ninth century.

We have in Cambodia a temple dedicated to Vālmīki. The image of Nithradevī (a form of Indian Durgā) was sculptured under orders of king Īśānavarman of Cambodia (Chopra et al. 1979: 214-20).

*Rāmāyaṇa* was so popular an epic that arrangements were made for its daily recitation along with *Mahābhārata* and Purāṇas and it was considered an act of great merit to present handwritten copies of these texts to the temples (Śaraṇa).

**Remnants of Indian Culture in Present Cambodia**

The influence of Indian culture in Cambodia is still depicted in the form of their worship, literary works, etc. The *Ramaker* is the Cambodian version of *Rāmāyaṇa*. There is evidence of the importance of Rāma's story in Cambodian culture that dates to the sixth century CE. The earliest references to the Rāma story are found in temple iconography and epigraphy. During the medieval centuries several versions of literary texts entitled *Ramaker* were written. Today we see evidence of *Ramakerti* in oral tales, visual, and performing arts, especially classical dance of the Cambodian court. Besides *Ramaker*'s instructional and religious importance, episodes from the *Ramaker* are often performed within villages for magical purposes. When there is a drought the people hope that the performance will produce rain. (http://orias.berkeley.edu/SEARama/RamaCam-bodia.htm)

## Efforts to Save Ancient Ruins

To save the ancient ruins of Kambuja capital from further destruction has been declared under the UNESCO has declared it as a protected site. Following the inscription of Angkor into the World Heritage List and the World Heritage List in Danger in 1992, UNESCO provided substantial assistance to Cambodia for the establishment and development of an appropriate national legal and institutional framework for the protection and management of the site (www.unesco.org).

## References

*Bulletin de L'École Française d'Extrême Orient* (*BEFEO*), 1961, vol. XLVIII, pp. 85-86.

Chatterjee, S., 1998, *Indian Civilization and Culture*, New Delhi: M.D. Publications.

Chopra, P.N., B.N. Puri and M.N. Das, 2004, *Bharat kā Sāmājik Sānskr̥tik aur Arthik Itihās*, I, New Delhi: Macmillan India.

Chopra, P.N., T.K. Ravindran and N. Subramanian, 1979, *History of South India*, **vol:** *Ancient Period*, New Delhi: S. Chand & Company.

Goedes, G., 1944, *Histoire Ancienne Des Etatas Hindouises D'Extrême*, Hanoi: Orient.

Luniya, B.N., 1994, *Life and Culture in Ancient India* (*From the Earliest Times to 1000* AD), Agra: Lakshmi Narain Agrawal Publishers.

Majumdar, R.C., 1994, *Ancient India*, New Delhi: Motilal Banarsidass.

Sharan, M.K., 2003, *Studies in Sanskrit Inscriptions of Ancient Cambodia*, New Delhi: Abhinav Publications.

Nayyar, S., 2002, *India's Relationship with South East Asia: Essays Series: Indian Influence Abroad*, eSamskriti (www.esamskriti.com), retrieved on 4 January 2013.

Nilkantha Shastri, K.A., 1976, *A History of South India from Pre-historic Time to Fall of Vijayanagar*, New Delhi: Oxford University Press.

Sen, S.N., 1999, *Ancient Indian History and Civilization*, New Delhi: New Age International Publishers.

Sengupta, A.B., 2005, *God & King: The Devaraja Cult in South Asian Art & Architecture*, New Delhi: Regency Publication.

Sethna, K.D., 1997, *Ancient India in New Light*, New Delhi: Aditya Prakashan.

Sharma, R.S., 1990, *Prachin Bharat*, New Delhi: Publication Division, National Council of Education Research and Training (NCERT).

Srivastav, K.C., 2007, *Prācīn Bhārat kā Itihās tathā Sanskr̥ti*, Allahabad: United Book Depot.

Tripathi, R.S., 1999, *History of Ancient India*, Delhi: Motilal Banarsidass.

Thakur, U., 1986, *Some Aspects of Asian History and Culture,* New Delhi: Abhinav Publications.

Vajpayee, K.D., 2002, *Bhāratīya Vāstukalā kā Itihās*, Lucknow: Uttar Pradesh Hindi Sansthan.

Varma, R.S., 1973, "Indian Culture in South East Asian Countries", *Triveni* (vol. 3, July–September), Madras: Triveni Foundation.

Vedalankar, H.D., 2004, *Bharat kā Sānskṛtik Itihās*, Delhi: Atma Ram & Sons.

## Internet Sources

http://orias.berkeley.edu/SEARama/RamaCambodia.htm

www.unesco.org

http://www.vietvisiontravel.com/viewer.asp?pgid=41&aid=2218

# 21

# Cultural Relationship between India and Thailand

*Shyam Sunder Sharma*

**Abstract**

India and Thailand, located in each other's extended neighbourhood, share unique civilizational links going back several millennia. The shared link of Buddhism is reflected in regular pilgrimages to places of Buddhist interest in India by a large number of Thai people. Hindu elements can be found reflected in Thai architecture, arts, sculpture, dance, drama and literature. The Thai language incorporates Pāli and Sanskrit influences. A large Indian Diaspora living and working in Thailand is another important bond.

About 7,90,000 Indian tourists visited Thailand in 2010, making India one of the fastest growing markets for Thailand for inbound tourism. In 2011, the number was about 8,30,000 for January–November 2011 (some slowdown in later part of the year is due to floods in Thailand). The number of Thai tourists to India is around 45,000 (mainly to Buddhist pilgrimage sites).

Both countries are important regional partners linking South and South-East Asia. They co-operate closely in the ASEAN, East Asia Summit (EAS) and BIMSTEC groupings as also Mekong Ganga Cooperation (MGC) and Asia Cooperation Dialogue (ACD).

## Introduction

THERE is a long history of the connection between Hinduism and South-East Asia. These links date back to 2,000 years and had resulted in the formation of Indian kingdoms on the Indo-Chinese peninsula and pre-modern Indonesia. The foundation of the first Indian settlements in this region was established with the migration of priests, traders and seamen from India to different parts of South and South-East Asia. This migration of Indian traders and immigrants resulted in the founding of Indian kingdoms which practised Indian arts, religion and customs who used Sanskrit as the sacred language. R.C. Majumdar notes a number of Indians had settled and established colonies in South-East Asia. There was also political domination exercised by Indian dynasties in this area. He shows the spread of Hindu kingdoms and the victory of Hindu culture over the region and the influence in almost every part of people's life in the region. He also notes that Buddhism had important centres and played an important role in the spread of Hindu culture in this region.[1] Bose also gave evidence of Indian settlement in Thailand and the Indian influence over the Thai society. Thomas A. Kirsch also points out the complexity in Thai Buddhism. He has shown how the Thai Buddhism comprises of animistic, Brahmanistic and Buddhist elements.

Thailand is a Buddhist country with almost 95 per cent of its population practising Theravāda Buddhism. Buddhism spread from India long before the Christian era to different parts of Asia. The Thai culture has two sources of origin, indigenous and foreign. The first comes from the ideas and inspiration of people while the later comes from the cultural contact with other civilizations like India and China. The customs, traditions, ceremonies and festivals were thus derived from these sources.[2]

Therefore it is common to find Buddhism and Hinduism practised together in Thailand. In addition even though Buddhism is the official religion in Thailand, there is a great religious tolerance for other religions. Therefore there is a mix of several practices from other religions with the Buddhist beliefs. As for the Hindu practices, they have become so common that Thais' sometimes are not being able to distinguish between Buddhism and Hinduism. It then becomes easy for them to practise both the religions at the same time. The reason behind this is that many of the Buddhist rituals and beliefs are the same as the Hindus rituals and beliefs. The purpose of this paper is

---

1 Majumdar 1955: 15-16.

2 Charuwan 1981: 12-13.

thus to study this similarity with an emphasis on the connections found between the Thai and Hindu festivals.

## Thai Festivals and Their Linkage with Hindu Festivals

India, a country of festivals, is the seventh largest country in the world and each month there is a festival celebrated in some part of the country. There is a festival to celebrate every season like harvests, commemorating historical people and events, and to express one's devotion to deities. All the festivals celebrated do have prayers, rituals, decorating homes, music, dance and sharing feasts. As mentioned earlier there are several festivals but among those there are a few that are the most important ones and are celebrated all over the country.

Similarly in Thailand there are lots of festivals that are celebrated throughout the country. Many of these festivals are celebrated at the same time of the year as the Hindu festivals and are celebrated in the similar manner as well. In this paper I will focus on four famous festivals as the examples to show the cultural connections through religion between the two countries.

### Holī

The festival of colours called Holī begins on *dvādaśī* (twelfth day) of the waxing moon of the month of Phālguna[3] or spring (the season of hope and new beginnings and marks the rekindling of the spirit of life). Phālguna is considered the last month of the year and spring starts from the next day of the new Indian year. Thus since ancient times, this festival is considered a festival of merrymaking announcing the commencement of the spring season. The festival is generally celebrated in northern part of India. There are several different stories associated with this festival. According to one of the stories from the Purāṇas,[4] it is said that this was the day when Lord Śiva opened his third eye and the spark from his third eye burned Lord Kāma (Lord of Love) into ashes. This perhaps explains the other names of this festival: Vasanta-Mahotsava and Kāma-Mahotsava.

Almost forty days before the start of this festival, a log of wood

---

3 Is the last month of the Hindu calendar.

4 Literary texts written in Sanskrit dating from fourth century BCE to around CE 1000.

is kept in a prominent public place and people throw twigs of trees and other things that make the log grow into a big heap. This heap is then set alight on the night of the Phālguna Pūrṇimā,[5] along with chanting of some *mantras* to ward away all the evil spirits. Singing and dancing also add to the celebration of this festival. On the next day people splash coloured powder and coloured water over each other. It is believed that even the enemies become friends on this day. The significance of this festival is to fill ones life with the colours of happiness and friendship. It marks the beginning of the Indian New Year.

### Songkran

A Thai festival celebrating the New Year is the same as the Indian festival of Holī. Songkran in Thailand is celebrated on 13 April every year and last for three days. The traditional celebration was pouring water to invite to Indra to descend to earth and bring rain for a good harvest for the farmers. The first day is known as the Maha Songkran Day which marks the end of the old year. The second day is known as the Wan Nao and the third and the last day is the Wan Thaloeng Sok which marks the beginning of the New Year itself. This festival offers valuable customs to the Thai community where everyone returns home in order to celebrate the festival with their family members. Everyone gathers together to pay respect to their elders by pouring scented water on to their hands and presenting gifts. Later together everyone celebrates this festival by splashing water over each other. Perhaps the only difference that can be found in Thailand would be that people pour scented water over others while in India it is more common to use colours which are sometimes mixed with water as well. This festival originating from India is celebrated not only in Thailand but also in other South-East Asian countries like Myanmar known as Feast of Thingyan, Bpee Mai in Laos, Chaul Chnam Thmey in Cambodia, Vietnam and Yunnan.[6]

### Kārttika Pūrṇimā and Dīpāvalī

Kārttika Pūrṇimā[7] is an Indian festival where devotees take a dip in

[5] Full moon day in the month of February to mid-March.

[6] Agarwal 2010: 11.

[7] Celebrates the power of Lord Śiva who killed the demon Tripura on this day. The month of Kārttika is considered to the holiest month of the Hindu calendar.

the holy river of Ganges to wash away all the sins and their effects. The whole month of "Kārttika", falling in around October to November according to the Indian calendar, is considered to be the most sacred among the twelve months of the year. During this month devoted Hindus refrain from non-vegetarian food. People take pre-dawn bath and visit temples as a matter of routine. The last five days called *pañcaka* are considered even more sacred, in which there is wide participation and the last day is "Kārttika Pūrṇimā".

Dīpāvalī on the other hand is the most popular and most celebrated festival of India which lasts for four days. During this festival people will light their houses with traditional *dīyā*s (oil lamps) and candles marking it as a night of enchantment. This festival falls in the holiest month of Kārttika and comes twenty to twenty-one days after Duśaharā (festival celebrated to mark the defeat of Rāvaṇa by Lord Rāma). The festival of Dīpāvalī is celebrated to mark the return of Lord Rāma along with his wife Sītā and brother Lakṣmaṇa to Ayodhyā after fourteen years of exile. The festival symbolizes the end of darkness of ignorance and the beginning of knowledge that enlightens the world. This festival is celebrated by people of all races and religion symbolizing unity is diversity. As part of the festivities, everyone would worship goddess Lakṣmī (goddess of wealth) along with Lord Gaṇeśa, play fireworks and exchange gifts and sweets among friends and family members. For businessmen, the festival marks the end of the financial year. The businesses would close their financial accounts and start with the new accounts only after worshipping goddess Lakṣmī during Dīpāvalī.

### Loy Krathong

The festival of Loy Krathong, one of the most popular festivals of Thailand, falls somewhere in November on the full moon day of the twelfth lunar month. The practices performed in this festival are to show gratitude to the river goddess "Mae Khong Kha" (Gaṅgā). *Loy* means "to float" and *krathong* is a "raft". The worshippers float the *krathong* in the river during the high tide at the end of the rainy season. The festival starts in the evening when people carry their *krathong*s (a lotus-shaped vessel made of banana leaves) to the nearby rivers. The *krathong* contain a candle, three joss-sticks, some flowers and coins. After lighting candles and joss-sticks and making a wish, each person gently places his/her *krathongs* on the water and drifts it away till they go out of sight. The general belief is that the *krathongs* carry away sins and bad luck, and the wishes that have been made for the new year due to start. This festival is the same as Kārttika Pūrṇimā, the festival celebrated in India around the same time of the year and is also known to be inspired by the festival of Dīpāvalī.[8] These festivals of lights mark the end of the rainy season and the beginning of winter. The festival is also celebrated in Myanmar and is known as Tazaung-mon.[9]

**Navarātri**

Navarātri is a festival dedicated to the goddess Durgā appearing on earth in nine materializations. This festival is celebrated twice a year, beginning of summer and beginning of winter. It is observed for nine days all over India and each day is considered to be sacred and auspicious. The festival is devoted to the worship of god in a female form. Out of these nine days, three are dedicated to Durgā (goddess of energy), three to Lakṣmī (goddess of wealth) and three days for Sarasvatī (goddess of knowledge). On the eighth and the ninth day, *yajña* (offerings to fire) is performed in every temple to give offerings to goddess Durgā and to bid her farewell. The tenth and the last day of this festival hold a lot of significance for the Hindus. This is the day when goddess Durgā killed demon Mahiṣāsura who defeated the gods and their king Indra and took over the throne. The defeated gods and Indra approached Brahmā, Viṣṇu and Śiva who then decided to combine their energies to give rise to Durgā who could destroy the evil demon. Even since then the day is celebrated as Daśaharā or Vijayadaśamī which is the victory of good over evil. Another common theme which celebrates the victory of good over evil is associated with the victory of Lord Rāma over Rāvaṇa. On Vijayadaśamī, Hindus all around the country burn effigies of Rāvaṇa, his brother Kumbhakarṇa and son Meghanād to celebrate this day. This festival of Navrātri holds the same significance of cleansing ones' self as does the Vegetarian Festival in Thailand. During this festival, devotees will observe a fast for seven to nine days depending on which region they come from. During this festival they will refrain from meat,

[8] Desai 2005: 32-33.

[9] Agarwal 2010: 17.

alcohol, and anything made from common salt or spices. Special meal is prepared to be consumed during this festival.

### Thai–Chinese Vegetarian Festival

The Thai–Chinese Vegetarian Festival falls at the same time as Navrātri. It falls during the first nine days of the ninth lunar month of the Chinese calendar. For nine days the Thai–Chinese community cleanse themselves spiritually and physically by abstaining from meat, alcohol, sexual encounters, lying, uncharitable thoughts and aggression. During these nine days, the Chinese Buddhists would wear white attire and visit temples in order to be part of the merit-making ceremonies. Other highlights of this festival include devotees performing incredible acts like fire-walking, climbing knife-blade ladders and a street procession where some have their cheeks pierced and bodies spiked with sharp objects. This festival is originally a Taoist rite which was introduced in early nineteenth century by a visiting Chinese opera troupe to Phuket. At that time there was a outbreak of malaria which quickly spread and affected everyone in Phuket. According to legend, the troupe performed a religious ceremony which involved a strict vegetarian diet and ritual self-mutilation. This allowed the troupe to quickly recover from their illness and this attracted the locals who then sent volunteers to China to learn more about the purification routine practised by the troupe. These rites then became part of an annual festival in Thailand since then.

### Oṇam

Oṇam is one of the greatest festivals and most important harvest festivals of Kerala, south India, and is considered as the time for sports and festivities after three months of heavy rains. It is a ten-day festival celebrated in the Malayalam month Chingam which falls around the end of August and the beginning of September. It is a festival to celebrate the reward of nature after a year of hard labour. During this festival people take their boats and country crafts to celebrate. Each snake boat in Kerala belongs to a village along the banks of the river Pambā and is worshipped like a deity. Only men are allowed to board or even touch a boat and that too just barefoot. The oarsmen usually dress in white *dhotī*s and turbans singing traditional boat songs as they splash their oars in the water along with the rhythm of the songs. Women on the other hand dress up in new clothes and heavy jewellery and make elaborate yet complex designs of *raṅgolīs* (most popular art forms in India) using coloured rice paste and flower mat in front of their homes. This colourful festival also draws several thousands of local and foreign spectators.

**Long-Boat Racing**

Long-Boat Racing is one of the most traditional rites that mark the end of the Buddhist Rains Retreat. The earliest records show king Ekathotsarot (1605-10) during the Ayutthaya period held a boat race. The purpose was to train the oarsmen with the soldiers so they can be used during war. King Chulalongkorn (1868–1910) also wrote about this festival in his "Royal Ceremonies of the Twelve Months". He mentions the race being held in the eleventh month between Samatthachai (boat of the king) and the Kraisonmuk (boat of the queen). The race was held to predict the future. If the race was won by Kraisonmuk, the nation would enjoy abundant harvest and on the other hand if it was defeated then there would be sufferings.

In ancient times the royal race would be held in the eleventh lunar month with the end of the rainy season when the Chao Phraya River was flooded annually in Ayutthaya region. Later the water level would subside and farmers could harvest their crops. However if the water level remains high, it would lead to hardship for the farmers. As a remedy to this, the king would also perform a Brāhmanic rite in the eleventh month to prevent floods in advance.[10]

The rites now take place during the eleventh and twelfth lunar months (September or October) when the water level is at its highest. In Thailand, Long-Boat Racing is considered a traditional annual event and is presently considered as a national sport. It is organized by provinces with major waterway flowing through like Phitsanulok, Nan, Pathumthani, Angthong, Surat thani, Ayutthaya and others. The Long-Boat Racing has historical significance as it can be traced back to 600 years. During the earlier periods, boat racing was a means to keep boat oarsmen physically and mentally strong for national defence. These races are very colourful and unique as the boats are nicely decorated and the oarsmen would wear dress of the same colour.

10 Wattana 2006.

This race draws thousands of local and foreign spectators enjoying the event from both sides of the riverbank. This festival shares a connection with the Indian festival of Oṇam which has been discussed above.

**Other Religious Similarities**

In addition to the festivals of India and Thailand, there are other similarities that one can find. Thai culture is deeply routed in the traditional religious practices. The Thai cultural habits are similar to those practised in the Hindu culture. First of all, the salutation to welcome or greet each other is *wai*, a gesture of bowing which is very common in India where people greet each other with *namaskāra*. In fact, this word is part of the Thai language and is pronounced in Thai as *namaskārn*.

It is also important to note that the Thai national and royal emblem is Garuḍa, the vehicle of Viṣṇu. The walls of the magnificent temple next to the king's Grand Palace are painted with stories from *Rāmāyaṇa*. The Hindu gods, Brahmā, Viṣṇu and Śiva are commonly worshipped by the Thais. Also every office and even the residential areas will have a spirit house with the statue of Brahmā and offerings of food, incense sticks and flowers will be made on a daily basis.

Yet another interesting influence can be seen at the new Suvarṇabhūmi airport's international departure hall. A famous Hindu sculpture of Samudra-Manthana (the churning of the Ocean of Milk) is located in the passenger departure hall. The Samudra-Manthana statue depicts a legend of the Hindu god Viṣṇu (Nārāyaṇa), who took the form of a tortoise and sat on the bottom of the sea. According to the myths, Viṣṇu's second incarnation on earth was of Kūrma (a tortoise), to help recover *amṛta* (nectar of immorality). Gods and demons together set about producing *amṛta* by churning the Ocean of Milk, using Mt. Mandara as a churning stick. The mountain along with Vāsukī (the serpent) used as a churning rope, was placed on Kūrma's back by other gods in order to proceed with the task.

Another common religious practice in both the cultures is the one related to making offerings or giving alms. One is not supposed to sniff flowers and incense sticks or taste food items as that will be considered as being used already and therefore unsuitable to be used in religious offerings.

Furthermore one can find a religious similarity when a *havana* or *homa* is conducted in which a *homa-kuṇḍa* (sacrificial pit) is sanctified by chanting *mantra*s before the fire-god Agni is invoked. Offering of various things are made along with chanting of *mantra*s into the fire. During this ritual, the brāhmaṇa will offer *ghee* (clarified butter) with a wooden stick into the fire and the leftover will be dropped in a vessel full of water just beside the *homa-kuṇḍa* chanting *namāmaḥ* along. This means that the offerings are made to god Indra and are not for one's own self. The water is considered sacred and is sprinkled over the worshippers at the end of the fire ceremony as a blessing from the gods and also to ward away evil spirits.

A similar ritual is practised in Thailand where the *Sangharath* (Supreme Patriarch) drops candle wax (instead of drops of oil as in Hindu ceremony) in water which is then considered *nam-mon* (holy water). The word *nam-mon* has originated from the Sanskrit word *namāmaḥ* itself. This sacred water is then sprinkled over worshippers as a blessing from god. As Nathaniel Altman mentions, water is commonly used in Thailand for ritual exorcism, which is performed by a specially trained Buddhist monk or Hindu brāhmaṇa whose ancestors were emigrated from India. The belief is that evil spirits are afraid of water and the worshippers who fear being possessed by spirits would undergo ritual bathing to ward away these spirits.

**Bilateral Treaties Agreements**

- Trade Agreement — 1968
- Bilateral Air Services Agreement — 1969
- Maritime Boundary Delimitation Agreement — 1969
- Cultural Agreement — 1977
- Agreement on the Delimitation of Sea Bed Boundary in the Andaman Sea — 1978
- Double Taxation Avoidance Agreement — 1985
- Establishment of Joint Trade Committee — 1985
- Protocol for Scientific & Technical Cooperation between Thailand Institute of Scientific & Technological Research (TISTR) and Centre for Scientific and Industrial Research (CSIR) — 1986

- Agreement between Government of Thailand and the Government of India on the Maritime Boundary in the Andaman Sea from Point 7 to the Trifurcation Point between Thailand, India and Myanmar, initiated in Bangkok — 1989
- Establishment of Joint Commission — 1989
- MoU between ONGC and Petroleum Authority of Thailand for mutual Cooperation in the field of exploration and exploitation of petroleum Resources and for training of personnel — 1989
- Agreement on Cooperation between the Federation of Indian Chambers of Commerce & Industry (FICCI) and the Board of Trade of Thailand — 1990
- Cooperation Agreement between the Federation of Thai Industries and the Federation of Indian Chambers of Commerce & Industry (FICCI) — 1991
- MoU between the Indian Council of Agricultural Research (ICAR) and the Asian Institute of Technology (AIT) — 1992
- Agreement on Peaceful Uses of Atomic Energy — 2000
- Bilateral Investment Promotion and Protection Agreement (BIPPA) — 2000
- MoU on Co-operation in Information Technology — 2001
- Agreement on Co-operation in the Exploration and Use of Outer Space for Peaceful Purposes — 2002
- Agreement on Scientific, Technical and Environmental Co-operation and Transfer of Technology — 2002
- Agreement for Exemption of Visas for Diplomatic and Official Passports — 2003;
- MoU on Co-operation in the Field of Agricultural Science, Technology and Economy — 2003
- Agreement on Tourism Co-operation — 2003
- Framework Agreement for Establishing a Free Trade Area between Thailand and India — 2003
- Programme of Co-operation in Biotechnology — 2003

- Framework Agreement on the BIMSTEC Free Trade Area — 2004
- Mutual Legal Assistance Treaty — 2004
- MoU between the Indian Navy and the Royal Thai Navy on Coordinated Patrol Procedures in the Areas Adjacent to International Maritime Boundary Line and Establishment of Lines of Communication — 2005
- MoU on Co-operation in the Field of Education — 2005
- MoU on Air Services — 2006
- Programme of Co-operation (POC) in Science and Technology — 2006
- MoU on Co-operation in the area of Renewable Energy — 2007
- MoU on Cultural Exchange Co-operation (2007-09) — 2007
- MoU on Defence Co-operation — 2012
- Treaty on Transfer of Sentenced Persons — 2012
- The 2nd Protocol to Amend the Framework Agreement for Establishing Free Trade Area between Thailand and India — 2012
- Programme of Co-operation in Science & Technology for 2012-14 — 2012
- Cultural Exchange Programme for 2012-14 — 2012
- MoU between Chulalongkorn University and ICCR for setting up a Chair at the India Studies Centre of the University — 2012

## Conclusion

This paper shows the cultural linkage of Thailand with India with an emphasis on four popular festivals celebrated in the two countries. There is a long historical linkage between India and the South-East Asian region. Therefore it is likely to find a lot of similarities to show the cultural linkage in this region. The diffusion of the Hindu religious practices has been made possible by the trade links, traders, priests and seamen. Over a period of time the cultural diffusion has become an integral part of the Thai society and it is sometimes difficult to know which practices are Hindu and Thais.

This study compared four major Hindu festivals, Holī, Kārttika Pūrṇimā and Dīpāvalī, Navarātri and Oṇam with the four Thai festivals of Songkran, Loy Krathong, Thai-Chinese Vegetarian Festival, and the Long-Boat Race. The four chosen festivals are celebrated around the same time of the year and the ways of celebration are also very similar. The festival of Holī and Songkran, the harvest festivals are celebrated by splashing water over one another and marks the beginning of the New Year. Kārttika Pūrṇimā, Dīpāvalī and Loy Krathong are also associated with water where people wash their sins by taking a dip in Ganges in India and by floating a *krathong* in Thailand. The festival marks the financial New Year in India. The Navarātri and the Vegetarian Festival mark the period of time where devotees discipline themselves by fasting, turning themselves into vegetarian for nine days. Lastly, the Oṇam and Long-Boat Race are traditional harvesting festivals that mark the end of the rainy season and are celebrated by having boat races.

It is also interesting to see other cultural links between the two countries. Some include the way of greeting, the Indian *namaskāra* and Thai *wai*, the national emblem of Thailand, Garuḍa which is the vehicle of Hindu god Viṣṇu, several Hindu sculptures that can be found around Thailand, and the practice of *homa* and the beliefs related to the sacred water, *nam-mon*. More research on the cultural and religious linkage can reveal several other elements that link the two regions of India and South-East Asia together.

## References

Agarwal, Ruchi, 2010, "Water Festivals of Thailand: The Indian Connection", *Silpakorn University International Journal*, **9-10**: 7-18.

Altman, Nathaniel, 2002, *The Spiritual Source of life: Sacred Water*, Hidden Spring, chap. 5, pp. 138-40.

Bose, P.N., 1927, *The Indian Colonies of Siam*, Lahore.

Charuwan, Chareonla, 1981, *Buddhist Arts of Thailand*, Buddha Dharma Education Association, chap. 1, pp. 12-13. http://www.buddhanet.net/pdf_file/budartthai2.pdf

Desai, S.N. 2001, *Hinduism in Thai Life*, Mumbai: Popular Prakashan.

Gupta, Shakti M., 1991, *Festivals, Fairs, and Fasts of India*, New Delhi: Clarion Books.

Kirsch, Thomas A., 1977, "Complexity in the Thai Religious System: An interpretation", *Journal of Asian Studies*, **36**(2).

Majumdar, R.C., 1955, *Ancient Indian Colonization in South East Asia,* Baroda: Oriental Institute, chap. 1, pp. 1-19.

Tansuchat, Roengchai & Panmanee, Chanita, *Tourist Motivation, Characteristic and Satisfaction in Night Festival: Loy Krathong Festival 2010*, Oral presentation at Maejo University. (http://iscthlr.turismo.wu-wien.ac.at/files/papers/p25_fullpaper.pdf) (retrieved on 16 September 2011)

Wattana, Thawat, 2006, "Boat Racing in Thailand", *Anura Thailand Tourism*, Thai Airways website, **23**(10) 25 August 2006 (http://www.thaiways magazine.com/thai_article/2310_boat_racing_in_thailand boat_racing_in_thailand.html)

http://www.thaiemb.org.in/en/index.php

http://www.mfa.go.th/main/en/home

http://www.sscnet.ucla.edu/southasia/Religions/texts/Puranas.html (retrieved on 10 September 2011)

http://www.enotes.com/food-encyclopedia/hindu-festivals (retrieved on 16 September 2011)

Stamboulis, Dave, *Thai Festival Primer: The weird, the Colorful, and the Fun,* http://www.davestamboulis.com/festival.pdf (retrieved on 16 September 2011).

# 22

# Reinventing the Connectedness
## Implications for India in Mainland South-East Asia

*Sarita Dash*

### Introduction

THIS paper tries broadly to look at the role of culture in harnessing India's potential in building a long-term understanding among the peoples of India and mainland South-East Asia. Keeping in mind the topic of the conference I have excluded Myanmar while discussing India's cultural interaction with the countries of Cambodia, Laos, Vietnam and Thailand.

India's relationship with the countries of South-East Asia is unique. In a way not many regions in the world can claim such age-old, uninterrupted and multifaceted ties. India's strong cultural presence in the form of religious, artistic and intellectual expressions, the presence of the migrant Indian communities in different parts of South-East Asia, architectural designs and motifs from Angkor Vat to literary heritage of *Rāmāyaṇa*, still convey the story of India's cross-cultural interaction with the region much before the age of globalization and communication technology. Significantly, these roots of India's cultural imprints are visible in the South-East Asian soil; even to this day.

The Indian influences on South-East Asia can be traced back to the first century CE. It continued until the Western hegemony was established in both the regions. India's relations with South-East Asia passed through many phases. India–South-East Asia trade relations extend much before the advent of colonialism and predates even the beginning of the Christian era. In fact, trade acted as a vehicle for cultural transmission leading to the development of "Indianized" states in South-East Asia. Medieval India did have cultural contacts with all those regions concerned whereas colonial India's cultural diplomacy became a handmaiden of British political diplomacy.

On the eve of India's Independence in 1947, Indian contacts and knowledge about South-East Asia were vague, illusory and uncertain. Except for a small number of area specialists and those closely related to the Indian immigrants in the area, very few Indians knew as much about their neighbours in South-East Asia as they knew of Europe or America. A vague memory of the ancient trading activities with South-East Asia and the close cultural contacts between the two regions was all that an average educated Indian's awareness of this region.[1]

Even though, the anti-colonial movement provided an impetus for both India and South-East Asia to come closer, this phase was a short one. The Bandung Conference of 1955 marked both the peak and the beginning of the decline of interest between the two regions. The Cold War again played a critical role in ensuring that both India and South-East Asia drifted apart with the two sides often being on opposite sides of the Cold War divide as did the different economic models that were adopted. It was only during the early 1990s; the end of Cold War together with India's own liberalized economic policies compelled New Delhi to look East. At the tenth ASEAN Summit in 1992, India was accepted as a sectoral dialogue partner, a status that enabled it to participate in areas such as trade and investment, joint ventures, science, technology, tourism and human resource development. In December 1995, India was admitted as a full dialogue partner of ASEAN and the following May 1996, New Delhi was admitted into the ASEAN Regional Forum (ARF).[2] The launching of Gaṅgā–Mekong co-operative initiative and the Ministry of Culture's efforts to collect and organize the variants of *Rāmāyaṇa* from South-East Asia; even the recently held summit on "ASEAN–India Partnership for Peace and Shared Prosperity" in New Delhi on December 2012 shows some further steps in this regard. India's Look East Policy has evolved in four different waves over centuries. The first wave of cultural and commercial engagement between India and

---

1 Sardesai 1996: 78-79.

2 Naidu 1998: 28.

its South-East Asian neighbours lasted until the twelfth/thirteenth century. The second wave was evolved by the British empire giving to a strong strategic dimension. Independent India's leaders like Jawaharlal Nehru took the lead in launching the third wave by focussing on East Asia as an important part of India's policy of Asian resurgence. However, the imperatives of the Cold War, intra-Asian conflict and rivalries, and India's weaknesses on economic and military fronts hindered her Asia policy to flourish. What is named as India's Look East Policy (LEP) since the early 1990s constitutes "the fourth wave of India's eastward (re)engagement". India has not only reinforced its economic and cultural relations with the countries of ASEAN and East Asia, but also firmed up strategic relations with them through its LEP.[3]

In the contemporary times, while states are trying to capture foreign markets for expansion of trade and economy by propagating their values, ideas, ways of life and culture in the other's space, India already has a rich legacy of these elements. In the new millennium, India is trying its best to expand its relations with the region within the framework of its Look East Policy. The data from India and South-East Asia is inseparably linked and a comprehensive study of one is meaningless without a thorough knowledge of the other. Against this backdrop, the present study is aimed at finding out and analysing the roots of India's cultural relations in the region.[4]

## Religions of Indian Origin

Hinduism, Buddhism and Islam the three dominant ancient religions of the region and these have for centuries influenced the social, moral and intellectual lives; ultimately leading to the evolution of society and politics in mainland South-East Asia. The pervasive role played by these religions, integrating each of these civilizations, makes an interesting subject of inter-disciplinary studies. There is no clear evidence suggesting the exact period of spread of these religions to the countries of Laos, Vietnam, Cambodia and Thailand. Both Hinduism and Buddhism are supposed to have gone there nearly at the same time, i.e. in the first-century CE through traders, priests or

---

[3] Muni 2011: 1-2.

[4] Dash 2003.

even monks. Later, they got patronized there by various rulers and had profound influences on the natives of the countries concerned.[5] However, after the eleventh-century conversion of a Burmese monarch Anawratha to Theravāda, Buddhism spread rapidly in mainland South-East Asia. This became the dominant faith of the people of Myanmar, Thailand, Laos and Cambodia while most of Vietnam followed a modified form of Māhāyana Buddhism.[6] Islam came to mainland South-East Asia later in thirteenth century CE.

## HINDUISM

Hinduism went to mainland South-East Asia with all its different sects and the whole pantheon. The most important sects those transmitted were Brāhmanism, Śaivism and Vaiṣṇavism.

## BRĀHMANISM

Even though, in mainland South-East Asia, Buddhism ultimately dominated, from early times, Brāhmanism and Buddhism mingled in the cultural legacy passed on to all the "Indianized" states. There was a two-way interaction between the ancient South-East Asian traditions with the traditions of imported religions. Many of them even got patronized by kings. Along with the dominance of Buddhism, the different cults and sects of Hinduism (Vaiṣṇavism, Śaivism, Devarāja Cult, etc.) persisted to a significant level.[7] From the beginning till recent times, there is the continuing importance of brāhmaṇas; even the Buddhist courts have engaged brāhmaṇas in astrological and ritual functions. As they had access to the sacred texts, the law books and other literature in Sanskrit, they were employed as priests, teachers, ministers and counsellors: the principal advisers of the kings. The epigraphic record of the mainland kingdoms demonstrates the powerful influence of *purohitas*, notably in Cambodia, where they often served under several successive rulers and provided continuity to the government in troubled times.[8]

---

5 Basham 1954: 451-52.

6 Sardesai 1997: 19-20.

7 Coedes 1968: 250-57.

8 Ibid.: 205.

Not only in the Hindu court in Angkor, but also in Buddhist court, in Sukhothai in Thailand, the brāhmaṇas conducted the great ceremonies, such as the royal consecration and functional as ministers and counsellors and had to share their influence with that of the Buddhist monks. From these functions it can be spoken of Brāhmanism as distinct from the specific cults of Śiva or Viṣṇu, or any of their innumerable kin.[9]

## ŚAIVISM

Cults of Śiva were strong in the ancient kingdoms of Cambodia and Champa (today's Vietnam). Two major roles played by Śiva were the political and the devotional. The political role was as the focus of *liṅga* cults. Different rulers sponsored these cults at the central shrines that constituted the ritual hub of their kingdom. State-sponsored Śiva cults were maintained in Cambodia till the twelfth century.[10] Śaivism as we find it in India with its numerous sects (Pāśupatas, Kālāmukhas, etc.) are also found in mainland South-East Asia. There are a number of Śivaliṅgas found in Laos even to this day.[11] On the top of Phou Lokan hill, a Sanskrit inscription mentions the erection of Śivaliṅga by king Mahendravarman.[12]

## VAIṢṆAVISM

In Angkor, several rulers gave honour to Viṣṇu, but by far the most conspicuous success of Vaiṣṇavism in gaining state support was embodied in the construction of Angkor Vat by king Sūryavarman II (CE 1130-50). The ritual and cosmological symbolism of the monument is richly embodied in every detail of Angkor Vat's art and design representing a devotional form of Viṣṇu worship.

In addition to the worship of Śiva and Viṣṇu, traces of worship of Durgā, Gaṇeśa, Indra, Brahmā and most of the other deities of Hindu

---

9 Coedes 1968: 253.

10 Tarling 1992: 278.

11 View expressed by S.D. Muni, former Indian Ambassador to Laos in a personal conversation.

12 P.P. Mishra, "Indo–Lao Cultural Rapprochement in Ancient and Medieval Times", available in: http://www.seasite.niu.edu/lao/laostudies/pmish1.htm

pantheon are also found. This reveals the intensity of Hindu influence on the religious life of mainland South-East Asia. Apart from mainstream Hinduism or Brāhmanism, South-East Asians also adopted the animistic cults and rituals like the worship of mountains as abodes of gods, snakes (Nāga Cult) and animals.[13]

Hinduism not only provided a way of life giving a particular belief system but also offered them certain related ideas on kingship, deification and divinity of the ruler along with law and administration. Hindu mythologies based on *Rāmāyaṇa*, *Mahābhārata* and Purāṇas have a profound influence on the South-East Asian minds. All these epics are still prevalent in Laos, Cambodia, Thailand and Vietnam even though in different forms. Hinduism with its mythology, epics and tradition and rituals had helped considerably in making a common psychological make-up of the peoples of the regions.[14]

## BUDDHISM

Buddha images and motive seals attest the introduction of the religion since early times. The record begins with a number of Buddhist statues found in various parts of mainland South-East Asia. Buddhism, with its universal values, came to be embodied even more than Brāhmanism; in the teachings of pilgrims and wandering scholars and monks from India. A Thai most likely thinks of the Buddhism of his country as a continuation of the Theravāda tradition, which was allegedly brought to the Golden Peninsula (Suvarṇabhūmi) by Aśoka's missionaries Sona and Uttara in the third century BCE. Modern scholarship explains that Buddhism was a prevalent religion in South-East Asia; mainly in present-day Myanmar, Thailand, Vietnam, Cambodia and Laos prior to the development of the classical South-East Asian states (Champa, Srivijaya, Majapahit, etc.) which occurred from the tenth or eleventh century to the fifteenth century CE. This early period of Buddhism in South-East Asia was diverse and eclectic, infused with elements of Hindu Dharmaśāstras and Brāhmanic deities, Mahāyāna Buddhas and Tāntric practices, Sanskrit Sarvāstivādin texts, as well as Pāli Theravāda tradition.[15]

---

13 Tarling 1992: 299-314.

14 Ray 1998: 142-62.

15 Ibid.: 243-62.

Buddhism competed successfully with indigenous terms of magical animism and Brāhmanism and got transformed in the process, during these early centuries. Its propagation supposed to have followed the same pattern that was seen in Central and East Asia. Monks like Padmasambhava would have accompanied traders and brought in objects of power and protection such as relics and images as well as literary tradition in the form of magical chants in sacred languages also written texts. The Buddhist chronicles in Pāli and South-East Asian vernacular languages associate Buddhism with a high continental way of life in contrast to the less developed life of tribal peoples. Buddhism provided the development of an urban culture, symbols of translocal values and articulated a world-view in which diverse communities could participate and find a new identity, a language in which they could communicate and institution in which an organized religious life could be pursued and systematically taught.[16]

The rulers of Champa in southern Annam (Vietnam) also patronized Buddhism. Although Hinduism was initially the dominant religion in Cambodia, there is some evidence of Buddhism from the fifth century CE. The evidence cited supports the contention that throughout much of mainland South-East Asia Buddhism was present as a part of the larger Indian cultural influence.[17]

The relationship between Buddhism and the rise of the monarchical states in the classical period of South-East Asian history is generally referred to as symbiotic, i.e. one of mutual benefit. Rulers supported Buddhism because it provided a cosmology in which the king was accorded the central place; and a view of human society in which the human community was dependent on the role of the king. Ideologically, Buddhism legitimated kingship, providing a meta-physical rationale and moral basis for its existence. The Buddhist Saṅgha, in turn, supported South-East Asian monarchs because the material well-being, success and popularity of institutional Buddhism depended to a significant degree on the approval, support and largest of the ruling classes.[18] Buddhism's contribution to the classical

[16] Kitagawa 2002: 119.

[17] Hall 1981: 256.

[18] Ibid.: 256-71.

conception of South-East Asian kingship is particularly noteworthy in its emphasis on *dharma* and on the role of the ruler as a moral exemplar. The *king* is a *cakkavatti,* one whose rule depends upon the universal *dharma* of cosmic, natural and moral law. This symbiotic relationship between political and religious leadership roles takes a particular mythic pattern in many of the classical South-East Asian chronicles. Architecturally it manifests itself in the great (*caitya* or *stūpa*) monuments of Angkor, Dagan and other ancient capitals.[19]

From the late eleventh century to the early thirteenth century South-East Asia experienced a shift to Sinhala Theravāda Buddhism, which has been a major component of the religious life of South-East Asia since then. The foundation of Mahāyāna, Tāntricism and Hīnayāna concepts still prevail on the substratum at Cambodia, Laos, Vietnam and Thailand even to this day. Even though, in the colonial and post-colonial phases Buddhism in those countries has undergone significant modification still it has been a critical component in the identity of the Thais, Laotians, Cambodians and Vietnamese contributing much to world culture.

### Synthesization of Indian Religions in South-East Asia

Interestingly, in states where Hīnayāna Buddhism prevailed, brāhmaṇas played an important ceremonial part, especially at courts. They still do so in Thailand and Cambodia, though themselves strikingly different from their counterparts in India.[20] Thus, some of the most significant synergetic developments in Indian religions took place on the soil of South-East Asia. The syncretism of Hindu and Buddhist cults was promoted by the mystical doctrines of Tāntricism. There is the image of Amoghapāśā; the primordial goddess of destination with her attendants, while there are also the Avalokiteśvaras in Thailand closely embracing their *śakti*s or Tārās, the latter being associated with Tāntric Buddhism.[21] The composite form of Śaṅkara–Nārāyaṇa in Champa represents the corresponding Indian image of Harihara; the amalgamation of the cults of Viṣṇu and Śiva. In Cambodia, as well we find mention of Hari-Hara and of Viṣṇu–

19 Tarling 1992: 273-79.

20 Jayapalan 1999: 5.

21 Hall 1981: 85.

Caṇḍeśvareṣaṇā *liṅga* and also the inclusion of the Buddha in a Trimūrti along with Brahmā and Viṣṇu, the whole together with a *liṅga* being dedicated to Śiva (CE 1067). The Cambodian Trimūrti marks, accordingly, a greater integration than the Trimūrti at Elephaṇṭā and elsewhere in India.[22]

The mysticism and magic of Indian religion, the aura of supernatural power, appears to have been the chief attraction for the South-East Asians. Moreover, a cosmic explanation of the universe and of man's place in it seems to have replaced the patchwork of animist practice and belief.[23] There was no dogmatic rigidity in the Indian tradition to avert the accommodation of local ideas and institutions within Hinduism or Buddhism. Similarly, the comforts of the old animistic ways were not denied but got mingled with the Indian traditions. Adding Viṣṇu or Maitreya to the pantheon enhanced rather than limited the strength of familiar spirits.[24] Some of the indigenous beliefs were in harmony with Indian traditions like worship of mountains, rivers and serpents. Many facets of life in India and South-East Asia are intertwined to such a degree that sometimes it becomes difficult to differentiate between them.[25] Ultimately it was the accommodative and synergetic quality of Indian religions with its tremendous adaptability seems to have found much appeal in the countries of South-East Asia.

Close religious affinity that provides a strong basis for friendly relations between India and South-East Asia is further reinforced by their commonalities in arts, architecture and cultural heritage. Along with the spread of different religions also went the arts, architectural styles of different parts of India. The erection of those monuments took place in areas where wet-rice cultivation had existed long enough for a leisured class to arise, supported by the taxes and services of the peasant communities who were interested in Indian culture.[26]

---

22 Ibid.: 114-20.

23 Sarkar 1970: 19-20, also see Tarling 1992: 280 n. 15.

24 William 1976: 23.

25 P.P. Mishra, op. cit.

26 Hall 1981: 60.

## ARTS AND ARCHITECTURE

Sir John Marshall, a noted connoisseur, rightly opines:

> To know Indian art in India alone is to know but half its story. To apprehend to the full we must follow it in the wake of Buddhism to Central Asia, China and Japan; we must watch it assuming new forms and breaking it into new beauties as it spread over Tibet, Burma and Siam; we must gaze in awe at the unexampled grandeur of its creations in Cambodia and Java. In each of these countries Indian art encounters a different racial genius, a different local environment and under their modifying influence it takes on a different garb.[27]

According to D.G.E. Hall, a prominent historian of South-East Asia:

> Under the stimulus of Indian influence, especially during the period of middle age in Europe, art and architecture developed to a pitch which bears comparison with anything the rest of the world can show.[28]

Except Vietnam in all the other countries of mainland South-East Asia, we find strong Indian influences even to this day. Of all the aspects of Indian influences the nature and extent of the evolution of arts particularly sculptures and architecture have been the most fully studied. This is because of the availability of evidences as shown on those monuments. Apart from inscriptional evidences, these monuments are the solid proof of India's cultural imprints on mainland South-East Asia.[29]

### Popular Monuments bearing Indian Roots

A detailed study of the significant architectural sites of mainland South-East Asia those represent strong Indian roots till this day is difficult due to lack of space. Still, a brief description of the important ones is provided here. Some of the most important monuments that depict religious and mythological themes of India in a splendid way refer to Beantey Srei (late tenth century), Phimeanakas (early eleventh century), Baphuon (third quarter of eleventh century), Angkor Vat (twelfth

---

27 Sharma 1993: 86.

28 Hall 1981: 62.

29 Sardesai 1986: 95.

century), Angkor Thom (end of twelfth century), Bayon (twelfth century) temples of Cambodia , Wat Phu in Laos and My Son in Vietnam.

Angkor Vat and Angkor Thom in Cambodia are the most important temple complexes that show a high Indian influence. Of all the Khmer monuments these are the best preserved. Angkor Vat is the largest religious building of the world. Of late, Indian government has realized India's cultural linkage with this Hindu temple. The Archaeological Survey of India (ASI) with UNESCO support has undertaken the charge of its restoration. Recently the ASI has taken charge of restoring another Hindu temple in Cambodia, i.e. Ta Prohm.[30] In My Son of Vietnam, there are about twenty temples, all of which have either received or still need restoration, and a host of scattered but imposing Śivaliṅgas.

Regarding the Indian art, Coedes writes:

> Indian art was mostly formal, external, that is why from the very first, it is more striking than the internal ties that unite the plastic arts of farther India to India we know no monument in India resembling even remotely the Bayon or Angkor Thom or Borobudur. And yet the monuments are the pure production of the Indian genius, the deep meaning of which is apparent only to the eyes of the Indianist.[31]

Among the Indian schools of art, those of the Amarāvatī, Gupta, Pallava and Pāla phases of art have left their impact in varying degrees on the specimens of the art and architecture of South-East Asia.[32] It was mainly the Gupta style, bulky and round, emerging in India after several centuries of development, that became adopted by most of the other peoples of Asia, including the Mons and Khmers. The individuality of the major art styles of South-East Asia (to a great extent, the result of interaction between Indian and pre-Indian indigenous South-East Asian components) is far or more difficult to define than the Indian.[33] R.C. Majumdar after discussing the

---

30 "Angkor: A Temple Town Awaits Indians", *The Hindu*, 13 May 2003.

31 Coedes 1968: 252.

32 Sarkar 1985: 325.

33 Basham 1999: 448.

controversy regarding the origin of Khmer art and architecture suggests that though the art had its Indian origin it developed indigenously. It must have undergone a process of evolution that we notice in different parts of India in different ages.[34]

During the late Gupta and the Pāla–Sena periods many parts of South-East Asia were greatly influenced by developments in Indian religious field, especially in the Buddhist field. Therefore, we find a strong late Gupta and Pāla influence in many manifestations of art and architecture of South-East Asia. Inscriptions show that there was also a very close contact between many South-East Asian regions and the Tamil kingdoms, particularly during the period of the Coḷa dynasty (ninth to thirteenth century CE). This finds explanation for the presence of a Coḷa element in many areas of South-East Asian art and architecture.[35] Highlighting such Indian influence R.C. Majumdar writes:

> If we remember that the Indians from the eastern part of India played a prominent part in the colonization of the Far East, and also the great extent to which Indian civilization had influenced that of Champa we need not hesitate to trace the origin of Cham style to Indian temples at Bādāmī, Cāñjīvaram and Mamallapuram, particularly as this part of India was the nearest by way of sea to the kingdom of Champa. It is quite true that Champa did not blindly imitate the Indian prototypes and added new elements of their own, but the fact that their style was throughout based upon the essential characteristic features of Indian style, seems to be beyond question.[36]

### Affinities

The art in South-East Asia, like its parent art in India may be described as the handmaid of religion. All the monuments of the art, so far discovered, are religious structures. Religion provides sole aim and inspiration from beginning to end.[37] Although most of these monuments are now in ruins, the few temples that are still present intact constitute the greatest and most durable heritage of the Indian culture and civilization in these far-off regions.

---

34 Ibid.: 449.

35 Majumdar 1963: 174.

36 Ibid.: 174-75.

37 Majumdar 1963: 102.

Thus the basic elements of Indian art, i.e. art associated with spirituality, symbolism, rhetoric, sensuality, etc. are all reflected in its South-East Asian counterpart. This implies that the latter did not go beyond that. This is where the similarity exists. Through art, architecture and aesthetics a certain type of high cultural value spread to South-East Asia, got accepted by its elite and took a modified shape in the different monuments.

## ART OF WRITING, LANGUAGE AND LITERATURE

Apart from arts, architecture and aesthetics, India contributed profoundly to the literary heritage of mainland South-East Asia. The art of writing; undoubtedly one of the greatest inventions of humanity, was introduced to South-East Asia by India. Introduction of this art of writing enabled the South-East Asians to get equipped with Indian linguistic materials to develop their own vernacular and compose many beautiful original works.[38] Highlighting the Indian influence in this regard, H.B. Sarkar writes:

> There is hardly any doubt that much of the cultural heritage of South-East Asia would have been lost forever if its people had not adopted at an early stage the Indian art of writing. It is indeed very difficult now for the uninitiated people to discern that all the major scripts of South-East Asia, which today look very much different from those of India, owe their common origin to the late variety of the Indian Brāhmī scripts.[39]

It needs to be mentioned here that unlike India, China could not be successful in influencing South-East Asia in the cultural sphere. The writing system is supposed to be the chief cause. Even though, the Chinese calligraphy was aesthetically admirable, it was too cumbersome to be learnt. The absence of alphabets or syllabery, more importantly the pictographic character of Chinese script could not attract the South-East Asians. Outside China only the Koreans and the Japanese, neither of whom had their own model to study; and the Vietnamese, who were under Chinese rule for a millennium, adopted Chinese writing. As far as Indian system is concerned, even the Mongols and the Tibetans, long in close contact with China, opted for

---

38 Sarkar 1985: 168.

39 Ibid.: 169

Indian alphabets. The matter of writing system is emphasized because it helped in transmitting ideas, beliefs, values and even literary expressions to mainland South-East Asia from Indian side. It is for the absence of the same reason that the Chinese ways (Confucianism, political institution, etc.) could not have any significant impact on South-East Asia.[40]

In *The Saga of Indian Culture in South-East Asia: Retrospect and Prospect*, Y. Yagamma Reddy writes:

> The legacy of Indian culture can be better understood from the linguistic evolution. It enriched vernacular speech through new words and grammatical forms of Sanskrit origin and through introducing the first form of writing which ultimately contributed immensely to the stabilization and development of main languages among Cambodians, Burmese, Siams, Thais and Laotians.[41]

Regarding the introduction of the art of writing, the credit goes to the "brāhmaṇa migrants".[42] It is supposed that through these brāhmaṇas went Sanskrit; the language of high culture, and Pāli went through the Buddhist preachers and other followers.

## INDIAN SOURCES

Regarding the sources of the early scripts of Funan, Cambodia and Champa (Vietnam), there are contradicting views. They variously affiliate these scripts to the central, western and southern parts of India. Here difficulty arises from the fact that in their earliest forms, the different types of Indian writing show their fewest divergences. Therefore, while R.C. Majumdar opines that the oldest Sanskrit inscription in Funan used Kuṣāṇa script from north India, K.A. Nilakantha Sastri argues that all the alphabets used in South-East Asia had a south Indian origin and that Pallava script has a predominant influence. Coedes, however, points out that the use of a pre-Nāgarī script for a short time at the end of the eighth and beginning of the ninth centuries is the implication of a wave of Bengali influence.[43] From the viewpoint of pallaeography and chronology of the early

40 Sardesai 1986: 37.

41 Reddy 1998: 17.

42 Sarkar 1985: 168.

43 Ibid.: 169.

inscription of South-East Asia, A. Christie has expressed a different view. From his analysis it can be drawn that the people of the Gujarat–Malabar region dominated in matters of immigration from fourth century to fifth century CE, but from fifth century to sixth century CE the people of south India took the lead in overseas activities. Even though he has traced the Pallava, west Cāḷukyan and Mulava styles of writing, he has not explained what he meant by south Indian style distinguished from the above styles.[44]

It is generally agreed that the earliest specimen of the Indian art of writing in mainland South-East Asia is provided by Vo-canh inscription of Funan, which had been written in the late Brāhmī script. Some scholars have assigned it to the second or third century CE. D.C. Sircar thinks it to be of a later period. This is because in the second or third century, Prākr̥t was used in the contemporary charters of India instead of Sanskrit (which came into vague only in the Gupta period).[45] The scripts of Rāma Khambaeng of Thailand now used by the Thais in Lanna, Laos, Mengtung and Tongking owe their origin to India.[46] To sum up, most of the scripts and writing styles of mainland South-East Asia which even though have been modified in the present times, owe their origin to Indian influence of Sanskrit, Pāli and Tamil.

## LANGUAGES

Regarding the influence of Sanskrit language on the languages of South-East Asia. H.B. Sarkar writes:

> The numerous inscriptions discovered in Kambuja and other countries prove that Sanskrit was highly cultivated all over the region and formed the court language and the language of the learned.[47]

In this regard Alistair Lamb, a reputed historian, writes that many South-East Asian languages contain an important proportion of words of Sanskrit or Draviḍian origin. Some of these languages, like Thai, are still written in scripts that are clearly derived from Indian models.[48]

---

44 Ibid.: 170.

45 G. Coedes 1968: 48.

46 Sarkar 1985: 175-76.

47 Ibid.: 179.

48 Basham 1999: 442.

Use of Sanskrit language is still prevalent in countries like Thailand, Laos and Cambodia. In the words of William J. Gurney who made an in-depth study of spoken Thai from the point of Indian influence on it: "there are as many words of Indian origin in spoken Thai as are Greek and Latin words in spoken English".[49] Thai language has incorporated a large number of polysyllabic words of Indian origin, at first through the intermediary of words borrowed from Cambodian, and later by the creative use of Sanskrit and Pāli roots.[50] In fact, Sanskrit and Pāli words have enriched Thai vocabulary considerably, and their use is to some extent a mark of upper-class status in Thai land.[51] It is in line with this that a big corpus of individual names and names of cities, towns and villages in Thailand is found to be of Indian origin. The Thai language is still written in scripts that are clearly derived from Indian models.[52]

Similarly Sanskrit and Pāli have made deep inroads into the script, language and literature of Laos. Majority of the Lao inscriptions has been in Sanskrit. Lao script was introduced by king Rāma Kampheng of Sukhodaya in CE 1283, which marked the common origin of Thai and Lao alphabets. In the same year, Pāli scriptures from Sri Lanka were introduced resulting in greater influence of Pāli. One type of Lao script known, as Toua-Lam is considered sacred and it is used for transcribing Pāli. In Lao language, there are about 60 per cent of words having Sanskrit and Pāli origin. There are many Lao words having Indian origin like: *kumara* (*kumāra*), *pativat* (*prativāda*), *pathet* (*pradeśa*), *prom* (*brahmā*), *pranam* (*praṇāma*), *rusi* (*ṛṣi*), *shanti* (*śānti*), *sri* (*śrī*), *sūt* (*sūtra*), *seṭṭhi* (*śreṣṭhi*), *youvatnari* (*yuvānārī*), *śabha* (*sabhā*), *champa* (*campā*), *naṅg mekhala* (*maṇi mekhalā*), *nang thorani* (*devī dhāraṇī*), *praya nak* (*nāgarāja*), etc. The names of some Indian flowers like *gulāb*, *campā* are exactly the same in Lao language. The words *dharmaśālā* in Sanskrit and *sala dham* in Lao language have exactly the same meanings.[53]

## LITERATURE

Apart from languages, Indian grammar contributed in the field of

---

49 Vohra 1998: 51.

50 Sarkar 1985: 109-15.

51 Ibid.: 114-19.

52 Basham 1999: 442.

53 Thakur 1986: 136.

grammatical politics a euphonic combination making some of the native languages richer. The vocabulary was considerably strengthened in all these countries by the introduction of Sanskrit words. This was significant in the field of abstract ideas, technical terms and many material objects.[54]

India also contributed largely by providing her Purāṇic literature (*Rāmāyaṇa, Mahābhārata*), Jātaka stories, etc. to the above-said countries, thereby giving her mythology, morals and values to the people concerned. The innumerable existing monuments and inscriptional references still attest to the tremendous Indian impact on Thailand, Cambodia and Laos. Episodes from the Purāṇas are not only referred to in the inscriptions of Indo-China, but have also been portrayed in the art and architecture of Cambodia.[55] After a brief review of the story of the introduction of Indian art of writing, language and literature to South-East Asia, we can quote G. Coedes:

> The native languages have not only been enriched and made more flexible by India, they have above all been stabilized, thanks to the use of Indian scripts. The common origin of the Mon, Burmese, Thai, Khmer, Cam, Javanese and Balinese systems of writing is still recognizable in an astonishingly divergent linguistic and literary milieu, which is hard to realise at first sight.[56]

The true classical Lao poetry is formed by translation of Indian poems, and Lao verses follow the metrics of Indian prosody. In folk songs, dramas and theatres, themes from Indian literature are in abundance. The Lao folklore had been influenced by Indian themes. Development of religious songs of Buddhist monks encouraged many stories becoming popular in both prose and poetry. In the classical Lao dance, one can find gestures and movements showing strong influence of various Indian dance forms.

*Rāmāyaṇa* is very popular in Laos. The country was earlier known as Lava, the son of Rāma. The story of Rāma or *Phra Lak Phra Lam* with its fundamental human value and social idea has contributed to the cultural life of people. The Lao have adopted the stories of *Rāmāyaṇa*

54 Sarkar 1985: 244.

55 Ibid.: 244.

56 Coedes 1968: 254-55.

as if it had happened in Laos. Names, titles and geographical settings were given local colour. The majority of Lao stories were derived from *Pañcatantra*. *Phra Saṁgharaja Vixula Mahāvihārathipati* in CE 1507 of *Wat Vixula Mahavihan* translated it into Lao language.

In the past it was through the visual and literary media that India was successfully sending her idea, values even knowledge. In the contemporary times while states are promoting cultural diplomacy through various media India has an age-old legacy in this regard. Promotion of these ancient arts and even restoration of the same in South-East Asia would help India in reviving the ancient cultural glory. India is having an emerging culture industry with a growing global appeal for its cultural goods, products even services. From Indian dance, drama, music to Hindi movies even to Indian tourist destinations, fashion and cosmetics, there is an array of cultural potentials bestowed upon India. Thus it can be safely said that South-East Asia is one region with which India has every reason to strengthen the ancient ties.[57]

In the first part of this paper I have discussed the various roots of India's cultural linkages in South-East Asia in different times. Can these roots be revived for greater co-operation? Do these roots have anything to play in enhancing India's relations with South-East Asia? The concluding lines are an attempt towards answering these questions.

Contemporary international politics is a war of ideas and a war of ideas can be won only by directly addressing to those ideas. It is through the cultural sphere that ideas are most rapidly expressed and the other cultures get the best opportunity to engage with each other and to recognize the splendour of them.

In an attempt to strengthen its relationship with South-East Asia, India has actively used culture as an important instrument of its Look East Policy. India's efforts to harmonize these cultural linkages within the overall objectives of the Look East Policy, has been further strengthened by modern cultural means, such as Indian films, fashion, arts, literature and cuisine. While these potent "exports" have succeeded in casting a strong Indian footprint in South-East Asia,

---

[57] Viswam 1997: 4.

their influence has also been reinforced by the presence of Indian diaspora in the region. Enhancing relations with ASEAN has been central to India's "Look East Policy" and there has been steady progress in the ASEAN–India relations since the policy was initiated in early nineties. ASEAN–India functional co-operation is diverse and includes co-operation across a range of sectors, such as trade, science and technology, human resource development, space sciences, agriculture, new and renewable energy, information and communication technology, telecommunications, transport and infrastructure, tourism and culture. Co-operation between India and ASEAN is being intensified, including in the cultural, educational and academic fields, through the promotion of people-to-people contacts, and initiatives such as Youth Exchange Programmes, Special Training Courses for ASEAN Diplomats, Media Exchange Programmes and the ASEAN–India Network of Think Tanks Meeting. India has established Centres for English Language Training (CELT) and Entrepreneurship Development Centres (EDC) in Cambodia, Lao PDR, Myanmar and Vietnam (CLMV countries). A MoU on Strengthening Tourism Co-operation between India and ASEAN was signed at the ASEAN–India Ministerial Meeting on Tourism on 12 January 2012, in Manado, Indonesia.[58]

India played host to the eighteen-member farmers' delegation from nine ASEAN member states through the ASEAN–India Farmers Exchange Programme for the first time in 2012. In August 2014, the India-ASEAN Free Trade Agreement (FTA) in Services & Investment is one step closer to implementation following approval by Thailand Ministry of Commerce to accept the terms outlined in the region-wide agreement. The annual trade volume between India and ASEAN is expected to rise from US $ 80 billion (Bt 2.4 trillion) in 2012 to US $ 100 billion in 2015 and to $ 200 billion in 2020 as India looks towards ASEAN for closer economic co-operation.

ASEAN and India are also supporting sub-regional developments, including the Mekong–Ganga Co-operation and Bay of Bengal Initiative for Multi-Sectoral Technical and Economic Co-operation frameworks. Other frameworks supported that are worth to mention here are the Cambodia–Laos–Vietnam Development Triangle Area,

---

58 http://www.aseanindia.com/about/history

Greater Mekong Sub-Region and ASEAN Mekong Basin Development Co-operation.[59]

### Indian Efforts towards Promoting Cultural Relations

India signed cultural agreements with Vietnam (1976), Thailand (1977), Laos (1994) and Cambodia (1996). Cultural Exchange Programmes (CEPs) also exist with Cambodia (2001-02) and Vietnam (2001-03). Cultural exchange programmes with Laos, Cambodia and Vietnam are intensive in nature, covering various fields under the sub-heads of education, health, culture, arts, youth affairs and sports and mass media.[60]

### Cultural Centres

Indian Cultural Centres (ICC) are important platforms to promote India's cultural diplomacy in South-East Asia. The Indian Council for Cultural Relations (ICCR) is in advanced stage to open a new Indian Cultural Centre in Hanoi (Vietnam). The Centre will beef up India's cultural presence in Vietnam and constitute an important dimension of the friendly partnership between the two countries. The Embassy has organized international conferences on Buddhism, on Tagore and on The Cham Civilizational Linkages in recent times. A "Joint Painting Workshop-cum-Exhibition" that brought together renowned Indian and Vietnamese artists was organized in April 2012. The "Kalpana Digitial Art Exhibition" was also held during April–May 2012. The Embassy, Indian Council of World Affairs and the Diplomatic Academy of Vietnam organized a very successful seminar on "India–Vietnam Strategic Partnership: Future Directions" in Hanoi in July 2012. It has been decided to open a new Vietnam–India Centre for English Language Training at the Diplomatic Academy of Vietnam.[61]

### Educational Scholarships and Cultural Diplomacy Initiatives

Educational assistance forms another important element in India's cultural diplomacy, offering generous scholarships to South-East Asian

---

[59] http://www.nationmultimedia.com/business/Trade-deals-set-to-open-new-erafor-Asean-India-30197024.html

[60] Cited in Sahai 2003: 143-44.

[61] http://meaindia.nic.inmeaxpsite/foreignrelation/vietnam.pdf

students for studying Indian language as well as pursuing other studies and researches in India. There are several important schemes, under which India provides scholarships for South-East Asian students to study in India. Under the General Cultural Scholarship Scheme (GCSS) of the ICCR, fifty-six scholarships are provided to South-East Asian countries (Thailand (10), Vietnam (6), Combodia (2), and Laos (8)). Thirty scholarships are provided to BIMSTEC countries. Among the AYUSH scholarship scheme for BIMSTEC countries only seven has been utilized out of fifteen slots in 2010-11 financial years. Similarly out of the total fifty slots for Mekong–Ganga Co-operation Scholarship Scheme only twenty has been utilized in the same year. Other than these schemes, ICCR also provides fellowship to South-East Asian students and scholars under some general schemes, such as Commonwealth Scholarship Scheme, Cultural Exchange Programme and the Colombo Plan. Only one fellowship has been awarded to Vietnam under Expansion Plan 2010-11 by the ICCR and only one academician visited India from Vietnam during the same financial year. Three distinguished visits; one from each of the countries of Cambodia, Laos and Vietnam have been possible in 2010-11. There has been no outgoing visitors programme nor any study visit by Indian scholars to none of the countries of Cambodia, Laos, Vietnam even Thailand, in 2010-11 financial year. In Cambodia, the Council organized a Buddhist Conference during 2010-11 as part of its policy to trace the roots of Buddhism in India and link it with the South-East Asian countries.[62] Apart from these scholarship schemes, the Indian government also helps in the establishment of chairs related to India, and its languages in various universities of mainland South-East Asia. For example, there is a Sanskrit chair at Silpakorn University, Bangkok, Thailand. Two new chairs have been established in the financial year 2010-11 in Cambodia (Sanskrit and Buddhist Studies) and Vietnam (Contemporary Indian Studies).[63] The first meeting of the India–Vietnam Joint Working Group on Educational Exchange was held in May 2012 in New Delhi. The meeting discussed measures to strengthen co-operation in the field of education between the two countries.

---

62 *ICCR Annual Report 2010-2011*, p. 12.

63 Ibid.: 10-11.

There have been a number of cultural delegations; mainly dance groups from India to Cambodia, Vietnam and Laos during 2010-11. The Indian Mission supports the Cambodia–India Entrepreneurship Development Centre (CIEDC) by providing literature, education scholarships and Indian Technical and Economic Cooperation (ITEC) training slots for CIEDC's students and staff. India contributed close to US $ 2 million to construct the Mecong-Ganga Cooperation (MGC) Asian Traditional Textiles Museum in Cambodia. Indians, nearly one million, comprise the largest number of South Asian tourists visiting Thailand every year. These visitors contribute a significant chunk of its income from tourism.[64]

## CONNECTIVITY

Delhi Dialogue IV on the theme "India and ASEAN: Partners for Peace, Progress and Stability" was held on 13-14 February 2012 in New Delhi which also flagged off ASEAN–India Commemorative Year celebration. The visit of the ASEAN Committee of Permanent Representatives (CPRs) to India during 12-17 February 2012 coincided with Delhi Dialogue IV. According to Indian Foreign Minister Salman Khurshid the latest summit represented a crucial "take off" point for connectivity between India and ASEAN countries. He cited the three-nation highway project linking India's north-east with Myanmar and Thailand as an example of land-transport connectivity. Additional sections of the 1,300-km highway near India's border with Myanmar and the Myanmar border with northern Thailand are under construction and will be joined with the existing route in Myanmar, where road conditions will be improved. The cross-border highway is scheduled for opening in 2016.

The Indian foreign minister also cited the potential linkages of India's Chennai seaport with Thailand's Laem Chabang deepsea port as another example of connectivity between India and ASEAN countries. From Thailand, the highways and seaports could be further linked with those in Laos, Cambodia and Vietnam, whose ports are in the South China Sea. The Thai government has also shown support in extending the trilateral highway to reach Laos and Cambodia.[65]

---

64 http://www.aseanindia.com/countries/asean/thailand

65 http://www.nationmultimedia.com/business/Trade-deals-set-to-open-new-erafor-Asean-India-30197024.html

Tourism could be a major revenue earner for both India and these South-East countries and also a very good way to promote people-to-people links. Many of these countries have huge Buddhist populations and India provides many important Buddhist heritage sites. At present, there are no direct flights between India and Vietnam. Vietnam Airlines and Jet Airways signed a MoU in October 2011 on comprehensive co-operation that includes commencing direct flights in the near future. At the 8th ASEAN–India Summit held in Hanoi, Vietnam, in October 2010, Prime Minister of India announced the extension of visa on arrival facility to Cambodia, Vietnam, Philippines and Laos with effect from 1 January 2011. Visa on arrival facility now stands extended to seven ASEAN countries (Lao PDR, Cambodia, Vietnam, Myanmar, Singapore, Indonesia and the Philippines).

### ROLE OF NORTH-EAST INDIA

The north-eastern states of India play an important role in India's Look East Policy as they share a land border with the ASEAN. However, it is a matter of regret that they have not been able to reap the benefits of India's Look East Policy. There is a need to increase trade between India's north-eastern states and the ASEAN countries, given their geographical contiguity. There is also a need to involve the people of this region in any initiative to foster closer ties with the ASEAN countries concerned. Also, the central government should take into confidence the chief ministers of this region while framing policies as part of India's Look East Policy.

### The ASI and the Conservation of Indian Heritage in South-East Asia

The conservation of Angkor Vat in Cambodia is supposed to be one of the most outstanding projects of ASI in any foreign country.[66] On Cambodia's request, India is also undertaking the restoration and conservation of the Ta Prohm Temple in Siem Reap. India will undertake a project for restoration of the Cham monuments in My Son. ASI will execute the project with a grant of US $ 3 million by India.[67] ASI should take more of such restoration projects and offer its skilled services.

66 http://asi.nic.in/asi_abroad.asp

67 http://meaindia.nic.in/meaxpsite/foreignrelation/vietnam.pdf

## BUDDHIST LINKAGES

In the recent times, Thailand happens to be a Hindu–Buddhist country.[68] Theravāda Buddhism is the religion of nearly all ethnic or "low land", constituting about 40-50 per cent of the overall population in Laos. Similarly, Buddhism is the state religion of Cambodia. An estimated 93 per cent of the population of Cambodia is Theravāda Buddhists. Even the Mahāyāna school of Buddhism claims over 34,000 followers and has 105 temples throughout the country.[69] Recognizing that Buddhism, the dominant religion in the countries of mainland South-East Asia, is a common socio-cultural and religious thread, India should make conscious efforts to project a Buddhist-friendly image by drawing attention to its Buddhist heritage. It is already trying to revive Buddhist linkages to strengthen its stakes in South-East Asia by promoting visits of Buddhist scholars and monks as well as developing Buddhist tourist circuits in India. This is also evident from the initiative to rebuild Nalanda University. This university, an initiative demonstrating India's eagerness to foster a culture of understanding and regional consciousness, is a project, which, if efficiently implemented, can establish India's reputation as a mover of big ideas and their concrete implementation. India's role in putting together a multilateral coalition of nations across East and South-East Asia for rebuilding the Nalanda University has not received as much attention as it should have.

## SENDING OF RIGHT MESSAGES

The whole process of Indian cultural influence was interaction between culture of India and South-East Asian countries. Any attempt to assign greater role either to India or to South-East Asia would be futile. Moreover, giving importance to terminologies like Indic, Indianization, Classical or Indigenization would result into semantic controversy.[70]

---

68 http://www.unhcr.org/refworld/country,,,,THA, 4562d8cf2,5021057d67,0.html

69 United States Department of State, 2011 Report on International Religious Freedom-Cambodia, 30 July 2012, Available at: http://www.unhcr.org/refworld/country,,USDOS,, KHM,,502105d249,0.html

70 http://www.seasite.niu.edu/lao/laostudies/pmish1.htm

India's culture has a global appeal given its long history and rich heritage. India does not have a record of precipitating forcible territorial occupations in its neighbourhood. This imparts India an advantage over China as far as initial conditions shaping a benign image are concerned. However, in reality, China is enjoying a more favourable perception in several parts of the region. This is probably due to India's failure in effective projections and influencing people and countries in a positive way whether through ideas, attraction of cultural heritage or even intellectual contribution.

Indian television channels are already popular in much of South-East Asia. It is time to encourage circulation of more print editions of prominent newspapers in the region. Both print and visual media representation is crucial to direct recognition and empirical understanding of each other. India appears to be a poor performer in highlighting its positive role in South-East Asia. Strategic literature and popular discourse should attempt to positively articulate India's image as a significant regional entity. Notwithstanding the overly critical bent of India's domestic media, the challenge for official agencies is to project detailed, accurate and convincing accounts of India's achievements.

## PROMOTING CULTURE IN AN INSTITUTIONAL MANNER

India should conceive of some better institutional role through ICCR. Bollywood films and music, Indian food, *yoga*, IT and higher education are the most potent Indian exports that have been earning it strategic gains. These exports have strong competitive advantages and can act as effective tools in furthering India's cultural presence in South-East Asian countries. Regular screening of Indian movies, promoting dance and music extravaganza, education fairs, *yoga* shows and IT exhibitions can serve India's objectives well. Hindi, Urdu, Gujarati, Punjabi, Bengali and Tamil languages may serve the purpose in a combined manner in South-East Asia.

## ROLE OF THE DIASPORA

Indian culture has captured the fancy of the entire world with its literature, art, films, fashion, arts and cuisine. While these potent "exports" have succeeded in casting a strong Indian footprint in South-East Asia, their influence has also been reinforced by the presence of

Indian diaspora in the region. Indians settled in the countries of South-East Asia can participate actively in spreading Indian culture and consolidating a benign image for India, a role similar to that played by the Chinese diaspora in South-East Asia. India can benefit by enhancing engagement with its large and diverse diaspora in South-East Asia. Estimated population of Indians living in Vietnam is 2000, mostly in Ho Chi Minh City.[71] According to the L.M. Singhvi Committee report on Indian diaspora, the total population of Indians in Thailand stands at 85,000, which is 0.07 per cent of total Thai population. Out of this, the number of Persons of Indian Origin (PIOs) is 70,000, while there are 15,000 Non-Resident Indians (NRIs). The Committee indicates that Thai Indians can play a possible role in the BIMSTEC and Mekong–Ganga Co-operation. According to this report, Thai Indians want greater interaction between the Thai Board of Investment (BOI) and Indian chambers of commerce like FICCI to promote understanding of markets. By addressing some of their concerns, e.g. increased air connectivity to north-east India from Thailand, the Indian establishment can help Thai Indians in exploring Indian markets and in expanding the area of bilateral economic co-operation.[72]

Indian efforts towards cultural diplomacy in South-East Asia have not been able to match the kind of cultural impact and local integration that the Chinese Confucius institutes have been able to achieve. Hanban — the public institution working in collaboration with the Chinese Ministry of Education for promoting the Confucius institutes — is a model worth studying by ICCR. It is widely believed that India's soft power potential is actually more than that of China. But India needs to polish its skills in getting the right message across, something that China is doing cleverly by spending large resources. India needs to learn from the Chinese experience in using soft power as a critical tool of regional strategy. While it does possess an edge in the cultural and educational dimensions, it is almost impossible for India to match China in economic assistance at this stage of economic development.

---

[71] http://meaindia.nic.in/meaxpsite/foreignrelation/vietnam.pdf

[72] Pranav Kumar, *Indian Diaspora in Thai–India Cooperation*, available at: http://www.ipcs.org/article/South-East-asia/indian-diaspora-in-thai-indiacooperation-2578.html

It therefore has to follow a carefully thoughtout strategy for optimizing its soft power leverage in the region. Financial limitations must be offset by cultural and educational advantages, with country-specific variations wherever required. All that has been discussed above is simply a revisiting of past findings and conclusions relating to the Indian experience in that area. Ultimately in the field of culture, its effective use in furthering relations and India's long-term aspirations; a lot needs to be done. Culturally, historically and from the civilizational point of view India should have shown more concern and involvement in the region. Merely setting up institutions for furthering cultural relations and hosting state to state functions under its aegis and within the confines and control of officialdom have neither served the purpose nor furthered the Indian effort at cultural diplomacy. The whole objective in undertaking a *tour d'horizon* of India's cultural sharing with the South-East Asian countries is to advocate an approach of greater cultural activism on the part of India. It is accepted that in the present state of world affairs "the most important distinctions among peoples are not ideological, political or economic [but] cultural".[73] In this context, efforts at resuming cultural linkages and forming cultural coalitions can assume a new geopolitical, historical and civilizational significance; at least for India and this region with which she has been umbilically connected. Such an effort on our part would be a true reinvention of India's potential in mainland South-East Asia.

## References

Basham, A.L., 1954, *The Wonder that Was India*; survey of the history and culture of the Indian subcontinent before the coming of the Muslims, London: Sidgewick Jackson.

——— (ed.), 1999, *A Cultural History of India*, New Delhi: Oxford University Press.

Coedes, G., 1968, *The Indianized States of Southeast Asia*, Honolulu: East West Publication, ed. Wolter F. Vella, tr. Susan Brown Coming.

Dash, Sarita, 2003, "Roots of India's Cultural Diplomacy in South-East Asia", M.Phil. Dissertation, New Delhi: Jawaharlal Nehru University.

---

[73] Anirban Ganguly, *The Necessity of Reinventing a Shared Cultural Past: India and South-East Asia;* available at: http://www.vifindia.org/article/2011/april/20/The-Necessity-of-Reinventing-a-Shared-Cultural-Past%E2%80%93India-and-South-East-Asia

Coedes, G., 1968, *The Indianized States of Southeast Asia,* Honolulu: East West Center.

Hall, D.G.E., 1981, *History of Southeast Asia,* Honolulu: Hawai University Press.

Jayapalan, N., 1999, *History of Southeast Asia,* New Delhi: Atlantic Publishers.

Kitagawa, Joseph M., 2002, *The Religious Tradition of Asia,* London: Collier Macmillan.

Majumdar, R.C., 1944, *Hindu Colonies in the Far East,* Calcutta: Firma K.L. Mukhopadhyay.

Muni, S.D., 2011, *India's "Look East" Policy: The Strategic Dimension,* ISAS Working Paper no. 121, Singapore: National University of Singapore.

Naidu, G.V.C., 1998, *"India and ASEAN" Strategic Analysis,* New Delhi: Institute of Defence and Strategy Analyses, October.

Ray, H.P., 1998, *The Winds of Change Buddhism and the Maritime Links of Early Southeast Asia,* New Delhi: Oxford University Press.

Reddy, Y.Y., 1998, "Need of Developing a New Outlook at Greater India Concept", in *The Saga of Indian Culture in South-East Asia: Retrospect and Prospect,* Centre for Studies on Indo-China and South Pacific, Sri Venkateswara University, Tirupati, Monograph Series no. IX.

Sahai, P.S., 2003, "Cultrual Diplomacy: India in Singapore" in N.N. Vohra (ed.) *Emerging Asia Challenges for India and Singapore,* New Delhi: Manohar.

Sardesai, D.R., 1986, *Southeast Asia: A History,* Boulder: Routledge.

———, 1996, "India and South-East Asia", in B.R. Nanda (ed.) *Indian Foreign Policy: The Nehru Years,* Delhi: Vikas Publishing House.

———, 1997, *Southeast Asia: Past and Present,* Boulder: Westview Press.

Sarkar, H.B., 1970, *Some Contribution of India to the Ancient Civilization of Indonesia and Malaysia,* Calcutta: Punthi Pustak.

———, 1985, *Cultural Relation Between Indian and Southeast Asian Countries,* Delhi: ICCR and Motilal Banarsidass.

Sharma, O.P., 1993, *Indian Culture: Ancient Glory and Present Gloom,* New Delhi: Intellectual Publishing House.

Tarling, Nicholas, 1992, *Comprehensive History of Southeast Asia,* London: Cambridge University Press.

Thakur, Upendra, 1986, *Some Aspects of Asian History and Culture,* New Delhi: Abhinav Publication.

Viswam, S., 1997, "India's Look-East Policy", *World Focus,* September, **18**(9): 4.

Vohra, N.N., 1998, *Religion, Politics and Society in South and Southeast Asia,* New Delhi: India International Centre.

William, Lea E., 1976, *Southeast Asia: A History,* New York: Oxford University Press.

# 23

## दक्षिणी-पूर्वी एशिया के देशों में राम का प्रभाव

*पवन कुमार*

जिस प्रकार से मर्यादा पुरुषोत्तम श्रीराम भारतीयता की पहचान हैं, उसी प्रकार से राम दक्षिणी-पूर्वी एशिया देशों की सभ्यता एवं संस्कृति के ललाट पर सोने की तरह चमकते दिखाई देते हैं। थाईलैंड, कम्बोडिया, मलेशिया, लोआस, म्यामांर आदि देशों में राम के आदर्शों का गहरा प्रभाव व असर देखा जा सकता है। कई देशों में तो लोग घरों में मुख्य आयोजनों पर रामकथा का पाठ करवाते हैं। रामकथा वहाँ के लोगों के लोक-जीवन में इतनी तारतम्यता के साथ जुड़ गई है, मानो वह उनकी अपनी संस्कृति क्यों न हो।

दक्षिणी-पूर्वी अलग-अलग देशों में रामकथा को अलग-अलग रूपों में प्रचारित किया जाता है। कम्बोडिया में इसे *रामकेर*, थाईलैंड में *रामकियन* तथा लाओस में *श्री लक्ष्मण–श्री राम* कहा जाता है। यहाँ सभी नामों के आगे *फ्र* अर्थात् श्री लगाया जाता है। म्यामांर में जब लोगों के बीच झगड़ा होता है तो कहा जाता है कि क्यों सुग्रीव और बाली की तरह लड़ रहे हो। इस बात से सहज अन्दाजा लग सकता है कि यहाँ के लोगों पर *रामायण* का कितना प्रभाव है। थाईलैंड में किसी की आँखों की सुन्दरता की उपमा सीताजी की आँखों से की जाती है। मलेशिया में सुल्तान की उपाधि में चरोन बाहुका (चरण पादुका) का इस्तेमाल भी होता है। इसके अलावा इन्डोनेशिया में रामकथा के लिए *रामायण* शब्द का प्रयोग किया जाता है। लाओस में *रामकथा* में श्रीराम के नाम के आगे श्रीलक्ष्मण जोड़ा जाता है।

दक्षिणी-पूर्वी एशिया के अधिकतर देशों में बौद्ध या मुस्लिम धर्म के अनुयायी हैं। इसलिए कई जगह *रामायण* में रावण को भगवान् शंकर की बजाए अल्लाह से वर माँगते दिखाया जाता है। वहाँ होने वाली रामलीलाओं में हनुमान् को काफी महत्त्वपूर्ण पात्र माना जाता है क्योंकि वह रावण की विभिन्न चालों को समय–समय पर काटता है। कई स्थानों पर श्रीराम के मन्दिर बनाए गए हैं, जहाँ पर श्रीराम, लक्ष्मण, सीता तथा हनुमान् की प्रतिमाएं लगाई गई हैं। थाईलैंड में "प्राच्य संस्कृति संस्थान" नाम से एक प्रतिष्ठान चलाया जा रहा है, जहाँ पर भारतीय संस्कृति तथा मर्यादा पुरुषोत्तम श्रीराम के आदर्शों का व्याख्यान होता है। वहाँ पर महात्मा गांधी, रबीन्द्रनाथ टैगोर की प्रतिमा

भी लगाई गई हैं। इस संस्थान में चीनी, थाई तथा संस्कृत भाषा के कोर्स शुरु किए गए हैं। इस प्रकार कई अन्य संस्थानों में भी वेद, उपनिषद् तथा अन्य शास्त्रों का ज्ञान दिया जाता है। इस प्रकार कहा जा सकता है कि दक्षिणी-पूर्वी एशिया के देशों में राम के नाम का डंका बजता है।

आजकल मेडागास्कर कहे जाने वाले द्वीप से लेकर आस्ट्रेलिया तक के द्वीप समूह पर रावण का राज्य था। राम-विजय के बाद इस सम्पूर्ण भू-भाग पर राम की कीर्ति फैल गई। राम के नाम के साथ रामकथा भी इस भाग में फैली और बरसों तक यहाँ के निवासियों के जीवन का प्रेरक अंग बनी रही।

श्रीलंका और बर्मा में *रामायण* कई रूपों में प्रचलित है। लोक-गीतों के अतिरिक्त रामलीला की तरह से नाटक भी खेले जाते हैं। बर्मा में बहुत से नाम राम के नाम पर है। रामावती नगर तो राम नाम के ऊपर ही स्थापित हुआ था। अमरपुर के एक विहार में राम, लक्ष्मण, सीता और हनुमान् के चित्र आज तक अंकित हैं।

मलेशिया में रामकथा का प्रचार अभी तक है। यहाँ मुस्लिम भी अपने नाम के साथ अक्सर राम, लक्ष्मण और सीता नाम जोड़ते हैं। यहाँ *रामायण* को *हिकायत सेरीराम* कहते हैं।

थाईलैण्ड के पुराने रजवाड़ों में भारत की भाँति राम की पादुकाएँ लेकर राज्य करने की परंपरा पाई जाती है। ये सभी अपने को रामवंशी मानते थे। यहाँ ''अजुधिया'' ''लवपुरी'' और ''जनकपुर'' जैसे नाम वाले शहर हैं। वहाँ पर रामकथा को ''रामकीर्ति'' कहते हैं और मंदिरों में जगह-जगह रामकथा के प्रसंग अंकित हैं।

थाईलैण्ड की *रामायण* के विषय में कहा जाता है कि यह भारत से नहीं बल्कि इण्डोनेशिया से कुछ 900 साल पहले यहाँ आई तथा रामकथा के चार रूपों – खोन, लाखोन नांग व हुन में प्रचिलत हुई। *रामाकीन* या *रामायण* में नवजात शिशु सम्बन्धी थाई व बौद्ध रिवाज़ों का प्रमुखता से उल्लेख है।

*फ्रा लाक फ्रा लाम* (प्रिय श्रीलक्ष्मण प्रिय श्रीराम) लाओस में लोकप्रिय *रामायण* के तीन रूपान्तरणों में से एक है। इसमें लाओस के खान-पान, वेश-भूषा, व्यवहार तथा परंपराओं की विस्तृत जानकारी है। कह सकते हैं कि यह लाओस के जनजीवन का "समग्र विश्वकोश" है। म्यांमार में ग्यारहवीं शताब्दी में राजा अंनावृथा का शासनकाल *रामायण* का प्रवेश काल माना जाता है। म्यांमार में 1973 में एक बौद्ध मठ से 80 ताडपत्रों पर *रामावथ्थु* नामक प्राचीन *रामायण* की पाण्डुलिपि मिली थी। इसके अतिरिक्त यहाँ अन्य पाँच विभिन्न प्रकार की *रामायण* प्रचलित हैं। म्यांमार की *रामायण* में भ्रातृ-प्रेम का स्वर प्रमुख है। जबकि लाओस में प्रचलित *रामायण* में आपसी स्नेह-सम्बन्धों को रेखांकित किया गया है। वहाँ के लोग राम-लक्ष्मण के प्रेम की मिसाल देते हैं।

हिंद चीन के अनाम में कई शिलालेख मिले हैं जिनमें राम का यशोगान है। यहाँ के निवासियों में ऐसा विश्वास प्रचलित है कि वे वानर कुल से उत्पन्न हैं और श्रीराम नाम के राजा यहाँ के सर्वप्रथम शासक थे। *रामायण* पर आधारित कई नाटक यहाँ के साहित्य में भी मिलते हैं। वहाँ इन नाटकों का मंचन भी विशेष कार्यक्रमों में किया जाता है।

कम्बोडिया में भी हिन्दू सभ्यता के अन्य अंगों के साथ-साथ *रामायण* का प्रचलन आज तक पाया जाता है। छठी शताब्दी के एक शिलालेख के अनुसार वहाँ कई स्थानों पर *रामायण* और *महाभारत* का पाठ होता था। वही परम्परा आज भी वहाँ कायम है।

जावा में रामचन्द्र राष्ट्रीय पुरुषोत्तम के रूप में सम्मानित हैं। वहाँ की सबसे बड़ी नदी का नाम सरयू है। *रामायण* के कई प्रसंगों के आधार पर वहाँ आज भी रात-रात भर कठपुतलियों का नाच होता है। जावा के मंदिरों में *वाल्मीकि रामायण* के श्लोक जगह-जगह अंकित मिलते हैं। वहाँ वाल्मीकि पूजन नाम से एक विशेष कार्यक्रम मन्दिर में होता है।

सुमात्रा द्वीप का *वाल्मीकि रामायण* में ''स्वर्णभूमि'' नाम दिया गया है। *रामायण* यहाँ के जनजीवन में वैसे ही अनुप्राणित है जैसे भारतवासियों के। बाली द्वीप भी थाईलैंड, जावा और सुमात्रा की तरह आर्य संस्कृति का एक दूरस्थ सीमा-स्तम्भ है। *रामायण* का प्रचार यहाँ भी घर-घर में है। यहाँ आर्य संस्कृति तथा वेद की बातें घरों में सुनी जा सकती हैं।

### "राम जातक" : लाओस की कथा

लाओस के निवासी और वहाँ की भाषा को "लाओ" कहा जाता है, जिसका अर्थ है "विशाल" अथवा "भव्य"। लाओ जाति के लोग स्वयं को भारतवंशी मानते हैं। लाओ साहित्य के अनुसार अशोक द्वारा कलिंग पर आक्रमण करने पर दक्षिण भारत के बहुत सारे लोग असम-मणिपुर मार्ग से हिंद चीन चले गए। लाओस के निवासी अपने को उन्हीं लोगों के वंशज मानते हैं। रमेश चंद्र मजुमदार नामक विद्वान् के अनुसार थाईलैंड और लाओस में भारतीय संस्कृति का प्रवेश ईसा पूर्व दूसरी शताब्दी में हुआ था। उस समय चीन के दक्षिण भाग की उस घाटी का नाम "गंधार" था।

लाओस की संस्कृति चाहे जितनी पुरानी हो, संसार के राजनीतिक मानचित्र पर वह मध्यकाल में ही अस्तित्व में आया। लाओ साहित्य के अनुसार राजकुमार फाल्गुन को लाओस का संस्थापक माना जाता है। एक क्षत्रिय सरदार ने किसी कारणवश अंकोर के राजदरबार में शरण ली थी। फाल्गुन उसी का पुत्र था। अंकोर नरेश ने अपनी पुत्री का विवाह उससे कर दिया। वह एक सैनिक टुकड़ी का स्वामी बन गया।

लाओस में रामकथा पर आधारित कई रचनाएँ हैं जिनमें मुख्य रूप से *फ्लक-फ्लाम* (रामजातक), *ख्वाय थोरफी, पोम्मचक* (ब्रह्मचक्र) और *लंका नाई* के नाम उल्लेखनीय हैं। *रामजातक* के नाम से विख्यात *फ्लक-फ्लाम* की लोकप्रियता का

रहस्य उसके नाम से अर्थ "प्रिय लक्ष्मण प्रिय राम" में समाहित है। *रामजातक* लाओस के आचार-विचार, रीति-रिवाज़, स्वभाव, विश्वास, वनस्पति, जीव-जंतु, इतिहास और भूगोल का विश्वकोश है। देहियर के अनुसार यह वास्तविक अर्थ में लाओ महात्मक है। *रामजातक* दो भागों में विभक्त है। इसके प्रथम भाग में दशरथ पुत्री चंदा और दूसरे भाग में रावण तनया सीता के अपहरण और उद्धार की कथा है। जातक कथाओं की तरह इसके अंत में बुद्ध कहते हैं कि पूर्वजन्म में ही वे ही राम थे और देवदत्त रावण था।

### "रामकियेन" : थाईलैंड की कथा

एक स्वतंत्र राज्य के रूप में थाईलैंड के अस्तित्व में आने के पहले ही इस क्षेत्र में रामायणीय संस्कृति विकसित हो गई थी। अधिकतर थाईवासी परंपरागत रूप से रामकथा से सुपरिचित थे। 1237 ई० में स्वतंत्र थाई राष्ट्र की स्थापना हुई। उस समय उसका नाम स्याम था। राजा बोरोमकोत (1732 ई०) के राजत्व काल की रचनाओं में रामकथा के पात्रों तथा घटनाओं का उल्लेख हुआ है। परवर्ती काल में जब तासकिन (1767 ई०) थोनबुरी के सम्राट् बने, तब उन्होंने थाई भाषा में *रामायण* को छंदोबद्ध किया जिसके चार खंडों में 2012 पद हैं। पुनः सम्राट् राम प्रथम (1721 ई०) ने अनेक कवियों के सहयोग से जिस *रामायण* की रचना करवाई। इसके अतिरिक्त थाईलैंड में रामकथा पर आधारित अनेक कृतियाँ हैं।

*रामकियेन* का आरंभ राम और रावण के वंश-विवरण के साथ अयोध्या और लंकी की स्थापना से होता है। तदुपरांत इसमें बालि, सुग्रीव, हनुमान्, सीता आदि की जन्म-कथा का उल्लेख हुआ है। विश्वामित्र के आगमन के साथ कथा की धारा सम्यक् रूप में प्रवाहित होने लगती है जिसमें राम-विवाह से सीता-त्याग और पुनः युगल जोड़ी के पुनर्मिलन तक की समस्त घटनाओं का समावेश हुआ है। *रामकियेन* वस्तुतः एक विशाल कृति है जिसमें अनेकानेक उपकथाएँ सम्मिलित हैं। इसकी तुलना हनुमान् की पूँछ से की जाती है। इसमें विभीषण पुत्री वेंजकाया द्वारा सीता का स्वांग रचाना, ब्रह्मा द्वारा राम और रावण के बीच मध्यस्थ की भूमिका निभाना आदि प्रसंग विशेष रूप से उल्लेखनीय हैं।

संपूर्ण *रामकियेन* इस प्रकार की विचित्र आख्यानों से परिपूर्ण है, किंतु इसके अंतर्गत रामकथा के मूल स्वरूप में कोई मौलिक अंतर नहीं दिखाई पड़ता। *रामकियेन* के अंत में सीता के धरती-प्रवेश के बाद राम ने विभीषण को बुलाकर समस्या के समाधान के विषय में पूछा। उसने कहा कि ग्रह का कुचक्र है। उन्हें एक वर्ष तक वन में रहना पड़ेगा। उसके परामर्श के अनुसार राम तथा लक्ष्मण हनुमान् के साथ एक वर्ष वन में रहे और उसके बाद अयोध्या लौट गए। अंत में इंद्र के अनुरोध पर शिव ने राम और सीता दोनों को अपने पास बुलाया। शिव ने कहा कि सीता निर्दोष हैं। उन्हें कोई स्पर्श नहीं कर सकता, क्योंकि उनको स्पर्श करने वाला भस्म हो जायगा। अंततः शिव की कृपा से सीता और राम का पुनर्मिलन हुआ।

रामजातक के आरंभ में भगवान् बुद्ध अपने शिष्यों से कहते हैं कि बाराह कल्प में ब्रह्मयुगल पृथ्वी पर आए। उन दोनों ने धरती की मधुर और सुगंधित माटी इतनी अधिक मात्रा में खा ली कि उनका शरीर भारी हो गया और वे उड़कर पुनः स्वर्ग नहीं जा सके। दक्षिण समुद्र तट पर घर बनाकर रहने लगे। उन्होंने एक सौ संतानों को जन्म दिया। इसी क्रम में इंद्रप्रस्थ नगर अस्तित्व में आया।

*रामजातक* में सीता का अपहरण विवाह के बाद रास्ते में हो जाता है। अपहरण के संदर्भ में स्वर्ण-मृग का प्रसंग हैं, किंतु शूर्पणखा की चर्चा नहीं हुई है। कैकेयी, भरत, शत्रुघ्न आदि की अनुपस्थिति के कारण वनवास का भी उल्लेख नहीं हुआ है। *राम-जातक* के द्वितीय खंड में सीता–हरण से उनके निर्वासन और पुनर्मिलन की सारी घटनाओं का वर्णन हुआ है, किंतु सब कुछ लाओस की शैली में हुआ है। अन्य जातक कथाओं की तरह इसके अंत में भी बुद्ध कहते हैं कि पूर्व जन्म में वे ही राम थे, यशोधरा सीता थी और देवदत्त रावण था।

इन देशों के अतिरिक्त फिलीपीन, चीन, जापान और प्राचीन अमेरिका तक राम-कथा का प्रभाव मिलता है। मैक्सिको और मध्य अमेरिका की मय सभ्यता और इंका सभ्यता पर प्राचीन भारतीय संस्कृति की जो छाप मिलती है उसमें रामायणकालीन संस्कारों का प्राचुर्य है। पेरू में राजा अपने को सूर्यवंशी ही नहीं ''राम'' वंशज भी मानते है। ''रामसीतव'' नाम से आज भी यहाँ ''राम सीता उत्सव'' मनाया जाता है।

इस प्रकार प्रत्येक देश में जहाँ-जहाँ भी राम-कथा पहुंची, अपने देश को सामाजिक प्राथमिकताओं को दृष्टिगत करते हुए राम को कहीं भगवान् के रूप में, कहीं एक रोमानी नायक की तरह, कहीं एक आदर्श पति, आकर्षक व्यक्तित्व, संयमी भाई के रूप में प्रमुखता दी है। राम की तरह सीता को भी कहीं प्रेम की देवी के रूप में प्रमुखता दी गई है, कहीं एक निष्ठावान पत्नी की, तो कहीं प्रतिशोध से भरी अर्द्धदेवी के चरित्र में ढाला गया है। रावण के चरित्र-चित्रण में भी देश के सामाजिक परिवेश के आधार पर अंतर दिखता है। जैसे लाओस में प्रचलित *रामायण* में रावण या ''राफनासुआन'' को बुरा व्यक्ति नहीं अपितु एक चतुर, विद्वान् तथा सुंदर व मोहक व्यक्तित्व वाले व्यक्ति के रूप में दिखाया जाता है।

इस प्रकार हम कह सकते हैं कि जिस प्रकार से भारत में राम-नाम का डंका बजता है उसी प्रकार से दक्षिणी-पूर्वी एशिया के देशों में राम-नाम का परचम लहराता है। इन देशों के लोग भी राम के सिद्धान्तों को आज भी प्रशासिक मानकर उनकी पालना करते हैं।

# 24

## भारतीय संस्कृति तथा रामायण का थाईलैंड पर प्रभाव

*मंजु बाला*

काबिले-गौर है कि थाईलैंडवासियों पर भारतीय संस्कृति की अमिट छाप है। दक्षिणी-पूर्वी एशिया के इतिहासविद् इस बात से अनभिज्ञ नहीं हैं कि खोम साम्राज्य, मध्यवर्ती थाईलैंड, लाओस तथा वियतनाम के कई भागों पर हमारी संस्कृति तथा सभ्यता का अत्यन्त प्रभाव था। 1000 ई० पू० में दक्षिणी थाईलैंड से श्री बिछाया साम्राज्य जिसके मुख्यालय छाया और सुमात्रा (अब इन्डोनेशिया में) थे, में बौद्ध धर्म का भारी प्रभाव रहा। कुछ समय के लिए लुफोरी राज्य में भी इस धर्म का बोल-बाला रहा। समय बीतता गया और धीरे-धीरे समूचे थाईलैंड में बौद्ध धर्म के दूसरे मत हीनयान का डंका बजने लगा। हीनयान का जन्म भारत में ही हुआ था, जो आज थाईलैंड का राजधर्म भी है। इसी प्रकार दबे पाँव भारतीय संस्कृति बौद्ध धर्म के सहारे वहाँ पहुँची। भारत की संस्कृति ने थाईलैंड की संस्कृति को इस प्रकार से प्रभावित कर दिया कि आज वहाँ दिन की शुरुआत से रात के अन्धेरे तक हमारी संस्कृति महकती और चहकती है। अगर बौद्ध धर्म के प्रति आस्था की बात करें तो आज वहाँ 90 प्रतिशत लोग बौद्ध धर्म के अनुयायी हैं। 15,000 से अधिक वहाँ पर बौद्ध मन्दिर बने हैं। थाईलैंड की भाषा में जिन्हें वाट कहा जाता है। मन्दिरों के दरवाजों पर भारतीय कला तथा वास्तुकला का नक्शा देखा जा सकता है। भारतीय संस्कृति के प्रतीक, गृहस्थी के लिए चार नियम, समाज की एकता और नियम तथा पूरे जीवन के लिए अड़तीस नियम बताए गए हैं। वहाँ के शासक के लिए नियम तथा गुण हैं।

थाईलैंड के पूर्व मुख्य न्यायाधीश कासेमसप वहाँ पर प्राच्य संस्कृति प्रतिष्ठान चलाते हैं। इस प्रतिष्ठान में भारतीय संस्कृति के रूप तथा पहलू देखे जा सकते हैं। वहाँ पर लोगों को हमारे देश के महापुरुषों के बारे में गहन जानकारी दी जाती है

थाईलैंड में *रामायण* का पाठ भी घरों में देखने को मिल सकता है, वहाँ पर एक अयोध्या के नाम से नगर भी है। मर्यादा पुरुषोतम श्रीराम के पुत्र लव के नाम से थाईलैंड में लवपुरी नामक जगह भी है। थाई के लोगों की सांस्कृतिक जीवन-धारा श्रीराम की जीवनदृष्टि में पूर्णतया समाहित है। बैंकाक के एक मन्दिर में नीलम की मूर्ति है। इस मन्दिर की दीवारों पर रामकथा भी चित्रित की गई है।

भारतीय मूल के लोगों में तो भारतीय त्यौहार, लोक नृत्य, लोक कथाओं तथा दूसरी कलाओं के प्रति घनिष्ठ प्रेम है, जो उनके शौक, रहन-सहन तथा त्यौहारों के मनाने के तौर-तरीकों आदि से पता चलता है।

## रामकियेन : थाईलैंड की कथा

एक स्वतंत्र राज्य के रूप में थाईलैंड के अस्तित्व में आने से पहले ही इस क्षेत्र में रामायणीय संस्कृति विकसित हो गई थी। अधिकतर थाईवासी परंपरागत रूप से रामकथा से सुपरिचित थे। 1237 ई० में स्वतंत्र थाई राष्ट्र की स्थापना हुई।

राजा बोरोमकोत (1732 ई०) के राजत्व काल की रचनाओं में रामकथा के पात्रों तथा घटनाओं का उल्लेख हुआ है। परवर्ती काल में जब तासकिन थोनबुरी के सम्राट् बने, तब उन्होंने थाई भाषा में *रामायण* को छंदोबद्ध किया जिसके चार खंडों में 2,012 पद हैं। पुनः सम्राट् राम प्रथम (1721 ई०) ने अनेक कवियों के सहयोग से *रामायण* की रचना करवाई। इसके अतिरिक्त थाईलैंड में रामकथा पर आधारित अनेक कृतियाँ हैं।

*रामकियेन* का आरंभ राम और रावण के वंश-विवरण के साथ अयोध्या और लंकी की स्थापना से होता है। तदुपरांत इसमें वालि, सुग्रीव, हनुमान्, सीता आदि की जन्म-कथा का उल्लेख हुआ है। विश्वामित्र के आगमन के साथ कथा की धारा सम्यक् रूप में प्रवाहित होने लगती है जिसमें राम-विवाह से सीता-त्याग और पुनः युगल जोड़ी के पुनर्मिलन तक की समस्त घटनाओं का समावेश हुआ है। *रामकियेन* वस्तुतः एक विशाल कृति है जिसमें अनेकानेक उपकथाएँ सम्मिलित हैं। इसकी तुलना हनुमान् की पूँछ से की जाती है। इसमें विभीषण पुत्री वेंजकाया द्वारा सीता का स्वांग रचाना, ब्रह्मा द्वारा राम और रावण के बीच मध्यस्थ की भूमिका निभाना आदि प्रसंग विशेष रूप से उल्लेखनीय हैं।

*रामकियेन* में दिखाया जाता है कि अयोध्या के निकट साकेत नामक एक नगर था। उसके सम्राट् कौदम थे। संतानहीन होने के कारण वे वन में तपस्या करने चले गए। हज़ारों वर्ष बाद उनकी लंबी और सफेद दाढ़ी के अंदर गौरैया की एक जोड़ी ने घोंसला बना लिया। एक दिन नर-पक्षी कमल पुष्प पर खाद्य सामग्री एकत्र करने के लिए बैठा था। उसी समय सूर्यास्त हो जाने के कारण कमल की पंखुड़ियाँ बंद हो गईं। पक्षी को रातभर उसी के अंदर रहना पड़ा। प्रातःकाल कमल खिलने पर वह अपनी पत्नी के पास पहुँचा, तो मादा-पक्षी ने उस पर विश्वासघात का आरोप लगाया। नर-पक्षी ने कहा कि यदि उसका आरोप यही है, तो वह ऋषि के सारे पाप का भागी होगा। ऋषि उसकी बात सुनकर चकित हो गए। उन्होंने पक्षी से अपने पाप के विषय में पूछा। पक्षी ने कहा कि निःसंतान होना पाप है।

ऋषि को जब अपनी भूल की जानकारी हुई, तब उन्होंने गृहस्थ आश्रम में प्रवेश करने का निर्णय लिया। उन्होंने तपोबल से एक सुंदरी का सृजन किया और उसे अपनी

पत्नी बना लिया। उसका नाम अंजना था। अंजना ने स्वाहा नामक एक पुत्री को जन्म दिया। गौतम एक दिन भोज्य सामग्री की तलाश में गए। इसी बीच अंजना का इंद्र से संपर्क हो गया जिसके फलस्वरूप उसने हरित देहधारी एक पुत्र को जन्म दिया। इस घटना के बाद एक बार सूर्य की दृष्टि अंजना पर पड़ी।

संपूर्ण *रामकियेन* इस प्रकार के विचित्र आख्यानों से परिपूर्ण है, किंतु इसके अंतर्गत रामकथा के मूल स्वरूप में कोई मौलिक अंतर नहीं दिखाई पड़ता। *रामकियेन* के अंत में सीता के धरती-प्रवेश के बाद राम ने विभीषण को बुलाकर समस्या के समाधान के विषय में पूछा। उसने कहा कि ग्रह का कुचक्र है। उन्हें एक वर्ष तक वन में रहना पड़ेगा। उसके परामर्श के अनुसार राम तथा लक्ष्मण हनुमान् के साथ एक वर्ष वन में रहे और उसके बाद अयोध्या लौट गए। अंत में इंद्र के अनुरोध पर शिव ने राम और सीता दोनों को अपने पास बुलाया। शिव ने कहा कि सीता निर्दोष हैं। उन्हें कोई स्पर्श नहीं कर सकता, क्योंकि उनको स्पर्श करने वाला भस्म हो जाएगा। अंततः शिव की कृपा से सीता और राम का पुनर्मिलन हुआ।

निष्कर्ष रूप से हम कह सकते हैं कि भारतीय संस्कृति तथा *रामायण* का थाईलैंड पर गहरा असर देखने को मिलता है। थाईवासी भारतीय संस्कृति को अपना अभिन्न अंग मानते हैं। तभी तो वे भारतीय संस्कृति के प्रतीक गृहस्थी के चार नियम और पूरे जीवन के लिए अड़तीस नियमों को अपने से दूर नहीं करते।

# Contributors


**Alexander V. Zorin**
(Institute of Oriental Manuscripts, The Russian Academy of Sciences)
Turku str., 3-66
ST PETERSBURG 192212
(Russia)
<kawi@yandex.ru>

**Anita Sharma**
Professor & Head
Department of East Asian Studies
Dean, Faculty of Social Sciences
University of Delhi
DELHI -110 007
<anitasharmadu@hotmail.com>
<asdeas@gmail.com>

**Asha Kadyan**
Vice-Chancellor
Bhagat Phool Singh Mahila Viswavidyalaya
KHANPUR KALAN- 131 305
District Sonepat (Haryana)

**Avadhesh Kumar Singh**
Professor & Director
School of Translation Studies & Training
Indira Gandhi National Open University
Maidan Garhi
NEW DELHI -110068
<avadhesh06@gmail.com>

**Bachchan Kumar**
Research Officer
South East Asian Studies
Indira Gandhi National Centre for the Arts
1, C. V. Mess, Janpath
NEW DELHI - 110 001
<bachchan_kumar@yahoo.com>

**Bal Ram Singh**
Executive Mentor,
School of Indic Studies
Professor and Director,
Botulinum Research Center
Institute of Advanced Sciences
78-540 Faunce Corner Mall Road
DARTMOUTH, MA 02747 (USA)
<bsingh@inads.org>

**D.R. Purohit**
Director
Centre for Folk and Performing Arts
HNB Garhwal University
Birla Campus Srinagar, Gharwal
SRINAGAR - 246 174
(Uttarakhand)

**Diljit Rana**
13, Malone Park

BELFAST, BT9 6NH
Northern Ireland (UK)
<lord.rana@googlemail.com>
<lord.rana@gmail.com>

**Do-Thu-Ha**
Vietnam National University
HANOI
<dothuha2000@gmail.com>

**Hawon Ku**
Assistant Professor, HOD
Department of Hindi
Hankuk University of Foreign Studies
107, Imun-ro, Dongdaemun-gu
SEOUL 130-791 (Korea)
<hawonku@gmail.com>
<hawonku@hufs.ac.kr>

**J.C. Sharma**
Former Diplomat
DELHI
<jcsharma000@yahoo.com>

**Kakali Ghoshal**
(Assistant Professor,
Department of Philosophy,
Budge Budge College)
Mayur Mahal, J.n. Basu Road
Harinavi, PS Sonarpur
KOLKATA - 700148
<Ghoshanamika62@Yahoo.in>

**Kapil Kapoor**
(Former Rector, Jawaharlal
Nehru University)
B-2/332, Ekta Garden
9 IP Extn., Near Mother Dairy
NEW DELHI - 110 092
<kapilkapoor1910@yahoo.com>

**Kavyashree G**
Assistant Professor, HOD
Kannada Department
Govt First Grade College
FARAHATABAD
Gulbarga Dist. (Karnataka)
<kavyasrinagbhushan@gmail.com>

**Komang Santhi Arsa**
Keyza Widiatmika
Dwi Warsiani
University of Indonesia
<komang.santhiarsa@gmail.com>

**M. Krzysztof Byrski**
University of Warsaw
POLAND
<m.k.byrski@uw.edu.pl>

**Madhu Kapoor**
(Associate Professor, Dept. of
Philosophy, Vivekananda
College)
1530, Garia Main Road
24 F, Shivam Apartment
KOLKATA - 700 084
<mattoo_k@yahoo.co.uk>

**Manju Bala**
Research Scholar from south India
<drpawan1982@gmail.com>

**P. Nagabhushanagoud**
Lecturer, Dept. of History and Archaeology
Davangere University
DAVANGERE - 577 002
(Karnataka)
<drnagbhushan@gmail.com>

**Pawan Kumar**
Research Director
C.M.J. University
SHILONG (Meghalaya)
<drpawan1982@gmail.com>

**Prapassorn Posrithong**
Independent Scholar in Art History, History and Museology
25/5 Soonthornkosa Rd., Klongtoey
BANGKOK 10110 (Thailand)
<pposrithong@live.com>

**Rajnish Kumar Mishra**
Special Centre for Sanskrit Studies
Jawaharlal Nehru University
NEW DELHI - 110 067
<Mishra_rajnish@yahoo.com>
<mishrarajnish@gmail.com>

**S. Ram Mohan**
(Formerly Special Secretary, Govt. of India)
687, 46th Street
9th Sector, K.K. Nagar West
CHENNAI 600 078 (T.N.)
<srammohan8@gmail.com>

**Sarita Dash**
(PhD student in South Asia Studies Division)
School of International Studies
Jawaharlal Nehru University
NEW DELHI - 110067
<saritadash1@yahoo.com>

**Shiva G. Bajpai**
Professor Emeritus,
Dept. of History
Former Director, Asian Studies
California State University
NORTHRIDGE, CA 91330-8250 (USA)
<Shiva.bajpai@csun.edu>
<bajpai.shiva@gmail.com>

**Shyam Sunder Sharma**
University of Delhi
DELHI - 110007
<sssharmasanskrit@gmail.com>

**Swati Raikhy**
313, Lajpat Puri
Lal Kurti
MEERUT CANTT. - 250 001 (U.P.)
<swatiraikhy@gmail.com>

**T.S. Satyanath**
(Retd. Professor of Linguistics, University of Delhi)
C-13, Maurice Nagar
DELHI - 110 007
<tssatyanath.du@gmail.com>

**Tran Phuoc Phuong Thao**
Asst. Professor
University of Buddhist studies
Department of Philosophy
HO CHI MINH CITY, (Vietnam)
<tambode108@gmail.com>

# Index